PLANTS OF
NORTHERN CALIFORNIA

Harmless, even kindly as botanists in general appear, how is it that they take delight in embittering the lives of laymen by their eternal juggling with the names of genera and species?

J. Smeaton Chase. 1919.

California Desert Trails: Two Years of Adventures.

Houghton Mifflin, Boston.

FALCONGUIDES®

PLANTS OF
NORTHERN
CALIFORNIA

A FIELD GUIDE TO PLANTS
WEST OF THE SIERRA NEVADA

EVA BEGLEY

FALCONGUIDES

GUILFORD, CONNECTICUT

FALCONGUIDES®

An imprint of The Rowman & Littlefield Publishing Group, Inc.

4501 Forbes Blvd., Ste. 200, Lanham, MD 20706

www.rowman.com

Falcon and FalconGuides are registered trademarks and Make Adventure Your Story is a trademark of The Rowman & Littlefield Publishing Group, Inc.

Distributed by NATIONAL BOOK NETWORK

800-462-6420

British Library Cataloguing-in-Publication Information available

Library of Congress Cataloging in Publication Data available

ISBN 978-1-4930-3184-9 (paperback)

ISBN 978-1-4930-3185-6 (e-book)

♾™ The paper used in this publication meets the minimum requirements of American National Standard for Information Sciences—Permanence of Paper for Printed Library Materials, ANSI/NISO Z39.48-1992.

Printed in the United States of America

This book is a work of reference. The author, editors, The Rowman & Littlefield Publishing Group, Inc., and all other parties involved in the creation and publication of this work have made every effort to provide accurate information, using sources believed to be reliable, and to follow standard practices acceptable at the time of publication. They do, not, however, warrant that the information is complete – that would be far beyond the scope of a field guide like this book – and they are not responsible for the consequences of any errors or omissions. They also do not assume any liability for personal accident, illness, or death related to any activities that readers might engage in related to the search for, handling, identification, collection, foraging, consumption, or any other use of any wild plant material, regardless of whether each plant species involved is or is not included in this book. Readers should understand that this book presents only a small fraction of the plant species in the geographic area covered by this book and that this book does not provide complete or detailed information for any plant species about its toxicity to humans or livestock or about other harmful properties it may have. Although in this book a few plant species are identified as being highly poisonous, many more have some level of toxicity in some or all of their parts. Moreover, readers should be aware that some plant species that are not toxic or harmful to certain animals can poison humans or harm humans in other ways. Should the need arise for complete certainty about the identity of a plant, readers should consult a knowledgeable botanist. Some university herbaria and the University of California's Agricultural Extension provide plant identification services. **In an emergency, contact a Poison Control Center (1.800.222.1222), a medical toxicologist, or another appropriate heathcare provider.**

CONTENTS

PREFACE AND ACKNOWLEDGMENTS

I've liked plants ever since I was a toddler. At age three, I got into big trouble for picking our landlady's prized blue hyacinths. In primary school, I got into more trouble for being late when I dawdled too long looking at weeds on my way to school. During northern England's short springs and summers, our home was always decorated with old jam jars full of flowers that I had found in nearby fields and hedgerows, although my mother would get quite upset with me if the next morning she found lots of aphids or other insects crawling around under one of my bouquets. Nonetheless, she encouraged my interest and saved enough of her weekly housekeeping money to buy me, for the then extravagant sum of five shillings, a little pocket guide to Britain's wildflowers, *The Observer's Book of Wild Flowers,* which still sits on my bookshelf.

As an adult, my idea of a good vacation has always included having time to check out some new plants. Eventually, it dawned on me that I knew more about the flora in some favorite vacation spots than in Sacramento, which by then had been my husband's and my home for 25 years. Sacramento boasts a 23-mile-long recreational trail along the Lower American River—that's the portion of the river between Nimbus Dam and its confluence with the Sacramento River. Most of the adjacent lands are far from pristine, and I confess that at first I was a bit of a botanical snob and mainly saw all the non-native grasses and infestations of yellow star-thistle and poison hemlock. But once I started looking more carefully, I found an unexpected diversity of native plants on the 5,000 acres adjacent to the river and trail: Almost half of the roughly 400 species I've encountered so far are native, and I keep finding more. That got me thinking about a book on local plants, which gradually evolved into this field guide.

California is home to more than 7,000 different species of plants. Some are easy to identify, others aren't. I'm grateful to the following people for helping me figure out some of them: Ihsan Al-Shehbaz, Missouri Botanical Garden, St. Louis; Mark Brunell, University of the Pacific, Stockton, California; Diana Chapman, Telos Rare Bulbs, Ferndale, California; Anita F. Cholewa, University of Minnesota, St. Paul; Ellen Dean, University of California, Davis; Peggy L. Fiedler, University of California Natural Reserve System; Sherri Laier, Oregon State Parks and Recreation; Richard Lis, California Department of Fish and Wildlife; Staci Markos, University of California, Berkeley; Melanie Parker, Sonoma County Regional Parks; Alan R. Smith, University of California, Berkeley; Genevieve K. Walden; Margriet

Wetherwax, University of California, Berkeley; and Marcia Wineteer, Bureau of Land Management, Utah.

I thank Andrew S. Doran of the University and Jepson Herbaria of the University of California at Berkeley for accepting my voucher specimens of some of the more unexpected or hard-to-identify plants along the Lower American River. I also thank Jennifer Carey, Julie Carville, Jordan Fisher Smith, Joe Medeiros, and Karen Wiese for their kind words of encouragement and good advice on how to get a book published, as well as my editors, David Legere and Julie Marsh, and everyone else at Globe Pequot involved in the publication process. And above all, it's hard to envision this book as ever having come to fruition without all the help and unflagging support of my husband and fellow photographer, Paul Begley—thank you, Paul!

INTRODUCTION

Geographic region covered by this guide

This book covers most of California north of San Francisco Bay and the Sacramento–San Joaquin River Delta and west of the Sierra Nevada. That includes the following regions:

- **The northern half of California's Central Valley, often called the Sacramento Valley.** Its elevation gradually rises from sea level at the Delta to about 300' near the city of Red Bluff. In terms of vegetation, its boundaries lie where woodlands of oak or pine form a "bathtub ring" around the Valley's grasslands, marshes, riparian forests, and agricultural lands.
- **The northern California coast.** For the purposes of this book, let's define this region as land close to the ocean that is not forested, be it dunes, grasslands, wetlands, or coastal scrub, that is, land covered with relatively low shrubs.
- **The North Coast Ranges.** These mountains consist predominantly of steep-sided ridges lying more or less parallel to the coast. The main vegetation types are oak woodland, conifer forest, and chaparral.
- **The Klamath Ranges.** In northwestern California, a few miles inland from the ocean, the parallel ridges of the North Coast Ranges are replaced by more randomly oriented mountains. These are the Klamath Ranges, composed of the Trinity Alps, Marble Mountains, and several other ranges, all of them supporting extensive conifer forests. To the east, Interstate 5 approximately runs along the geological boundary between the mainly metamorphic Klamath Ranges and the mainly volcanic Cascades.
- **The Cascade Ranges.** A lot of the Cascades' terrain is actually relatively low in elevation—most passes are in the 4,000–5,000' range, compared to the Sierra Nevada's 7,000' to above 10,000' passes—but the Cascades give an impression of great height because, starting with Mount Lassen near their southern end, they're dotted with major, often snowcapped volcanos. The Cascades support many different plant communities, and there's no abrupt change in vegetation as you travel north from the Sierra Nevada into the Cascades. The geological boundary between the two more or less follows the North Fork of the Feather River.

Excluded from this book is northeastern California's Modoc Plateau, which geographers consider part of the Great Basin that extends eastwards to the Rocky Mountains. Its sagebrush and pinyon-juniper vegetation, replaced by conifer forest at high elevations, resembles that of much of northern Nevada and eastern Oregon.

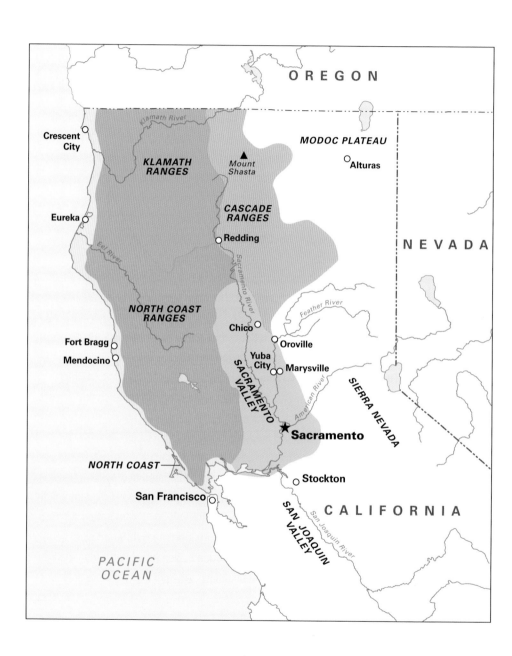

The geology of the region covered in this guide is incredibly complex, elevations range from sea level to Mount Shasta's 14,179', and average annual rainfall varies from 15–20" at the southern end of the Sacramento Valley to more than 100" in some coastal areas. As a result, the region supports many different habitats, sometimes within just a few miles or even yards of each other, containing a huge diversity of plants. In this book, I've concentrated on species growing in locations that are fairly easy to get to, on public lands, and generally within a mile or so of a trailhead.

Kinds of plants covered by this guide

This book is a field guide; that is, it includes some common, conspicuous species along with some less common ones and others that aren't very showy but that intrigued me for one reason or another; but it's not intended to be what botanists call a flora: a complete inventory of everything that grows in the region. Since plants in the wild don't come with labels telling you where they originally came from, I've included both native and non-native species.

Some groups of plants are underrepresented in this book. Conifers are one such group; for a much more thorough treatment, I recommend Ronald M. Lanner's exquisitely illustrated *Conifers of California*. Ferns are another. And then there are California's hundreds of species of grasses (family Poaceae), sedges (family Cyperaceae), and rushes (family Juncaceae), most of them notoriously challenging to identify and, except for a few sedges, not included here. If you're interested in grasses, you may find James P. Smith's *Field Guide to California Grasses* useful. I especially like *Weeds of California and Other Western States* by Joseph M. DiTomaso and Evelyn A. Healey; although it focuses primarily on weedy species, it includes lots of exceptionally good photos of the details needed for identification of many sedges, rushes, and grasses.

There are other large, difficult groups. They include the carrot family (Apiaceae), sunflower family (Asteraceae), borage or waterleaf family (Boraginaceae), and the many species of manzanita (*Arctostaphylos*), ceanothus (*Ceanothus*), and willow (*Salix*). To identify some species, you need fruit or seeds as well as flowers. For others, you need underground parts. Since I don't think it's good practice to dig plants up unless I have a scientific need to know *exactly* which species I'm looking at, I often just list such plants by their genus in my field notes.

In short, dear reader, you may find it hard to identify all the plants you encounter in northern California, and you certainly won't find every one in this book. By organizing the book according to families, though, rather than flower color, I hope to help you at least to place many plants not included here in their correct family or genus. That, in turn, will make it easier to figure out what an unknown plant is if you decide to consult some of the references listed near the end of this book, the most thorough of them being the 2012 edition of *The Jepson Manual: Vascular Plants of California*, edited by Bruce G. Baldwin and others, and its online equivalent, the *Jepson e-Flora* at http://ucjeps.berkeley.edu/eflora. And even if you can't identify something, I hope that won't discourage you from enjoying all the plants that you *can* identify. (If it's any comfort, there are times when I too eventually give up and can only say, "It's one of these two or three species" or even "Well, all I know it that it's such and such a genus.")

Some naturalized or weedy species not further described in this guide

Roughly half the plants now found in California's natural or seminatural areas were intentionally or unintentionally brought here by humans. Many of these non-natives have become widespread or even weedy, freed from whatever insects, pathogens, or other factors kept them in check in their homeland and now crowding out California natives. Especially near old homesteads or urban areas, though, you may find non-native plants that have escaped into the wild but don't proliferate to the point of becoming invasive. Botanists call such plants "naturalized." Plates 1 and 2 show a few of northern California's hundreds of naturalized species along with a few invasive ones.

Oleander (*Nerium oleander*; dogbane family, Apocynaceae) can have white, pink, salmon, or red flowers.

Greater periwinkle (*Vinca major*; dogbane family, Apocynaceae) is an extremely invasive groundcover.

Japanese honeysuckle (*Lonicera japonica*; honeysuckle family, Caprifoliaceae) has flowers that change from white to butter-yellow as they age.

Silver wattle (*Acacia dealbata*; pea family, Fabaceae) is one of the first trees to bloom in spring.

Silk tree (*Albizia julibrissin*; pea family, Fabaceae) is native to tropical Asia.

Rattlebush or red sesbania (*Sesbania punicea*; pea family, Fabaceae) is beautiful but highly invasive.

In fall, the leaves of sweet gum (*Liquidambar styraciflua*; witch-hazel family, Hamamelidaceae) turn yellow, pink, scarlet, or purple, often all on the same tree.

The fruit of sweet gum is a hard, prickly ball roughly 1–1.5 inches in diameter.

These new leaves of sweet fig (*Ficus carica*; mulberry family, Moraceae) will soon turn darker green but already show their highly distinctive shape.

Olive (*Olea europea*; olive family, Oleaceae) has become naturalized in the Sacramento Valley and southern part of the North Coast Ranges.

Almond (*Prunus amygdalus*; rose family, Rosaceae), shown here, and several other members of the rose family such as plum, cherry, peach, apple, and pear sometimes become naturalized.

Chinese firethorn (*Pyracantha fortuneana*; rose family, Rosaceae) is one of three invasive species of firethorn.

In fall, the upper side of the leaves of silver maple (*Acer saccharinum*; soapberry family, Sapindaceae) turns pale yellow, the underside beige or almost white.

Garden flowers like summer snow (*Leucojum aestivum*; amaryllis family, Amaryllidaceae) are sometimes the only sign that there used to be a homestead nearby.

Ixia (*Ixia flexuosa*; iris family, Iridaceae), native to southern Africa, is an uncommon escapee from gardens.

Cape buttercup (*Sparaxis elegans*; iris family, Iridaceae), another southern African species, attracts native butterflies such as pipevine swallowtails.

The life and structure of plants, in a nutshell

Plants come in a continuum of shapes and sizes, and it's not always easy to plug them into the pigeonholes of botanical terminology. Moreover, botanical vocabulary can be discouragingly complex, but it does make communication easier, just as, if you're a car mechanic, it helps to know the names of all the bits and pieces that make a car run. Here are the basics on plant structure and the botanical terms used in this book. Terms in **bold text** are included in the glossary.

Annuals germinate from seed, grow, bloom, produce a new crop of seeds, and die in a single growing season. **Biennials** germinate and grow leaves in their first year, often in a tight cluster at ground level called a **rosette**. The leaves die at the end of the growing season, but the underground parts survive and, during the plant's second year, produce more leaves plus a flowering stem. Then the whole plant dies. **Perennials** live longer than two years, some only a few years, others centuries or even millennia. A perennial with a stem that thickens into a single woody trunk is a **tree**. If, near ground level, a woody perennial divides into a few woody trunks it's a multi-trunked tree; if it divides into many branches it's a **shrub** (or bush). (And where, you may ask, is the dividing line between "a few" and "many"? Answer: It's really up to you.) If the branches are woody only near the base and their upper portions die back at the end of each growing season, botanists call the plant a **subshrub**. If all aboveground parts die back every year but the underground parts live on, the plant is a **herbaceous perennial**. Sometimes, although by no means always, you can distinguish herbaceous perennials from annuals and biennials by the presence of last year's dead stems among the current year's new growth. **Vines** are plants that climb into taller vegetation (or trail across the ground when there's nothing tall nearby). They can be woody perennials like California grape (*Vitis californica*), herbaceous perennials like California man-root (*Marah fabacea*), or annuals like many species of pea (*Lathyrus*).

Some species refuse to stick with one category: Telegraph weed (*Heterotheca grandiflora*), for example, can be annual, biennial, or perennial, while poison oak (*Toxicodendron diversilobum*) usually is a shrub but occasionally grows into a woody vine.

Regardless of how long a plant will live, when its seeds germinate, they're taking their first baby steps towards becoming mature plants that will produce more seeds. Each seed uses the nutrients stored inside it—the same nutrients that make nuts and grains tasty and nourishing to all sorts of creatures, including us—to produce first a root, then a stem and leaves. In dry climates, the germinating seed may initially put most of its energy into growing a long root to reach moist soil. I've pulled up valley oak seedlings (courtesy of the

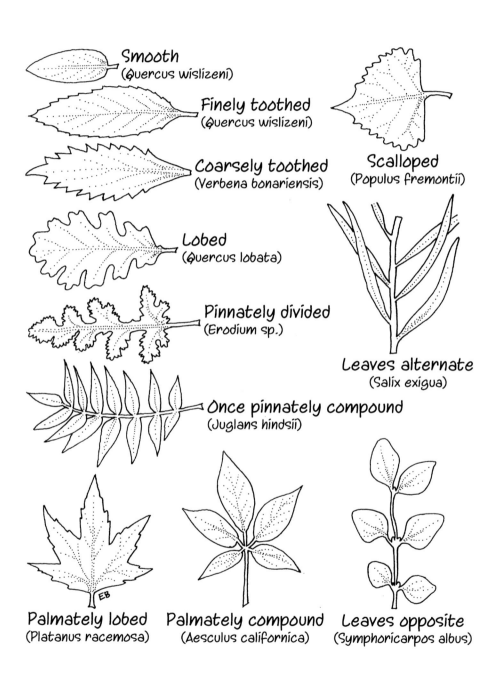

Smooth
(Quercus wislizeni)

Finely toothed
(Quercus wislizeni)

Coarsely toothed
(Verbena bonariensis)

Scalloped
(Populus fremontii)

Lobed
(Quercus lobata)

Pinnately divided
(Erodium sp.)

Leaves alternate
(Salix exigua)

Once pinnately compound
(Juglans hindsii)

EB

Palmately lobed
(Platanus racemosa)

Palmately compound
(Aesculus californica)

Leaves opposite
(Symphoricarpos albus)

neighborhood's jays and squirrels) from my backyard that had just two tiny leaves but an 18-inch-long root.

Leaves come in many different forms, and there's a bewildering array of terms to describe the innumerable variations. Many have a lower, stalk-like part called the **petiole**; the expanded, flattened part at the far end of the petiole is called the **blade**. If there's no petiole and the blade attaches directly to the stem, the leaf is **sessile**. Many species have a single blade per leaf. In others, the blade is divided into several smaller units, making the leaf **compound**; each little segment of blade is called a **leaflet**. If the leaflets radiate outwards from a common point, the leaf is **palmately** compound. If the leaflets are attached in two rows to the continuation of the petiole, the leaf is **pinnately** compound. This pattern can be repeated several times, giving you twice compound leaves, three-times compound leaves, and so on. So how do you tell a compound leaf from a stem with several leaves? The answer lies at the junction of the leaf and stem, where you'll find one or more buds—sometimes tiny and hard to find—that potentially can grow into a branch or flower, if they haven't done so already.

Leaf margins can be more or less straight or **smooth** (called "entire" by botanists), toothed, scalloped, or lobed. If they're so deeply lobed that the leaf is almost but not quite compound, the leaf is considered **divided,** or **dissected**. How the leaves are arranged on the stem is also important in identification. If the leaves are attached one by one, they're **alternate**, if in pairs, **opposite**. If three or more are attached at the same level, they're **whorled**.

Eventually, it's time to reproduce. Flowering plants do this by means of flowers. In what I call the "textbook flower" there's an outer whorl of **sepals**—flattened structures that protect the rest of the flower while it's developing. Above them is a whorl of **petals**, collectively called the **corolla**, which tend to be relatively showy in species pollinated by insects or other animals; you might say they're like billboards advertising the presence of good eats. The next whorl consists of the male parts of the flower, the **stamens**. Each stamen has a relatively thin stalk called the **filament** and an **anther**, whose function is to produce **pollen**. Right at the center of the flower, you'll find one or more **pistils**, which are the female parts. Each pistil is topped by one or more **stigmas**. Those are the surfaces where the pollen needs to wind up. When the right pollen grain meets the right stigma, it germinates and sends a long tube down through a neck-like part of the pistil called the **style** into the **ovary**. The ovary contains one or more **ovules**, which, after they've met up with a pollen tube and been fertilized, mature into **seeds**. As the seeds develop, the rest of the ovary ripens into some type of **fruit**, sometimes juicy and fleshy like apples or tomatoes, sometimes dry like acorns, each tiny "parachute" in a dandelion seed head, or unshelled peanuts.

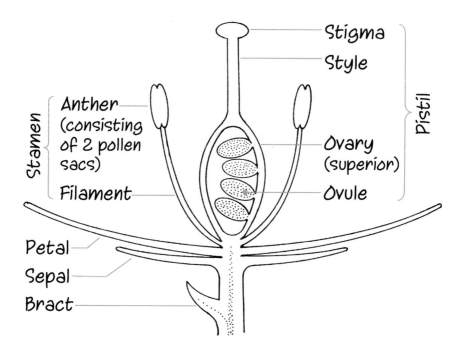

There are almost as many variations on this theme as there are species of flowering plants. Parts can be **free** from one another, or they can be **fused** together. Unlike the "text-book flower," in some species the sepals, petals, and stamens appear attached to the *top* of the ovary. That's because the lower portion of each sepal, petal, and stamen has fused with the walls of the ovary, resulting in what's called an **inferior ovary**. That's inferior in the sense of "below other flower parts,, not "worse than." (Conversely, the "textbook flower" has a **superior ovary** in the sense of "above other flower parts," just as Lake Superior was so named by French explorers because it's more northerly than the other Great Lakes, hence above them when mapped with north at the top.)

Some flowers lack stamens, or at least functional ones; they're called **female or pistillate flowers. Male or staminate** flowers lack functional pistils. Other flowers, especially wind-pollinated ones, may lack sepals or petals or both. Conversely, certain species have additional more or less leaf-like structures called **bracts** just below the sepals; bracts can be green or some other color. A cluster of flowers is referred to as an **inflorescence**.

A special case: the sunflower family

Exceptionally complex inflorescences are what unite the sunflower family, or Asteraceae. This huge family, with around 23,000 species in 1,500 genera worldwide, includes just about the whole gamut of growth forms. Some members, such as sunflowers, are hard to miss; others, such as burweed (*Soliva sessilis*) and slender woolly marbles (*Psilocarphus tenellus*), are so small that they're easy to walk across without noticing. And many, like coyote brush (*Baccharis pilularis*), fall somewhere in the middle in terms of overall conspicuousness, but it may take a bit of detective work to recognize their affinities—you have to look closely to see that their flowers are in fact built on the same general plan as sunflowers. What at first glance looks like a single blossom is in fact a whole cluster of precisely arranged small flowers, hence the old scientific name for the family, Compositae, the family of composite flowers.

Often each inflorescence, or **head**, consists of two types of flowers an outer ring of **ray flowers**, the center of which is filled with smaller **disk flowers**. Each ray flower has five petals, but they're all swept to one side and fused, so that they resemble a single petal. Disk flowers have more normal-looking corollas, typically with five petals. The anthers of the five stamens in each flower, but not their filaments, are fused into a tube around the style and stigma. Both ray and disk flowers have inferior ovaries. The sepals of each flower are so highly modified that they're no longer recognizable as sepals and collectively termed the **pappus**, which may consist of scales, barbs, bristles, or feathery hairs. To accommodate all these flowers, the top of the stem is enlarged into what's called the **receptacle**, which can be plate-like, hemispherical, spherical, conical, or columnar. The lower, outer part of the receptacle is wrapped by one to many rows of bracts, called **phyllaries** in this family.

Some family members only produce ray flowers, others only disk flowers. An artichoke is a good example of the latter. The "leaves" are the phyllaries; the fuzz that you scrape away from the center consists of immature disk flowers, each with a bristly pappus, along with a whole bunch of additional bristly hairs attached directly to the receptacle; and the tasty "artichoke bottom" is the receptacle.

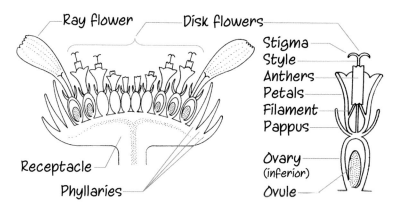

What's a species?

In theory, a species consists of all those individuals that are related closely enough to be able to produce fertile offspring. Thus, horses and burros are different species because their hybrid offspring—mules—are sterile.

In actual practice, it's a bit trickier to decide what constitutes a species, and there's a constant tug-of-war in scientific circles between the splitters and the lumpers—those scientists who consider small differences as significant enough to constitute separate species and those who don't. Yarrow (*Achillea millefolium*), for example, used to be split into two, later three hard-to-distinguish species, and you often ended up identifying a particular plant based simply on the elevation at which you found it. Since yarrow grows everywhere from coastal grasslands to high

Ryegrass (*Festuca perennis*) flowers, showing pale yellow anthers dangling from thread-like filaments. Two small, fuzzy, white stigmas are just barely visible.

mountain meadows, and the differences between the three "species" overlap, it makes a lot of sense to consider it a single species. But what would you do about two groups of plants that look somewhat similar but occur only in widely separated locations, where there's no possibility of pollen or seeds being transported by natural processes from one site to the other? Are they one species or two? The situation is further complicated by human introduction of plants from other regions. The new arrivals sometimes hybridize with related local species—and the hybrids aren't always sterile but may keep on crossing with each other or one or both parent species. DNA studies can sort out a lot of these muddles, but I doubt that folks in academic circles will ever run out of topics for dissertations and grant proposals.

Lest you think that disagreements between splitters and lumpers are purely academic, consider the following case: What DNA analysis recently revealed to be a single species of grass, ryegrass, now classified as *Festuca perennis*, used to be split into Italian ryegrass (*Lolium multiflorum*) and perennial ryegrass (*Lolium perenne*). The first had long, spiky extensions on some of the bracts enclosing its flowers, the second didn't. So what, you may say. But Italian ryegrass was considered to be a plant of dry, upland habitats and perennial ryegrass a plant of moister habitats that are legally protected under Section 404 of the federal Clean Water Act as "Waters of the United States." Suppose you owned acreage covered with perennial ryegrass and you wanted to develop your land. Until recently, you might not have received permission to go ahead until you had carried out or paid for all sorts of extra steps to mitigate the damage you were going to inflict on your "wetland"—but if you were lucky and had mainly Italian ryegrass, the law would not have required any mitigation. In short, how the experts define a species can, on occasion, have a big impact on your wallet.

A couple of notes on the species descriptions in this book

The differences between similar species, as described in this book, may seem picayune. In reality, there usually are additional visible differences (as well as differences in their DNA), but you may need a microscope to see them; in the interest of brevity, I've focused on the one or two most easily observed features.

For most species, the geographic range pertains only to northern California; again, in the interest of brevity, I generally omit occurrences elsewhere.

Why bother with scientific names?

Granted, at first glance scientific names appear complicated, unpronounceable, cumbersome. But let's consider some of the disadvantages of common names, that is, names in the local language. Is that pretty blue flower wally baskets, grass nut, or Ithuriel's spear? And those pale yellow flowers nearby: Are they wild turnip, wild kale, wild radish, jointed wild radish, jointed charlock, white charlock, or cadlock? It doesn't help that there's a related, blue- or purple-flowered species that's also called wild radish. Another example: We all know that a lime is a small green fruit in the citrus family, good for making margaritas and key lime pie. But in England, lime also refers to the tree that most Americans call basswood (one of several species in the genus *Tilia*) or linden (actually, its German name).

Names like "oak" or "rose" can be just as confusing. Yes, valley oak, blue oak, red oak, willow oak, and pin oak are all related and all produce a particular type of fruit: acorns. But she-oak and poison oak are completely different, unrelated plants, just as, except for their names, rock rose, moss rose, sun rose (also called rush rose), rose-of-Sharon, rose-of-Siam, and Malay rose have little in common with the rose bushes you may have in your garden. The situation gets even more complicated when you switch to other languages. Oak is *roble* in Spanish, *chêne* in French, *Eiche* in German, *eg* in Danish, *derw* in Welsh, *haritz* in Basque, *tammi* in Finnish … you get the picture. And what do you call all those plants, usually small, inconspicuous ones, that don't have any common name at all?

Enter the scientific name. It's a two-part name: The first, called the genus (plural: genera), applies to all members of a closely related group. For example, almost all plants that bear acorns belong to the genus *Quercus*. The second part of the scientific name, called the specific epithet, tells you exactly which member of that group. Together, the two names constitute the name of the species, and a Spanish, French, Basque, or for that matter Russian, Chinese, or Hmong botanist will know exactly which species you mean by *Quercus lobata*—valley oak—and understand right away that it's quite different from she-oak (a species of the genus *Casuarina*) or poison oak (*Toxicodendron diversilobum*). By convention, the name of the genus is always capitalized, the specific epithet always lowercase, and both words are italicized or underlined. If there's a subspecies (abbreviated subsp. or, in older books, ssp.) or variety (abbreviated var.), that word too is italicized or underlined. The names are based on Latin (or sometimes Greek) because in the 18th century when the Swedish botanist Carolus Linnaeus (also known as Carl von Linné) devised this system of nomenclature, Latin was the international language used by European scholars. Even when a species is named after a person or place, the name is given a Latin form. Each known plant species has a scientific name, and there's one and only one valid scientific name for each species.

Note that little word, *valid*. Despite what I've just said, plants sometimes end up being given more than one scientific name. That can happen several ways. Sometimes two botanists, each unbeknownst to the other, find and name the same new species—and almost inevitably they give it different names. Once it's clear, though, that the two names refer to the same kind of plant, whichever name was first formally published becomes the valid one. Other times, a botanist studying a group of related plants may decide that what seemed to be one variable species actually represents several distinct species or, conversely, that what, like *Achillea millefolium*, looked like a cluster of similar species is in fact one species. In the latter case, the botanist may reclassify what used to be considered distinct species as subspecies or varieties (the distinction between subspecies and varieties is rather nebulous). Occasionally a botanist may decide that a species has been completely misclassified and belongs in a different genus or even a different family. As a result, one or more scientific names will be changed. To help keep track of these changes, the last name or initials of the botanist assigning the name is often appended to the scientific name. There's an International Code of Botanical Nomenclature that lays out the rather

Lasthenia californica subsp. *californica*? Or *Lasthenia gracilis*? The two can be impossible to distinguish visually, but their DNA is quite different.

complicated rules for naming and renaming plant species; the rules themselves are made by an International Botanical Congress, established in 1864, which at first met rather sporadically but since the 1950s has convened every six years or so. For many years, new or revised scientific names had to be published in print, but in 2011 the International Botanical Congress approved electronic publication. Ultimately, only one name is considered *the* valid name. Older names are termed synonyms, but they're no longer deemed valid and not used in new scientific publications.

Similar, presumably related genera are grouped into families, similar families into orders, and so on. In the last two decades, quite a few species names and assignments into families have been revised based on DNA sequencing and other molecular technologies. Instead of relying primarily on the appearance of a plant and perhaps some microscopic internal features or the presence or absence of particular chemicals, botanists can now classify plants based on the similarity of their DNA; that is, how closely they're genetically related. While in theory that sounds very reasonable, assuming your goal is to group plants by their evolutionary relationships, it does occasionally cause practical problems, for example, when two genetically distinct species of plants look almost identical, such as *Lasthenia californica* subsp. *californica* and *Lasthenia gracilis*.

Pronunciation of scientific names

The way I see it, scientific names are intended for *communication*, not for showing off or playing one-upmanship games. As long as the other person understands what you mean, who cares exactly how you pronounce the vowels or which syllables you stress? Some folks will tell you to give the names their Latin pronunciation—but what's "correct" Latin? My father, born and raised in Germany, was horrified by the Latin spoken at British universities, and no doubt his British colleagues snickered behind his back at his Continental Latin. And some mycologists (people who study fungi—and, by the way, should that be foong-ee or funj-eye?) say that they can tell who had studied under which professor, simply based on his or her pronunciation of the scientific names of certain fungi.

Some books provide detailed instructions on pronunciation; I don't worry about them a whole lot—probably most of my pronunciations are based on my various professors'. Here are my "rules of thumb"—which, incidentally, I break plenty of times myself:

- Usually both "c" and "ch" are hard, like a "k."
- Usually "g" is hard.
- If the name starts with an almost-impossible-to-say combination of consonants, such as tm (as in *Tmespiteris*) or ct (as in *Ctenolophon*), just enunciate the second one.
- Conversely, if you see several vowels in a row, try to pronounce as many of them as you can without getting your tongue hopelessly tied in knots. So, for example, "ie" is two syllables and, depending on your preference, becomes "eye-ee" or "ee-eh." Exceptions: "oi" almost always sounds like "oy" as in "boy"; "ae" can sound like "ee" or "eh"; and "oe" usually sounds like "ee."
- Most family names end in –aceae, often pronounced ace-ee-ee in English. (So much for the "rule of thumb" that "c" is usually hard!)

So don't let language snobs spoil your day. If you can manage *Rhododendron*, *Chrysanthemum*, and *Impatiens* (which, incidentally, I pronounce "im-PAY-shee-ens" rather than "im-PAH-tee-ens"—so much for consistency!), you'll do just fine with most other scientific names! As for specific epithets like *tshawytscha* or *vexillocalyculatum*: I doubt that anyone can say them gracefully without some practice!

Why are plants arranged by family in this book?

In many wildflower guides, plants are arranged by flower color. Some flowers, however, are multicolored or come in more than one color, or the colors are intermediate—is cream-colored yellow, or is it white? Also, everyone sees color differently: One person's purple is someone else's pink or blue. And of course flower color is of no help whatsoever when all you have is the fruit. You can partially figure out a flower's structure by examining the fruit—think of the stem and remnants of sepals and stamens on a typical apple—but you can't deduce its color. As a result, I often find myself having to leaf through most of the book anyway when it's organized by flower color.

In this guide, plants are presented in the same sequence as in many botanical reference books: first grouped into the major categories of ferns and horsetails, conifers, and flowering plants (which in turn are broken down into two groups, called dicotyledons and monocotyledons by botanists); then, within each of these major categories, alphabetically by families; and finally, by each plant's scientific name. The advantage of this arrangement is that it helps you recognize the characteristic features of many families. For example, if you find a plant with five-petalled flowers borne in flat spirals that gradually uncoil as the fruit matures, there's a good chance that it's in the Boraginaceae (borage family), regardless of what color the flowers are. If it has four or six petals and lots of stamens, it's probably in the Papaveraceae (poppy family); if it has four petals and six stamens, it's probably in the Brassicaceae (mustard family). Recognizing families gets you to genera and species more quickly, which in turn adds to the pleasure of plant-hunting.

All that said and done, now go and enjoy the plants!

FERNS AND HORSETAILS

MEXICAN MOSQUITO FERN

As small as Mexican mosquito fern is, it dwarfs the single duckweed plant (*Lemna* sp.) near the lower right-hand corner.

This plant is about half an inch in diameter. Against a light background, some translucent, almost white roots are apparent mainly by their shadows; the yellowish brown roots get their color from a coating of minute, hitchhiking algae.

Mexican mosquito fern floating in calm water.

Family: Azollaceae (mosquito fern family)

Scientific name: *Azolla microphylla* Kaulf.

Overall appearance: Small aquatic plants, free floating, with unbranched roots up to about 1" long that dangle in the water; stems branched multiple times, all the branches lying in one plane, the plant as a whole more or less isodiametric with a width of 0.4–0.5".

Leaves: 0.02–0.3" long, oval to almost round, densely crowded and overlapping each other, with tiny bumps (called papillae by botanists) on the upper side that give the plants a velvety look.

Elevation: Sea level to 4,000'.

Habitat: Slow-moving water and ponds.

Comments: It's hard to believe that this little plant, native from South America to British Columbia, is a fern, but like all ferns its life cycle includes production of spores. In winter, the plants often turn reddish; it seems to me that they also do so when stressed by summer heat. They're often so abundant that they completely cover the surface of the water. Once my dog spotted something to chase on the other side of an *Azolla*-covered irrigation canal and dashed off onto the brick-colored mat, then looked totally indignant when she found herself swimming.

Mosquito fern (*Azolla filiculoides*) plants are slightly larger, up to 1.2" long by 0.8" wide with oval leaves 0.05–0.08" long; other than that, they differ from Mexican mosquito fern in various all-but-microscopic details. Classification of species of *Azolla* is still an unresolved issue—there seem to be half a dozen or so of them worldwide—and future DNA research may provide better insight.

The tiny leaves of *Azolla* are actually quite complex. Each has two lobes: a lower, colorless, cup-shaped lobe that traps air and provides buoyancy, and an upper, photosynthetic lobe. A cavity inside the upper lobe contains microscopic strands of a bacterium, *Anabaena azollae*, that coverts nitrogen gas in the air into a form of nitrogen usable by plants. The bacteria (formerly classified as blue-green algae) fix enough nitrogen to feed themselves and their *Azolla* host; in return, the host provides *Anabaena* with carbohydrates. The upshot of this collaboration is that the fern can grow incredibly fast, doubling its weight every three to five days when conditions are right. Rice farmers in southeast Asia and other tropical regions make good use of *Azolla*'s fast growth and high nitrogen content; in fact, a Chinese agricultural text published in AD 540 already mentions *Azolla*. Vietnamese farmers grow one or two crops of *Azolla* in flooded fields and incorporate the nitrogen-laden ferns into the muddy soil, then plant their rice. Elsewhere, the rice is planted before the fields are inoculated with *Azolla*; as the rice grows tall and dense, the light-starved ferns die and decay, releasing nitrogen and other nutrients.

Sterile leaves of deer fern.

Underside of a fertile leaf of deer fern, with a sterile leaf in the background.

DEER FERN

Family: Blechnaceae (deer fern family)

Scientific name: *Blechnum spicant* (L.) Roth

Height: Up to about 3'.

Leaves: Of two types: sterile and fertile. Sterile leaves in clusters; each leaf up to 3.5' long by 0.8–4" wide, deeply lobed to once pinnately compound, usually with 20–80 pairs of lobes or leaflets. Fertile leaves (when present) emerging from the center of a cluster of sterile leaves, once pinnately compound, the leaflets less than 0.1" wide. Spore-producing structures (called sporangia) arranged in 2 long, narrow, closely spaced rows running lengthwise along the underside of each leaflet.

Elevation: Sea level to 5,000'.

Habitat: Moist, shady areas.

Comments: Worldwide, there are more than 200 species of *Blechnum*; this is the only one in northern California, where it grows mainly in the North Coast Ranges, Sierra Nevada, and coastal areas. As in most ferns, individual sporangia are tiny, best seen with a hand lens. Giant chain fern (*Woodwardia fimbriata*), California's only other representative of Blechnaceae, is 3–6' tall. Its leaves aren't differentiated into sterile and fertile leaves and are once pinnately compound with deeply lobed leaflets and narrow clusters of sporangia in two rows on the underside of each lobe.

Underside of a mature leaf of giant chain fern (*Woodwardia fimbriata*).

Bracken in fall.

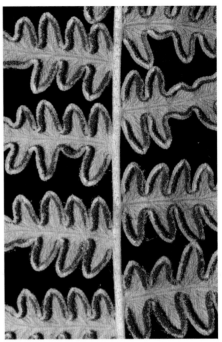

Bracken sporangia change from light green to dark brown as they mature.

BRACKEN

Family: Dennstaedtiaceae (bracken family)

Scientific name: *Pteridium aquilinum* (L.) Kuhn var. *pubescens* Underw.

Height: 10" to 5'.

Leaves: Overall shape a broad triangle, the blade 6" to 5' long, with a leaf stalk anywhere from 4" to more than 3' long. Lower part of blade usually 3-times pinnately compound; upper part less highly compound. Spore-producing structures (called sporangia) arranged in a more or less continuous line on the underside of the leaves parallel to the margins, which curl down to protect the delicate sporangia while they're maturing.

Elevation: Sea level to above 10,000'.

Habitat: Meadows and pastures, woodland, and forest; can tolerate both full sun and deep shade.

Comments: Bracken is the only species of *Pteridium* in California, where it's widespread except in the Central Valley and the deserts. It grows from creeping underground stems, regrows quickly after forest fires, and can form dense stands, sometimes becoming invasive. In fall, the leaves turn a beautiful golden yellow; then the dead brown leaves persist well into the following year. Young fronds are considered an asparagus-like delicacy in some places; nonetheless, the species is toxic to livestock and people. Cooking removes the vitamin B1–destroying enzymes that raw plants contain but not the carcinogens that are also present, and evidence from Japan suggests a link between frequent consumption of bracken and stomach cancer.

Upper half of a leaf.

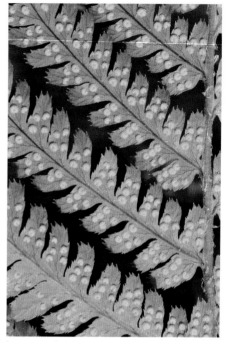

Immature sori.

CALIFORNIA WOOD FERN

Family: Dryopteridaceae (wood fern family)

Scientific name: *Dryopteris arguta* (Kaulf.) Maxon

Height: 1' to more than 3'.

Leaves: Usually in compact clusters. Overall shape of each leaf a narrow triangle, the blade 1' to more than 3' long by 5–12" wide, once or twice pinnately compound, the longest leaflets near the base of the blade; leaflet margins toothed with a vein running into the tip of each tooth. Sporangia borne in round clusters (called sori), each sorus covered by a delicate, kidney-shaped flap of leaf tissue until the sporangia are mature and ready to shed their spores.

Elevation: Sea level to above 8,000'.

Habitat: Shaded gullies, caves, and open wooded slopes.

Comments: This fern is native from southern California to British Columbia and eastwards to Arizona. In the Sacramento Valley it occurs in the Sutter Buttes; I've also found it along the Lower American River in dense oak woodland along with California maidenhair fern (*Adiantum jordanii*) and lots of poison oak. The little flaps that protect the immature sporangia in each sorus remind me of the kidney-shaped backyard swimming pools that were trendy in the 1950s and 60s. After the sporangia have matured, you have to look closely to find remnants of these protective flaps. Common wood fern (*Dryopteris expansa*) occurs mainly along the coast, in the western part of the North Coast Ranges, and in caves on the Modoc Plateau and has more or less 3-times pinnately compound leaves. Male fern (*Dryopteris filix-mas*) is rare in California.

Old sori after the spores have been shed.

WESTERN SWORD FERN

Family: Dryopteridaceae (wood fern family)

Scientific name: *Polystichum munitum* (Kaulf.) C. Presl

Height: 20" to more than 6'.

Leaves: Usually in clumps of up to 75 or even 100 leaves per clump. Each leaf 20" to 4' or occasionally 6' long, once pinnately compound, more or less evergreen; texture often coarse or leathery. Sori round, in 2 rows on the underside of the leaflets, each young sorus protected by a small, round, stalked outgrowth of leaf tissue, a bit like a miniscule umbrella, that shrivels as the sporangia mature.

Elevation: Sea level to 2,500', occasionally as high as 5,200'.

Habitat: Moist, shady woods, forests, and caves.

Comments: As in most ferns, the leaves of this species start out as tight coils, then unfurl as they grow bigger. At maturity the tiny sporangia abruptly pop open, flinging out the spores; the empty husks of the sporangia turn golden brown, as shown here. Western sword fern often forms dense stands on the forest floor. Look for it in northwestern California, the Cascades, the Sierra Nevada, and caves on the Modoc Plateau. It's the most common of northern California's eight species of *Polystichum*.

Like most ferns, western sword fern produces leaves that start out as tight coils, then unfurl as they grow bigger.

Leaf sheaths and spore-producing cones of common scouring rush (*Equisetum hyemale* subsp. *affine*).

Leaf sheaths of smooth scouring rush (*Equisetum laevigatum*).

COMMON SCOURING RUSH

Family: Equisetaceae (horsetail family)

Scientific name: *Equisetum hyemale* L. subsp. *affine* (Engelm.) Calder & Roy L. Taylor

Height: 2–7'.

Leaves: Hardly recognizable as leaves; in whorls, thin, slender, and fused by their lateral margins into 0.3–0.7"-long sheaths that wrap around the hollow, finely ridged, mostly unbranched stem; usually with two dark bands and a whitish one in between, each of the 22–50 teeth at the top of the sheath representing one leaf.

Elevation: Sea level to above 8,000'.

Habitat: Places with sandy or gravelly, moist soil.

Comments: This common herbaceous perennial typically forms dense stands from creeping underground stems. At the tip of the generally unbranched aboveground stems, you may find a small cone-shaped structure consisting of stalked, hexagonal plates, a bit like tiny 6-sided umbrellas packed together. That's where the spores are produced; when the spores are mature, the plates separate to release them. In smooth scouring rush (*Equisetum laevigatum*), a widespread annual, each sheath of leaves has only a single narrow dark band. Common horsetail (*Equisetum arvense*) and giant horsetail (*Equisetum telmateia* subsp. *braunii*) produce numerous small, regularly spaced branches.

In the Pacific Northwest, *Equisetum* is notoriously invasive, even thrusting up through asphalt paving. Native Americans and other people used the rough-textured stems like sandpaper and for scrubbing pots, hence the common name "scouring rush." All of today's species are herbaceous, but during the Carboniferous age, 345–280 million years ago, some of their now long-extinct relatives became woody and tree-like, 60' or more in height, and were a prominent component of the earth's vegetation.

Inch-long insect in one of the branched horsetails, probably common horsetail (*Equisetum arvense*).

WATER CLOVER

Family: Marsileaceae (marsilea family)

Also called: Hairy pepperwort

Scientific name: *Marsilea vestita* Hook. & Grev. subsp. *vestita*

Height: Up to 6" when growing on muddy soil.

Leaves: Palmately compound, each leaf consisting of 4 hairy leaflets and resembling a 4-leaved clover; leaf stalk slender, 2–15" long in plants growing in water, 1–6" in plants growing on exposed mud; leaf margins generally smooth.

Elevation: Sea level to above 7,000'.

Habitat: Vernal pools, pond margins, creek beds, and other muddy places.

Comments: This odd little fern grows from creeping underground stems; its leaves may form in clusters or be spread out along the stem. Its spores are produced inside oval, dark brown, hard-sided cases that are about 0.1–0.3" long and borne on short stems nestled among the leaf stalks. In northern California, the species occurs in the Sacramento Valley, Cascades, Sierra Nevada, the eastern part of the North Coast Ranges, and on the Modoc Plateau. At elevations of 4,500–6,500' in the Klamath Ranges and Cascades, you may find a rather similar-looking species, *Marsilea oligospora*; its leaflets have faintly scalloped margins.

NESTED POLYPODY

New leaves soon after their emergence in late fall.

Underside of leaf with almost mature sori, which will turn golden or rusty brown after the spores have been shed.

Underside of leaf with pale green, immature sori.

Family: Polypodiaceae (polypody family)

Also called: Intermediate polypody

Scientific name: *Polypodium calirhiza* S. A. Whitmore & A. R. Sm.

Height: Usually 4–8", sometimes up to 16".

Leaves: Strung out along long, creeping underground stems; the blades typically 4–8" long, less often as short as 2" or as long as 16", deeply pinnately lobed but not compound; the leaf midrib hairy on the upper side; margins toothed. Spore-producing structure (called sporangia) borne in round to oval or oblong clusters, 0.06–0.2" long, called sori; immature sporangia are fully exposed and not protected by a curled-under leaf margin or any other structure.

Elevation: Sea level to about 4,500'.

Habitat: Cliffs, rocky outcrops, and road cuts; sometimes also on tree trunks, branches, or mounds of dredger tailings.

Comments: Look for nested polypody in northwestern California, the Cascade foothills, and the Sierra Nevada. It's generally uncommon in the Sacramento Valley but abundant on mossy dredger tailings shaded by oak trees along the Lower American River. The leaves die quickly in the Valley's summer heat, and by June or July you really have to search for their shriveled remains. New leaves emerge soon after the first winter rains, and their bright green color makes them conspicuous in the wintry landscape.

Licorice fern (*Polypodium glycyrrhiza*) looks rather similar; it grows from California's Coast Ranges to Alaska but not in the Sacramento Valley. In places where licorice fern and nested polypody grow together, they often hybridize; in fact, the hybrid offspring frequently outnumber the two parent species (for example, at Point Reyes), making identification a challenge. Northern California is also home to two species in which the upper side of the leaf is hairless along the midrib: western polypody (*Polypodium hesperium*) and the aptly named leatherleaf fern (*Polypodium scouleri*). They too can hybridize with other polypodies.

CALIFORNIA MAIDENHAIR FERN

Family: Pteridaceae (brake family)

Scientific name: *Adiantum jordanii* Müll. Hal.

Height: 8–20", occasionally taller.

Leaves: Loosely to tightly clustered, 8–20" or longer including the thin, shiny, reddish brown to black leaf stalk; twice or 3-times pinnately compound; each fan-shaped leaflet irregularly lobed, the sides converging at an angle of 90–180°, the lobes usually less than one-quarter of the leaflet's length. Spore-producing structures (called sporangia) borne in a discontinuous row near the leaf margins, which curl down to protect them.

Elevation: Sea level to 4,000'.

Habitat: Moist, shady areas.

Comments: This dainty fern grows from creeping underground stems along the coast; it's fairly common in the North Coast Ranges and the foothills ringing the Sacramento Valley. Southern maidenhair fern (*Adiantum capillus-veneris*) is less frequent. Its leaflets are more deeply lobed and their sides converge at an angle of 45–90°. Five-finger fern (*Adiantum aleuticum*) has leaves whose first division is more or less palmately compound (although there aren't necessarily five such divisions or "fingers"); each "finger" is further divided on a pinnate pattern. Native American basket weavers use the leaf stalks of California maidenhair and five-finger fern to create dark patterns on a background of lighter-colored basketry materials.

 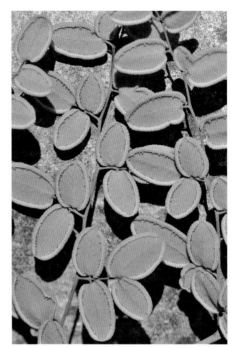

COFFEE FERN
Family: Pteridaceae (brake family)

Scientific name: *Pellaea andromedifolia* (Kaulf.) Fée

Height: Up to about 30".

Leaves: Loosely clustered, 8–30" long including the leaf stalk, 4–12" wide, usually 3-times pinnately compound, occasionally twice or 4-times compound; leaflets oval, medium to dark green, blue-green, or purplish red, not shiny, the tip of each rounded, slightly indented, or notched but never coming to an abrupt point. Leaf stalk slender, shiny, tan or reddish, somewhat brittle and easily snapped. Spore-producing structures (called sporangia) in a row parallel to the margins of the leaflets, which curl down to protect them.

Elevation: Sea level to 6,000'.

Habitat: Dry or rocky, sunny or shaded areas.

Comments: Coffee fern grows from creeping underground stems, sometimes as floppy bunches of leaves sprawling down a steep bank or entangled in other vegetation, other times more upright. The dead leaves persist for a while, turning dark rust or purplish brown, their leaflets curling inwards from both sides as they dry out. It's fairly common in the North Coast Ranges, Cascades, and Sierra Nevada. Bird's-foot fern (*Pellaea mucronata*) has dark brown to black leaf stalks and narrow leaflets that come to a small abrupt point at the tip. Three additional species of this genus occur in northern California: Brewer's cliff-brake (*Pellaea breweri*) has once pinnately compound leaves, each leaflet deeply cleft into two or three lobes, while Sierra cliff-brake (*Pellaea brachyptera*) and Bridges' cliff-brake (*Pellaea bridgesii*) have twice pinnately compound leaves.

GOLDBACK FERN

Family: Pteridaceae (brake family)

Scientific name: *Pentagramma triangularis* (Kaulf.) Yatsk. et al. subsp. *triangularis*

Height: 4–16".

Leaves: Overall shape broadly triangular to pentagonal, the blade 1–7" long and almost as wide on a slender, shiny, dark or reddish brown, somewhat brittle leaf stalk that's about twice as long as the blade; once pinnately compound except for the lowest part, which is twice pinnately compound; all leaflets deeply lobed. On the lower side of the leaf, the spore-producing structures (called sporangia) more or less follow the veins (easiest to see in young leaves); the rest of the surface is covered with little granules of a waxy, cream-colored to bright yellow exudate.

Elevation: Sea level to 7,500'.

Habitat: Woodland and shaded rocky areas.

Comments: Goldback fern grows from short underground stems, and its leaves are usually more or less clustered. It's widespread in northern California except in the Sacramento Valley. Two other subspecies of *P. triangularis* are restricted to southern California. Silverback fern (*Pentagramma pallida*), which has been reported from Butte, Shasta, and Mendocino counties, resembles goldback fern except that its leaf stalks are dark brown to black and its leaves produce a white exudate on both sides; in older manuals, it's considered another subspecies of *P. triangularis*.

Underside of an old leaf. Numerous mature, golden brown sporangia almost hide the pale yellow, waxy exudate on the leaves.

To add to the confusion, all these plants used to be classified in the genus *Pityrogramma*. To quote the 2012 *Jepson Manual*, the whole group is "a puzzling complex of intergrading chemical, chromosomal, and morphological variants."

CONIFERS

Pollen cones, which around December release huge clouds of yellow pollen.

Four mature seed cones along with some dead branchlets.

INCENSE CEDAR

Family: Cupressaceae (cypress family)

Also called: Post cedar, white cedar, or bastard cedar

Scientific name: *Calocedrus decurrens* (Torr.) Florin

Height: 60–225'.

Leaves: Evergreen, opposite, 0.1–0.4" long, scale-like, overlapping, closely appressed to flat sprays of small, drooping branches (often called branchlets), bright yellowish green to olive-green.

Seed cones: 0.7–1.5" long, hanging from the upper branches, reddish brown; technically composed of 6 scales, but most noticeable is the woody center partition sandwiched between 2 woody scales that at maturity curl away to release 4 seeds; of the 2 seeds on each side, one is flanked by a long, skinny, diamond-shaped wing, the other by a shorter, narrower wing.

Elevation: Usually 1,000' to above 8,000'.

Habitat: Forest.

Comments: This widespread tree has fibrous reddish bark resembling that of coast redwood (*Sequoia sempervirens*). Redwood bark, though, can be almost a foot thick; except at the base of the tree, incense cedar's rarely exceeds an inch in thickness and consequently isn't nearly as fire-resistant. You'll find both pollen and seed cones on the same tree. Older books refer to incense cedar as *Libocedrus decurrens*. Port Orford cedar (*Chamaecyparis lawsoniana*) and Alaska cedar (*Callitropsis nootkatensis*, also called Alaska cypress or yellow cypress because of its sulfur-yellow wood) have somewhat similar foliage; Port Orford cedar's is deep yellow-green and smooth-textured, while Alaska cedar's is blue-green in color and feels harsh and prickly. Both species produce small, round seed cones resembling those of *Hesperocyparis*. Port Orford cedar is restricted to the Klamath Ranges and southwestern Oregon; Alaska cedar grows all the way from Siskiyou and Del Norte counties to southeastern Alaska.

Seed cones of an unidentified species of *Hesperocyparis*.

CYPRESS

Family: Cupressaceae (cypress family)

Scientific name: *Hesperocyparis* (formerly called *Cupressus*)

Height: Generally less than 80'. Siskiyou cypress (*Hesperocyparis bakeri*) can reach 130'; pygmy cypress (*Hesperocyparis pygmaea*) is a 3–6' shrub on poor soil but a 30–160' (!) tree on rich soil.

Leaves: Evergreen, opposite, scale-like, overlapping, closely appressed to branchlets.

Seed cones: 0.4–2" wide, woody, more or less spherical, consisting of 6–12 abutting plates, usually borne in clusters, often remaining on the plants for several years.

Elevation: Sea level to 6,000', depending on the species.

Habitat: Chaparral, woodland, forest, or coastal terraces, depending on the species.

Comments: Unlike the flat sprays of incense, Alaska, and Port Orford cedar, the branchlets of *Hesperocyparis* are three-dimensional. Each shrub or tree produces both pollen and seed cones. Monterey cypress (*Hesperocyparis macrocarpa*), native to Monterey County, has been widely planted and become naturalized, especially near the coast. At various times, botanists have divided California's members of this genus into anywhere from 8–15 species, several of them, no matter how you split or lump them, native to northern California. Common names can be confusing, and some conifers called "cypress" or "cedar" actually belong to completely different genera or even families.

WESTERN JUNIPER

Family: Cupressaceae (cypress family)

Scientific name: *Juniperus occidentalis* Hook.

Height: 15–65'.

Leaves: Evergreen, opposite or in whorls of 3, scale-like, overlapping, closely appressed to young branches.

Seed cones: 0.3–0.5" wide, more or less spherical, somewhat fleshy and resembling a berry, initially blue-green, maturing blue-black.

Elevation: 2,000–7,500'.

Habitat: Dry open areas, woodland, and sagebrush.

Comments: Western juniper produces pollen and seed cones on the same tree; it occurs from the Cascades and Modoc Plateau north and east into Washington, Idaho, and Nevada. Sierra juniper (*Juniperus grandis*) and California juniper (*Juniperus californica*) are more widespread in northern California; the former is a tree, the latter can be a shrub or small tree, and both generally produce pollen and seed cones on separate plants. Common juniper (*Juniperus communis*) is almost always a low shrub; unlike other junipers, its 0.3–0.8"-long leaves are needle-shaped and spreading. Many different birds and mammals feed on the berry-like seed cones of all the junipers, inadvertently dispersing the digestion-resistant seeds in their droppings.

COAST REDWOOD

Family: Cupressaceae (cypress family)

Scientific name: *Sequoia sempervirens* (D. Don) Endl.

Height: Up to about 360'.

Leaves: Evergreen, mostly alternate and flattened into one plane, 0.2–1" long, very narrow. On especially fast-growing branches and those bearing pollen or seed cones, the leaves are shorter, no more than 0.3" long, and may be appressed to the branches or spread away from them.

Seed cones: 0.5–1.5" long, woody, spherical to oval, composed of 15–20 or more stalked, wrinkled plates.

Elevation: Usually sea level to 2,000'; rarely as high as 3,600'.

Habitat: Conifer forest, generally within 5–25 miles of the coast, in areas with a lot of summer fog.

Comments: The trunk of this iconic tree can attain 30' in diameter. Trees 1,000–1,200 years old are not uncommon in old-growth forest, and some have lived up to 2,200 years. Seed cones and the small yellowish pollen cones grow on the same tree. Unlike other conifers, coast redwood can regenerate from dormant buds encircling the base of the trunk if a tree dies or is felled. You'll find the resulting rings of trees here and there in old-growth forest where the parent died from a lightning strike or other natural causes; second-growth forest has many such rings around cut stumps. Today, coast redwood is widely planted but occurs naturally only from Monterey County to southern Oregon. Researchers, though, have found fossil *Sequoia* as far away as Montana and Wyoming from periods when western North America's climate was very different.

White fir (*Abies concolor*) sapling already showing the tiers of branches that characterize most firs.

Immature seed cone of grand fir (*Abies grandis*) exuding, as is typical of many firs, copious amounts of resin.

FIR

Family: Pinaceae (pine family)

Scientific name: *Abies*

Height: Generally no more than 250', although noble fir (*Abies procera*) can reach 280'.

Leaves: Evergreen, 0.8–3.5" long, depending on the species, very narrow, leaving circular scars on the twigs when they break off.

Seed cones: No more than 9" long, woody, more or less cylindrical with a rounded top, borne upright on the tree's upper branches, the scales shed one by one to release the seeds.

Elevation: Generally 3,000' to above 10,000', depending on the species, except for grand fir (*Abies grandis*), which grows from sea level to about 2,000'.

Habitat: Generally found in forest.

Comments: Of northern California's six species of fir, only grand fir (*Abies grandis*) grows right along the coast, where it can vary from a scraggly shrub in coastal scrub to a majestic, 240'-tall forest tree. Unlike most conifers, firs carry their cones upright. The cones disintegrate on the tree when the seeds are ripe, and the only intact cones you'll find on the ground are those gnawed off by Douglas squirrels, which dismantle them on the ground to feed on the seeds or stash them away intact for winter supplies. Some species of *Abies* hybridize, which can make identification tricky. Douglas-fir (*Pseudotsuga menziesii* var. *menziesii*) is easily distinguished by its completely different seed cones, which hang from the branches, are shed intact, and have long, 3-pointed bracts interspersed among the cone scales.

SITKA SPRUCE

Family: Pinaceae (pine family)

Also called: Tideland spruce

Scientific name: *Picea sitchensis* (Bong.) Carrière

Height: Usually under 220', rarely up to 320'.

Leaves: Evergreen, arranged spirally on the branches and bristling in all directions, 0.4–1.5" long, stiff, narrow, more or less flat on the upper side, somewhat rounded on the lower side, with a sharp tip.

Seed cones: 2–4" long, hanging from the upper branches; core woody but scales stiffly papery, with irregularly toothed margins.

Elevation: Sea level to 1,500'.

Habitat: Coastal forest and moist to swampy areas near the coast.

Comments: Like coast redwood (*Sequoia sempervirens*), Sitka spruce is restricted to moist, foggy coastal areas, but its range extends from California's north coast 1,800 miles northwards into Alaska. In windy sites, it may just form low, tangled hedges; where more sheltered but not crowded by other trees, it can become candelabra-like with a trunk exceeding 16' in diameter; elsewhere it can form dense stands of straight, columnar trees. It grows very fast, and trees only 100 years old may already be 200' tall. Nonetheless, the wood is exceptionally strong. As in many other trees adapted to cool or cold climates, new leaves begin developing in fall inside buds protected by small brown scales; the following spring the scales drop off and the leaves emerge. Sitka spruce seems to produce especially many light, papery bud scales, which for a while can carpet the ground. Brewer spruce (*Picea breweriana*), found in hard-to-get-to places high in the Klamath Ranges and southwestern Oregon, has long, drooping branches with exceptionally dark green foliage that give it its alternate common name, weeping spruce. California's only other spruce, Engelmann spruce (*Picea engelmannii*) grows in a few remote locations in Siskiyou and Shasta counties; it's more common farther north and east.

Typical stand on a marshy shore.

LODGEPOLE PINE

Family: Pinaceae (pine family)

Also called: Tamarack

Scientific name: *Pinus contorta* Loudon subsp. *murrayana* (Grev. & Balf.) Critchf.

Height: Up to about 110'.

Leaves: Evergreen, in bundles of 2, 1–3.5" long, needle-like.

Seed cones: 0.8–2.5" long, woody, fairly symmetrical in shape, with prickly scales, sometimes borne in pairs or small clusters, dropping off the tree soon after opening.

Elevation: 3,000' to above 11,000'.

Habitat: Forest, lake margins, and the borders of wet meadows; also fairly dry sites in the upper part of its elevational range or after a forest fire.

Comments: Northern California is home to about 10 species of pine, some with two or more subspecies or varieties. Here, I've only included two representatives of the group. Although lodgepole pine does well on wet soils, you'll sometimes also find it on much drier ground, especially after a forest fire, when it can form almost impenetrable "dog-hair thickets." As in other members of the pine family, pollen and seed cones are borne on the same tree. In northern California, this subspecies occurs in the Klamath Ranges, Cascades, and Sierra Nevada. Three other subspecies retain their cones on the tree for many years. Two of them, shore pine (*Pinus contorta* subsp. *contorta*) and the rare Bolander's beach pine (*Pinus contorta* subsp. *bolanderi*), can be found near sea level along the northern California coast; both have asymmetrical seed cones. The fourth subspecies grows in the Rocky Mountains.

FOOTHILL PINE

Family: Pinaceae (pine family)

Also called: Gray pine or ghost pine

Scientific name: *Pinus sabiniana* D. Don

Height: Up to 125'.

Leaves: Evergreen, in drooping bundles of 3, 4–15" long, needle-like, dull gray-green.

Seed cones: 4–12" long by 5–7" wide, woody, taking until the fall of their second year of growth to mature, then persisting on the tree for a few more years; cone scales thick, sharp-pointed, the scales near the base of the cone bearing stout hooked spurs.

Elevation: 500–5,000', occasionally lower.

Habitat: Woodland, chaparral, dry slopes and ridges, and infertile soils in mixed conifer-deciduous forest.

Comments: This is the first pine you'll encounter as you head out of the Sacramento Valley into the surrounding foothills. Its sparse, gray-green foliage and unusual branching pattern make it easy to identify. Like most pines, young trees have a single straight trunk. After 20–30 years, though, they start

On the tree, this seed cone would be hanging from its branch.

producing thick branches all growing steeply upwards so that it can be hard to figure out which one was the original trunk, and the trees may start leaning at all sorts of odd angles as if, as one botanist put it, they're not entirely sober. Fully grown but still green seed cones can weigh 4–4.5 pounds each and are the second heaviest of any North American pine; only Coulter pine (*Pinus coulteri*), native to southern California and Baja California, has heavier ones. Sugar pine (*Pinus lambertiana*), widespread in northern California's mountains, produces cones up to 2' long, but they have thin scales and so are much lighter in weight.

BLUE ELDERBERRY

Family: Adoxaceae (muskroot family)

Scientific name: *Sambucus nigra* L. subsp. *caerulea* (Raf.) Bolli

Height: 6' to more than 25'.

Leaves: Deciduous, opposite, once pinnately compound with 3–9 leaflets per leaf, each leaflet 1–8" long; margins toothed.

Flowers: Borne in fairly flat-topped clusters of numerous small creamy white flowers, the entire cluster 1.5" to more than 12" in diameter; each flower with 5 sepals, 5 spreading petals fused at their bases, and 5 stamens; ovary inferior.

Blooms March through September.

Elevation: Sea level to almost 10,000'.

Habitat: Stream banks, flood plains, and open areas in woodland and forest.

Comments: Even in winter, these shrubs or small multi-trunked trees are easy to identify by the many new vertical shoots growing out of older, leaning or arching branches. In mild winters, the plants may start leafing out as early as January. Later, each small flower produces a berry-like fruit roughly 0.2" in diameter, almost black but covered with so much waxy bloom that it looks light blue. In late spring and summer, plants often bear flowers and fruit simultaneously. Older texts place *Sambucus* in the Caprifoliaceae (honeysuckle family).

The valley elderberry longhorn beetle (*Desmocerus californicus dimorphus*, sometimes called VELB for short) lives only in the Sacramento Valley and northern San Joaquin Valley and is completely dependent on blue elderberry. The colorful red and black males have bodies up to 0.8" long and equally long antennae; the females are mainly black, with shorter antennae. Between March and June, the adults feed on elderberry leaves and flowers. Then they mate. Each female lays anywhere from 8 to more than 100 eggs, and the larvae that hatch from the eggs tunnel into young elderberry branches and feed on the soft interior tissues for a year or two. Eventually each larva transforms into an immobile pupa; about a month later a new adult emerges from the pupa. The beetles became rare as California's riparian forests were cut down for agricultural and urban development, construction of levees and highways, and other reasons, and so now both beetles and elderberry plants in the beetles' home range are protected by the federal Endangered Species Act.

RED ELDERBERRY

Family: Adoxaceae (muskroot family)

Scientific name: *Sambucus racemosa* L. var. *racemosa*

Height: 3–20'.

Leaves: Deciduous, opposite, once pinnately compound with 5–7 leaflets per leaf, each leaflet 1.5" to more than 6" long, oval; margins toothed.

Flowers: Borne in elongated or strongly domed clusters of numerous small creamy white flowers, the entire cluster less than 5" in diameter; each flower with 5 sepals, 5 petals fused at their bases and often curved downwards, and 5 stamens; ovary inferior.

Blooms May through July.

Elevation: Sea level to almost 11,000'.

Habitat: Moist sites in forest or open terrain.

Comments: This red-fruited shrub grows in much of northern California except in the Sacramento Valley and the eastern part of the North Coast Ranges. In older texts it's called *Sambucus microbotrys* and, like all the elderberries, included in the Caprifoliaceae (honeysuckle family). Black elderberry (*Sambucus racemosa* var. *melanocarpa*) occurs at elevations of 6,000–11,000'. It's similar to red elderberry except that its inflorescences usually are less than 3" wide and its fruit is glossy black, lacking the waxy bloom that gives blue elderberry its common name.

FREEWAY ICEPLANT

Family: Aizoaceae (iceplant or fig-marigold family)

Scientific name: *Carpobrotus edulis* (L.) N. E. Br.

Height: A few inches, with stems up to 10' long sprawling across the ground.

Leaves: Succulent, opposite, 2.5–4" long, sharply triangular in cross-section, hairless, without a waxy bloom.

Flowers: 3–4" in diameter; sepals 5; petals numerous, initially cream-colored or light yellow but turning pink with age; stamens numerous; ovary inferior.

Blooms mainly April through October, but you can often find a few flowers almost all year long.

Elevation: Sea level to about 350'.

Habitat: Coastal grassland, scrub, chaparral, dunes, beaches, and roadsides.

Comments: This invasive perennial, native to southern Africa, has been widely planted along freeways and in coastal areas. Unfortunately, it smothers any native vegetation in its path, produces lots of seeds, and can regrow from small, broken-off fragments of stem. In short, nowadays most biologists consider it bad news. Sea fig (*Carpobrotus chilensis*) has smaller leaves with a waxy bloom and a more rounded-triangular shape in cross-section and magenta flowers that are only 1–2" wide, but it too is invasive. The two species can hybridize.

40

WILD PISTACHIO

Family: Anacardiaceae (sumac or cashew family)

Also called: Mount Atlas mastic tree

Scientific name: *Pistacia atlantica* Desf.

Height: 10–35'.

Leaves: Deciduous, alternate, once pinnately compound, typically with 7–9 leaflets per leaf (occasionally as few as 3 or as many as 15), each leaflet 2–4" long and up to almost 1" wide, upper side glossy, covered with short soft hairs at least when young, petiole D-shaped in cross-section; margins smooth and flat.

Flowers: Male and female flowers borne on separate trees; sepals and petals not differentiated, tiny, greenish brown; male flowers with 4–7 stamens; female flowers with vestigial or no stamens and a superior ovary with 3 styles that ripens into a fleshy, red, egg-shaped fruit 0.2–0.3" long.

Blooms February through April.

Elevation: Sea level to 300'.

Habitat: Floodplains, open woodland, and disturbed areas.

Comments: This tree is native from northern Africa to Pakistan, and its resin has been harvested nondestructively for millennia for medicinal uses. The pistachio nuts you find in the store come from a related Middle Eastern species, *Pistacia vera*, which is often grafted onto *Pistacia atlantica* rootstock. Chinese pistache (*Pistacia chinensis*), widely planted horticulturally, has leaflets with slightly wavy, upward-curved margins. In California, wild pistachio is occasionally found in the Sacramento Valley.

PEPPER TREE

Family: Anacardiaceae (sumac or cashew family)

Also called: Peruvian pepper tree, false pepper, escobilla, or molle de Peru

Scientific name: *Schinus molle* L.

Height: 15–60'.

Leaves: Evergreen, alternate, 4–12" long, once pinnately compound with 15–59 leaflets per leaf; leaflets generally less than 0.5" wide, matte to satiny; margins smooth or slightly toothed.

Flowers: Borne in big, loose clusters, with male and female flowers on separate trees; each flower roughly 0.1" wide with 5 sepals, 5 white, greenish, or pale yellow petals, and 10 stamens or a superior ovary with 3 styles.

Blooms June through August.

Elevation: Sea level to above 2,000'.

Habitat: Disturbed ground, roadsides, and riparian areas.

Comments: This attractive albeit weedy tree is native to South America. Its twigs are flexible and drooping, which together with the drooping leaves gives the trees a distinctive "weeping" look. Its aromatic leaves can cause dermatitis. Brazilian pepper tree (*Schinus terebinthifolius*), which has been reported from the San Francisco Bay region, has stiff twigs that angle upwards and fewer but wider leaflets; it resembles wild pistachio (*Pistacia atlantica*) but is evergreen. Both species of *Schinus* produce small, red, berry-like fruits. Those of Brazilian pepper tree are dried and used as "pink peppercorns," especially in South American cuisines, but some people are highly allergic to them.

POISON OAK

Family: Anacardiaceae (sumac or cashew family)

Also called: Western poison oak

Scientific name: *Toxicodendron diversilobum* (Torr. & A. Gray) Greene

Height: 20" to 15' as a shrub, even taller in its vine-like form.

Leaves: Deciduous, alternate, once pinnately compound, usually with 3 or rarely 5 shiny leaflets, the terminal leaflet 0.4" to more than 5" long by 0.4–3.5" wide; leaflet margins smooth, wavy, or lobed. Young leaves often bronze-colored.

Flowers: Borne in loose, arching sprays, with male and female flowers usually on separate plants; each flower 0.2–0.3" wide with 5 small green sepals, 5 white or yellowish green petals, and 5 stamens or 1 pistil with a single style.

Blooms March through June.

Elevation: Sea level to almost 5,500'.

Habitat: Woodland, chaparral, partly shaded grassland, and coastal scrub.

Comments: This notorious species, called *Rhus diversiloba* in older texts, can be a shrub or woody vine. Contact with any part of the plant, including leafless twigs in winter, can cause severe dermatitis. Most Native Americans seem to have been immune to poison oak and used the twigs in basketry and for smoking salmon, the leaves for making a deep black dye. Individuals of mixed Native American and European ancestry, however, are more likely to lack immunity. Deer relish the leaves, eating as much as 20 percent of each year's growth in some areas; horses like it too. The roughly spherical white fruits, up to 0.3" in diameter, are eaten by mourning doves, crows, Nuttall's woodpeckers, and other birds. Box elder (*Acer negundo*) has similar-looking leaves, but they're always opposite, never alternate. Skunk bush (*Rhus aromatica*, formerly called *Rhus trilobata*) resembles poison oak but has yellow petals and orange fruit. Many other members of this largely tropical and subtropical family, which includes cashews, pistachios, and mangoes, also produce irritant chemicals.

BREWER'S ANGELICA

Family: Apiaceae (carrot family)

Scientific name: *Angelica breweri* A. Gray

Height: 3' to more than 6'.

Leaves: Alternate, overall shape somewhat triangular, the blade up to more than 3' long and equally wide, twice or 3-times pinnately compound; leaflets 2.4–4" long, fairly narrow, bright green, usually hairless; margins toothed.

Flowers: Borne in compound umbels; sepals tiny or not evident at all; petals 5 per flower, white, hairy on their lower side; stamens 5, also white; ovary inferior, densely hairy.

Blooms June through August.

Elevation: 2,500' to almost 10,000'.

Habitat: Conifer forest and open areas in forest.

Comments: Look for Brewer's angelica in the Cascades and Sierra Nevada. It's one of seven species of *Angelica* found in northern California, all of them herbaceous perennials that grow from a taproot.

COAST ANGELICA

Family: Apiaceae (carrot family)

Scientific name: *Angelica hendersonii* J. M. Coult. & Rose

Height: 30" to more than 6'.

Leaves: Alternate, the blade up to 2' long, twice to 3-times pinnately compound; leaflets 2–4" long, narrow to oval, thick, their upper side bright green or a more muted gray-green, their lower side paler and usually covered with dense woolly hairs; margins toothed or scalloped.

Flowers: Tightly packed together in compound umbels; sepals tiny or not evident at all; petals 5 per flower, white to purplish pink, densely hairy on their lower surface; stamens 5, white; ovary inferior, densely hairy.

Blooms June through July.

Elevation: Sea level to about 500'.

Habitat: Coastal bluffs and coastal scrub.

Comments: Coast angelica can tolerate wind and salt spray, and so you may find these rather sturdy herbaceous perennials sprawling right on the edge of coastal bluffs from Monterey County to southern Washington.

BUR-CHERVIL

Family: Apiaceae (carrot family)

Scientific name: *Anthriscus caucalis* M. Bieb.

Height: 18–40".

Leaves: Alternate, the blade 2–6" long on a petiole about half as long, twice or 3-times pinnately divided or compound, sparsely to moderately hairy, with a nice herbal scent when crushed, a bit like parsley but sweeter; the lower part of the petiole flattened and wrapped around the stem, with shaggy white hair along the margins.

Flowers: Borne in relatively few-flowered, fairly open compound umbels, usually with only 4–6 stalks composing the primary umbel; no sepals; petals 5 per flower, white; stamens 5, filaments white, anthers off-white to beige; ovary inferior, covered with tiny, Velcro-like hooks.

Blooms March through June.

Elevation: Sea level to 5,000'.

Habitat: Somewhat moist, lightly to deeply shaded places.

Comments: Bur-chervil is native to Eurasia. It can be annual or biennial, resprouting from a taproot in its second season, and often grows in dense patches. It's the only representative of its genus found in California.

POISON HEMLOCK

Family: Apiaceae (carrot family)

Also called: Poison stinkweed, poison parsley, or carrot fern

Scientific name: *Conium maculatum* L.

Height: 20" to 10'.

Leaves: Alternate, the blade 6–12" long, usually twice pinnately compound, hairless, with an unpleasant musty smell when bruised.

Flowers: Borne in compound umbels; no sepals; petals 5 per flower, white; stamens 5, also white; ovary inferior, with longitudinal ribs that become prominent as the fruit dries, hairless.

Blooms April through July.

Elevation: Sea level to 5,000'.

Habitat: Riparian and disturbed areas.

Comments: This weedy European biennial was introduced to North America in the 1800s as a fern-like garden plant—in early spring, when the new growth is a couple of feet tall, it does look a bit like bracken from a distance. Close up, it looks quite different, and of course bracken, being a true fern, never flowers. The stems of poison hemlock are hollow, and both they and the petioles are typically spotted or streaked reddish purple. All parts of the plant are extremely poisonous to humans and other mammals when ingested, and some people get dermatitis just from handling the plants. Water hemlock (*Cicuta maculata*), native to California, is just as poisonous. It too can have purple-streaked stems, but its leaves are only once or twice pinnate; it grows mainly in the Klamath Ranges and the Sacramento–San Joaquin River Delta. Western water hemlock (*Cicuta douglasii*), another highly toxic species, is similar to water hemlock but has plain green stems.

QUEEN ANNE'S LACE

Family: Apiaceae (carrot family)

Also called: Carrot, wild carrot, bird's nest, or devil's plague

Scientific name: *Daucus carota* L.

Height: 6" to 4'.

Leaves: Alternate, the blade 2–6" long, typically 3- or 4-times pinnately dissected with very narrow leaf segments, hairless to bristle-haired.

Flowers: Borne in compound umbels several inches wide, a whorl of pinnately lobed bracts just below each main umbel; sepals often not evident; petals 5 per flower, white, except for one rose, purple, or almost black flower at the center; stamens 5, also white except in the dark central flower; ovary inferior, bristly.

Blooms May through September.

Elevation: Sea level to 5,500'.

Habitat: Disturbed areas such as roadsides and flood plains.

Comments: This widespread European species can be an annual, biennial, or short-lived herbaceous perennial. The dark center flower is easy to miss: At first glance you might think it's a small insect. One plant I found had four lavender central flowers, and a few inflorescences lack a dark central flower entirely. In immature umbels, the bracts temporarily extend beyond the flowers so that the inflorescences resemble southwestern carrot (*Daucus pusillus*), but the bracts lack *D. pusillus*'s bristly hairs, and in any case the flowers of Queen Anne's lace soon catch up with the bracts and hide them when viewed from above. When fruiting, the branches of the umbel curl upwards into a "bird's nest" shape, revealing the bracts again. The only other species I know of that forms a similar "bird's nest" when fruiting is toothpick ammi (*Ammi visnaga*). The seed heads of greater ammi (*Ammi majus*) stay flat and open. Both species of *Ammi* are hairless, and neither has a dark central flower.

SOUTHWESTERN CARROT

Family: Apiaceae (carrot family)

Also called: American wild carrot

Scientific name: *Daucus pusillus* Michx.

Height: 1.5" to more than 3'.

Leaves: Alternate, the leaf blade 1.2" to more than 4" long, usually 3-times pinnately dissected with very narrow leaf segments and rough, bristly hairs.

Flowers: Borne in compact compound umbels up to 1.5" in diameter, including a whorl of bristly bracts under each inflorescence, never with a dark central flower; sepals often not evident; petals 5 per flower, white; stamens 5, also white; ovary inferior, very bristly.

Blooms April through June.

Elevation: Sea level to 5,500'.

Habitat: Dry, rocky or sandy open areas in grassland, coastal scrub, and chaparral; disturbed sites such as roadsides.

Comments: This inconspicuous annual is easy to overlook; once your eyes have become attuned to it, though, you're likely to discover that it can be quite abundant. The stems of southwestern carrot branch less than those of Queen Anne's lace (*Daucus carota*), sometimes not at all. When fruiting, its umbels stay flat, and in locations supporting both species, southwestern carrot seems to bloom about a month earlier than Queen Anne's lace. Southwestern carrot is native from South America to British Columbia.

Personally, I'd like to see the English name of this entire family changed to "poison hemlock family" as a reminder that even though many of its members are delicious to eat—they include carrots, celery, fennel, parsley, dill, and cilantro—others are deadly poisonous.

COASTAL BUTTON-CELERY

Family: Apiaceae (carrot family)

Scientific name: *Eryngium armatum* (S. Watson) J. M. Coult. & Rose

Height: Often just a few inches, with stems 4–20" long lying flat on the ground; sometimes growing more upright.

Leaves: Basal leaves with blades 4–12" long, narrow, usually hairless, sessile or with a short, wide petiole; margins toothed or irregularly incised, each tooth tipped with a spine; stem leaves alternate and smaller.

Flowers: Nestled among spine-tipped, light green, gray, or purple-tinged bracts that form domed heads 0.2–0.6" wide, most bracts edged white; sepals 5, spine-tipped, colored like the bracts; petals 5, white or purplish; stamens 5, anthers also white or purplish, drying tan after the pollen has been shed; ovary inferior.

Blooms May through August.

Elevation: Sea level to 650'.

Habitat: Coastal grassland, bluffs, coastal scrub, and marsh edges.

Comments: If you've ever sat down on the ground in coastal grassland, then jumped up again in a hurry, this painfully spiny biennial or herbaceous perennial may have been the reason. It grows along the coast from Santa Barbara County to Humboldt County and also in the Sacramento–San Joaquin River Delta and the southern part of the North Coast Ranges.

GREAT VALLEY COYOTE THISTLE

Family: Apiaceae (carrot family)

Scientific name: *Eryngium castrense* Jeps.

Height: 8" to 2'.

Leaves: Basal leaves with blades 4–12" long, narrow, hairless, sessile or with a very short petiole; margins deeply pinnately lobed, sometimes twice pinnately lobed, spiny; stem leaves smaller.

Flowers: Nestled among spiny, light green, gray-green, or blue-green bracts that form nearly spherical heads 0.3–0.6" wide; sepals 5, the same color as the bracts, tapering to a spine at the tip, with toothed spiny margins; petals 5, white or purplish; stamens 5, anthers blue or white; ovary inferior.

Blooms April through July.

Elevation: Sea level to 3,000'.

Habitat: Vernal pools, swales, and beds of intermittent streams.

Comments: This heavily branched biennial or herbaceous perennial occurs mainly on the eastern side of the Central Valley, in the Cascade and Sierra Nevada foothills, and in the San Francisco Bay region. Bee thistle (*Eryngium articulatum*) has much showier, bright purplish blue flower heads, each head 0.4–1" wide and perched on a "plate" of long spiny bracts; it can bloom as late as September. Northern California's nine additional representatives of the genus, several of which are rare, are as unobtrusive as *Eryngium castrense*.

FENNEL

Family: Apiaceae (carrot family)

Scientific name: *Foeniculum vulgare* Mill.

Height: 3–10'.

Leaves: Alternate, the blade up to 16" long and 12–16" wide, divided several times into fine, thread-like segments, hairless, with an anise or licorice scent when bruised.

Flowers: Borne in flat-topped compound umbels; no sepals; petals 5 per flower, yellow; stamens 5, anthers yellow; ovary inferior, longitudinally ribbed, hairless. Blooms May through September.

Elevation: Sea level to above 5,000'.

Habitat: Disturbed ground, grassland, and riparian areas.

Comments: Fennel, native to southern Europe, is a weedy herbaceous perennial that grows from a taproot; it has become widespread in northern California. It's easily recognized even when not flowering by its distinctive leaves, scent, and slightly zigzag stems. New growth starts appearing among the previous year's dead stems in late winter or early spring, and even stems that look dead may produce new leaves. Unlike wild fennel, the varieties of fennel that are cultivated as a vegetable are seldom invasive, and their fruit is the fennel "seed" used in Mediterranean cooking. Parsnip (*Pastinaca sativa*), a Eurasian species, also has yellow flowers and can grow to more than 6' tall, but its leaves are once pinnately compound with fairly wide leaflets. It shows up here and there throughout northern California but isn't nearly as invasive as fennel.

COW PARSNIP

Family: Apiaceae (carrot family)

Also called: Giant hogweed

Scientific name: *Heracleum maximum* W. Bartram

Height: 3–10'.

Leaves: Alternate, the blade 8–20" long and about equally wide, pinnately compound with 2 short-stalked lateral leaflets and 1 long-stalked terminal leaflet; leaflets wide, lobed with coarsely toothed margins; petioles 4–16" long, longer than the blades of the uppermost leaves on each stem, flattened and clasping the stem, sometimes inflated, generally hairy.

Flowers: Borne in big compound umbels; no sepals; petals 5 per flower, white; stamens 5, filaments white, anthers pale yellow; ovary inferior, longitudinally ribbed, often slightly hairy.

Blooms April through July.

Elevation: Sea level to 9,500'.

Habitat: Sunny or partly shaded sites with moist soil.

Comments: This herbaceous perennial has hollow but very stout stems. In coastal scrub and grasslands, you'll see it towering over surrounding vegetation, and the dead stems and seed heads can persist all winter. Some Native American tribes made flutes and whistles from the hollow stems; others prepared a yellow dye from the roots. It's the only North American species in its genus and is native from California to Alaska and farther east. In older references, it's called *Heracleum lanatum*.

FOOTHILL LOMATIUM

Family: Apiaceae (carrot family)

Also called: Caraway-leaved lomatium or alkali desert-parsley

Scientific name: *Lomatium caruifolium* (Hook. & Arn.) J. M. Coult. & Rose var. *denticulatum* Jeps.

Height: 6–18".

Leaves: In a basal cluster, the blade 2–12" long and about equally wide, usually dissected 1–3 times into very narrow, pointed segments.

Flowers: Borne in small compound umbels on upright or spreading, leafless flowering stalks; sepals usually not evident; petals 5 per flower, light yellow or sometimes purplish; stamens 5, anthers white or cream-colored; ovary inferior, hairless.

Blooms April through May.

Elevation: 200–1,600'.

Habitat: Vernal pools and grassland.

Comments: This variety of foothill lomatium grows from a slender taproot; it occurs on the eastern side of the Sacramento Valley, in the adjacent foothills, and in the higher parts of the North Coast Ranges. Another variety, *Lomatium caruifolium* var. *caruifolium*, is mainly found farther south. Northern California is home to many species of *Lomatium*, some of them rare, others widespread, all of them herbaceous perennials. To be certain of your identification, you need the whole plant, including roots, leaves, flowers, and the small, seed-like fruits.

BUTTE DESERT-PARSLEY

Family: Apiaceae (carrot family)

Also called: Yellow Hartweg's lomatium

Scientific name: *Lomatium marginatum* (Benth.) J. M. Coult. & Rose var. *marginatum*

Height: 6–20".

Leaves: In a basal cluster, the blade 2–8" long and about equally wide, usually dissected 1–3 times into very narrow or even thread-like, pointed segments.

Flowers: Borne in small compound umbels on leafless, more or less spreading flowering stalks; sepals usually not evident; petals 5 per flower, yellow, sometimes turning purple as they age and dry out; stamens 5, anthers yellow; ovary inferior, hairless.

Blooms March through May.

Elevation: 50' to above 3,000'.

Habitat: Grassland, woodland, yellow pine forest, and chaparral.

Comments: This variety of butte desert-parsley is most common in the Sacramento Valley, Sierra Nevada foothills, Cascades, and Klamath Ranges. It grows from a slender taproot. *Lomatium marginatum* var. *purpureum* has reddish purple flowers and grows in the North Coast Ranges. As with other members of this genus, you need the whole plant, including underground parts, leaves, flowers, and fruit, to be certain of its identity.

BISCUIT ROOT

Family: Apiaceae (carrot family)

Also called: Hog fennel, bladder parsnip, or common lomatium

Scientific name: *Lomatium utriculatum* (Torr. & A. Gray) J. M. Coult. & Rose

Height: 4–20".

Leaves: Alternate, the blade 2" to more than 6" long, usually several times pinnately dissected into very narrow, pointed segments; the lower part of the 0.6–4"-long petiole flattened and wrapped around the stem, the middle part often wide and boat-shaped.

Flowers: Borne in relatively showy compound umbels; sepals 5 per flower, very small or not evident at all; petals 5, yellow; stamens 5, anthers yellow; ovary inferior, hairless or covered with minute hairs.

Blooms February through May.

Elevation: 150' to above 5,000'.

Habitat: Grassland, woodland, yellow pine forest, chaparral, and coastal scrub.

Comments: This herbaceous perennial grows from a more or less slender taproot. Unlike many species of *Lomatium*, in which all the leaves grow in a basal rosette, it has leafy stems, and the lower part of the stem tends to be purplish. The species occurs throughout northern California and is especially common in the southern half of the North Coast Ranges and around the perimeter of the Sacramento Valley.

FOOTSTEPS OF SPRING

Family: Apiaceae (carrot family)

Also called: Yellow mats

Scientific name: *Sanicula arctopoides* Hook. & Arn.

Height: 1–2", with stems up to 8" long lying flat on the ground.

Leaves: Mainly basal, the blade 0.8" to about 2.5" long, deeply 3-lobed; margins coarsely toothed or with additional lobes.

Flowers: Borne in compound umbels, each secondary umbel head-like and nestled into a circle of 8–17 conspicuous, unlobed or 3-lobed, greenish yellow bracts; 10–12 bisexual flowers per head, each with 5 inconspicuous sepals, 5 yellow petals, 5 yellow stamens, and an inferior, hairless or prickly ovary; in addition, 10–13 male (that is, lacking a functional pistil) flowers per head.

Blooms February through May.

Elevation: Sea level to about 800'.

Habitat: Coastal grassland, coastal scrub, and dunes.

Comments: At first glance you might mistake this herbaceous perennial for a member of the sunflower family. It grows from a taproot and despite its small stature visually jumps out at you from surrounding vegetation by its intense chartreuse color. Northern sanicle (*Sanicula graveolens*) and turkey pea (*Sanicula tuberosa*) can also be quite low-growing, but the plants are less flamboyantly colored and have twice or 3-times compound leaves.

PURPLE SANICLE

Family: Apiaceae (carrot family)

Also called: Shoe buttons

Scientific name: *Sanicula bipinnatifida* Hook.

Height: 4.5" to 2'.

Leaves: Mainly basal, the blade 1.5" to nearly 8" long, once or twice pinnately divided, the segments narrow, green or purplish, often with a waxy bloom; margins toothed; a few smaller leaves arranged alternately on the stem.

Flowers: Borne in compound umbels consisting of 3–5 very compact, head-like secondary umbels on fairly long stalks; 8–10 bisexual flowers per head, each with 5 greenish sepals fused at the base, 5 reddish purple or yellow petals, 5 stamens with off-white or purplish anthers, and an inferior, prickly ovary; in addition, 10–12 male (that is, lacking a functional pistil) flowers per head.

Blooms March through May.

Elevation: 50–6,000'.

Habitat: Grassland, woodland, and chaparral.

Comments: This taprooted herbaceous perennial grows in the Sacramento Valley, northern and central Sierra Nevada and its foothills, Cascades, northwestern California, and as far away as Baja California and British Columbia. Its common name notwithstanding, purple sanicle can have yellow flowers. It's one of nine species of *Sanicula* found in northern California.

RANGER'S BUTTONS

Family: Apiaceae (carrot family)

Also called: Swamp white heads

Scientific name: *Sphenosciadium capitellatum* A. Gray

Height: 20" to 6'.

Leaves: Alternate, the blade 4–16" long, usually once or twice pinnately compound, the leaflets 0.4" to nearly 5" long, fairly narrow; margins toothed, irregularly jagged, or pinnately lobed; petioles flattened and clasping the stem.

Flowers: Borne in compound umbels with densely hairy stalks, the secondary umbels forming dense, spherical heads; no sepals; petals 5 per flower, white or purplish; stamens 5, white; ovary inferior, covered with woolly white hairs.

Blooms July through August.

Elevation: Generally 3,000' to above 11,000'.

Habitat: Wet meadows, swampy areas, lake shores, and stream banks.

Comments: This herbaceous perennial grows from tuber-like roots. Look for it in the Cascades, Klamath Ranges, and the eastern part of the North Coast Ranges. It also occurs in the high Sierra Nevada and as far away as eastern Oregon, Idaho, and Baja California. It's the only species in its genus.

TALL SOCK-DESTROYER

Family: Apiaceae (carrot family)

Also called: Upright hedge-parsley or field hedge-parsley

Scientific name: *Torilis arvensis* (Huds.) Link

Height: 1' to more than 3'.

Leaves: Alternate, the blade 2–5" long, the lower leaves twice or 3-times pinnately compound, the upper ones generally once pinnately compound; leaflets covered with short, hard, flat-lying hairs that give them a rough texture; margins coarsely toothed or pinnately lobed.

Flowers: Borne in long-stalked, fairly flat compound umbels; sepals tiny or not evident at all; petals 5 per flower, heart-shaped or asymmetrically lobed, the petals around the outside of each secondary umbel bigger than the ones facing the center, white; stamens 5, white; ovary inferior, with curved maroon bristles that turn into tiny, tan, hooked burs covering the fruit.

Blooms April through July.

Elevation: Sea level to above 5,000'.

Habitat: Disturbed, sunny to shady sites.

Comments: This wispy, even dainty-looking, invasive annual, native to Europe, is easy to miss until you (or your dog) have walked through a patch of it and become acquainted with its burred, 0.1–0.2"-long fruits. Short, stiff, flat-lying hairs make the stems feel sandpapery, which zigzag slightly between branching points. Short sock-destroyer (*Torilis nodosa*, sometimes called knotted hedge-parsley) only gets 4–20" tall and has small, very dense to head-like umbels borne close to the stem; it's native to Eurasia but has become widespread in California.

BITTER DOGBANE

Family: Apocynaceae (dogbane family)

Also called: Spreading dogbane

Scientific name: *Apocynum androsaemifolium* L.

Height: 6–12", occasionally up to 3'.

Leaves: Opposite, the blade 1.5–2.5" long, oval to almost round, drooping from thin wiry branches, upper side nearly hairless, lower side sometimes finely woolly; petiole short; margins smooth.

Flowers: Borne in loose, fairly upright clusters; sepals 5, small, green with pink margins or tips; petals fused into a 5-lobed bell, from less than 0.2" to 0.3" long, very pale pink to bright purplish pink, often striped deeper pink; stamens 5, anthers pinkish; ovaries 2, superior, their stigmas fused.

Blooms May through October.

Elevation: 600' to above 8,000'.

Habitat: Rocky slopes, chaparral, and dry openings in conifer forest.

Comments: This low-growing herbaceous perennial is native from southern California to British Columbia and eastern North America and widespread in most of northern California except in the Sacramento Valley. The plants rarely seem to produce fruit; when they do, the two ovaries grow into a pair of reddish brown parentheses, 3–5" long and touching each other top and bottom, that eventually split open to release the seeds inside. A short tuft of brownish hairs on each seed facilitates dispersal by wind. In fall, the leaves turn golden yellow.

INDIAN HEMP

Family: Apocynaceae (dogbane family)

Scientific name: *Apocynum cannabinum* L.

Height: 1–4'.

Leaves: Opposite or occasionally whorled, the blade 2–4" long, fairly narrow, often angled upwards from rather stout stiff stems, usually hairless, upper side matte medium green with light yellowish green veins, lower side light green; petiole short; margins smooth.

Flowers: Borne in compact to loose upright clusters; sepals 5, green; petals 5, fused into a tube at the base, white or greenish white; stamens 5, anthers bright yellow; ovaries 2, superior, their stigmas fused.

Blooms April through October.

Elevation: Sea level to 6,500'.

Habitat: Moist soil; occasionally in drier spots.

Comments: This herbaceous perennial, widespread throughout northern California, can form dense stands that sprout from creeping underground stems. It prefers moist areas, but I've also found it in dry uplands surrounded by yellow star-thistle. Like many members of this family, it has sticky, milky white sap. Although the flowers seem fairly inconspicuous, they attract many insects, including buckeye butterflies, western tiger swallowtails, and honeybees. The odd-looking fruits, 2–8" long, initially resemble a pair of green parentheses touching each other top and bottom; later they separate, turn reddish brown, and split open to release the small seeds, each topped by an inch-long tuft of whitish hairs. Many Native American tribes made string, rope, fishing nets, and textiles from this species, usually gathering the dead stems in late fall or winter. A foot of string required five stems, a 40' by 6' net for trapping deer 7,000' of string or 35,000 stems. To obtain such huge quantities, big patches were carefully managed, primarily with fire, to reduce competing vegetation and encourage growth of long, straight, new stems. Today, ranchers consider the species undesirable because it's poisonous to livestock.

PURPLE MILKWEED

Family: Apocynaceae (dogbane family)

Scientific name: *Asclepias cordifolia* (Benth.) Jeps.

Height: 1–3'.

Leaves: Opposite, 2–6" long, oval to heart-shaped, sessile, the leaf base clasping the stem, hairless to slightly hairy; margins smooth.

Flowers: Borne in loose, sometimes floppy umbels; sepals 5, small, reddish; petals 5, dark reddish purple, swept backwards, with hairy margins; the rest of the flower pale pink.

Blooms May through July.

Elevation: Sea level to 6,500'.

Habitat: Foothill woodland, chaparral, and rocky slopes.

Comments: This herbaceous perennial, which grows from a stout woody root, occurs in most of northern California except along the coast and in the Sacramento Valley. Its stems, often tinged purple near the top, tend to lean sideways (what botanists call "ascending") and, as in many members of this family, contain a white, sticky sap. The fruit is a smooth capsule, 4–6" long, borne pointing upwards on stalks that abruptly bend downwards. See showy milkweed (*Asclepias speciosa*) for more details about the complicated flower structure and pollination mechanism common to all members of this genus.

Monarch butterflies (*Danaus plexippus*) are the only species of butterfly known to migrate long distances; they're also totally dependent on milkweed. Adults overwinter in a few locations in Mexico's mountains and coastal southern and central California, then head north when the weather warms up. It takes several successive, short-lived generations each spring and summer to reach the butterflies' north-ernmost feeding grounds—some migrate as far as Hudson Bay. Along the way, the females lay their eggs on whatever species of *Asclepias* they can find, the only food that the black-, yellow-, and white-banded caterpillars will eat. Milkweed contains bitter, poisonous compounds that accumulate in the caterpillars and persist in the adult butterflies, making them distasteful to insectivorous birds. Each year's final genera-tion is longer-lived and makes it all the way back to the butterflies' winter grounds. Several other species of butterfly that don't feed on milkweed have evolved wing patterns resembling monarchs—black-and-orange with white dots—which presumably lessens their risk of being eaten by birds.

NARROW-LEAVED MILKWEED

Family: Apocynaceae (dogbane family)

Also called: Mexican whorled milkweed

Scientific name: *Asclepias fascicularis* Decne.

Height: 20" to 4'.

Leaves: Opposite or whorled in 3s–6s, 1.5–5" long but no more than 0.2" wide, usually folded upwards along the midrib, hairless to slightly hairy; petiole very short; margins smooth.

Flowers: Borne in compact, domed or more or less flat-topped umbels; sepals 5, green or pink, inconspicuous; petals 5, greenish white or pale pink, swept backwards.

Blooms May through October.

Elevation: Sea level to above 7,000'.

Habitat: Dry or moist, open or lightly shaded areas, including stream banks and ditches.

Comments: This herbaceous perennial can be found in most of northern California. It grows from creeping underground stems and, when conditions are right, can form big, dense patches; elsewhere you may only see widely scattered plants. From a distance, its overall "gestalt" often resembles mugwort (*Artemisia douglasiana*), but close up the two species are completely different. The fruit is a skinny capsule, 2–4" long, that splits open to release flat brown seeds, each crowned with a tuft of inch-long white hairs that facilitate dispersal by wind. See showy milkweed (*Asclepias speciosa*) for more details about the complicated flower structure and pollination mechanism common to all members of this genus.

Like other milkweeds, all parts of the plant contain compounds that are highly poisonous to livestock; the animals usually avoid it unless there's not much else to eat, but poisoning can occur through contaminated hay. Some Native Americans chewed the dried sap like gum, which seems rather surprising given the plants' toxicity. Other tribes used the stem fibers for string and rope, sometimes combining them with those of Indian hemp (*Apocynum cannabinum*).

SHOWY MILKWEED

Family: Apocynaceae (dogbane family)

Scientific name: *Asclepias speciosa* Torr.

Height: 20" to 4'.

Leaves: Opposite, the blade 3–6" long, oval or oblong, hairless or covered with short, velvety hairs, leaf bases rounded or heart-shaped; petiole short; margins smooth.

Flowers: Borne in almost spherical umbels; sepals 5, yellowish green, inconspicuous; petals 5, dusky pink, swept backwards, the pale pink "hoods" (see Comments) forming a 5-pointed star.

Blooms May through September.

Elevation: Sea level to above 6,000'.

Habitat: Many habitats, including riparian areas and roadsides; often but not always on dry or gravelly soil.

Comments: This herbaceous perennial grows throughout northern California except near the coast. Its fruit, up to 4" long, is covered with silky to woolly hairs as well as scattered, large, soft spines. It's one of six or seven species of milkweed in the region.

Milkweed flowers are complicated. The swept-back petals more or less hide the sepals, and what look like five cupped petals are actually outgrowths from the stamens, called hoods. In some species a slender projection, called a horn, emerges from each hood. The anthers and stigma are fused into a single central structure with five vertical slits around its perimeter. Pollination is equally complicated. When an insect crawls over a milkweed flower looking for nectar, one of its legs may accidentally slip into one of the vertical slits, then pull out two little lumps of pollen as it frees itself. (You can extract the pollen masses yourself by careful probing with a pin.) Then, *if* this insect visits another milkweed flower from which a previous visitor already removed some of the pollen, and *if* the leg carrying the first flower's pollen happens to slip into a "vacant" slit in the second flower, and *if* in tugging its leg out, the insect leaves the pollen behind, and *if* the pollen mass was inserted right side up (yes, these little lumps of pollen actually have a top and a bottom!), then the second flower may set seed. That's a lot of *if*s—no wonder that *Asclepias* usually doesn't produce much fruit compared to the numerous flowers on each plant.

MARSH PENNYWORT

Family: Araliaceae (ginseng family)

Scientific name: *Hydrocotyle umbellata* L.

Height: Usually no more than 2", with creeping or floating stems.

Leaves: Alternate, the blade 0.4–2" long, round, a 0.2–2"-long petiole attached to the center of the underside of the leaf like the handle of an umbrella; margins scalloped or lobed.

Flowers: Borne in simple, nearly spherical umbels of 10–60 flowers; sepals 5, minute; petals 5, white, greenish, or pale yellow; stamens 5, with white filaments and beige anthers; ovary inferior.

Blooms March through October.

Elevation: Sea level to 4,500'.

Habitat: Marshes, muddy soil, and shallow water along the margins of rivers and lakes.

Comments: You can find this little herbaceous perennial creeping across muddy ground or its leaves floating in shallow water, occasionally forming big mats, in the Sacramento Valley, the Sierra Nevada foothills, and farther south and east. Two other native pennyworts grow in similar habitats but seem to be a bit more widespread, occurring along the coast and the western part of the North Coast Ranges as well as farther inland. *Hydrocotyle ranunculoides* has deeply 3- to 7-lobed, kidney-shaped leaves and dense umbels of 5–10 flowers. *Hydrocotyle verticillata*'s leaves resemble those of marsh pennywort, but its flowers are borne in several small, widely spaced whorls on 0.6–8"-long flowering stems. Lawn pennywort (*Hydrocotyle sibthorpioides*), native to Asia, has shallowly lobed, kidney-shaped leaves. As its common name implies, it grows in moist places, including overwatered lawns, and so far has only been reported from a few urban sites in northern California. Older references include *Hydrocotyle* in the Apiaceae (carrot family).

PIPEVINE

Wide-open flowers.

Almost mature flower, the sepal lobes just about ready to separate.

Fully grown but still green fruit. Later, it will split vertically in several places to release the seeds. Dark brown or blackish remnants of the fruit often remain on the vines until spring.

Family: Aristolochiaceae (pipevine family)

Also called: California pipevine or Dutchman's pipe

Scientific name: *Aristolochia californica* Torr.

Height: Woody vine that can climb to about 15'.

Leaves: Deciduous, alternate, not emerging until after flowering has begun, the blade 1.2–6" long, oval to heart- or arrow-shaped, covered with soft, sometimes silky hairs; petiole 0.8–2" long.

Flowers: Sepals 3, fused into a U-shaped tube with 3 lobes at the tip, the tube ranging from pale green to tan to maroon with darker veins, the inner surface of the lobes thickened and yellowish, burnt orange, or red; no petals; 6 stamens and a 3-lobed stigma hidden inside the sepal tube; ovary partly inferior.

Blooms January through April.

Elevation: Usually sea level to 1,500', occasionally as high as 2,300'.

Habitat: Riparian forest, woodland, and chaparral.

Comments: This woody vine, which climbs by twining its stems around its support, grows mainly in the eastern part of the Sacramento Valley, the adjacent foothills, and the southern portion of the North Coast Ranges. Its strange-looking flowers are pollinated by fungus gnats. Later in the year, you may see boldly patterned black-and-orange caterpillars feeding voraciously on pipevine leaves and immature fruit—they're the larvae of pipevine swallowtail butterflies (*Battus philenor hirsuta*), and pipevine is the only plant they eat. Eventually each caterpillar turns into an immobile chrysalis, from which an adult butterfly will emerge. The butterflies seem to prefer blue or purple flowers such as blue dicks (*Dichelostemma capitatum*), winter vetch (*Vicia villosa*), and coyote mint (*Monardella villosa*), but when those aren't available, they make do with whatever nectar-bearing flowers they can find, including filaree (*Erodium* spp.), button bush (*Cephalanthus occidentalis*), and even yellow star-thistle (*Centaurea solstitialis*). After mating, the females lay their eggs on pipevine leaves, and the cycle repeats itself. Pipevine contains chemicals that are poisonous to many animals but not to pipevine swallowtails. The caterpillars accumulate the toxins in their bodies, making both the caterpillars and adult butterflies unpalatable to predators, which instinctively know or quickly learn to avoid the butterflies' bold colors.

    California doesn't have any other plants that even remotely resemble pipevine, and the butterflies are California's only large, black swallowtail, so they too are easy to recognize. Elsewhere in the United States and in both the New World and Old World tropics, though, there are numerous other species of *Aristolochia*, most or perhaps all of them poisonous, as well as other species of *Battus* whose caterpillars feed exclusively on these plants. In addition, some completely unrelated butterfly species that *aren't* poisonous have evolved similar colors to fool would-be predators. Why no other Californian butterflies mimic the pipevine swallowtail's defensive coloration is still a bit of a scientific mystery.

Pipevine swallowtail caterpillar. See blue dicks (*Dichelostemma capitatum*) for a photo of adult butterflies.

YARROW

Family: Asteraceae (sunflower family)

Also called: Common yarrow, milfoil, bloodwort, plumajillo, or carpenter's weed

Scientific name: *Achillea millefolium* L.

Height: Usually 4" to 3', occasionally up to 6'.

Leaves: Blades of basal leaves 4–8" long and up to 1.2" wide, 3-times pinnately dissected into very narrow to thread-like segments, almost hairless to densely soft-haired; stem leaves alternate, smaller, sessile; with a strong herbal scent when bruised.

Flowers: Borne in numerous small heads grouped in flat-topped clusters; each head with 3–4 rows of phyllaries, 5–8 ray flowers, and 15–40 disk flowers, both types of flowers with white or sometimes light pink petals.

Blooms April through September.

Elevation: Sea level to above 11,000'.

Habitat: Many habitats.

Comments: This highly variable herbaceous perennial, common throughout northern California, grows from creeping underground stems. Plants range from nearly hairless to covered with enough soft white hairs to make them appear gray. Fernleaf yarrow (*Achillea filipendulina*), native to the Caucasus, is a garden ornamental with golden yellow flowers; it has escaped from cultivation here and there in Humboldt County and in southern California but doesn't seem to have become invasive.

BLOW-WIVES

Family: Asteraceae (sunflower family)

Scientific name: *Achryachaena mollis* Schauer

Height: 1.5" to 2'.

Leaves: Opposite on the lower part of the stem, alternate higher up, 0.8–6" long by less than 0.3" wide, more or less sessile, covered with soft hairs; margins smooth or toothed.

Flowers: Heads often borne singly, each head 0.6–0.8" long, narrow; phyllaries 3–8 in a single row, with long, soft, spreading hairs; ray flowers 3–8, barely projecting beyond the phyllaries, yellow or red; disk flowers 4–35, with yellow or reddish petals and dark purple anthers.

Blooms March through June.

Elevation: Sea level to 4,000'.

Habitat: Grassland.

Comments: The round, glistening white seed heads, up to 1.2" in diameter, of this little annual are more conspicuous than its flowers. It's common in the Sacramento Valley and the southern half of the North Coast Ranges but occasionally appears in other locations as well. This is the only species in its genus.

WESTERN RAGWEED

Family: Asteraceae (sunflower family)

Scientific name: *Ambrosia psilostachya* DC.

Height: 1' to more than 6'.

Leaves: Lower leaves opposite, the blade 0.8" to nearly 5" long, typically once pinnately lobed or divided, bristly, petiole up to 1" long; margins coarsely toothed; upper leaves alternate, smaller, more or less sessile.

Flowers: Male and female flowers borne in separate heads on the same plant; male heads 0.1–0.2" wide, nodding and evenly spaced on upright flowering stalks, each with fused phyllaries that resemble an upside-down bowl with the yellow anthers projecting from the lower side; female heads farther down the stem among the leaves, very inconspicuous, each containing a single flower, the phyllaries fusing into a spiny bur around the single-seeded fruit inside.

Blooms June through November.

Elevation: Sea level to above 3,000'.

Habitat: Dry ground.

Comments: This widespread herbaceous perennial grows in big clumps from creeping roots; its stems don't branch a lot. Common ragweed (*Ambrosia artemisiifolia*), native to eastern North America, is annual, with a slender taproot and much more branched stems; it's less common in northern California. Beach bur-sage (*Ambrosia chamissonis*) is a low-growing herbaceous perennial that can form big mats on beaches and dunes.

MAYWEED

Family: Asteraceae (sunflower family)

Also called: Dillweed, dog-fennel, dog's chamomile, fetid chamomile, stinking daisy, or stinkweed

Scientific name: *Anthemis cotula* L.

Height: Usually less than 2'.

Leaves: Alternate, the blade 0.4–2.5" long by 0.6–1.2" wide, once to 3-times pinnately divided into very narrow or thread-like segments, sparsely hairy, with or without a petiole; with a strong, unpleasant smell when crushed.

Flowers: Heads up to 0.4–1" wide; phyllaries in 3–5 rows; each head with 10–15 sterile ray flowers with strap-shaped white petals and numerous yellow disk flowers.

Blooms April through October.

Elevation: Sea level to 8,500'.

Habitat: Grassland, woodland, chaparral, dunes, and disturbed areas.

Comments: This weedy European annual occurs in most of northern California. Its stems branch mainly near the top, or the entire stem can be branched. Corn chamomile (*Anthemis arvensis*), another European annual, is less common and lacks mayweed's unpleasant smell; its ray flowers are female, and the stems branch mainly near ground level. The leaves of pineapple weed (*Matricaria discoidea*) resemble those of mayweed except for their sweet, pineapple-like scent; its flower heads are completely different, consisting just of a pointed dome of greenish yellow disk flowers.

Mugwort (*Artemisia douglasiana*) inflorescence.

Tarragon (*Artemisia dracunculus*) inflorescence and foliage.

MUGWORT

Family: Asteraceae (sunflower family)

Scientific name: *Artemisia douglasiana* Besser

Height: 20" to more than 8'.

Leaves: Alternate, the blade 0.4–6" long, upper side sparsely to moderately hairy, lower side woolly; margins smooth or with 3–5 pointed lobes near the tip of the leaf; with a pleasant sagebrush-like scent when bruised.

Mugwort foliage.

Flowers: Heads loosely to densely clustered; individual heads less than 0.2" wide, upright or nodding, bell-shaped, with several rows of woolly phyllaries with translucent margins; no ray flowers; 5–9 female flowers and 6–25 bisexual disk flowers per head, inconspicuous except for their bright yellow stamens and curved yellow stigmas.

Blooms May through November.

Elevation: Sea level to above 7,000'.

Habitat: Riparian and other open to shady areas, often with moist soil.

Comments: This herbaceous perennial grows from creeping underground stems. On a breezy day, it's easy to identify from a distance: The leaves' light underside makes them shimmer as they flutter in the wind. The aboveground stems usually grow upright and often stay unbranched, and the dead stems may persist all winter. It occurs throughout northern California. Tarragon (*Artemisia dracunculus*) is less common. In spring, its new growth starts out upright but then gets floppy, and its leaves are much narrower, hairless, and either unscented or tarragon-scented. Northern California's several species of sagebrush belong to the same genus.

COYOTE BRUSH

Family: Asteraceae (sunflower family)

Scientific name: *Baccharis pilularis* DC. subsp. *consanguinea* (DC.) C. B. Wolf

Height: 3' to almost 15'.

Leaves: Evergreen, alternate, the blade 0.6–1.6" long by 0.1–0.6" wide, hairless, often sticky, petiole short or none; margins smooth or with 5–9 teeth.

Flowers: Male and female flowers borne on separate shrubs in heads consisting of disk flowers only; male heads (above left) roughly 0.2" wide and equally long, with 4 or 5 rows of phyllaries overlapping like shingles on a roof and 20–34 flowers with white petals and yellow stamens; female heads (above right) narrower, 19–43 flowers per head, petals and stigmas white.

Blooms July through December.

Elevation: Sea level to 2,500', occasionally higher.

Habitat: Riparian areas, grassland, woodland, coastal bluffs, and disturbed sites.

Comments: This rounded, densely branched shrub is widespread in northern California except on the Modoc Plateau. The flowers have an odd, not entirely pleasant scent but are rich in nectar that attracts numerous

Female shrub in early January, covered in fruit.

honeybees, butterflies, and other insects. In winter, female shrubs can be almost hidden under a blanket of fluffy seed heads. A prostrate form with smaller leaves, *Baccharis pilularis* subsp. *pilularis*, occurs naturally near the ocean; it's widely used in landscaping in the Sacramento Valley and elsewhere.

MULE FAT

Family: Asteraceae (sunflower family)

Also called: Seep willow

Scientific name: *Baccharis salicifolia* (Ruiz & Pav.) Pers. subsp. *salicifolia*

Height: Up to about 13'.

Leaves: Evergreen, alternate, up to 6" long by 0.1–0.8" wide, sessile or with the base tapered to a short petiole, hairless to minutely hairy, often shiny as if freshly varnished, sometimes a bit sticky; margins smooth or slightly toothed.

Flowers: Male and female flowers borne on separate shrubs in conical, rounded, or flat-topped clusters of small heads of disk flowers; male heads (above left) roughly 0.2" long, with 4 or 5 rows of light green, pink-edged, or purplish phyllaries overlapping like shingles on a roof and 10–48 flowers with white or pink-tipped petals and white stamens; female flowers similar, 50–150 flowers per head, stigmas white.

Blooms mainly in spring and fall.

Elevation: Sea level to almost 8,000'.

Habitat: Stream banks, riparian woodland, coastal scrub, and moist disturbed sites.

Comments: Older texts call this shrub *Baccharis viminea*; in northern California it occurs near the coast and in the North Coast Ranges, Klamath Ranges, Sacramento Valley, and the foothills of the Cascades and Sierra Nevada. The branches tend to be long, upright or leaning, and loosely branched. Mulefat doesn't bloom as prolifically as coyote brush (*Baccharis pilularis*), but honeybees like the flowers nonetheless. A small "parachute" of white hairs lets the seed-like fruits (above right) be dispersed by wind. Marsh baccharis (*Baccharis glutinosa*, also called seep willow or water-wally) has upright, mostly unbranched stems up to about 6' tall and creeping underground stems that create thickets; it likes marshes and stream banks, as its common names imply, and grows from sea level to about 4,000'. Several additional species of *Baccharis* can be found in southern California.

DEVIL'S BEGGARTICK

Family: Asteraceae (sunflower family)

Also called: Sticktight

Scientific name: *Bidens frondosa* L.

Height: 6" to 4'.

Leaves: Opposite, once pinnately compound with 3–5 leaflets per leaf, each leaflet 0.8–3.5" long, more or less hairless; margins toothed.

Flowers: Heads with 5–8 green, spreading, narrow, slightly hairy outer phyllaries and an inner circle of short, upright, yellowish green phyllaries; ray flowers, if any, barely longer than the inner phyllaries, yellow; disk flowers yellow to orange and no longer than the inner phyllaries.

Blooms June through October.

Elevation: Sea level to almost 7,000'.

Habitat: Flood plains and disturbed sites with damp soil.

Comments: This rather uncommon native annual shows up here and there throughout northern California; it can also be found in southern and eastern North America and from northern Europe to the tropics worldwide. It gets its common name from its 0.2–0.4"-long fruits, each of which is armed with two barbed prongs that easily snag fur or feathers. Tall beggartick (*Bidens vulgata*) occurs in freshwater wetlands; its flower heads have 10–20 outer phyllaries, and its disk flowers are distinctly longer than the inner phyllaries. Nodding beggartick (*Bidens cernua*) and bur marigold (*Bidens laevis*) have showy yellow ray flowers.

YELLOW CARPET

Family: Asteraceae (sunflower family)

Scientific name: *Blennosperma nanum* (Hook.) S. F. Blake var. *nanum*

Height: Usually 1.2–5", sometimes up to 1'.

Leaves: Alternate, lower leaves generally 1.5–2.5" long, sessile, pinnately divided into 5–15 very narrow lobes, hairless to sparsely hairy, often slightly succulent; upper leaves smaller, sometimes undivided.

Flowers: Heads borne singly, usually no more than 0.5" wide; phyllaries generally in 2 rows; ray flowers 5–13 per head, petals light yellow or rarely white and often drooping slightly; disk flowers numerous, each flower with light yellow petals and a knob-like, fuzzy, white stigma.

Blooms January through May.

Elevation: Sea level to 5,000'.

Habitat: Grassland, seeps, and the margins of vernal pools.

Comments: Wherever it grows, this annual is one of our earlier spring wildflowers and, as its common name implies, can bloom in great profusion. Look for it in the Sacramento Valley, North Coast Ranges, and Cascade and Sierra Nevada foothills. The rare Point Reyes blennosperma (*Blennosperma nanum* var. *robustum*) occurs only at Point Reyes and near Fort Bragg. California's only other species of *Blennosperma*, Sonoma sunshine (*Blennosperma bakeri*), is also rare; it's restricted to a few sites in Sonoma County.

CALIFORNIA BRICKELLBUSH

Family: Asteraceae (sunflower family)

Scientific name: *Brickellia californica* (Torr. & A. Gray) A. Gray

Height: 20" to more than 6'.

Leaves: Deciduous, usually alternate, lower leaves sometimes opposite, the blade 0.4–4" long by 0.4–3.5" wide, hairless or covered with short fine hairs, petiole 0.1" to more than 2.5" long; margins toothed or scalloped.

Flowers: Heads borne singly or clustered along the branches, each head slender, up to 0.5" long; phyllaries in 5 or 6 rows; no ray flowers; disk flowers 8–18, petals greenish yellow, each flower with 2 long, club-shaped, yellow style branches that flop in all directions.

Blooms July through December.

Elevation: Sea level to almost 9,000'.

Habitat: Dry open flats, rocky slopes, dry woodland, chaparral, and coastal bluffs.

Comments: This nondescript shrub or subshrub occurs in most of northern California except along the coast and on the Modoc Plateau. In early spring, bright green new growth emerges from the plants' woody bases among the previous year's dead, grayish stems. Two other species in this genus grow in the region, both of them herbaceous perennials. *Brickellia grandiflora* has nodding flower heads; *Brickellia greenei* has several small but leaf-like bracts directly beneath each flower head and off-white petals.

ROSIN WEED

Family: Asteraceae (sunflower family)

Also called: Sticky calycadenia

Scientific name: *Calycadenia multiglandulosa* DC.

Height: 4" to more than 2'.

Leaves: Usually alternate, occasionally opposite, the blade 1.5 to more than 3" long, very narrow, with short rough hairs that make the leaves feel sandpapery, petiole short or none; lower leaves often withered by the time the plants bloom; margins smooth or toothed.

Flowers: Heads spaced out along the stems or clustered near the top; phyllaries with long or short white hairs and scattered glandular hairs, each of the latter like a short pin with a glistening, dark reddish to almost black head; ray flowers 2–6 per head, petals 0.2–0.4" long, usually 3-lobed with a relatively narrow middle lobe flanked by two wider lobes, most often white but occasionally cream, yellow, or tinged rose; disk flowers 4–20 per head, each with 5 petals and dark maroon anthers.

Blooms May through October.

Elevation: 150–3,600'.

Habitat: Open, dry areas and rocky slopes.

Comments: In northern California, this common annual grows in the North Coast Ranges, Sacramento Valley, and Sierra Nevada. It's one of seven *Calycadenia* species in the region, all preferring dry habitats and with white, yellow, or pink flowers.

ITALIAN THISTLE

Family: Asteraceae (sunflower family)

Scientific name: *Carduus pycnocephalus* L. subsp. *pycnocephalus*

Height: 8" to more than 6'.

Leaves: Alternate, basal leaves 4–6" long with 4–10 lobes and sharp spines that stick out in all directions from the wavy margins; stem leaves smaller, with woolly or cobwebby hairs and long extensions that run down the stem as spiny "wings."

Flowers: Heads generally in clusters of 2–5, each head cylindrical, 0.4–0.8" wide; phyllaries spine-tipped and wrapped in cobwebby hairs; no ray flowers; disk flowers numerous with purplish pink petals and light blue pollen.

Blooms March through July.

Elevation: Sea level to 4,000'.

Habitat: Disturbed areas and woodland.

Comments: This annual or biennial thistle is one of four *Carduus* species in northern California, all invasive, native to Europe, and with a pappus of minutely barbed bristles. Confusingly, slender-flowered thistle (*Carduus tenuiflorus*) is also sometimes called Italian thistle, but its basal leaves have 12–20 lobes and its flower heads are borne in clusters of 5–20. Plumeless thistle (*Carduus acanthoides*) and musk thistle (*Carduus nutans*) have nearly spherical flower heads, those of musk thistle nodding and up to 3" in diameter. Bull thistle (*Cirsium vulgare*), another weedy non-native, has a pappus of feathery hairs.

YELLOW STAR-THISTLE

Family: Asteraceae (sunflower family)

Scientific name: *Centaurea solstitialis* L.

Height: 4" to nearly 5'.

Leaves: Alternate, lower leaves 2–6" long, deeply pinnately lobed, usually covered with short bristles and fuzzy gray hairs, often withered by the time the plant blooms; upper leaves smaller, narrow, unlobed, sessile, their bases running down the stem like "wings."

Flowers: Heads solitary or borne in loose clusters, phyllaries collectively shaped like a narrow-necked but spine-studded vase, the longest spines 0.4–1" long, straw-colored; no ray flowers; disk flowers numerous, yellow.

Blooms May through November.

Elevation: Sea level to almost 4,500'.

Habitat: Grassland and disturbed areas.

Comments: In fall, this annual's stems may look all but dead, yet still bear flowers. It occurs throughout northern California. Tocalote or Malta star-thistle (*Centaurea melitensis*) and Sicilian star-thistle (*Centaurea sulphurea*) are superficially similar but differ in numerous details; neither one is quite as pervasive (yet) in northern California as yellow star-thistle. All three are native to Europe, where local insects and pathogens keep them in check, but invasive here. The genus includes several other notoriously weedy species, such as purple star-thistle (*Centaurea calcitrapa*) and diffuse knapweed (*Centaurea diffusa*). *Centaurium* is a completely unrelated member of the Gentiana-ceae (gentian family).

FITCH'S TARWEED

Family: Asteraceae (sunflower family)

Also called: Fitch's spikeweed

Scientific name: *Centromadia fitchii* (A. Gray) Greene

Height: 2–20".

Leaves: Lower leaves opposite, up to 6" long, pinnately lobed, densely hairy, with numerous additional stalked, yellow to dark brown glandular hairs, often withered by the time the plant blooms; upper leaves alternate, smaller, narrow, unlobed, spine-tipped.

Flowers: Each head nestled in a star-like cluster of leaves; phyllaries like small leaves but held more vertically; 10–20 ray flowers per head, yellow; disk flowers numerous, with yellow petals, a pappus of 8–12 whitish scales, and red to purplish brown anthers.

Blooms May through November.

Elevation: Sea level to about 3,000'.

Habitat: Disturbed areas, grassland, vernal pools, and woodland.

Comments: The large, sticky glands of this annual are easily visible even without a hand lens. The smell of the resin they exude reminds me of turpentine and vinegar; I find it unpleasant. Picking a specimen for closer examination is painful, thanks to all the spines. Even where abundant, the plants tend to be scattered, not forming big patches the way common spikeweed (*Centromadia pungens*) does; as one author put it, Fitch's spikeweed is "not gregarious." In older texts it's called *Hemizonia fitchii*.

COMMON SPIKEWEED

Family: Asteraceae (sunflower family)

Scientific name: *Centromadia pungens* (Hook. & Arn.) Greene subsp. *pungens*

Height: 4" to 4'.

Leaves: Lower leaves opposite, 2–6" long, once or twice pinnately divided into narrow segments, hairless to coarsely hairy, often withered by the time the plant blooms; upper leaves alternate, smaller, narrow, unlobed, spine-tipped.

Flowers: Each head nestled in a cluster of leaves; phyllaries spine-tipped; 5–75 or more yellow ray flowers per head; 6–200 or more disk flowers, with yellow petals, no pappus, and yellow, brown, or reddish anthers.

Blooms April through November.

Elevation: Sea level to about 4,000', occasionally higher.

Habitat: Grassland and disturbed sites with dry or moist soil.

Comments: This annual has rigid, straw-colored stems and can form big patches. The plants are painfully spiny to handle but, unlike Fitch's tarweed (*Centromadia fitchii*), not sticky because they generally lack glandular hairs; even when a few glandular hairs are present, they're tiny. Often you'll see several to many small, spine-tipped, green or yellow scales among the disk flowers. Some older texts call this species *Hemizonia pungens*. *Centromadia parryi* is similar, but its disk flowers have a pappus consisting of 3–5 scales.

SKELETON WEED

Family: Asteraceae (sunflower family)

Also called: Rush skeleton weed, devil's grass, hogbite, or gum succory

Scientific name: *Chondrilla juncea* L.

Height: 16" to 5'.

Leaves: Basal leaves and those on the lower part of the stem 1.5–5" long, hairless or nearly so; margins toothed or slightly lobed, the lobes pointing back towards the base of the leaf; upper leaves alternate, much smaller, narrow to thread-like.

Flowers: Heads borne singly or in clusters of 2–5 at intervals along the stems, each head 0.5–1.5" wide with 7–15 flowers; phyllaries in 2 rows, the outer much shorter than the inner; petals strap-shaped with 5 teeth at the tip, pleated lengthwise, yellow.

Blooms June through January.

Elevation: Sea level to 2,000'.

Habitat: Disturbed ground; grows best in well-drained soil but tolerates a wide range of conditions.

Comments: This invasive, biennial or herbaceous perennial is native to the Old World's Mediterranean region. The lower parts of its stiff, heavily branched stems are covered with bristly, downward-pointing hairs; the upper parts are often hairless. Like chicory, dandelion, and other related species, the plants contain milky sap, but you may have to squeeze a cut stem to see it.

CHICORY

Family: Asteraceae (sunflower family)

Scientific name: *Cichorium intybus* L.

Height: 16" to more than 6'.

Leaves: Alternate, the blades of the lower leaves 4–8" long, hairless to covered with short rough bristles, petioles winged; upper leaves smaller, sessile; margins nearly smooth to slightly lobed, the lobes pointing sideways or forwards.

Flowers: Clusters of heads borne at intervals along the stems, each head 1–2" wide with 10–25 flowers; phyllaries in 2 rows, the outer row spreading and shorter than the inner; petals strap-shaped with 5 teeth at the tip, usually Wedgewood-blue, sometimes white or purplish pink; anthers a darker shade of blue; pappus reduced to minute scales.

Blooms April through October.

Elevation: Sea level to 5,000'.

Habitat: Disturbed sites and pastures; prefers moist or poorly drained, calcium-rich soil.

Comments: Chicory, widespread throughout northern California but native to Europe, has hollow stems and milky sap. It can be annual, biennial, or perennial; the woody taproot is sometimes roasted and used as a coffee flavoring or substitute. Radicchio is a cultivated, red-leaved variety of chicory. Blue lettuce (*Lactuca tatarica* subsp. *pulchella*) also has blue flowers, but its pappus consists of numerous long white bristles.

BULL THISTLE

Family: Asteraceae (sunflower family)

Scientific name: *Cirsium vulgare* (Savi) Ten.

Height: 12" to more than 6'.

Leaves: Alternate, 4–16" long, slightly to deeply pinnately lobed, upper side covered with flat-lying slender prickles, lower side usually woolly, leaf bases extending down the stem as fiercely spiny wings; margins edged with spines up to 0.6" long.

Flowers: Heads borne singly or in small clusters, each head about 2–3" long; phyllaries numerous, collectively forming a bell-shaped to narrow-necked structure, their bases entangled in cobwebby hairs, each phyllary tapering to a long, outwards-curved spine; no ray flowers; numerous disk flowers per head; petals purple; pollen white.

Blooms May through October.

Elevation: Sea level to above 7,500'.

Habitat: Disturbed areas.

Comments: California is home to lots of species of *Cirsium*, many of them native, some rare. Bull thistle, though, is a weedy biennial from Europe. It's the only California *Cirsium* that has prickles on the upper leaf surface *and* spiny-winged stems. Thistles in the genus *Carduus* also have spiny-winged stems, but their pappus consists of minutely barbed bristles, the barbs so small that you may need a hand lens to see them, while in *Cirsium* the pappus consists of feathery hairs.

SOUTHERN BRASS BUTTONS

Family: Asteraceae (sunflower family)

Also called: Australian waterbuttons, carrot weed, or southern cotula

Scientific name: *Cotula australis* (Spreng.) Hook. f.

Height: 1–8", occasionally taller.

Leaves: Alternate, the blade usually 0.8–2.5" long, twice or 3-times pinnately divided, typically sparsely covered with long, soft hairs, sometimes with minute harsh hairs, with or without a petiole.

Flowers: Heads borne singly on stalks 0.4" to more than 3" long; each head fairly flat and 0.1–0.2" wide; phyllaries in 2 or 3 rows; 8–40 inconspicuous greenish female flowers that lack both petals and pappus in 1–3 concentric circles surrounding 12–40 or more white or pale yellow bisexual disk flowers, each disk flower with a 4-lobed corolla, 4 stamens, and no pappus.

Blooms January through May.

Elevation: Sea level to above 5,000'.

Habitat: Disturbed sites with relatively moist soil.

Comments: Despite its tiny flower heads, this weedy annual from Australia can be so abundant in early spring when not much else is in bloom that it becomes relatively easy to spot. Mexican brass buttons (*Cotula mexicana*) is similar but has once or twice pinnately divided leaves and disk flowers with 3-lobed corollas and three stamens; it can be a troublesome weed on golf courses.

BRASS BUTTONS

Family: Asteraceae (sunflower family)

Scientific name: *Cotula coronopifolia* L.

Height: 1.5" to more than 16".

Leaves: Alternate, the blade 0.4" to nearly 3" long, narrow, somewhat fleshy, hairless, sessile, the base expanded into a pale green sheath encircling the stem; margins smooth, irregularly toothed, or lobed.

Flowers: Heads upright or nodding, borne singly on stalks 0.8–4" long; each head fairly flat and 0.2–0.6" wide; phyllaries in 2 or more rows; a ring of 12–40 or more inconspicuous, pale green female flowers that lack both petals and pappus encircling 12–200 or more bright yellow bisexual disk flowers.

Blooms March through December.

Elevation: Sea level to 1,000', occasionally higher.

Habitat: Vernal pools, marshes, and other sites with moist soil; can tolerate saline conditions.

Comments: This herbaceous perennial is from southern Africa; in northern California, it's common in the Sacramento Valley, northern Sierra Nevada foothills, greater San Francisco Bay region, and along the coast. Its stems are often reddish; sometimes they grow upright, other times they sprawl across the ground and root where they touch the soil.

STINKWORT

Family: Asteraceae (sunflower family)

Scientific name: *Dittrichia graveolens* (L.) Greuter

Height: 8" to 3'.

Leaves: Basal leaves 0.8" to nearly 3" long, fairly narrow, covered with sticky glandular hairs, camphor-scented, withering early; margins smooth or finely toothed; stem leaves alternate, 0.4–1.5" long, often very narrow.

Flowers: Heads borne at intervals along the stems, each head 0.2–0.3" wide; phyllaries in 3 or 4 rows, the outer ones shorter than the inner, covered with sticky glandular hairs; ray flowers 10–12 per head, petals yellow, turning brownish orange as they wilt; disk flowers 9–14, yellow or reddish.

Blooms September through November.

Elevation: Sea level to above 2,000'.

Habitat: Disturbed areas, riparian woodland, and the margins of salt marshes.

Comments: This heavily branched, weedy annual from the Old World's Mediterranean region can form thicket-like patches; if you push your way through, you'll end up covered with the sticky resin and whatever debris sticks to it. Some people get contact dermatitis from handling the plants. Currently the species occurs mainly south of Mendocino and Shasta counties and from the coast to the western slope of the Sierra Nevada, but it appears to be spreading.

FALSE DAISY

Family: Asteraceae (sunflower family)

Scientific name: *Eclipta prostrata* (L.) L.

Height: 4" to more than 3'.

Leaves: Opposite, 0.8–4" long, narrow, sessile, covered with short, hard, flat-lying hairs; margins smooth or finely toothed.

Flowers: Heads roughly 0.3–0.5" wide; phyllaries in 1 or 2 rows; ray flowers 20–40, white; disk flowers 15–30 or more, petals white, anthers brown with yellow pollen.

Can bloom any time of year.

Elevation: Sea level to 4,500'.

Habitat: Shorelines and other places with damp soil.

Comments: Older references may call this annual *Eclipta erecta*, *Eclipta alba*, or *Verbesina alba*. Some plants sprawl; others grow more upright into a bushy shape. Regardless of the plants' shape, their purplish stems covered with white, hard, flat-lying hairs and the sandpapery feel of the leaves are distinctive. The green "button" in the photo is an immature seed head. In northern California, false daisy occurs mainly in the Sacramento Valley and is considered a native species, but it's a nearly worldwide weed. In India, a blue-black dye derived from the plants was traditionally used to color hair. The dye was, or perhaps still is, also used for tattoos.

HORSEWEED

Family: Asteraceae (sunflower family)

Also called: Canada fleabane, colt's tail, mare's tail, or butterweed

Scientific name: *Erigeron canadensis* L.

Height: 8" to 7', rarely up to more than 11'.

Leaves: Alternate, the blade 0.8–4" long by 0.2–0.4" wide, occasionally wider, hairless to hairy, lower leaves with tapered bases or short petioles, upper leaves sessile; margins straight or toothed, often fringed with bristly hairs.

Flowers: Heads numerous, inconspicuous, usually less than 0.2" long, borne on short branches on the upper half of the stem; 20–45 or more ray flowers per head with white, greenish, or pink petals that just barely project beyond the phyllaries and 7–30 or more disk flowers with yellow, 4-lobed corollas.

Can bloom nearly all year.

Elevation: Sea level to about 2,500'.

Habitat: Disturbed sites.

Comments: Older texts call this widespread native annual *Conyza canadensis*. Its branches stay shorter than the main stem. Hairy or flax-leaved fleabane (*Erigeron bonariensis*) is similar but tends to branch near the base, the branches growing taller than the main stem; unlike horseweed, it's covered with short, stiff hairs as well as longer, soft ones. Tropical horseweed (*Erigeron sumatrensis*) is less common in northern California; it has disk flowers with 5-lobed corollas.

77

WANDERING DAISY

Family: Asteraceae (sunflower family)

Also called: Wandering fleabane or subalpine fleabane

Scientific name: *Erigeron glacialis* (Nutt.) A. Nelson var. *glacialis*

Height: 3–18".

Leaves: Basal leaves 2–8" long, narrow to spoon-shaped, hairless or sparsely long-haired; margins smooth; stem leaves smaller, alternate, narrow to oval, sessile, their bases often clasping the stem.

Flowers: Heads borne singly or in loose clusters of up to 8, each roughly 1" in diameter; phyllaries densely covered with stalked glandular hairs; ray flowers 30–105 per head, lavender or purple, their petals drying into tight brown coils; disk flowers numerous, yellow.

Blooms July through September.

Elevation: 4,000' to above 11,000'.

Habitat: Alpine meadows, open areas in forest, and talus slopes.

Comments: This herbaceous perennial grows in the Klamath Ranges, Cascades, and Sierra Nevada. It spreads by means of rather short, creeping underground stems. Some older texts call it *Erigeron peregrinus* var. *angustifolius*. *Erigeron glacialis* var. *hirsutus* has bristly to softly long-haired leaves. About a dozen additional species of *Erigeron* with lavender, pink, or purple ray flowers can be found in northern California at elevations above 4,000'.

SEASIDE DAISY

Family: Asteraceae (sunflower family)

Scientific name: *Erigeron glaucus* Ker Gawl.

Height: 2–16".

Leaves: Alternate, the blade 0.8" to more than 5" long, spoon-shaped to widely oval, somewhat fleshy, hairless to densely hairy, lower leaves with winged petioles, upper leaves sessile; margins smooth or slightly toothed near the tip.

Flowers: Heads borne singly or in clusters of up to 15, each head roughly 1" wide; phyllaries densely covered with long, soft hairs; ray flowers 80–165 per head, lavender, pink, or rarely white; disk flowers numerous, sometimes green as buds, then turning yellow as they open.

Blooms May through July.

Elevation: Sea level to about 60'.

Habitat: Coastal grassland, dunes, and beaches.

Comments: This fairly common, strictly coastal subshrub or herbaceous perennial spreads from creeping underground stems and sprawling aboveground branches that root where they touch the ground; as a result, seaside daisy can grow into low mounds many feet in diameter. Supple daisy (*Erigeron supplex*), an inconspicuous coastal species that lacks ray flowers, is considered rare because its habitat is threatened by development. About 10 additional species of *Erigeron* with white, pink, or lavender ray flowers occur at fairly low elevations elsewhere in northern California.

LARGE-FLOWERED WOOLLY SUNFLOWER

Family: Asteraceae (sunflower family)

Scientific name: *Eriophyllum lanatum* (Pursh) J. Forbes var. *grandiflorum* (A. Gray) Jeps.

Height: Up to about 3'.

Leaves: Alternate, the blade 1" to more than 3" long, very narrow to oval, upper side hairless to moderately hairy, lower side with dense woolly or cobwebby hairs; margins rolled under and smooth or pinnately lobed.

Flowers: Heads borne singly on flower stalks 4–12" long that thicken at the top; phyllaries in a single row, their tips turned outwards, woolly; usually 12 or 13 yellow ray flowers per head, their petals 0.4–0.8" long, along with numerous yellow disk flowers. Blooms April through July.

Elevation: Sea level to 5,500'.

Habitat: Gravelly flood plains, grassland, woodland, chaparral, pine forest, and dry, rocky sites.

Comments: This biennial or short-lived herbaceous perennial grows in most of northern California except along the coast and on the Modoc Plateau. It's one of several varieties of woolly sunflower in northern California; they differ in leaf shape, size, degree of woolliness, and of course flower size. Near the ocean you may find seaside woolly sunflower (*Eriophyllum staechadifolium*), a densely branched subshrub with tight clusters of 5–15 or more small, bright yellow flower heads. Golden yarrow (*Eriophyllum confertiflorum*), which grows in the North Coast Ranges, resembles *Achillea filipendulina*, a horticultural species that occasionally escapes into the wild and confusingly is also called golden yarrow.

Seaside woolly sunflower (*Eriophyllum staechadifolium*).

GOLDEN ASTER

Family: Asteraceae (sunflower family)

Also called: Brewer's aster

Scientific name: *Eucephalus breweri* (A. Gray) G. L. Nesom

Height: 4" to more than 3'.

Leaves: Alternate, the largest leaves 0.8–2" long, fairly narrow to oval, more or less sessile, almost hairless to woolly or glandular-haired on both sides; margins smooth or toothed.

Flowers: Heads borne on long stalks in very open clusters; heads narrow, each with 3–6 rows of narrow phyllaries; no ray flowers; disk flowers bright yellow.

Blooms July through September.

Elevation: 4,000' to above 10,000'.

Habitat: Dry rocky slopes, open conifer forest, and subalpine meadows.

Comments: This herbaceous perennial used to be called *Aster breweri* or *Chrysopsis breweri*. Individual plants can have anywhere from 1 to more than 20 upright stems. It grows in the Klamath Ranges, Cascades, and Sierra Nevada and is the most common of northern California's six species of *Eucephalus*; but except for the rare wayside aster (*Eucephalus vialis*), the others generally have at least one or two, often more, white, lavender, or purple ray flowers. Several species of the big genus *Erigeron*, however, lack ray flowers and look similar to golden aster, as does rayless golden aster (*Heterotheca oregona* var. *compacta*).

WESTERN GOLDENROD

Family: Asteraceae (sunflower family)

Also called: Grass-leaved goldenrod

Scientific name: *Euthamia occidentalis* Nutt.

Height: Up to more than 6'.

Leaves: Alternate, up to 4" long and no more than 0.4" wide, sessile, with 3–5 fairly conspicuous main veins running the length of the leaf; margins edged with tiny hard teeth.

Flowers: Numerous heads borne on upwards-angled branches in dense, domed to flat-topped clusters; each head generally less than 0.5" long with 3 or 4 rows of phyllaries, 15–25 or more yellow ray flowers, and 6–18 yellow disk flowers.

Blooms July through November.

Elevation: Usually sea level to 2,000', occasionally up to 7,500'.

Habitat: River banks, wet meadows, irrigation ditches, and freshwater or saltwater marsh.

Comments: This widespread herbaceous perennial, called *Solidago occidentalis* in older references, is California's only species of *Euthamia*. It grows from creeping underground stems and sometimes forms big patches. Hold a leaf up against bright light to see the parallel veins. Although the leaf margins *look* smooth, you can feel the tiny teeth by running a finger back and forth along the edge. The phyllaries and upper sides of the leaves can be very shiny, almost as if varnished, but are neither sticky nor scented.

CUDWEED

Family: Asteraceae (sunflower family)

Scientific name: *Gnaphalium palustre* Nutt.

Height: 1–6", rarely up to 1'.

Leaves: Alternate, 0.4–1.5" long by 0.1–0.4" wide, densely covered with long, white, shaggy hairs, more or less sessile with a tapering base; margins smooth.

Flowers: Heads in dense clusters at the tips of the stems, with smaller clusters lower down the stem; phyllaries in 3–5 rows; what look like ray flowers are actually the stiff, white or beige tips of the inner phyllaries; each head with a ring of 40–130 or so ultra-slender female flowers surrounding 4–7 slightly larger bisexual disk flowers with bright yellow anthers.

Blooms April through October.

Elevation: Sea level to almost 10,000'.

Habitat: Flood plains, sandy streambeds, and damp depressions.

Comments: This small, ghost-like annual tends to branch near the base, the branches growing more or less horizontally for a short distance before turning upright. It occurs throughout northern California and is the state's only species of *Gnaphalium*. Older texts include several more, but those have now been reassigned to other genera. Members of the genus *Pseudognaphalium* tend to be a lot taller and less woolly, have less densely clustered flower heads, and prefer drier habitats than cudweed; some, unlike cudweed, have scented foliage. Cottontop (*Micropus californicus* var. *californicus*), not a close relative, looks similar to cudweed but grows in drier habitats, is minimally branched, and has even less conspicuous flower heads with hard, woolly phyllaries that curve inwards, almost completely hiding the minute flowers at their center.

GREAT VALLEY GUMWEED

Family: Asteraceae (sunflower family)

Also called: Common gumplant

Scientific name: *Grindelia camporum* Greene

Height: 1–4', occasionally taller.

Leaves: Alternate, the blade 0.8–6" long, narrow to oval, yellowish green to gray-green, usually hairless, sometimes sandpapery to the touch or sticky, the base clasping the stem or narrowed into a short petiole; margins smooth or toothed.

Flowers: Heads borne singly on fairly long flowering stalks; each head roughly 1–1.5" wide with 5–7 rows of spreading to outwards-curled phyllaries, the center of the head filled with sticky white resin until the flowers begin opening; 25 to about 40 yellow ray flowers and numerous yellow disk flowers per head.

Blooms May through December.

Elevation: Sea level to 4,500'.

Habitat: Grassland and open, dry, sandy or rocky flats; can tolerate somewhat saline or alkaline soil.

Comments: In northern California, this herbaceous perennial occurs in the Sacramento Valley, North Coast Ranges, Cascade foothills, and Sierra Nevada. It's one of six species of *Grindelia* found in the region; in all of them, a sticky white exudate accumulates among the phyllaries of unopened flower heads. They differ from one another in the shape of the leaves, flower head, and phyllaries. Intermediate forms are not unheard of, especially where species' ranges overlap.

BEACH GUMWEED

Family: Asteraceae (sunflower family)

Scientific name: *Grindelia stricta* DC. var. *platyphylla* (Greene) M. A. Lane

Height: 4" to more than 3'.

Leaves: Alternate, 0.4–6" long, narrow to oval, yellowish green, usually sessile and often clasping the stem, hairless or sparsely hairy, somewhat fleshy; margins toothed.

Flowers: Heads often nestled among several leaf-like bracts, each head typically 1.5–2" wide with 4–6 rows of spreading to outwards-curled phyllaries, the center of the head filled with sticky white resin until the flowers begin opening; 16–60 yellow ray flowers and numerous yellow disk flowers per head.

Blooms all year.

Elevation: Sea level to 1,000'.

Habitat: Coastal bluffs and dunes.

Comments: This herbaceous perennial or subshrub grows along the coast from Santa Barbara County to southern Oregon. Although it occasionally becomes shrub-like, you'll most often see it forming a mat-like groundcover. The stems tend to be pale, and the lowest 4" or so can be woody. *Grindelia stricta* var. *stricta*, also coastal, has leaves that taper to a petiole; it occurs in sloughs and salt marshes as well as on bluffs and dunes. *Grindelia stricta* var. *angustifolia* is a subshrub found in tidal wetlands around San Francisco Bay.

SNEEZEWEED

Family: Asteraceae (sunflower family)

Also called: Rosilla

Scientific name: *Helenium puberulum* DC.

Height: 20" to more than 5'.

Leaves: Basal leaves withered by the time the plants bloom; margins smooth; stem leaves 1.5–6" long by 0.2–1.6" wide, sessile, hairless or sparsely hairy.

Flowers: Heads borne singly on long stalks; each head almost spherical, 0.4–0.8" wide, lacking ray flowers or with 5–15 small yellow ray flowers that can be almost hidden by the hundreds of yellow, reddish brown, or purplish disk flowers.

Blooms May through August.

Elevation: Sea level to 4,000'.

Habitat: Stream banks, wet meadows, marshes, and seeps.

Comments: This annual, biennial, or short-lived herbaceous perennial can be easy to miss even when it's 5' tall, but its small, doorknob-like flower heads, often with a short ruffle of ray flowers, are unmistakable. The stems have pronounced longitudinal flanges, or wings, running down them and branch mainly in the upper part of the plant. Sneezeweed occurs in most of northern California except on the Modoc Plateau. It's one of four northern California species of *Helenium*, but the others have much more conspicuous ray flowers.

83

COMMON SUNFLOWER

Family: Asteraceae (sunflower family)

Scientific name: *Helianthus annuus* L.

Height: Up to 10'.

Leaves: Lower leaves sometimes opposite, upper leaves alternate, the blade 4–16" long, oval to heart-shaped, lower side covered with stiff hairs that make it feel sandpapery; margins smooth to coarsely toothed.

Flowers: Heads borne singly or in clusters of 2–9; phyllaries in 1–3 rows; ray flowers 15–30 or more, yellow; numerous disk flowers, their petals tipped yellow, red, or purplish brown.

Blooms June through October.

Elevation: Sea level to 6,500'.

Habitat: Grassland and disturbed sites.

Comments: This widespread annual is especially common in the Sacramento Valley. It hybridizes with other annual species of *Helianthus*, and so it's highly variable. California sunflower (*Helianthus californicus*) is a herbaceous perennial with yellow disk flowers that prefers wet sites such as marshes and stream banks. Texas blueweed or yerba parda (*Helianthus ciliaris*), an invasive, 2'-tall herbaceous perennial native to northern Mexico and the south-central United States, has blue-green foliage and red-lobed disk flowers; it grows in fairly moist areas and can tolerate saline soil. *Helianthus annuus* var. *macrocarpus*, with flower heads sometimes well over 1' in diameter, is widely cultivated for its oil-rich seeds.

BRISTLY OX-TONGUE

Family: Asteraceae (sunflower family)

Scientific name: *Helminthotheca echioides* (L.) Holub

Height: 1' to more than 6'.

Leaves: Alternate, the blade 2–8" long, fairly narrow, lower leaves with bases that taper into winged petioles, upper leaves sessile and sometimes clasping the stem, upper side covered with blister- or pimple-like bumps and hard, barbed hairs or prickles; margins smooth, toothed, or pinnately lobed.

Flowers: Heads borne singly or in clusters, 0.8–1.6" wide; phyllaries in 2 rows, the outer forming a somewhat bowl-like structure, the shorter inner row more upright, all of them coarsely hairy; numerous flowers per head, corollas strap-shaped and angled upwards or spread flat as in a dandelion head, yellow, often with an orange or brown streak on the lower side.

Can bloom nearly all year.

Elevation: Sea level to almost 3,500'.

Habitat: Disturbed areas, especially those with heavy soil.

Comments: This unattractive weedy annual or biennial has milky sap and stems covered with stiff, barbed hairs that are shaped like tiny palm trees. It's from Europe and used to be called *Picris echioides*. In northern California it occurs along the coast and in the North Coast Ranges, Sacramento Valley, and Sierra Nevada foothills.

TELEGRAPH PLANT

Family: Asteraceae (sunflower family)

Also called: Telegraph weed

Scientific name: *Heterotheca grandiflora* Nutt.

Height: 4" to more than 8'.

Leaves: Alternate, the blade 0.8" to nearly 3" long, oval to narrow, rather thick, densely covered with stiff, flat-lying to spreading hairs, some with glandular hairs as well, lower leaves with petioles, upper leaves sessile; margins smooth or toothed.

Flowers: Heads numerous near the top of the stem, tightly clustered or borne on fairly long flower stalks; additional heads often present farther down the stem; each head roughly 0.5–0.7" wide with 3–6 rows of narrow, overlapping phyllaries; ray flowers 25–40 per head with yellow petals that sometimes curl downwards; disk flowers 30–75, also yellow.

Blooms mainly in summer and fall, but a few flowers may be present nearly all year.

Elevation: Sea level to about 3,600'.

Habitat: Flood plains, dry streambeds, woodland, dunes, and sandy, dry, disturbed areas.

Rayless golden aster (*Heterotheca oregona* var. *compacta*).

Comments: This taprooted annual, biennial, or short-lived herbaceous perennial is common in the Sacramento Valley and Sierra Nevada foothills. Normally the densely leafy, bristly stems branch only near the top, but damaged plants branch much lower. Three other species of *Heterotheca* grow in northern California; rayless golden aster (*Heterotheca oregona*, called *Chrysopsis oregona* in older texts) is the only one that lacks ray flowers. It's a smaller, bushy plant and likes flood plains and seasonally dry streambeds at elevations below 3,000'.

PITGLAND TARWEED

Family: Asteraceae (sunflower family)

Also called: Sticky tarweed or narrow tarplant

Scientific name: *Holocarpha virgata* (A. Gray) D. D. Keck subsp. *virgata*

Height: 8" to 4'.

Leaves: Basal leaves 2–6" long by 0.1–0.4" wide, often withered by the time the plants bloom; upper leaves generally alternate, much smaller, very narrow, crowded on short side branches, most with both non-glandular and stalked glandular hairs and a conspicuous resin-exuding pit at the tip.

Flowers: Heads numerous, borne at the tips of the branches and along the stem; phyllaries in a single row, each phyllary with several lobes tipped with resin-secreting pits; 3–8 yellow ray flowers per head plus 9–15 or more disk flowers with yellow corollas and maroon or dark purple anthers.

Blooms May through December.

Elevation: Sea level to above 3,000'.

Habitat: Grassland and open woodland.

Comments: This annual, formerly called *Hemizonia virgata*, can form dense stands. The sweet-smelling, sticky resin makes the plants unpalatable to livestock; bees, though, love the nectar-rich flowers, and many birds and small mammals feed on the seeds. Pitgland tarweed grows in the Sacramento Valley and around its perimeter and is northern California's only species of *Holocarpha*.

SMOOTH CAT'S EAR

Family: Asteraceae (sunflower family)

Also called: False dandelion or flatweed

Scientific name: *Hypochaeris glabra* L.

Height: 4" to 2'.

Leaves: Basal leaves in a rosette, the blade 0.8–4" long, more or less hairless; margins smooth, shallowly lobed, or toothed; stem leaves alternate, very small, scale-like.

Flowers: Heads borne singly on slender stems, each head roughly 0.2–0.5" wide; phyllaries in several uneven rows; flowers dandelion-like with bright yellow, strap-shaped petals, their lower side sometimes reddish.

Blooms March through June.

Elevation: Sea level to above 5,000'.

Habitat: Grassland, sparse woodland, and disturbed sites.

Comments: This annual is common throughout northern California except on the Modoc Plateau. Sometimes the leaves, especially the first ones, have scattered coarse hairs on the upper side and along the margins. Rough cat's ear (*Hypochaeris radicata*), on the other hand, always has foliage that's covered with coarse hairs and feels rough. It too is widespread in northern California but is a herbaceous perennial with a fleshy taproot and flower heads approximately 0.6–1" wide. Both species contain milky sap, are native to Europe, and sometimes grow side by side.

PRICKLY LETTUCE

Family: Asteraceae (sunflower family)

Also called: Common wild lettuce, China lettuce, or compass plant

Scientific name: *Lactuca serriola* L.

Height: 20" to 10'.

Leaves: Alternate, 1.5" to more than 6" long, sessile, often with 2 basal lobes that clasp the stem, coarsely hairy with prickly bristles on the lower side and along the margins, midrib pale and unusually stiff; margins unlobed or slightly to deeply lobed.

Flowers: Heads usually well spaced on widely spreading branches, typically only a few heads in bloom at any given time; each head less than 0.3" wide, with 2–4 rows of phyllaries and 9–14 butter-yellow flowers. Blooms May to October.

Elevation: Sea level to almost 9,000'.

Habitat: Disturbed sites, annual grassland, and seasonal wetlands.

Comments: This homely-looking, milky-sapped, annual or biennial weed from Europe is widespread throughout northern California and is one of several species of *Lactuca* in the region, most of them non-native. It forms surprisingly beautiful seed heads, much daintier than those of dandelions, that fall apart in the slightest breeze. Unlike the sowthistles (*Sonchus asper* and *Sonchus oleraceus*), prickly lettuce has a solid stem. Its 3'-deep taproot helps it survive the dry season. The leaves can vary wildly in shape, even in the same patch of plants, but regardless of shape they often twist at the base so that the blade is held more or less vertically.

HARE-LEAF

Family: Asteraceae (sunflower family)

Scientific name: *Lagophylla glandulosa* A. Gray

Height: 4" to 3', occasionally up to 5'.

Leaves: Lower leaves opposite, withered by the time the plants bloom; upper leaves alternate, 1.2–5" long by 0.2–0.5" wide, more or less sessile, green or gray-green, with dense soft hairs and small, golden-headed, stalked glandular hair; margins smooth or toothed.

Flowers: Heads borne in small clusters, often with only 1 or 2 heads open at a time; each head roughly 0.7–1.5" wide with 5 phyllaries in a single row, 3–5 additional green bracts below it, 5 yellow 3-lobed ray flowers, and 6 disk flowers with yellow corollas and maroon anthers.

Blooms April to November.

Elevation: Sea level to 3,000'.

Habitat: Grassland and openings in woodland or chaparral.

Comments: Hare-leaf, which grows in the North Coast Ranges, Sacramento Valley, and Cascade and Sierra Nevada foothills, has straight stems. In little hare-leaf (*Lagophylla minor*) the main stem is zigzagged; the bright green leaves may have purple- or yellow-headed glandular hairs or none at all. A third northern California species, *Lagophylla ramosissima*, can have straight or zigzagged stems, but its foliage is grayish and the flowers are smaller. All three are annual.

NIPPLEWORT

Family: Asteraceae (sunflower family)

Scientific name: *Lapsana communis* L.

Height: 8" to 5'.

Leaves: Alternate, the blade 0.8–8" long, oval, with or without a petiole; margins smooth or toothed.

Flowers: Heads borne in open clusters, each head on a long, very slender stalk; 2 rows of phyllaries per head, the outer phyllaries tiny, the inner ones up to 0.4" long, each with a longitudinal ridge like the keel of a boat; 6–15 flowers per head; corollas 0.2–0.4" long, strap-shaped with 5 small teeth at the tip, yellow.

Blooms May through September.

Elevation: Sea level to above 5,000'.

Habitat: Riparian forest, other moist, shady sites, and disturbed ground.

Comments: This easily overlooked annual or biennial from Europe is the only species in its genus. In northern California it occurs along the coast and in the North Coast Ranges, Klamath Ranges, Sacramento Valley, and Sierra Nevada. Unlike many other non-native members of its family, it's not invasive.

Unidentified species of *Lasthenia* at Boggs Lake, Lake County.

Fremont's goldfields (*Lasthenia fremontii*).

FREMONT'S GOLDFIELDS

Family: Asteraceae (sunflower family)

Scientific name: *Lasthenia fremontii* (A. Gray) Greene

Height: Up to 14".

Leaves: Mainly opposite, 0.4–2.5" long, very narrow, hairless to sparsely hairy; margins smooth or with a few very narrow pinnate lobes.

Flowers: Heads borne singly, each head 0.5–1" wide; phyllaries 8–16 per head in 1 row, not fused, hairy; ray flowers 6–13, bright yellow; disk flowers numerous, anthers yellow.

Blooms March through May.

Elevation: Sea level to above 2,000'.

Habitat: Wet meadows and vernal pools.

California goldfields (*Lasthenia californica* subsp. *californica*) or common goldfields (*Lasthenia gracilis*).

Comments: Northern California is home to about 13 species of *Lasthenia*, all native, all annual. Most of them used to be included in the genus *Baeria*. Smooth goldfields (*Lasthenia glaberrima*) and small-ray goldfields (*Lasthenia microglossa*) have minute ray flowers or lack them entirely, but the others all look rather alike. They're differentiated from each other by details such as whether the phyllaries are free or fused, the shape of the receptacle, what kind of pappus they have, and whether the petals turn red when treated with an alkaline solution such as lye. Fremont's goldfields grows mainly in the Central Valley and the foothills of the Cascades and Sierra Nevada. California goldfields (*Lasthenia californica* subsp. *californica*) and common goldfields (*Lasthenia gracilis*) often occur in the same places as Fremont's goldfields as well as in coastal areas and the North Coast Ranges but prefer somewhat drier ground, which for a short time in spring they can carpet bright yellow. In both these species, the flowers may or may not have a pappus; when it's absent, the two species are indistinguishable except at a molecular level.

FREMONT'S TIDY-TIPS

Family: Asteraceae (sunflower family)

Scientific name: *Layia fremontii* (Torr. & A. Gray) A. Gray

Height: Up to 16".

Leaves: Basal leaves in a rosette or opposite, less than 3" long, usually with rough bristly hairs, deeply pinnately lobed with up to 29 lobes; stem leaves alternate, smaller, with smooth, toothed, or lobed margins.

Flowers: Heads borne singly, each head 1–1.5" wide; phyllaries in 1 row, hairy; ray flowers 3–15, petals bright yellow except for pure white or occasionally pale yellow tips; disk flowers 4–100 or more, each with a small bract next to it, petals yellow, anthers maroon.

Blooms February through May.

Elevation: Sea level to 2,600'.

Habitat: Grassland and foothill woodland.

Comments: Fremont's tidy-tips grows mainly in the Central Valley and the foothills of the Cascades and Sierra Nevada. It's one of seven species of *Layia* native to northern California, all of them annual. Smooth tidy-tips (*Layia chrysanthemoides*) and coastal tidy-tips (*Layia platyglossa*) have equally pretty yellow-and-white flowers and, as a result, are sometimes used rather indiscriminately in seed mixes, with the result that you may find them along highways and in other revegetated areas way outside their native range.

HAIRY HAWKBIT

Family: Asteraceae (sunflower family)

Also called: Lesser hawkbit

Scientific name: *Leontodon saxatilis* Lam. subsp. *longirostris* (Finch & P. D. Sell) P. Silva

Height: 4–12".

Leaves: In a basal rosette, 0.8–10" long, slightly to densely hairy or bristly, with smooth, toothed, or deeply lobed margins, the lobes pointing outwards or slightly forwards; stem leaves, if present at all, reduced to small scales.

Flowers: Heads borne singly; phyllaries in 2 or more rows, the outer row short and very narrow, the inner phyllaries much longer, slightly wider, and often purple-tipped; flowers bright yellow, dandelion-like.

Blooms April through October.

Elevation: Sea level to 3,200'.

Habitat: Grassland, vernal pools, and disturbed areas.

Comments: Some books call this small annual or biennial *Leontodon taraxacoides* subsp. *longirostis*. It grows along the coast and in the Sacramento Valley, Cascades, Sierra Nevada foothills, and San Francisco Bay region. The fruits of the inner flowers have a slender neck about 0.1" long between the main body of the fruit, containing the single seed, and the bristly pappus. *Leontodon saxatilis* subsp. *saxatilis* can be biennial or perennial and has shorter-necked fruit. Its range largely overlaps with that of the other subspecies. Both are native to Europe and have several unbranched, thin, solid or hollow stems per plant with milky sap. Common dandelion (*Taraxacum officinale*) has similar-looking flowers but hollow, relatively thick stems and almost or completely hairless leaves with backward-pointing lobes.

STICKY LESSINGIA

Family: Asteraceae (sunflower family)

Scientific name: *Lessingia pectinata* Greene var. *tenuipes* (J. T. Howell) Markos

Height: 2–28".

Leaves: Alternate, typically 0.1–1.2" long, sometimes as long as 2.5", fairly narrow, with minute stalked glandular hairs and larger bead-like resin-secreting glands; margins smooth, toothed, or pinnately lobed.

Flowers: Heads borne singly on wiry green or tan branches, each head roughly 0.3" wide with about 6 rows of phyllaries overlapping like shingles on a roof, phyllaries green, edged with bead-like glands; 15–30 flowers per head; petals yellow with a maroon throat; stamens yellow.

Blooms May through October.

Elevation: Sea level to 5,200'.

Habitat: Flood plains, open sandy ground, dry grassland, coastal scrub, and chaparral.

Comments: This annual grows mainly in central California but does make it as far north as Sacramento County. Sometimes the sticky resin produced by the glands smells like sagebrush or thyme; other times it's unpleasantly sharp and turpentiney. I once found what at first glance seemed to be a patch of strangely hairy plants; upon closer inspection they turned out to have lots of fluffy, wind-dispersed willow seeds stuck to them. Northern California's eight additional species of *Lessingia* have white to lavender flowers.

DAGGERLEAF COTTONROSE

Family: Asteraceae (sunflower family)

Scientific name: *Logfia gallica* (L.) Coss. & Germ.

Height: 0.8–20".

Leaves: Alternate, the largest generally 0.8–1.2" long by about 0.05" wide, stiff, sharply pointed, covered with cobwebby white hairs; margins smooth.

Flowers: Heads borne in clusters of 2–10 or more at branching points and at the tips of the branches, each head flask-shaped, less than 0.2" long, with 5 short, translucent phyllaries; 9–12 corolla-less female flowers per head, each almost hidden by a hard, keeled bract folded around it; 3–5 bisexual disk flowers with 4-lobed, brownish yellow corollas.

Blooms March through July.

Elevation: Sea level to 3,600'.

Habitat: Open, sandy or gravelly flood plains and other dry, open areas.

Comments: The pale grayish color and slender shape of this annual, native to the Old World's Mediterranean region, make it easy to miss. Older books call it *Filago gallica*. Its stems fork several times, like repeated Ys. The bracts wrapped around the female flowers are attached to the upper surface of the receptacle; they don't cup the flower head from below the way phyllaries do. California cottonrose (*Logfia filaginoides*), a California native, has wider, flexible leaves and 0–4 phyllaries per flower head.

92

COMMON MADIA

Family: Asteraceae (sunflower family)

Also called: Common tarweed

Scientific name: *Madia elegans* D. Don

Height: 2.5" to more than 8'.

Leaves: Lower leaves opposite, upper leaves alternate, usually 1.2–8" long by 0.1–0.8" wide, sessile, covered with soft or occasionally coarse hairs along with sticky glandular hairs that consist of a slender stalk surmounted by a round, yellowish brown, purple, or black head; margins usually smooth.

Flowers: Heads showy, generally 1–2" wide, borne in open clusters; phyllaries in a single row, hairy; each head generally with 5–20 or more bright yellow ray flowers, the lower part of their corollas often dark red, the tip deeply 3-lobed, and 25–80 or more yellow disk flowers with yellow, brown, or dark purple anthers. Blooms April through November.

Elevation: Sea level to above 11,000'.

Habitat: Grassland and open disturbed sites.

Comments: You have be a morning person to see this beauty: By 10 a.m. or so, its ray flowers start curling up. It's said that the flowers uncurl again in the late afternoon and stay open throughout the night. Even within a single patch, the inflorescences can vary tremendously in the number of ray flowers and how much red, if any, they have: The two shown above were from adjacent plants, while other plants nearby had inflorescences with numerous all-yellow ray flowers or just a few yellow-and-red ones. The disk flowers are functionally male, only producing pollen, then withering and dropping off; and so each seed head consists of a circle of tiny, seed-like black or brown fruits produced by the ray flowers around a bald center where the disk flowers used to be. The smell of the resin produced by the glandular hairs reminds me of turpentine with a whiff of wintergreen. Typically the upper half of the plant branches quite a bit, but the branches don't overtop the main stem. It's the showiest of northern California's nine species of *Madia* and occurs throughout the region, although it seems to be less frequent near the coast and on the Modoc Plateau.

GUMWEED

Family: Asteraceae (sunflower family)

Also called: Slender tarweed

Scientific name: *Madia gracilis* (Sm.) Applegate

Height: 2" to more than 3'.

Leaves: Lower leaves opposite, upper leaves alternate, 0.4–6" long by 0.1–0.4" wide, sessile, covered with long hairs and lots of sticky glandular hairs similar to those of common madia (*Madia elegans*); margins usually smooth.

Flowers: Heads not showy, usually 0.7" or less in width; phyllaries in a single row, hairy; each head generally with 3–10 lemon-yellow or greenish yellow ray flowers, the tip of their corollas 3-lobed, and 2–16 or more greenish yellow disk flowers with brown, black, or dark purple anthers.

Blooms April through August.

Elevation: Sea level to above 8,000'.

Habitat: Grassland, open woodland, chaparral, and other partly shaded areas.

Comments: This inconspicuous annual is common throughout northern California. The flower heads are spaced out along the often slightly zigzag stems, not crowded near the top as in coast tarweed (*Madia sativa*). Also, although the entire stem of gumweed is hairy, only in the upper part are glandular hairs interspersed among the non-glandular hairs. Both ray and disk flowers produce seeds. The common name is easy to confuse with gumplant (*Grindelia* spp.), a very different-looking member of this family.

COAST TARWEED

Family: Asteraceae (sunflower family)

Also called: Chile tarweed

Scientific name: *Madia sativa* Molina

Height: 1–3', occasionally up to more than 6'.

Leaves: Lower leaves opposite, upper leaves alternate, 0.8–7" long by 0.1–0.7" wide, occasionally much wider, sessile, covered with long hairs along with lots of very sticky glandular hairs similar to those of common madia (*Madia elegans*); margins usually smooth.

Flowers: Heads not showy, typically 0.5" or less wide; phyllaries in a single row, hairy; each head generally with 5–13 butter-yellow ray flowers, the tip of their corollas 3-lobed, and 11–14 greenish yellow disk flowers with brown or dark purple anthers.

Blooms May through October.

Elevation: Sea level to 3,200'.

Habitat: Grassland and open, disturbed sites.

Comments: Despite its common name, this annual doesn't just grow near the coast but also far inland in the North Coast Ranges and even the Sacramento Valley. It can occur in the same locations as the far more widespread gumweed (*Madia gracilis*) but tends to bloom a little later. The two look rather similar, but the entire stem of coast tarweed is covered with glandular hairs, and most of its flower heads are crowded together at the tip of the stem.

PINEAPPLE WEED

Family: Asteraceae (sunflower family)

Also called: Rayless chamomile

Scientific name: *Matricaria discoidea* DC.

Height: Usually 4–12".

Leaves: Alternate, 0.4–2" long, twice or 3-times pinnately divided into very slender or thread-like segments, sessile, hairless, sweet-scented when crushed.

Flowers: Heads borne singly or in small clusters; each head a pointed dome less than 0.5" wide; phyllaries in 2 or 3 rows, their margins papery and translucent; no ray flowers; numerous yellowish green disk flowers.

Blooms February through August.

Elevation: Sea level to above 7,000'.

Habitat: Flood plains, stream banks, and disturbed sites.

Comments: Some older texts refer to this inconspicuous but very common annual as *Chamomilla suaveolens* or *Matricaria matricarioides*; it's widespread in northern California but native to northwestern North America and northeastern Asia. Valley mayweed (*Matricaria occidentalis*) is very similar but is a California native that grows in undisturbed wetlands, including vernal pools, alkali flats, and the margins of salt marshes; the two species also differ in some minute features of the fruit. German chamomile (*Matricaria chamomilla*), native to Europe and used in herbal teas, has 10–25 white, often drooping ray flowers per head.

COTTONTOP

Family: Asteraceae (sunflower family)

Scientific name: *Micropus californicus* Fisch. & C. A. Mey. var. *californicus*

Height: 0.4–20".

Leaves: Alternate, 0.2–0.6" long, narrow, sessile, covered with woolly white hairs; margins smooth.

Flowers: Heads often borne in small clusters, sometimes singly; each head roughly 0.2" wide, spherical, generally with 5 small, papery phyllaries; 4–8 very slender female flowers per head, each almost completely enclosed in a thick, hard, bloated, densely woolly bract; 2–5 male flowers in the center, with short, generally 5-lobed corollas and yellow or reddish anthers.

Blooms March through June.

Elevation: Sea level to 5,200'.

Habitat: Dry, open ground and disturbed areas.

Comments: This small annual is widespread in northern California; it usually has one main stem with a few short side branches. Mount Diablo cottonseed (*Micropus amphibolus*) occurs in the southern part of the North Coast Ranges but is rare. At first glance, cudweed (*Gnaphalium palustre*) looks similar to cottontop, but each of its fuzzy heads has a ring of stiff, papery, petal-like bracts encircling the flowers; its stems tend to branch near the base, the bottom inch or two of each branch sprawling along the ground before turning upright.

FRAGRANT CUDWEED

Family: Asteraceae (sunflower family)

Scientific name: *Pseudognaphalium beneolens* (Davidson) Anderb.

Height: 1' to nearly 4'.

Leaves: Alternate, 1–2.5" long, very narrow, sessile, with a dense coat of shaggy or woolly hairs; margins smooth; older leaves twist and coil in all directions.

Flowers: Heads borne in fairly loose clusters; each head somewhat elongated and with 4–7 rows of white, matte or shiny, opaque phyllaries that overlap like shingles on a roof, a ring of about 40 to about 70 very narrow, pale yellow female flowers, and a central cluster of 5–11 bisexual disk flowers with yellow anthers.

Blooms June through October.

Elevation: Sea level to about 3,000'.

Habitat: Gravelly flood plains and dry, open areas.

Comments: The leaves of this annual or short-lived perennial have a pleasant scent that reminds me of curry powder but sweeter and less pungent. The plants' pale, ghost-like color often blends into their surroundings, making it easy to overlook them. In northern California, they grow mainly in the southern part of the North Coast Ranges and in the Sacramento Valley and Sierra Nevada foothills. Five additional species of *Pseudognaphalium* occur in the region. Older texts assign them to the genus *Gnaphalium*.

CALIFORNIA CUDWEED

Family: Asteraceae (sunflower family)

Also called: Ladies' tobacco

Scientific name: *Pseudognaphalium californicum* (DC.) Anderb.

Height: 8" to more than 4'.

Leaves: Alternate, 1.4–4" long, usually 0.2–0.4" wide, sessile, with stalked glandular hairs that produce a sticky, sweet-smelling resin, some plants with additional long wavy or woolly hairs; margins smooth or wavy, sometimes curled downwards.

Flowers: Heads borne in large, flat-topped or domed clusters; each head with 7–10 rows of white or pinkish, matte or shiny, opaque phyllaries that overlap like shingles on a roof, a ring of 105–140 very slender female flowers, and a central cluster of 7–12 bisexual disk flowers.

Blooms April through July.

Elevation: Sea level to above 2,500'.

Habitat: Partly shaded grassland, dry woodland, chaparral, and disturbed areas; often on sandy, sloping sites.

Comments: California cudweed can be annual, biennial, or perennial. Its foliage tends to look much greener than that of other species of *Pseudognaphalium*. Viewed up close, each flower head is shaped like a miniature artichoke. When ready for pollination, the top of the "artichoke" is crowned with a ruff of lemon-yellow stigmas that emerge from the female flowers. The species occurs mainly from Butte, Glenn, and southern Humboldt counties southwards.

RED-TIP RABBIT-TOBACCO

Family: Asteraceae (sunflower family)

Also called: Jersey cudweed

Scientific name: *Pseudognaphalium luteoalbum* (L.) Hilliard & B. L. Burtt

Height: 4" to 2'.

Leaves: Alternate, the lower leaves crowded together on the stem, the upper leaves more widely spaced, 0.4–2.5" long, usually less than 0.3" wide, sessile, covered with a dense coat of woolly hairs; margins generally curled downwards.

Flowers: Heads borne in compact clusters; each head with 3 or 4 rows of pale green, silvery gray, or tan, translucent, hairless or densely woolly phyllaries, a ring of about 135–160 very narrow female flowers with translucent red-tipped corollas, and a central cluster of 4–10 bisexual disk flowers with red- or yellow-tipped corollas and yellow anthers.

Blooms April through August.

Elevation: Sea level to nearly 3,000'.

Habitat: Disturbed areas, streambeds, and drying muddy sites.

Comments: In northern California, this Eurasian annual grows in coastal areas, the Sacramento Valley, and the Cascade and Sierra Nevada foothills. Although it occurs in streambeds, it can also thrive in ultra-dry sites such as the edges of levee-top roads. Its foliage is unscented; cottonbatting plant (*Pseudognaphalium stramineum*), which has yellow flowers, is the only other species of *Pseudognaphalium* in the region without scented foliage.

PINK CUDWEED

Family: Asteraceae (sunflower family)

Scientific name: *Pseudognaphalium ramosissimum* (Nutt.) Anderb.

Height: 20" to 5'.

Leaves: Alternate, 1" to nearly 3" long, usually no more than 0.2" wide, sessile, sometimes with a rather sparse coat of woolly hairs with stalked glandular hairs underneath the woolly ones; margins generally wavy and curled downwards.

Flowers: Heads borne in big, fairly open clusters; each head cylindrical, with 4 or 5 rows of translucent pink phyllaries that overlap like shingles on a roof, a ring of about 40–60 very narrow, pale to bright yellow female flowers, and a central cluster of 2–7 bisexual disk flowers with yellow anthers.

Blooms July through September.

Elevation: Sea level to 2,000'.

Habitat: Dunes, sandy fields, chaparral, and woodland.

Comments: In northern California, pink cudweed can be found near the coast and in the San Francisco Bay region; it's more common in central and southern California. It's biennial and has sweet-scented foliage. Occasionally the phyllaries are white or greenish rather than pink.

DWARF WOOLLY MARBLES

Family: Asteraceae (sunflower family)

Also called: Dwarf woollyheads

Scientific name: *Psilocarpus brevissimus* Nutt. var. *brevissimus*

Height: About 1", with stems up to 4" long lying flat on the ground.

Leaves: Mainly opposite, the longest 0.3–0.6" long, narrow, sessile, densely woolly; margins smooth.

Flowers: Heads single or in clusters of 2–4, the largest heads 0.2–0.4" wide, snuggled in a "nest" of leaves at the tip of the stem; 8–80 female flowers per head, each wrapped in a densely woolly bract; 2–10 male flowers per head, their petals fused into a 5-lobed, pale or reddish tube; all flowers tiny and almost completely hidden by woolly hairs.

Blooms May through June.

Elevation: Sea level to above 8,000'.

Habitat: Almost or completely dry beds of vernal pools, mud flats, and drainage channels.

Comments: This annual occurs in most of northern California. Technically, it lacks phyllaries; the woolly bracts associated with the female flowers functionally replace them. Delta woolly marbles (*Psilocarpus brevissimus* var. *multiflorus*) only grows in the Sacramento Valley as far north as Glenn County; its silky-haired flower heads can be up to 0.6" wide. Tall woolly marble (*Psilocarpus elatior*), also rare, is restricted to the Cascades and Modoc Plateau.

SLENDER WOOLLY MARBLES

Family: Asteraceae (sunflower family)

Scientific name: *Psilocarpus tenellus* Nutt.

Height: Up to 1".

Leaves: Opposite, the longest 0.2–0.6" long, narrow to oval, widening towards the tip, sessile, covered with cobwebby to silky or woolly hairs; margins smooth.

Flowers: Heads borne singly or in clusters of 2–4, each about 0.1–0.2" wide, nestled among the leaves at the tip of the stem; 25 to about 50 female flowers per head, each wrapped into a white-haired bract, corollas very short and very slender; 2–10 male flowers per head, corollas 5-lobed.

Blooms March through July.

Elevation: Sea level to almost 8,000'.

Habitat: Seasonally moist ground and compacted soil such as the margins of trails.

Comments: Another diminutive annual, it's widespread throughout most of northern California except the northernmost region. Young plants start out upright, then begin sprawling across the ground and forming flat mats. Round woolly marbles (*Psilocarpus chilensis*) resembles slender woolly marbles in many ways but has male flowers with 4-lobed corollas, and its stems usually stay upright. Oregon woollyheads (*Psilocarpus oregonus*) also has tiny flower heads and male flowers with 4-lobed corollas, but its leaves are very narrow, 6–12 times as long as they are wide.

DOUGLAS' THREADLEAF RAGWORT

Family: Asteraceae (sunflower family)

Also called: Shrubby butterweed or bush groundsel

Scientific name: *Senecio flaccidus* Less. var. *douglasii* (DC.) B. L. Turner & T. M. Barkley

Height: 1–4'.

Leaves: Alternate, 1.5" to almost 5" long, very narrow to thread-like or pinnately divided into very narrow or thread-like lobes, sessile or with short petioles, sparsely covered with short lint-like hairs; margins smooth.

Flowers: Heads borne in open, often flat-topped clusters; phyllaries in 2 rows, the lower spreading, the upper longer, upright, and arranged side by side like a picket fence; each head with 8, 13, or 21 ray flowers, their strap-shaped corollas 0.4–0.8" long, and 40–50 disk flowers; all flowers yellow.

Blooms June through October.

Elevation: Sea level to nearly 5,000'.

Habitat: Gravelly flood plains, grassland, woodland, chaparral, and open, dry, well-drained, disturbed sites.

Comments: This subshrub or shrub has upright to arching or even floppy branches; its large flowers and brilliant white, dandelion-like seed heads make it fairly noticeable. It grows in the North Coast Ranges, Sacramento Valley, Cascades, and Sierra Nevada as well as farther south. It's one of many species of *Senecio* in California, some native, some introduced; most are annuals or herbaceous perennials. Worldwide, the genus encompasses more than 1,000 species. German or Cape ivy, native to southern Africa, is an invasive perennial vine in coastal California, the San Francisco Bay region, and parts of the North Coast Ranges. It used to be called *Senecio mikanioides* but has been reclassified as *Delairea odorata*.

ARROWLEAF RAGWORT

Family: Asteraceae (sunflower family)

Also called: Tall ragwort or arrowleaf groundsel

Scientific name: *Senecio triangularis* Hook.

Height: Usually 8" to 4', occasionally up to almost 7'.

Leaves: Alternate, the blade 1.5" to more than 4" long by 1–2.5" wide, narrowly to widely triangular, usually hairless, lower leaves with petioles, upper leaves more or less sessile; margins toothed.

Flowers: Heads borne in loose to fairly dense, elongate, rounded, or flat-topped clusters of 10–60; phyllaries in 2 rows, the lower black-tipped, often very short and at most half as long as the upper; about 8 yellow ray flowers and 35–45 yellow disk flowers per head.

Blooms June through September.

Elevation: 300' to almost 11,000'.

Habitat: Rocky stream banks and damp sites in conifer forest.

Comments: This herbaceous perennial grows in the Klamath Ranges, Cascades, and Sierra Nevada. It likes moist to wet sites and blooms relatively late in the growing season. Lamb's-tongue ragwort (*Senecio integerrimus* var. *major*) can sometimes be found in drier forest or sagebrush scrub in the same general locations. It blooms earlier in the growing season, has stems densely covered with cobwebby hair, and produces fewer but somewhat larger flower heads.

COMMON GROUNDSEL

Family: Asteraceae (sunflower family)

Scientific name: *Senecio vulgaris* L.

Height: 4" to 2'.

Leaves: Alternate; lower leaves with blades 0.8–4" long by 0.1–1.5" wide and short petioles, often slightly fleshy, hairless or covered with loose, wavy hairs; margins toothed to deeply pinnately lobed; upper leaves smaller, sessile.

Flowers: Heads borne singly or in dense to loose, upright to nodding clusters of 8–20 or more; phyllaries in 2 rows, the lower black-tipped and much shorter than the upper; no ray flowers; 30–65 yellow disk flowers per head.

Blooms February through July.

Elevation: Sea level to above 4,000'.

Habitat: Disturbed areas.

Comments: This widespread, weedy annual with hairless or sparsely hairy stems is native to Eurasia. Woodland groundsel (*Senecio sylvaticus*), another Eurasian species, has hairy stems, and its lower phyllaries, if present at all, have green tips. Unlike common groundsel, in which all flowers are bisexual, each flower head of woodland groundsel has 1–8 female flowers around its perimeter— that is, the flowers lack stamens—but it's hard to figure that out without a microscope. Sometimes these female flowers have a short, strap-shaped corolla, sometimes they don't.

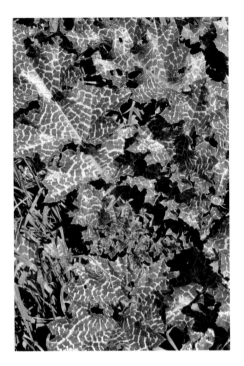

MILK THISTLE

Family: Asteraceae (sunflower family)

Also called: St. Mary's thistle or blessed milkthistle

Scientific name: *Silybum marianum* (L.) Gaertn.

Height: 8" to 10'.

Leaves: Leaves in basal rosette 6" to more than 2' long with winged petioles; stem leaves smaller, alternate, sessile, their bases clasping the stem; all leaves hairless or nearly so, dark green with large, irregular white blotches; margins lobed, wavy, and very spiny.

Flowers: Heads borne singly; each head with 4–6 rows of stiff, spine-tipped phyllaries that radiate star-like from the head, no ray flowers, and numerous disk flowers with slender pink to purple corollas; anthers purple; pollen light blue.

Blooms February through June.

Elevation: Sea level to 3,000'.

Habitat: Disturbed areas.

Comments: This invasive annual or biennial is native to the Old World's Mediterranean region; in northern California it occurs mainly along the coast and in the North Coast Ranges, Sacramento Valley, and Cascade and Sierra Nevada foothills. The conspicuous white blotches on the leaves, which look as if someone had spilled milk onto the plant, and hollow, wingless and spineless stems make it easy to identify. The seed-like fruits can survive nine or more years in the ground; they're crowned with a tuft of 0.6 0.8"-long hairs but often don't seem to get carried very far away by the wind, with the result that new plants frequently grow in dense, almost impenetrable stands. The leaves of Italian thistle (*Carduus pycnocephalus*) can be weakly variegated in green and white, but its stems are spiny-winged and the flower heads less than half the width of those of milk thistle.

CALIFORNIA GOLDENROD

Family: Asteraceae (sunflower family)

Scientific name: *Solidago velutina* DC. subsp. *californica* (Nutt.) Semple

Height: 8" to 5'.

Leaves: Alternate; lower leaves up to 5.5" long, narrow, with toothed margins; upper leaves much smaller with smooth margins; all covered with short, velvety hairs.

Flowers: Heads borne in elongate clusters; phyllaries in several rows that overlap like shingles on a roof; each head with 6–11 ray flowers and 6–17 disk flowers, all flowers yellow.

Blooms May through November.

Elevation: Sea level to above 8,000'.

Habitat: Woodland, grassland, coastal scrub, chaparral, and disturbed sites.

Comments: This subspecies of California goldenrod occurs throughout northern California. The inflorescences, each usually consisting of numerous rather tightly clustered flower heads, can vary from slender to wide; occasionally you'll also find plants with just a few flower heads on each stem. The seed heads just look like beige, slightly fluffier versions of the flower heads. It's one of seven native species of *Solidago* that grow in the region, all of them herbaceous perennials. Coast goldenrod (*Solidago spathulata*) stands out by the shiny, varnish-like coating on its leaves and phyllaries and its narrow, club-like inflorescences.

BURWEED

Family: Asteraceae (sunflower family)

Also called: Carpet burweed or lawn burweed

Scientific name: *Soliva sessilis* Ruiz & Pav.

Height: Less than 3", often with stems 0.5–6" long lying flat on the ground.

Leaves: Alternate or whorled, usually less than 0.8" long, twice or 3-times pinnately divided into narrow lobes, bright yellowish green; hairless or covered with short, soft hairs.

Flowers: Heads borne singly, greenish, generally 0.2–0.4" wide, ultra-inconspicuous and partly hidden by leaves; phyllaries in 1 or 2 rows, spine-tipped; each head with a ring of 5–12 or more corolla-less female flowers surrounding 4–9 or more male disk flowers with white or pale yellow, 3- or 4-lobed corollas.

Blooms April through July.

Elevation: Sea level to 5,000'.

Habitat: Disturbed sites, especially those with compacted soil.

Comments: This mat-forming little annual is another of those easy-to-walk-over-without-seeing-it plants. After pollination and fertilization, each female flower turns into a small, flat, sharp-pointed fruit that can easily get caught in fur or feathers (or socks). It grows in the North Coast Ranges, Klamath Ranges, Sacramento Valley, and Sierra Nevada foothills but is native to South America. Pineapple weed (*Matricaria discoidea*) and southern brass buttons (*Cotula australis*) have similar leaves but quite different flower heads.

SPINY SOW THISTLE

Family: Asteraceae (sunflower family)

Also called: Prickly sow thistle

Scientific name: *Sonchus asper* (L.) Hill subsp. *asper*

Height: 4" to 4'.

Leaves: Alternate, 2.4–12" long, shiny; upper leaves with rounded, downwards-curved or coiled lobes at their bases that clasp the stem; margins toothed, edged with fairly soft spines, sometimes lobed.

Flowers: Heads borne in small clusters; phyllaries usually in 3 rows, the innermost row the longest, forming a vase-like structure with a bulbous base and narrow neck and studded with soft, often gland-tipped spines; each head with numerous light yellow flowers.

Can bloom at almost any time of the year.

Elevation: Sea level to above 6,000'.

Habitat: Stream banks, riparian areas, and some-what moist disturbed ground.

Comments: This common, weedy annual is native to Europe. Its smooth, stout, typically unbranched stems are hollow, which you can feel by gently squeezing them, and both the stems and the main veins in the leaves are often colored purple. The sap is milky. I'm not sure how pigs, male or female, come into the picture—maybe they like to eat the plants? Anyway, the *ow* in sow thistle is pronounced like the *ow* in *owl*, not as in *sow*.

COMMON SOW THISTLE

Family: Asteraceae (sunflower family)

Also called: Smooth sow thistle, colewort, or hare's lettuce

Scientific name: *Sonchus oleraceus* L.

Height: 4" to almost 5'.

Leaves: Alternate, the blade 2–14" long, soft to the touch, upper side matte or satiny; margins toothed or lobed, the lobe at the tip of the leaf often arrow-shaped; upper leaves sessile with pointed, straight or only very slightly curved lobes at their bases.

Flowers: Heads borne in small clusters, sometimes with a patch of soft woolly hairs just below each head; phyllaries usually in 3 rows, forming a vase-like structure with a bulbous base and narrow neck, hairless or with scattered glandular hairs; each head with numerous light yellow flowers.

Can bloom at almost any time of the year.

Elevation: Sea level to above 8,000'.

Habitat: Disturbed sites and riparian areas.

Comments: Like spiny sow thistle (*Sonchus asper*), this widespread, hollow-stemmed, weedy annual may have been introduced centuries ago by Spanish settlers. The two species are most easily differentiated by their leaves. Also, spiny sow thistle usually doesn't branch much, while common sow thistle plants tend to branch near the base. Two other species of *Sonchus* are less common in northern California.

WHITE-PLUME WIRE LETTUCE

Family: Asteraceae (sunflower family)

Also called: Small wire lettuce

Scientific name: *Stephanomeria exigua* Nutt. subsp. *coronaria* (Greene) Gottlieb

Height: 3' to more than 6'.

Leaves: Basal leaves and those near the bottom of the stem 0.8–2" long, narrow, with toothed to deeply pinnately lobed margins, often withered by the time the plants bloom; upper stem leaves alternate, small, bract-like.

Flowers: Heads borne singly or in clusters along the stem and branches; phyllaries in 2 rows; each head with 5–11 light purplish pink flowers, their strap-shaped corollas tipped with 5 small teeth.

Blooms May through November.

Elevation: Sea level to above 9,000'.

Habitat: Grassland, forest openings, and disturbed sites, especially those with sandy or volcanic soil.

Comments: This annual or biennial mainly grows farther south but does make it into northern California along the Lower American River and perhaps in some other locations. Its branches are stiffly angled upwards, and the seed-like, 0.1–0.2"-long, light brown fruits look a bit like miniature ears of corn. "White-plume" refers to the pappus that tops each fruit with feathery white hairs. Five additional species of *Stephanomeria* occur in northern California, some annual, some perennial, all pink- or white-flowered.

WESTERN MOUNTAIN ASTER

Family: Asteraceae (sunflower family)

Scientific name: *Symphyotrichum spathulatum* (Lindl.) G. L. Nesom var. *spathulatum*

Height: 8" to 2'.

Leaves: Alternate, the blade 2–6" long, narrow, usually hairless, basal leaves with petioles, stem leaves sessile; margins more or less smooth.

Flowers: Heads borne on long stalks in very open clusters of 3–10; phyllaries in several rows, their tips curved outwards; each head with 15–40 lavender ray flowers and numerous yellow disk flowers.

Blooms June through August.

Elevation: 4,000' to above 9,000'.

Habitat: Meadows and open conifer forest.

Comments: Older texts call this herbaceous perennial *Aster occidentalis* var. *occidentalis*; it grows from long, creeping underground stems. *Symphyotrichum spathulatum* var. *intermedium* can get up to 3' tall and produces 10–50 flower heads per stem. Western bog aster (*Symphyotrichum spathulatum* var. *yosemitanum*) is rather uncommon; it has extremely narrow leaves, less than 0.2" wide. All three varieties can be found in the Klamath Ranges, Cascades, Sierra Nevada, and farther north. Several additional species of *Symphyotrichum* also occur in northern California, all with white, lavender, or purple ray flowers and yellow disk flowers, their habitats ranging from sea-level salt marshes to high mountain forests and meadows.

YELLOW SALSIFY

Family: Asteraceae (sunflower family)

Also called: Western salsify or western goat's beard

Scientific name: *Tragopogon dubius* Scop.

Height: 12" to more than 3'.

Leaves: Alternate, 8–20" long, grass-like, sessile, sometimes hairy near the base when young, later becoming hairless; margins smooth.

Flowers: Heads borne singly on stalks that widen noticeably just below the head; phyllaries in 1 row, their long narrow tips flaring outwards; petals lemon-yellow, the strap-shaped corollas of the peripheral flowers in each head much shorter than the phyllaries; anthers brown or purplish.

Blooms May through September.

Elevation: Sea level to nearly 9,000'.

Habitat: Grassland, disturbed sites, and open areas in woodland or conifer forest.

Comments: This annual or biennial occurs mainly in the Sacramento Valley, San Francisco Bay region, and Sierra Nevada. In meadow salsify (*Tragopogon pratensis*), the corollas of the peripheral flowers are at least as long as the phyllaries, and the stems widen only slightly below the flower heads, if at all. Oyster plant or common salsify (*Tragopogon porrifolius*) has purple flowers. All three are native to Europe. They have milky sap, usually close their flowers by mid-day (in England, meadow salsify is called Jack-go-to-bed-at-noon), and produce huge, beige or tan, but otherwise dandelion-like seed heads.

Woolly mule's ears (*Wyethia mollis*).

WOOLLY MULE'S EARS

Family: Asteraceae (sunflower family)

Also called: Mountain mule's ears

Scientific name: *Wyethia mollis* A. Gray

Height: 12–20", occasionally taller.

Leaves: Basal leaves present while plants are flowering, their blades 8–16" long, fairly narrow to oval, initially densely woolly on both sides but losing most hair with age, the hairs giving the leaves a gray-green or blue-green appearance; margins smooth; stem leaves alternate, smaller, sessile.

Gray mule's ears (*Wyethia helenioides*), showing its wide, almost leaf-like phyllaries.

Flowers: Heads borne singly or in 2s or 3s, each head typically 2–4" wide; phyllaries in 2 or 3 rows, 0.6" to nearly 1.5" long and relatively narrow; each head with 6–15 ray flowers and 35–100 or more disk flowers, all flowers bright yellow.

Blooms May through August.

Elevation: 3,000' to above 11,000'.

Habitat: Meadows, dry rocky slopes, open conifer forest, and sagebrush scrub.

Comments: This species occurs in all of northern California's mountains; like other members of the genus, it's a herbaceous perennial with a sturdy taproot. Gray mule's ears (*Wyethia helenioides*) grows in grassland and chaparral up to about 6,500' throughout much of northern California. Its common name notwithstanding, its foliage is usually much brighter green than that of woolly mule's ears, and its rather wide phyllaries have wavy margins. Other northern California species of *Wyethia* include *Wyethia angustifolia*, which has very narrow to almost triangular basal leaves with short, rough hairs, and *Wyethia bolanderi*, in which the basal leaves wither before the plants bloom. *Wyethia glabra*, found in the southern part of the North Coast Ranges, has shiny, usually hairless leaves and prefers shady sites.

COMMON COCKLEBUR

Family: Asteraceae (sunflower family)

Scientific name: *Xanthium strumarium* L.

Height: Generally 4" to 5'.

Leaves: Alternate, the blade usually 1.5–5" long by 1.2–4" wide, triangular or palmately 3- to 5-lobed, covered with rough hairs that make the leaves feel sandpapery; margins smooth or toothed.

Flowers: Male and female heads borne on the same plant, the female heads below the male heads; male heads with 1–3 rows of minute phyllaries or without phyllaries, with 20–150 or more whitish or cream-colored disk flowers that lack functional pistils; female heads with 6–12 or more rows of green, sharp, hooked phyllaries enclosing 2 flowers.

Blooms July through October.

Elevation: Sea level to 4,500'.

Habitat: Riparian areas, seasonal wetlands, and disturbed sites with moist soil.

Comments: This widespread, weedy annual seems to be native throughout the Americas. The stems usually have lots of dark streaks or spots. As the two seeds in each female head mature, the phyllaries fuse around them into a hard, brown or black bur that easily gets entangled in fur or feathers. The burs float and hence can also be dispersed by water. Spiny cocklebur (*Xanthium spinosum*) has narrower leaves and golden yellow spines on its stems.

OREGON GRAPE

Family: Berberidaceae (barberry family)

Also called: Hollyleaf mahonia

Scientific name: *Berberis aquifolium* Pursh var. *aquifolium*

Height: 3' to more than 6'.

Leaves: Evergreen, alternate, pinnately compound with 5–9 leaflets per leaf, petiole usually 0.4–1" long; leaflets 1.4–3" long by 0.8–2" wide, the upper side shiny; margins flat to slightly wavy with 12–24 spine-tipped teeth along each edge.

Flowers: Borne in fairly tight clusters, each flower with 9 sepals in 3 whorls of 3, 6 petals in 2 whorls of 3, 6 stamens, and a superior ovary, all parts bright yellow.

Blooms March through June.

Elevation: 1,300–7,500'.

Habitat: Conifer forest.

Comments: Northern California has three varieties of this shrub; they differ in features such as number of leaflets per leaf, petiole length, number of spines on the leaf margins, and whether the shrubs are upright or creeping. Several additional species of *Berberis* also grow in the region; identifying them can be tricky because some species and varieties intergrade. The fruit of most of them is a small, blue-black berry. In some older references the genus is called *Mahonia*. It's one of the few dicotyledons whose sepals and petals come in 3s rather than 4s or 5s.

WHITE ALDER

White alder (*Alnus rhombifolia*).

Immature male catkins of white alder along the Lower American River in November.

Male catkins of white alder on the same tree as above right in late January.

Red alder (*Alnus rubra*).

Family: Betulaceae (birch family)

Scientific name: *Alnus rhombifolia* Nutt.

Height: Up to 115'.

Leaves: Deciduous, alternate, the blade 2" to more than 4" long by 1.5–2" wide, oval or diamond-shaped; upper side dark green and hairless or finely hairy; lower side lighter green and finely hairy; margins toothed and usually flat.

Flowers: Male and female flowers borne on the same tree; male flowers in long, hanging clusters called catkins, each flower tucked under a small yellowish green bract and consisting of 3–5 tiny fused sepals and 3–5 stamens with bright red anthers, like miniature pomegranate seeds; female flowers in smaller clusters borne at various angles, each flower consisting of a small bract and a pistil with 2 deep pink stigmas.

Blooms January through April.

Elevation: Sea level to 5,000', occasionally to almost 8,000'.

Habitat: Banks of streams that flow all year.

Comments: White alder grows in most of northern California except in the western Sacramento Valley; on the Modoc Plateau it's uncommon. Even when not crowded by other trees, it tends to be relatively narrow in shape. The flowers are wind-pollinated; after fertilization, each female inflorescence matures into a small cone-like fruit, about 0.5–0.8" long. The following spring's inflorescences begin forming in late summer, and so a tree can simultaneously bear immature green catkins, the current year's maturing fruit, and old "cones" persisting from the previous year.

Red alder (*Alnus rubra*), also a tree, has leaves with rolled-under margins. It sometimes forms extensive groves on wet soils near the coast and in the western part of the North Coast Ranges and Klamath Ranges. Three other northern California alders are thicket-forming shrubs or small trees that can grow to about 30' tall: mountain alder (*Alnus incana* subsp. *tenuifolia*), which grows at elevations of 4,000–8,000', Siberian alder (*Alnus viridis* subsp. *fruticosa*), and thinleaf

Female catkins of white alder with protruding pink stigmas.

or Sitka alder (*Alnus viridis* subsp. *sinuata*). The latter two are sometimes just lumped together as "green alder"; all three have leaves with margins that are variously described as double-toothed or as having small, toothed lobes. Curiously, in the fall all alders shed their leaves while still green; they don't change color first like most deciduous species. Their roots harbor nitrogen-fixing bacteria that help them thrive in wet, nitrogen-poor soil. Native Americans make a red dye from the bark of both red and white alder and use their roots in basketry.

Mature fruit of white alder.

NORTHERN CATALPA

Family: Bignoniaeae (trumpet-creeper family)

Also called: Western catalpa or cigar tree

Scientific name: *Catalpa speciosa* (Warder) Engelm.

Height: Up to 100'.

Leaves: Deciduous, opposite or whorled, the blade 6–12" long, heart-shaped with a long pointed tip, lower side softly hairy, no disagreeable odor when bruised; margins smooth.

Flowers: Borne in showy upright clusters; each flower 1.6–2.5" long by 2–2.5" wide; petals fused into a broad tube topped by 5 frilly lobes, white with yellow and purplish brown spots and stripes in the tube's "throat."

Blooms April through July.

Elevation: Sea level to 5,000'.

Habitat: Riparian areas and disturbed sites.

Comments: The inflorescence shown here is just starting to bloom; soon it will turn into a frothy white cluster of blossoms, which in turn will be replaced by dangling, skinny, foot-long seed capsules. The trees are native from Illinois to Arkansas; in northern California, they've naturalized mainly near urban areas. Southern catalpa (*Catalpa bignonioides*) has slightly smaller leaves with an unpleasant odor when bruised; its flowers don't exceed 1.4" in length. It's native to the southeastern United States, where it thrives in wetlands; oddly, where naturalized in California it seems to prefer dry locations.

BUGLOSS-FLOWERED FIDDLENECK

Family: Boraginaeae (borage or waterleaf family)

Scientific name: *Amsinckia lycopsoides* Lehm.

Height: 8" to about 3'.

Leaves: Alternate, 1–4" long, lower leaves very narrow, upper leaves somewhat wider, with both flat-lying and stiff, bristly or prickly, spreading hairs; margins smooth.

Flowers: Borne in flat spirals that uncoil as the flowers age and set seed; sepals 5, their bases fused, green, very hairy; petals yellow to orange, fused into a 5-lobed tube with a darker orange spot on each lobe, the opening of the tube blocked by stiff hairs, the lower half of the tube abruptly constricted; stamens 5, attached to the narrow part of the tube.

Blooms March through June.

Elevation: Sea level to 2,800', occasionally higher.

Habitat: Grassland, sparse woodland, and disturbed sites.

Comments: Peel back the sepals to see the narrow part of the petal tube, which is shaped like one of those super-size coffee mugs or soda cups with a narrowed base to make them fit into a standard-size cup holder. Northern California is home to several additional species of *Amsinckia*. All are annual and several hybridize, but only in bugloss-flowered fiddleneck are the stamens hidden by dense hairs.

WHISPERING BELLS

Family: Boraginaeae (borage or waterleaf family)

Scientific name: *Emmenanthe penduliflora* Benth. var. *penduliflora*

Height: 2" to nearly 3'.

Leaves: Alternate, 0.4–5" long, the blade usually less than 1.5" wide with soft, spreading, non-glandular hairs and minute glands that produce a sticky but pleasantly scented resin; lower leaves with short petioles, upper leaves sessile; margins toothed to deeply pinnately lobed.

Flowers: Borne on thread-like stalks 0.2–0.6" long; sepals 5, green, hairy; petals light yellow or cream-colored, fused into a 5-lobed bell; stamens 5; ovary superior.

Blooms April through July.

Elevation: Sea level to above 7,000'.

Habitat: Chaparral and rocky or sandy sites, often under shrubs.

Comments: In northern California, this inconspicuous annual grows in the eastern part of the North Coast Ranges and in the Sierra Nevada foothills in El Dorado County. After pollination and fertilization, the flower stalks grow longer and bend down, and the petals fade and become dry and papery, so that the spent flowers resemble a row of tiny, creamy white bells. Except for a second variety that grows farther south, with white to pink petals and often reddish stems, there's nothing else quite like this species in California.

CALIFORNIA YERBA SANTA

Family: Boraginaeae (borage or waterleaf family)

Scientific name: *Eriodictyon californicum* (Hook. & Arn.) Torr.

Height: 3–10'.

Leaves: Evergreen or deciduous, alternate, often crowded near the tips of the branches, the blade 2–6" long by 0.4–2" wide, tapering to a short petiole, leathery; upper side dark green, hairless, covered with a shiny, sticky exudate; lower side paler with short matted hairs between the veins; margins rolled downwards and either smooth or toothed.

Flowers: Borne in loose to fairly compact clusters; sepals 5, narrow; petals fused into a trumpet-shaped, 5-lobed tube 0.3–0.7" long, white or lavender; stamens 5, filaments white, anthers gray or purplish; ovary superior, densely hairy.

Blooms April through July.

Elevation: Sea level to 6,000'.

Habitat: Grassland with poor, rocky soil; woodland and chaparral.

Comments: This variable, sometimes scragglylooking shrub occurs in most of northern California except on the Modoc Plateau. A black mold often attacks the leaves. The only other northern California member of the genus is matted yerba santa (*Eriodictyon lobbii*, called *Nama lobbii* in some older texts), which has bright purple flowers and forms patches a foot tall but several feet wide at elevations of 4,000–7,000' in the Klamath Ranges and Cascades.

SPOTTED HIDESEED

Family: Boraginaeae (borage or waterleaf family)

Also called: Common eucrypta

Scientific name: *Eucrypta chrysanthemifolia* (Benth.) Greene var. *chrysanthemifolia*

Height: Up to 3'.

Leaves: Opposite on the lower part of the stem, the blade 0.8–4" long by 0.4–2" wide, twice or 3-times pinnately lobed, with long spreading hairs and glandular hairs that produce a sticky, sweet-scented resin, petiole fairly short; upper leaves alternate, smaller, less lobed, sessile.

Flowers: Borne in loose clusters of 8–15 flowers on thread-like stalks; sepals 5, hairy; petals about twice as long as the sepals, fused into a 5-lobed bell, white with purple streaks and a glistening yellow center; stamens 5, white; ovary superior.

Blooms March through June.

Elevation: Sea level to about 3,000'.

Habitat: Chaparral, coastal bluffs, and recently burnt areas, usually in partial shade.

Comments: This annual occurs in the southern part of the North Coast Ranges but is more common farther south. Another variety, *Eucrypta chrysanthemifolia* var. *bipinnatifida*, grows in central and southern California. Its flowers are borne in clusters of 4–8; the plain white petals are about the same length as the sepals. The only other species in the genus is a small, purple-flowered desert plant.

ALKALI HELIOTROPE

Family: Boraginaeae (borage or waterleaf family)

Also called: Seaside heliotrope

Scientific name: *Heliotropium curassavicum* L. var. *occulatum* (A. Heller) Tidestr.

Height: Stems 4" to 2' long but often lying more or less flat on the ground.

Leaves: Alternate, the blade 0.4–2.5" long, oval to fairly narrow, fleshy, blue-green, hairless and covered with a waxy bloom, sessile or with a short petiole; margins smooth.

Flowers: Borne in tight flat spirals that gradually uncoil as the flowers age and set seed, each flower 0.1–0.3" wide; sepals 5, fleshy, hairless; petals fused into a bell-shaped tube with 5 white lobes and a star-like purple or greenish yellow center; stamens 5; ovary superior.

Blooms February through October.

Elevation: Sea level to above 7,000'.

Habitat: Moist or dry soil; tolerates saline or alkaline conditions.

Comments: This herbaceous perennial spreads by creeping roots that send up new stems here and there. It grows throughout the Sacramento Valley, along the coast, and in scattered locations elsewhere in northern California. It's one of only two species of *Heliotropium* found in the region; two more occur in central and southern California.

EUROPEAN HELIOTROPE

Family: Boraginaeae (borage or waterleaf family)

Scientific name: *Heliotropium europaeum* L.

Height: 2–16".

Leaves: Alternate, the blade 0.6–2" long, oval, gray-green or blue-green, hairy, with prominent pinnate veins; margins smooth.

Flowers: Borne in tight flat spirals that gradually uncoil as the flowers age and set seed, each flower 0.1–0.2" wide; sepals 5, narrow, very hairy; petals fused into a white, 5-lobed, bell-shaped tube; stamens 5; ovary superior.

Blooms April through August.

Elevation: Sea level to 4,500'.

Habitat: Open, disturbed areas.

Comments: European heliotrope is annual; it's native to southern and eastern Europe and northern Africa. In California, it occurs throughout the Sacramento Valley and the Cascade and Sierra Nevada foothills. Its leaves remind me of oregano, except that they're alternate instead of opposite and lack oregano's scent and flavor, and I've found it thriving in some exceptionally hot, dry places such as levee-top gravel roads. The plant shown here has almost finished blooming; earlier in the season the flowering stems are much shorter and tightly coiled.

CALIFORNIA HESPEROCHIRON

Family: Boraginaeae (borage or waterleaf family)

Scientific name: *Hesperochiron californicus* (Benth.) S. Watson

Height: Less than 4".

Leaves: In a basal rosette, the blade no more than 3.2" long, nearly hairless to velvety or hairy on both sides, base tapered to a fairly short petiole; margins smooth.

Flowers: 0.4–0.8" wide, borne on slender stalks 0.4–4" long; sepals 5, hairy; petals fused into a bell- or funnel-shaped, 5-lobed tube, white or tinged blue, the inside of the tube densely hairy; stamens 5; ovary superior.

Blooms May through July.

Elevation: 2,500–8,500'.

Habitat: Wet meadows and moist pockets in otherwise drier open locations.

Comments: This herbaceous perennial has a short, thick, vertically growing root; look for the plants in the Klamath Ranges, Cascades, and Sierra Nevada. Dwarf hesperochiron (*Hesperochiron pumilus*) occurs in the same areas and also the eastern part of the North Coast Ranges. It grows from slender creeping underground stems and has narrower leaves that usually are hairless at least on the lower side; its petals are white with purple veins, and the inside of the petal tube is bright yellow.

BAY FORGET-ME-NOT

Family: Boraginaeae (borage or waterleaf family)

Scientific name: *Myosotis laxa* Lehm.

Height: 4–16".

Leaves: Alternate, the blade 0.6–3.5" long by 0.1–0.6" wide, hairy, lower leaves with petioles, upper leaves usually sessile; margins smooth.

Flowers: Borne in flat spirals that gradually uncoil as the flowers age and set seed, each flower 0.1–0.2" wide; flower stalks and sepals with short, harsh, flat-lying hairs *without* hooked tips; petals 5, fused at the base, robin-egg-blue except for a prominent, yellow, raised rim around the opening of the petal tube; stamens 5, hidden inside the tube; ovary superior.

Blooms May through September.

Elevation: Sea level to 7,000', occasionally higher.

Habitat: Moist soil and shallow water.

Comments: This California native can be an annual or a short-lived herbaceous perennial. As in many members of its family, the ovary is deeply 4-lobed and after pollination and fertilization ripens into four "nutlets," each containing one seed. Northern California has several other species of forget-me-not, but they're all native to the Old World. They differ in the size and shape of the sepals, whether the hairs on the sepals lie flat or not and have hooked or straight tips, and the color of the petals.

CANYON NEMOPHILA

Family: Boraginaeae (borage or waterleaf family)

Also called: White nemophila or variable-leaved nemophila

Scientific name: *Nemophila heterophylla* Fisch. & C. A. Mey.

Height: Usually a few inches, with weak stems up to 1' long.

Leaves: Lower leaves opposite, the blade 0.4–1.6" long with an equally long petiole, deeply pinnately lobed with 5–7 usually widely spaced lobes; margins smooth or with a few teeth; upper leaves alternate, smaller, sessile, unlobed or with 3–5 lobes.

Flowers: 0.2–0.5" wide; sepals 5, hairy, with little downward-pointing "ears"; petals 5, fused at their bases into a bowl, pure white or bluish; stamens 5, anthers grayish blue to dark purple; ovary superior.

Blooms February through July.

Elevation: 100–5,500'.

Habitat: Woodland, forest, stream banks, chaparral, and talus, typically in light shade.

Comments: The bristly stems of this small annual often sag onto the ground, forming flower-dotted patches a foot or more in diameter. It's common in much of northern California except in the Sacramento Valley, where it only seems to grow in the Sutter Buttes, and on the Modoc Plateau. Small-flowered nemophila (*Nemophila parviflora*) also has plain white flowers, but they're no more than 0.2" wide.

FIVESPOT

Family: Boraginaeae (borage or waterleaf family)

Scientific name: *Nemophila maculata* Lindl.

Height: A few inches.

Leaves: Opposite, the blade of lower leaves 0.3–1.5" long by 0.1–0.6" wide with an equally long or longer petiole, deeply 5- to 9-lobed; margins smooth or with a few teeth at the tip; upper leaves smaller, unlobed, sessile.

Flowers: 0.4–2" wide; sepals 5, hairy, with little downward-pointing "ears"; petals 5, fused at their bases into a shallow bowl, white with purple veins and a conspicuous purplish blue spot at the tip of each petal; stamens 5, filaments white or lavender, anthers initially dull red or purple, later turning grayish; ovary superior.

Blooms March through July.

Elevation: 100–10,000".

Habitat: Grassland, woodland, and forest.

Comments: This little beauty grows along the eastern edge of the Sacramento Valley and in the Sierra Nevada. Two related species occasionally have a blue or purple spot at the tip of each petal: Sierra baby blue-eyes (*Nemophila spatulata*), which, despite its name, also occurs in the Cascades, has winged petioles and flowers 0.1–0.4" wide. Littlefoot nemophila (*Nemophila pedunculata*) grows throughout northern California; its flowers are 0.1–0.3" wide and sometimes have a small, light purple blotch on each petal.

The small yellow flower is California burclover (*Medicago polymorpha*).

Nemophila menziesii var. *atomaria*.

BABY BLUE-EYES

Family: Boraginaeae (borage or waterleaf family)

Scientific name: *Nemophila menziesii* Hook. & Arn. var. *menziesii*

Height: 4–12".

Leaves: Opposite, lower leaves 0.4–2" long on equally long petioles, deeply 6- to 13-lobed, lobes with smooth margins or a few teeth at the tip, margins with fewer lobes or merely toothed; upper leaves smaller with short petioles.

Flowers: 0.4" to more than 1.5" wide; sepals 5, hairy, with little downward-pointing "ears"; petals 5, fused at their bases into a shallow bowl, medium blue except for a white center, sometimes with blue veins, black speckles, or both; stamens 5, filaments white, anthers gray to chocolate brown; ovary superior.

Blooms February through June.

Elevation: Sea level to 5,200'.

Habitat: Grassland, woodland, coastal scrub, and chaparral.

Comments: This eye-catching, slightly succulent annual occurs naturally from Mendocino and Tehama counties to southern California. It's often included in wildflower seed mixes, though, and so you may find it in unexpected places. The petals of *Nemophila menziesii* var. *atomaria*, restricted to coastal areas and the western part of the North Coast Ranges and Klamath Ranges, can be almost pure white or decorated with blue veins and little black or purple dots and streaks, rather like fivespot (*Nemophila maculata*) without the big purple spots. *Nemophila menziesii* var. *integrifolia* grows mainly in central and southern California and the northern Sierra Nevada; although its lower leaves have five to seven lobes, its upper leaves are sessile and unlobed with smooth or toothed margins. Its flowers resemble those of variety *menziesii* in color but only get 0.2–0.6" wide.

Note the tiny white flowers. The penny is 0.75" wide.

SLEEPING COMBSEED

Family: Boraginaeae (borage or waterleaf family)

Also called: Winged combseed or northern pectocarya

Scientific name: *Pectocarya penicillata* (Hook. & Arn.) A. DC.

Height: 1–10".

Leaves: Alternate, 0.4–1.5" long by less than 0.1" wide, sessile, covered with hard, flat-lying white hairs.

Flowers: Borne in small coils that straighten out as the flowers age and set seed, usually only 1 flower open at a time at the tip of each branch, each flower 0.1" or less in diameter; sepals 5, hairy; petals 5, their bases fused into a short tube, white except for a light yellow "throat"; stamens 5, hidden inside the tube; ovary superior.

Blooms February through May.

Each X-shaped fruit, about 0.2" long, is derived from one ovary, often with the dry remnants of the style and stigma at the center of the X.

Elevation: Sea level to almost 7,000'.

Habitat: Disturbed sites and dry, sandy or gravelly grassland.

Comments: This is another one of those miniscule annuals that, frankly, I might never have noticed if I hadn't stopped on a late March day to look at some contorted sun cups (*Camissonia contorta*) blooming in a shallow depression that a few weeks earlier had been full of sand pygmyweed (*Crassula connata*) and common sandweed (*Athysanus pusillus*). The sandweed was gone, but in its place was another plant new to me with minute white flowers and the oddest little fruit: sleeping combseed. As in many species of Boraginaceae, the ovary is deeply 4-lobed, each single-seeded lobe maturing into what botanists call a nutlet. The species is widespread in northern California except near the coast and on the Modoc Plateau.

Little combseed (*Pectocarya pusilla*), also widespread in northern California, has fruit consisting of four tiny, wedge- or diamond-shaped nutlets forming a cross rather than an elongated X. Moth or round-nut pectocarya (*Pectocarya setosa*) is primarily a southern California species but has been reported from a few sites in Glenn and Lassen counties; its nutlets are roundish to oval and rimmed with a thin, translucent wing.

117

IMBRICATE SCORPIONWEED

Family: Boraginaeae (borage or waterleaf family)

Scientific name: *Phacelia imbricata* Greene subsp. *imbricata*

Height: 8" to 4'.

Leaves: Mainly basal, the blade 2–6" long, undivided, pinnately divided, or pinnately compound with 7–15 leaflets, bright light green to dark gray-green, with spreading stiff hairs and shorter glandular hairs that secrete a pleasantly scented sticky resin, petiole nearly as long as the blade; the few stem leaves smaller.

Flowers: Borne in flat spirals that uncoil but don't elongate very much as the flowers set seed; sepals 5, hairy; petals fused into a 5-lobed cylinder, white or lavender; 5 stamens and a forked style projecting well beyond the petals; ovary superior.

Blooms April through July.

Elevation: Sea level to 7,500'.

Habitat: Woodland, chaparral, and dry, sparse grassland.

Comments: OK, I admit it, I'm not fond of phacelias, largely because the 95 or so species in California can be so darn hard to identify. Some hybridize, making identification even more challenging. Also, some are covered with bristly hairs that cause contact dermatitis. Imbricate scorpionweed, a herbaceous perennial, has hairs that vary from merely stiff to painfully needle-like. Look for it in the North Coast Ranges, Sacramento Valley, and Sierra Nevada.

LACY PHACELIA

Family: Boraginaeae (borage or waterleaf family)

Also called: Tansy-leafed phacelia

Scientific name: *Phacelia tanacetifolia* Benth.

Height: 6" to more than 3'.

Leaves: Alternate, the blade of the lower leaves 0.8–8" long, usually once or twice pinnately compound, hairy, petiole shorter than the blade; leaflet margins toothed or lobed; upper leaves smaller, nearly sessile.

Flowers: Borne in flat spirals that uncoil but don't elongate very much as the flowers set seed; sepals 5, densely bristly; petals fused into a wide, 5-lobed bell, lavender or light to medium blue; stamens 5, filaments longer and a little darker than the petals, anthers initially lavender, later turning gray or tan; ovary superior, style branched into 2 long, spreading arms.

Blooms March through May.

Elevation: Sea level to above 8,000'.

Habitat: Grassland and other open areas with sandy or gravelly soil.

Comments: In northern California, this annual *Phacelia* occurs in the Sacramento Valley, Cascade foothills, and the eastern and southern parts of the North Coast Ranges. Sometimes the spiral inflorescences are packed together so tightly that collectively they form a kind of lumpy knob. The fruit is an oval capsule. Wild heliotrope (*Phacelia distans*) is similar, but its fruit is a spherical capsule.

VALLEY POPCORNFLOWER

Family: Boraginaeae (borage or waterleaf family)

Scientific name: *Plagiobothrys canescens* Benth. var. *canescens*

Height: 4" to 2'.

Leaves: Basal leaves in a rosette, the blade 0.6–2" long, narrow to very narrow, soft-haired; margins smooth; stem leaves alternate, smaller.

Flowers: Borne in flat spirals that uncoil and elongate as the flowers set seed, each flower roughly 0.1" wide; sepals 5, hairy, often with some rusty brown hairs; petals 5, their bases fused, white except for a yellow, raised rim around the opening of the petal tube that fades to white with age; stamens 5, hidden inside the tube; ovary superior.

Blooms February through June.

Elevation: Sea level to above 4,500'.

Habitat: Grassland, woodland, and coastal scrub.

Comments: California has about 40 species of *Plagiobothrys* and more than 60 species of the very similar genus *Cryptantha*. To identify them, you need the tiny fruits, or nutlets, as well as flowers. Valley popcornflower is slightly different from many, although not unique, in that it has leaves interspersed among its flowers, which is easiest to see as the plants set fruit and the flowering stems uncoil and elongate. Its stems often sprawl, forming low mounds a foot or more in diameter.

RUSTY POPCORNFLOWER

Family: Boraginaeae (borage or waterleaf family)

Scientific name: *Plagiobothrys nothofulvus* (A. Gray) A. Gray

Height: 8" to more than 2'.

Leaves: Basal leaves in a rosette, the blade 1.2–4" long, narrow, hairy; margins smooth; the few stem leaves alternate, smaller, narrower.

Flowers: Borne in small clusters of flat spirals that uncoil and elongate as the flowers set seed, each flower 0.1–0.3" wide, sometimes fragrant; sepals 5, with bristly, rusty brown hairs; petals 5, their bases fused, white except for a yellow, raised rim around the opening of the petal tube that fades to white with age; stamens 5, hidden inside the tube; ovary superior.

Blooms February through May.

Elevation: Sea level to 5,000'.

Habitat: Grassland, open woodland, and coastal scrub.

Comments: This annual, common throughout northern California, has upright stems. The upper part of the sepals (which are fused below the middle) breaks away from the ripening fruit like a small crown or cap. As typical of most species in the genus, only a few small bracts (if any) are interspersed among the flowers and flower buds. Rusty popcornflower sometimes intergrades with valley popcornflower (*Plagiobothrys canescens* var. *canescens*) and Arizona popcornflower (*Plagiobothrys arizonicus*).

119

VERNAL POOL POPCORNFLOWER

Family: Boraginaeae (borage or waterleaf family)

Also called: Stalked popcornflower or Great Valley popcornflower

Scientific name: *Plagiobothrys stipitatus* (Greene) I. M. Johnst. var. *micranthus* (Piper) I. M. Johnst.

Height: 4–20".

Leaves: Alternate, 0.8–4.5" long, fairly to very narrow, upper side usually hairless, lower side with short, flat-lying hairs, each hair often with a small, blister-like base; margins smooth.

Flowers: Borne along only slightly coiled stems, each flower less than 0.2" wide; sepals 5, hairy; petals 5, their bases fused, white except for a yellow, raised rim around the opening of the petal tube that fades to white with age; stamens 5, hidden inside the tube; ovary superior.

Blooms March through July.

Elevation: Sea level to 4,000'.

Habitat: Vernal pools and wet places in grassland, conifer forest, and sagebrush scrub.

Comments: This little annual lacks a basal rosette of leaves; its stems tend to be fleshy and more or less hollow. It occurs in most of northern California except near the coast. Showy Great Valley popcornflower (*Plagiobothrys stipitatus* var. *stipitatus*), found mainly in vernal pools and other wet spots in the Sacramento Valley, Cascade and Sierra Nevada foothills, and San Francisco Bay region, has flowers 0.2–0.5" in width.

MOUSE-EAR CRESS

Family: Brassicaeae (mustard family)

Also called: Thale cress

Scientific name: *Arabidopsis thaliana* (L.) Heynh.

Height: 2–12", occasionally taller.

Leaves: Mainly in a basal rosette, the blade 0.3–2" long by 0.1–0.6" wide, sparsely covered with unbranched and 2- to 4-branched hairs, petioles 0.4–1.5" long; margins smooth or minutely toothed; the few stem leaves alternate, smaller, sessile.

Flowers: Clustered at the top of the stem; sepals 4; petals 4, white; stamens 6, 2 of them shorter than the others, all with yellow anthers; ovary superior, turning into a skinny fruit 0.4–0.6" long.

Blooms February through May.

Elevation: Sea level to above 5,000'.

Habitat: Disturbed sites, especially those with sandy soil.

Comments: In northern California, this Eurasian annual is especially common in the eastern part of the Sacramento Valley; it's also widespread in the eastern United States. Partly because of its small number of chromosomes—only five pairs—and partly because it's easy to grow, it's often used in genetic research. Common rock cress (*Planodes virginicum*, previously called *Sibara virginica*)—which, despite its common name, is frequent in the Central Valley—is a native species that looks similar, but its hairs, if it has any at all, are unbranched.

COMMON SANDWEED
Family: Brassicaeae (mustard family)

Scientific name: *Athysanus pusillus* (Hook.) Greene

Height: 1–12", rarely up to 20".

Leaves: Basal leaves in a rosette, the blade 0.2–1" long, narrow, hairy, petiole usually short; margins smooth or toothed; the few stem leaves alternate, smaller, sessile.

Flowers: Clustered at the top of the stem, which elongates a lot as the fruit matures; sepals 4; petals 4, roughly 0.1" long, white, spoon-shaped; stamens 6, almost equal in length; ovary superior, turning into a disk-shaped fruit about 0.1" wide.

Blooms February through June.

Elevation: Sea level to 6,500'.

Habitat: Flood plains, sparse grassland, chaparral, and rocky outcrops.

Comments: The most noticeable feature of this diminutive annual (or perhaps it would be more accurate to say the least inconspicuous feature) is its fruits, which seem to hover just above the ground like tiny pale dots. They can be hairless or densely fringed with tiny hooked hairs around the margin, with fewer hairs on the flat faces; when backlit the hairs form a small white halo around each fruit. The species occurs throughout northern California. Lady's-tongue mustard (*Athysanus unilateralis*) is less common; it grows in the Sacramento Valley and Cascade foothills. Its flowers and fruits are borne on one side of the stem, and each little fruit has a slight twist to it.

121

FIELD MUSTARD

Family: Brassicaeae (mustard family)

Also called: Birdsrape mustard or wild turnip

Scientific name: *Brassica rapa* L.

Height: 1' to more than 3'.

Leaves: Blade of basal leaves 4–8" long, pinnately lobed, the lobe at the end bigger than the 2–6 pairs of lateral lobes with widely scattered hairs; margins toothed and wavy; leaves on the upper part of the stem smaller, sessile, hairless, unlobed, their bases clasping the stem.

Flowers: Sepals 4, yellowish; petals 4, 0.2–0.5" long by 0.1–0.3" wide, bright yellow; stamens 6, 2 of them shorter than the others; ovary superior, turning into a slender fruit 1" to more than 4" long that angles away from the stem.

Blooms January through May.

Elevation: Sea level to 5,000'.

Habitat: Disturbed areas in full sun or light shade.

Comments: This weedy annual or biennial is native to Europe. It can be distinguished from several other species of *Brassica* found in northern California, all with equally bright yellow flowers, by its sessile, non-fleshy stem leaves with clasping bases, the scattered hairs on its basal leaves, and the length of its petals. Cultivated varieties produce turnips and rutabagas. Cultivated forms of other species of *Brassica* include cabbage, cauliflower, broccoli, brussels sprouts, kale, bok choy, and several more leafy greens. The seeds of rapeseed (*Brassica napus*) yield canola oil; those of Chinese or Indian mustard (*Brassica juncea*) are the main ingredient in the condiment. *Rapistrum rugosum*, another naturalized European member of the Brassicaceae that's also called wild turnip, has completely different fruits that consist of a squat cylindrical or conical base topped by a much bigger ribbed sphere and a long pointy tip, the whole affair about 0.5" long and pressed against the stem. The family includes many other yellow-flowered species; you usually need leaves, flowers, and fruit to identify them.

Sea rocket (*Cakile maritima*).

American sea rocket (*Cakile edentula*): Note the slightly lobed leaf margin and the cylindrical shape of the lower segment of each fruit.

SEA ROCKET

Family: Brassicaeae (mustard family)

Scientific name: *Cakile maritima* Scop.

Height: Up to about 30".

Leaves: Alternate, the blade 1.5" to more than 3" long, pinnately divided into narrow finger-like segments, petioled, fleshy, hairless.

Flowers: Sepals 4, pinkish green; petals 4, 0.3–0.6" long, pink or lavender; stamens 6, 2 of them shorter than the others, anthers yellow; ovary superior, turning into a 2-segmented fruit, the lower segment with 2 short, flattened or horn-like, vertical lobes at the top, the upper segment more or less egg-shaped to conical.

Blooms May through November.

Elevation: Sea level to about 300'.

Habitat: Seaside dunes and sandy beaches.

Comments: You'll find this European annual growing in low mounds on beaches and dunes all along the coast from southern California to British Columbia. American sea rocket (*Cakile edentula*), native to eastern North America, seems less common in northern California; its leaves have toothed, scalloped, or only slightly lobed rather than deeply divided margins, its petals are 0.2–0.4" long, and the lower segment of the fruit is a simple cylinder, lacking the two lobes characteristic of *Cakile maritima*.

Sea rocket (*Cakile maritima*).

123

SHEPHERD'S PURSE

Family: Brassicaeae (mustard family)

Scientific name: *Capsella bursa-pastoris* (L.) Medik.

Height: Usually 2–20", occasionally taller.

Leaves: Mainly in a basal rosette, the blade 1–4" long, narrow, sparsely covered with unbranched and 3- to 5-branched hairs, petiole short; margins smooth, toothed, or pinnately lobed; the few stem leaves alternate, usually smaller, sessile with bases that clasp the stem.

Flowers: Clustered at the top of the stem; sepals 4, green or purplish; petals 4, 0.1–0.2" long, white or pale pink; stamens 6, 2 of them shorter than the others, anthers yellow; ovary superior, turning into a flat, purplish, heart-shaped to triangular fruit.

Blooms January through October.

Elevation: Sea level to above 9,000'.

Habitat: Disturbed areas.

Comments: This inconspicuous little annual or biennial, native to Eurasia but common throughout northern California, is one of our earliest spring flowers and continues blooming for a long time. The flowers are similar to those of mouse-ear cress (*Arabidopsis thaliana*), little western bittercress (*Cardamine oligosperma*), lacepod (*Thysanocarpus curvipes*), and various other small, weedy family members, but the heart-shaped or triangular fruit is unique. Buried seeds can survive for at least 15 years.

HEART-LEAVED BITTERCRESS

Family: Brassicaeae (mustard family)

Scientific name: *Cardamine cordifolia* A. Gray

Height: Usually 8" to 2', occasionally taller.

Leaves: Alternate, the blade 2–6" long, mostly heart- or kidney-shaped, often hairless, petiole 1–5" long; margins smooth, coarsely toothed, coarsely scalloped, or slightly wavy.

Flowers: Sepals 4, greenish; petals 4, 0.3–0.5" long, white; stamens 6, 2 of them shorter than the others, filaments green, anthers yellow; ovary superior, turning into a slender fruit 1–1.6" long.

Blooms February through August.

Elevation: 600' to above 11,000'.

Habitat: Moist, shady woodland, forest, wet meadows, and stream banks.

Comments: This herbaceous perennial grows from slender, creeping underground stems. Although mainly found at elevations above 2,000' from the Klamath Ranges, Cascades, and Sierra Nevada northwards to British Columbia, it also occurs in at least one shady canyon in Solano County. It's one of 11 species of *Cardamine* in northern California, all native except for hairy bittercress (*Cardamine hirsuta*), all with white or pale pink flowers except for rock toothwort (*Cardamine pachystigma*), which usually has bright lavender or pink flowers. You need the whole plant, including underground parts and seeds, to identify some of these species.

LITTLE WESTERN BITTERCRESS

Family: Brassicaeae (mustard family)

Also called: Idaho bittercress

Scientific name: *Cardamine oligosperma* Nutt.

Height: Usually 2–12", rarely up to 16"

Leaves: Mainly in a basal rosette, the blade 0.8" to nearly 4" long, once pinnately compound with 5–13 leaflets, the leaflet at the end bigger than the others, petiole short; leaflet margins smooth, toothed, or with 3–5 lobes; 3–8 smaller but otherwise similar alternate leaves per flowering stem.

Flowers: Sepals 4, green or reddish; petals 4, about 0.1" long, white; stamens 6 or occasionally only 4, filaments green or white, anthers white or cream; ovary superior, turning into a flattened, very slender fruit 0.5" to a little over 1" long that's held almost upright.

Blooms January through July.

Elevation: Sea level to nearly 11,000'.

Habitat: Wet meadows and other places with moist to wet soil.

Comments: Unlike most species of *Cardamine*, this inconspicuous annual or biennial is rather weedy and often invades landscaped areas. It grows from a thin taproot, and each plant only produces one or a few flowering, very upright stems. Hairy bittercress (*Cardamine hirsuta*) is similar but usually produces several flowering stems per plant that spread outwards from the base before turning upright.

WHITLOW GRASS

Family: Brassicaeae (mustard family)

Also called: Spring draba

Scientific name: *Draba verna* L.

Height: Usually 1–8", rarely up to 1'.

Leaves: All in a basal rosette, the blade usually 0.1–0.7" long, very narrow to oval, with branched hairs on both sides; margins smooth or toothed.

Flowers: Sepals 4, green; petals 4, 0.1–0.2" long, white, each deeply cleft into 2 lobes so that at first glance the flower seems to have 8 petals; stamens 6, anthers yellow; ovary superior, turning into a flattened, oval to elongate fruit 0.1–0.5" long.

Blooms February through May.

Elevation: Sea level to above 8,000'.

Habitat: Open or disturbed sites, woodland, and forest.

Comments: This annual is native to Eurasia and northern Africa but widespread in northern California. Even in drought years the tiny flowers can be so abundant that here and there a few square yards may look as if they were lightly dusted with snow. Several native species of *Draba* occur in the region, some of them rare; all have yellow flowers except for *Draba breweri*, which has white but unlobed petals and gray-green, densely woolly stems and leaves. It grows above timberline in the Cascade Ranges and Sierra Nevada.

SHORTPOD MUSTARD

Family: Brassicaeae (mustard family)

Also called: Hoary mustard

Scientific name: *Hirschfeldia incana* (L.) Lagr.-Fossat

Height: 8" to 5', occasionally taller.

Leaves: Blade of basal leaves 2–16" long, pinnately lobed or compound, the lobe at the end the biggest, lightly to densely covered with stiff hairs; margins smooth, toothed, or lobed; stem leaves alternate, smaller, often more or less sessile but without a lobed or clasping base.

Flowers: Sepals 4, narrow, yellowish; petals 4, about 0.2" long, yellow; stamens 6, 2 of them shorter than the others; ovary superior, turning into a slender fruit 0.3–0.7" long held parallel to the stem.

Blooms mainly April through October, but a few flowers may be present almost any time of year, sometimes on plants that look all but dead.

Elevation: Sea level to 6,500'.

Habitat: Disturbed sites.

Comments: This annual, biennial, or herbaceous perennial species is called *Brassica geniculata* in older texts; it's native to the Old World's Mediterranean region. The plants tend to be heavily branched and often grow wider than they're tall. Black mustard (*Brassica nigra*) also has fruit oriented parallel to the stem, but the plants aren't nearly as heavily branched; its inflorescences are bigger and the petals 0.3–0.5" long.

WATERCRESS

Family: Brassicaeae (mustard family)

Scientific name: *Nasturtium officinale* W. T. Aiton

Height: Usually 4" to 4', occasionally up to more than 6'.

Leaves: Alternate, once pinnately compound with 3–9 or more leaflets per leaf, each leaflet typically 0.4–2" long by 0.3–1.5" wide, usually more or less hairless; margins smooth or toothed.

Flowers: Sepals 4, rather wide, green; petals 4, 0.1–0.2" long, white; stamens 6, 2 of them shorter than the others, all with green filaments that turn purplish with age and yellow anthers; ovary superior, maturing into a slender fruit that's usually 0.4–1" long, angled away from the stem, constricted between adjacent seeds.

Blooms March through November.

Elevation: Sea level to 10,000'.

Habitat: Shallow, standing or flowing water such as lake margins, streams, marshes, and springs.

Comments: This aquatic herbaceous perennial, cultivated for its tasty leaves, used to be classified as *Rorippa nasturtium-aquaticum*. It's widespread in northern California and elsewhere in the northern hemisphere's temperate regions. Confusingly, the vine-like nasturtium grown in gardens for its bright orange or yellow flowers (*Tropaeolum majus*) and naturalized in the San Francisco Bay region and coastal California, belongs to a completely different family, the Tropaeolaceae (nasturtium family).

WILD RADISH

Family: Brassicaeae (mustard family)

Scientific name: *Raphanus sativus* L.

Height: Usually 1–4', sometimes as short as 4" or up to 6'.

Leaves: Blade of lower leaves 0.8" to 2' long, pinnately lobed or divided, the lobe or leaflet at the end the biggest, hairless or sparsely hairy, petiole long; margins toothed; upper stem leaves alternate, smaller, sessile or short-petioled.

Flowers: Sepals 4, greenish; petals 4, 0.6–1" long, purple, lavender, pink, or white with purplish veins; stamens 6, 2 of them shorter than the others, anthers yellow; ovary superior, turning into a fairly slender fruit 1.5–2.5" long.

Blooms February through July.

Elevation: Sea level to 5,000'.

Habitat: Disturbed areas and sparse grassland.

Comments: Jointed charlock (*Raphanus raphanistrum*, confusingly also called wild radish, wild kale, or wild turnip) is very similar except that its fruits are strongly constricted between adjacent seeds and its petals start out yellow. With time, though, the petals fade to white, making them harder to distinguish from wild radish; moreover, the two species hybridize freely, resulting in a kaleidoscope of petal colors. Both species can be annual or biennial and are native to Europe but common in most of northern California.

WESTERN YELLOW CRESS

Family: Brassicaeae (mustard family)

Also called: Curvepod yellow cress

Scientific name: *Rorippa curvisiliqua* (Hook.) Britton

Height: 2" to 2'.

Leaves: Lower leaves withering by the time the plants bloom; upper leaves alternate, the blade 1" to more than 5" long, hairless or sparsely hairy, with or without a petiole; margins coarsely toothed or pinnately lobed or divided.

Flowers: Sepals 4, about 0.1" long, narrow, yellow or greenish yellow; petals 4, no longer than the sepals, narrow, yellow or greenish yellow; stamens 6, anthers yellow; ovary superior, maturing into a slender, pod-like fruit 0.2–0.7" long that curves upwards.

Blooms April through September.

Elevation: Sea level to above 11,000'.

Habitat: Shallow water, stream banks, lake shores, marshy areas, mud flats, and meadows.

Comments: This annual seems to be the most widespread of several species of *Rorippa* in northern California, all with small yellow flowers, all growing in moist to wet places. Watercress (*Nasturtium officinale*), another shallow-water species, used to be included in the genus; it has white petals.

127

LACEPOD

Family: Brassicaeae (mustard family)

Also called: Fringepod or hairy fringepod

Scientific name: *Thysanocarpus curvipes* Hook.

Height: Usually 4" to 2', occasionally taller.

Leaves: Blade of basal leaves 0.4" to more than 5" long, widest near the tip, tapering to the petiole, usually sparsely hairy; margins smooth, toothed, or wavy; stem leaves alternate, smaller, sessile with basal lobes that clasp the stem.

Flowers: Sepals 4, greenish or light grayish purple with broad white margins, spreading, petal-like; petals 4, less than 0.1" long, white, the lower side sometimes lavender; stamens 6, anthers pale lavender, pollen cream-colored; ovary superior, turning into a flat, oval, hairless or hairy disk 0.1–0.4" wide that usually has lacy, perforated margins.

Blooms February through June.

Elevation: Sea level to above 8,000'.

Habitat: Grassland, woodland, and stream banks.

Comments: This annual is common throughout northern California. It was recently split into several subspecies, but the Sacramento-area plants that I've examined didn't seem to fit neatly into any one of them. The flowers are very small, and you're more likely to notice the plants when they're fruiting. Sometimes each fruit is edged with spoon-shaped lobes instead of being perforated.

SPOKEPOD

Family: Brassicaeae (mustard family)

Scientific name: *Thysanocarpus radians* Benth.

Height: 6" to 2'.

Leaves: Blade of basal leaves 0.6–2" long, widest near the tip, tapering to the petiole, hairless or sparsely hairy; margins wavy and toothed or pinnately lobed; stem leaves smaller, sessile with basal lobes that clasp the stem.

Flowers: Sepals 4, greenish with a white tip, spreading, petal-like; petals 4, about 0.1" long, white; stamens 6, anthers yellow; ovary superior, turning into a round, flattened, hairless or hairy disk 0.3–0.4" wide with spoke-like thickenings extending to the smooth or scalloped, often pink rim.

Blooms March through April.

Elevation: Sea level to about 2,500'.

Habitat: Grassland and moist hillsides.

Comments: This annual is widespread in northern California except on the Modoc Plateau. Unlike the region's other two species of *Thysanocarpus*, in spokepod the thin stalk holding the fruit often bends abruptly near the tip, although the fruits shown here have fairly evenly curved stalks. The third species, narrow-leaved lacepod (*Thysanocarpus laciniatus*) usually has hairless lower leaves and very narrow upper leaves. Its anthers are pale lavender; the fruits are 0.1–0.2" wide, round or oval, and have lobed, perforated, or solid margins.

SPICE-BUSH

Family: Calycanthaceae (sweet-shrub family)

Also called: Sweet-shrub

Scientific name: *Calycanthus occidentalis* Hook. & Arn.

Height: 3' to more than 10'.

Leaves: Deciduous, opposite, the blade 2–6" long by 0.8" to more than 3" wide, upper side shiny but slightly sandpapery to the touch, lower side hairless to hairy, with a pleasant scent when bruised, petiole 0.1–0.4" long; margins smooth.

Flowers: Borne singly on short branches, each flower about 2" wide with an unpleasant odor reminiscent of overripe fruit; no distinction between sepals and petals, the numerous petal-like parts brownish red; stamens numerous, the filaments shorter than the anthers, the innermost stamens sterile; pistils numerous, very slender, tightly packed.

Blooms March through August.

Elevation: Sea level to about 5,000'.

Habitat: Riparian forest, stream banks, and other moist, shady places.

Comments: In northern California, this native shrub grows mainly around the perimeter of the Sacramento Valley and in the southern part of the North Coast Ranges. It's pollinated by a small beetle, *Colopterus truncatus*, which feeds on protein-rich little outgrowths, brown or tan in color, at the tips of the stamens and innermost petals. The flowers close at night, trapping the beetles inside and giving them plenty of time to get themselves dusted with pollen, which they'll carry along to the next flower they visit the following day. Later the base of the flower enlarges into a leathery cup, 1–2" long, that encloses numerous small, dry, seed-like fruits, each derived from one pistil and containing one seed. These brown to almost black cups persist all winter, making the bushes easy to identify even when they're leafless.

129

SWAMP HAREBELL

Family: Campanulaceae (bellflower family)

Scientific name: *Campanula californica* (Kellog) A. Heller

Height: 4–12".

Leaves: Alternate, the blade 0.4–0.8" long, oval, with or without a short petiole; margins scalloped and edged with short, stiff hairs.

Flowers: 0.4–0.6" long; sepals 5, narrow, spreading, edged with short, hard hairs; petals fused into a 5-lobed bell, light to medium blue with darker veins; stamens 5, rather short; ovary inferior with a long, white or lavender style and 3-lobed white or pale lavender stigma.

Blooms June through September.

Elevation: Sea level to 1,300'.

Habitat: Marshy areas and wet stream banks in forest.

Comments: This rare herbaceous perennial only occurs near the coast from Santa Cruz County to Mendocino County. Its rather weak, four-angled stems tend to lean against nearby vegetation. They're covered with short, hard, downward-pointing hairs that are easy to detect by running your fingers upwards along the stem.

BLUEBELL

Family: Campanulaceae (bellflower family)

Also called: Alpine harebell or round-leaved harebell

Scientific name: *Campanula rotundifolia* L.

Height: 4" to 2'.

Leaves: Blade of basal leaves 1.5–2.5" long, a few of them usually oval to round, the others narrow, hairless, with toothed margins, petioled; stem leaves alternate, very narrow, almost grass-like, sessile, with smooth margins.

Flowers: 0.4–0.8" long, nodding on a slender stalk; sepals 5, narrow; petals fused into a 5-lobed bell, light to dark blue, occasionally white; stamens 5, filaments fairly short; ovary inferior, style shorter than the petals.

Blooms July through September.

Elevation: 4,000' to above 8,000'.

Habitat: Wet meadows, moist sites in conifer forest, and riparian areas.

Comments: This dainty herbaceous perennial occurs throughout the northern hemisphere's boreal regions; in California, it grows in the Klamath Ranges and Cascades. It's one of several species of *Campanula* in northern California, all with 4-angled stems and blue or white flowers. Scouler's harebell (*Campanula scouleri*) stands out by its style, which is much longer than the petals; it occurs in shady woodland and forest and along streams at elevations of a few hundred feet to above 6,000'.

TWO-HORNED DOWNINGIA

Family: Campanulaceae (bellflower family)

Scientific name: *Downingia bicornuta* A. Gray var. *picta* Hoover

Height: 2–10".

Leaves: Alternate, 0.2–0.6" long, narrow, sessile, hairless; margins smooth.

Flowers: Sepals 5; petals 5, their bases fused into a short tube, the upper 2 purple marbled with darker veins near the base, the lower 3 bigger, white, with a broad purple margin, two yellow or greenish spots, and a dark purple band with 2 small bumps or "horns" next to the opening of the petal tube; anthers lavender, fused into a tube around the style and stigma, with 2 long, white, twisted-together bristles at the end; ovary inferior.

Blooms April through July.

Elevation: Sea level to 300'.

Habitat: Vernal pools, lake shores, other wet places.

Comments: Like other *Downingia* species, this Sacramento Valley annual's slender ovary looks like a stem, but if you split it open, you'll find it full of tiny ovules. In the variety shown here, the "throat" of the petal tube is marbled with dark blue or purple veins. In *Downingia bicornuta* var. *bicornuta*, the throat is plain blue. You have to look closely to see the "horns" and other details; a hand lens helps.

MAROON-SPOTTED DOWNINGIA

Family: Campanulaceae (bellflower family)

Scientific name: *Downingia concolor* Greene var. *concolor*

Height: 2–8".

Leaves: Alternate, 0.2–0.7" long, narrow, sessile, hairless; margins smooth.

Flowers: Sepals 5; petals 5, their bases fused into a short tube, the upper 2 lavender, the lower 3 bigger, white, with a broad lavender margin and a relatively big, somewhat rectangular, dark maroon or purple spot next to the opening of the petal tube; anthers lavender, fused into a tube around the style and stigma; ovary inferior.

Blooms April through July.

Elevation: Sea level to 1,800'.

Habitat: Vernal pools, lake shores, mud flats, and other wet places.

Comments: This annual grows in the southern Sacramento Valley and southern North Coast Ranges. At Solano County's Jepson Prairie, which has more than half a dozen *Downingia* species, maroon-spotted downingia flowers are less than half the size of cupped downingia's (*Downingia insignis*); I don't know if they're always that small. Sometimes, next to the throat, you'll see two smaller yellow spots superimposed on the dark maroon spot.

TOOTHED DOWNINGIA

Family: Campanulaceae (bellflower family)

Also called: Toothed calicoflower

Scientific name: *Downingia cuspidata* (Greene) Rattan

Height: 2–10".

Leaves: Alternate, 0.1–0.6" long, narrow, sessile, hairless; margins smooth.

Flowers: Sepals 5; petals 5, their bases fused into a short tube, the upper 2 lavender, the lower 3 bigger, white, with a broad lavender margin, and a relatively big, 2-lobed, yellow spot next to the opening of the petal tube; anthers lavender, fused into a tube around the style and stigma; ovary inferior.

Blooms March through June.

Elevation: Sea level to 5,500'.

Habitat: Vernal pools, meadows, and lake shores.

Comments: This annual occurs in the Sacramento Valley, North Coast Ranges, Cascades, and Sierra Nevada foothills. Occasionally the flowers are all white except for the yellow central spot; this white form is abundant at Butte County's Table Mountain. The species is called "toothed" because of a minute tooth-like bump on three of the five fused anthers, which is all but impossible to see without a hand lens. Horned downingia (*Downingia ornatissima*, also called folded calicoflower) looks similar except that its two upper petals are usually strongly curled or folded back with a small backward-pointing pleat or "horn" between them.

CUPPED DOWNINGIA

Family: Campanulaceae (bellflower family)

Also called: Harlequin calicoflower

Scientific name: *Downingia insignis* Greene

Height: 4–10".

Leaves: Alternate, 0.2–0.6" long, narrow, sessile, hairless; margins smooth.

Flowers: Sepals 5; petals 5, their bases fused into a short tube, bright blue prominently marbled with darker blue, the lower 3 with a central white area that has 2 yellow or green spots next to a dark purple area, which is next to 2 yellow bumps or folds at the petal tube opening; stamens with dark blue filaments and light blue anthers, fused into a tube around the style and stigma; ovary inferior.

Blooms March through May.

Elevation: Sea level to almost 5,500'.

Habitat: Vernal pools, lake shores, other wet places.

Comments: All downingias carry their anthers at an angle to the filaments; in cupped downingia, this angle is often almost a right angle. The dark purple area on the lower petals can consist of a single band or a row of 2 or 3 spots. The main color can be pink or lavender. The species is common in the Sacramento Valley and also occurs on the Modoc Plateau.

VALLEY DOWNINGIA

Family: Campanulaceae (bellflower family)

Also called: Flatface calicoflower

Scientific name: *Downingia pulchella* (Lindl.) Torr.

Height: 2–10".

Leaves: Alternate, 0.2–0.5" long, narrow, sessile, hairless; margins smooth.

Flowers: Sepals 5; petals 5, bright blue, their bases fused into a short tube, the upper 2 angled away from each other in a very wide V, the lower 3 bigger, with a central white area that has 2 yellow spots next to a row of 3 dark purple spots or a single dark purple band, which in turn is next to 2 yellow folds that lead down into the dark purple petal tube; anthers lavender, fused into a tube around the style and stigma; ovary inferior.

Blooms April through June.

Elevation: Sea level to above 1,000'.

Habitat: Vernal pools, coastal salt marsh, and moist areas in grassland and foothill woodland.

Comments: Sometimes the two yellow spots merge into one big one. Look for this species in the Sacramento Valley and the inner North Coast Ranges. About 13 species of *Downingia* grow in northern California, not counting varieties, all annuals with a slender, stem-like inferior ovary. The rare dwarf downingia (*Downingia pusilla*), with petals less than 0.2" long, is the smallest.

TWINBERRY HONEYSUCKLE

Family: Caprifoliaceae (honeysuckle family)

Also called: Double honeysuckle or purple-flowered honeysuckle

Scientific name: *Lonicera conjugialis* Kellogg

Height: 2–6'.

Leaves: Deciduous, opposite, the blade 0.8" to more than 3" long, oval to almost round, finely hairy; margins smooth.

Flowers: Borne in pairs, each flower 0.2–0.3" long; sepals tiny; petals fused into a 4-lobed upright upper lip and an unlobed curled-down lower lip, dark red to almost black, the inside of the fused portion (the "throat") densely hairy; stamens 5, purplish; ovary inferior, the 2 ovaries of each pair of flowers fused for at least half their length.

Blooms May through August.

Elevation: 400' to almost 11,000'.

Habitat: Riparian areas, moist sites in conifer forest, and open rocky slopes.

Comments: In the dappled light of a conifer forest, you really have to search for this shrub's dark flowers. The brilliant red, translucent berries, on the other hand, are hard to miss even though they're only about 0.2–0.3" long. The berries vary in shape depending on the degree to which the two ovaries were fused, but each one has two little dots where the styles used to be attached. The species is widespread in northern California's mountains.

PINK HONEYSUCKLE

Family: Caprifoliaceae (honeysuckle family)

Also called: Hairy honeysuckle

Scientific name: *Lonicera hispidula* (Lindl.) Torr. & A. Gray

Height: 6–20'.

Leaves: Deciduous to semi-evergreen, opposite, the blade 1.5" to more than 3" long, fairly narrow to oval, hairy; margins smooth; upper leaves typically fused, forming a plate-like structure or sometimes a shallow cone around the stem.

Flowers: Borne in whorls; sepals small and inconspicuous; petals 5, fused into a slender 2-lipped tube, the upper lip 4-lobed, the lower consisting of a single lobe, both lips curled back, rose to purple, hairy; stamens 5, filaments white, anthers rose to orange, pollen yellow; ovary inferior.

Blooms April through July.

Elevation: Sea level to 3,600'.

Habitat: Forest, woodland, and riparian areas.

Comments: Pink honeysuckle can be a sprawling shrub or, if there's anything nearby for it to climb into, a woody vine. Hummingbirds like the nectar-rich flowers; birds like the fruits, which are round red berries, about 0.3" wide, similar to those of chaparral honeysuckle (*Lonicera interrupta*). The species is widespread in northern California except in the Sacramento Valley and on the Modoc Plateau. *Lonicera tatarica*, a Siberian shrub that has escaped from cultivation here and there, also has pink flowers, but they're borne in pairs and the petals are straight, not curled back.

CHAPARRAL HONEYSUCKLE

Family: Caprifoliaceae (honeysuckle family)

Scientific name: *Lonicera interrupta* Benth.

Height: Up to 10'.

Leaves: Evergreen, opposite, the blade 0.8–1" long, oval to almost round, hairless or hairy; margins smooth; the uppermost 1–3 pairs of leaves often fused around the stem.

Flowers: Borne in whorls; sepals 5, tiny, pale green; petals fused into a 2-lipped tube, the upper lip 4-lobed, the lower consisting of a single lobe, both lips curled back, cream-colored to lemon-yellow; stamens 5, anthers yellow; ovary inferior.

Blooms April through May.

Elevation: Sea level to 4,500'.

Habitat: Oak woodland, chaparral, flood plains, pine forest, and dry, open areas.

Comments: In northern California, this woody vine grows primarily in the Sacramento Valley, Cascades, Sierra Nevada, and the eastern part of the North Coast Ranges and Klamath Ranges. The fruit is a round, bright orange

or red, slightly translucent berry, 0.4" or less in diameter. Orange honeysuckle (*Lonicera ciliosa*), another woody vine found mainly in the Klamath Ranges and Cascades, has yellow, orange, or red-orange flowers so densely clustered at the ends of its branches that they sometimes form a sphere. Blue fly honeysuckle (*Lonicera cauriana*) has white petals and yellow to orange anthers; it's a shrubby plant that grows in bogs and wet meadows at elevations of 7,000–10,000' in the Cascades and Sierra Nevada. Japanese honeysuckle (*Lonicera japonica*), a vine cultivated for its scented flowers that start out white, then turn butter-yellow, occasionally escapes from gardens and can become invasive.

BLACK TWINBERRY

Family: Caprifoliaceae (honeysuckle family)

Also called: Bearberry honeysuckle

Scientific name: *Lonicera involucrata* (Richardson) Spreng. var. *ledebourii* (Eschsch.) Jeps.

Height: 5–12'.

Leaves: Deciduous, opposite, the blade 1.2–5" long, oval, hairless or hairy, petiole 0.1–0.5" long; margins smooth.

Flowers: Borne in pairs snuggled up against 2 pairs of relatively large bracts; petals fused into a cylindrical, 5-lobed tube, yellow or orange, usually flushed reddish; stamens 5, shorter than the petals; ovary inferior. Blooms May through July.

Elevation: Sea level to 5,000'.

Habitat: Moist sites.

Comments: This fairly tall shrub never becomes vine-like. Hummingbirds visit its flowers, and it's the only northern California honeysuckle in which the stamens are hidden inside the petal tube. It occurs mainly near the coast and in the North Coast Ranges. *Lonicera involucrata* var. *involucrata*, which grows in the Cascades and Sierra Nevada and on the Modoc Plateau, is said to differ in having strictly yellow petals, but I photographed the yellow-petalled flowers shown here right on the coast. As the shiny black berries mature, the bracts below the flowers turn a deep, rich red. This color combination attracts fruit-eating birds, whose eyes are especially well attuned to red and black. Bears and some small mammals also relish the berries, but there are conflicting reports on whether the berries are edible, mildly toxic, or downright poisonous for humans.

Twig turned upside down to show flowers hidden under the leaves.

Ripe berries.

COMMON SNOWBERRY

Family: Caprifoliaceae (honeysuckle family)

Also called: Waxberry

Scientific name: *Symphoricarpos albus* (L.) S. F. Blake var. *laevigatus* (Fernald) S. F. Blake

Height: 2–6'.

Leaves: Deciduous, opposite, the blade 0.4–1.2" long on mature plants, oval to almost round, hairy or hairless; margins smooth or lobed; leaves on new stems larger and more irregularly shaped.

Flowers: Sepals small, green; petals about 0.2" long, fused about half their length into a 5-lobed bell with a small asymmetrical bulge on one side, greenish pink on the outside, paler and densely hairy on the inside; stamens 5, anthers yellowish, almost hidden by hairs; ovary inferior.

Blooms May through July.

Elevation: Sea level to 4,000'.

Habitat: Shaded stream banks, woodland, mixed evergreen forest, and yellow pine forest.

Comments: Older texts call this shrub *Symphoricarpos rivularis*. It grows in much of northern California except in the Sacramento Valley and on the Modoc Plateau. Bees like the small flowers because, under the tangled hairs on the petals, they hold a surprising amount of nectar. The white berries, 0.3–0.5" in diameter, ripen in summer and often stay on the bare branches all winter; birds don't seem to find them appealing. The plants can produce numerous root suckers that form extensive thickets, and the Pomo Indians used to encourage this tendency by burning the shrubs in the fall. They then harvested the straight new suckers that emerged the following spring to make arrow shafts. The Costanoans made brooms from more brushy twigs.

Creeping snowberry (*Symphoricarpos mollis*) has sprawling branches that root wherever they touch the ground, hence another of its common names: trip vine. It occurs from sea level up to 10,000'. Mountain snowberry (*Symphoricarpos rotundifolius* var. *rotundifolius*) can be found above 4,000' in the Cascades and Sierra Nevada and has narrow pink flowers, their petals 0.3–0.4" long, that superficially resemble those of wax currant (*Ribes cereum* var. *cereum*).

STICKY MOUSE-EAR CHICKWEED

Family: Caryophyllaceae (pink family)

Scientific name: *Cerastium glomeratum* Thuill.

Height: 1–16".

Leaves: Opposite, 0.2–1.5" long, narrow to oval, sessile, hairy; margins smooth.

Flowers: Borne in open to fairly compact clusters, each cluster with a small green bract just below it; sepals 5, up to 0.2" long, green, sticky-haired, with narrow translucent margins; petals 5, 0.1–0.2" long, 2-lobed, narrow enough for the sepals to be clearly visible from above, white except for a greenish base; stamens 10, anthers creamy white; ovary superior with 5 styles.

Blooms February through May.

Elevation: Sea level to above 5,000'.

Habitat: Disturbed sites, grassland, and chaparral.

Comments: This widespread weedy annual has hairy, more or less upright stems that often fork near the top. The slender, thin-walled seed capsules are translucent, letting you see the tan seeds inside. The species is native to Europe and used to be called *Cerastium viscosum*. Big or common mouse-ear chickweed (*Cerastium fontanum* subsp. *vulgare*), another European species, is a perennial weed in lawns, marshy areas, and damp, disturbed sites. The translucent margins on its sepals are wider, and it has two kinds of stems, some low-growing, mat-forming, and flowerless, others upright and flowering.

FIELD CHICKWEED

Family: Caryophyllaceae (pink family)

Also called: Western field mouse-ear chickweed

Scientific name: *Cerastium viride* A. Heller

Height: 6–18".

Leaves: Opposite, 0.4" to nearly 2" long, fairly narrow, sessile, hairless or hairy; margins smooth.

Flowers: Sepals 5, 0.2–0.3" long, hairy; petals 5, 0.4–0.6" long, deeply lobed so that they almost look like 10, the base greenish yellow, the rest pure white; stamens 10, anthers creamy white; ovary superior with 5 styles.

Blooms February through August.

Elevation: Sea level to 1,600'.

Habitat: Coastal grassland, dunes, and rocky slopes.

Comments: Western field mouse-ear chickweed (formerly classified as *Cerastium arvense* subsp. *maximum*) grows along the coast from central California to Oregon; I photographed the plant shown here near sea level in Marin County. *Cerastium arvense* subsp. *strictum*, which occurs from the Klamath Ranges to the San Francisco Bay region and also in the Sierra Nevada foothills, is a slightly smaller plant with petals 0.3–0.4" long; it grows at elevations above 1,600'. Both are herbaceous perennials with non-flowering, sprawling, mat-forming stems and upright flowering stems; the two species can be hard to tell apart. Regardless of exactly what they are: If you find these cute little spring wildflowers, enjoy!

CALIFORNIA SANDWORT

Family: Caryophyllaceae (pink family)

Scientific name: *Minuartia californica* (A. Gray) Mattf.

Height: 0.5–5".

Leaves: Opposite, 0.1–0.2" long by less than 0.1" wide, sessile, hairless, often slightly fleshy; margins smooth.

Flowers: Sepals 5, about 0.1" long, hairless; petals 5, 0.1–0.2" long, white; stamens 10; ovary superior, light greenish yellow, with 3 white styles.

Blooms March through June.

Elevation: Sea level to 5,000'.

Habitat: Crumbling rock, grassy slopes, and chaparral.

Comments: It's easy to miss this dainty annual with its thread-like, hairless, much-branched stems and small flowers; once you start noticing it in a particular location, though, you'll often find it quite abundant. Older texts call it *Arenaria californica* or *Arenaria brevifolia* var. *californica*. It grows in most of northern California except on the Modoc Plateau. Douglas' sandwort (*Minuartia douglasii*) is similar except that it's hairy and has leaves 0.2–1.2" long. It too is widespread in northern California, and the two species sometimes occur in the same place. Annual sandwort (*Minuartia pusilla*) doesn't get more than 2" tall, and if it has any petals at all, they're shorter than the sepals; its common name isn't very helpful because it's not the only annual *Minuartia*. The rare Howell's sandwort (*Minuartia howellii*), another annual, occurs only in the Klamath Ranges and southern Oregon and has rigid, very narrow, mainly basal leaves. Nuttall's sandwort (*Minuartia nuttallii*) and reddish or red-seeded sandwort (*Minuartia rubella*) are herbaceous perennials that grow at elevations above 2,000' and form dense, flower-sprinkled clumps or mats.

The dry remains of several flowers are visible at the top of each seed head.

GRASS PINK

Family: Caryophyllaceae (pink family)

Also called: Wild carnation or proliferous pink

Scientific name: *Petrorhagia dubia* (Raf.) G. López & Romo

Height: 4" to 2'.

Leaves: Opposite, the bases of each pair fused around the stem into a sheath that's 2–3 times as long as it is wide, the blade 0.4–2.5" long, narrow to very narrow; margins smooth.

Flowers: Buds clustered inside several brown, papery bracts, only 1 flower emerging at a time; sepals 5 but completely hidden by the bracts; petals 5 per flower, heart-shaped to rather deeply 2-lobed, bright pink with several darker veins; stamens 10, anthers light blue or lavender; ovary superior with 2 styles.

Blooms in spring and early summer.

Elevation: Sea level to almost 6,000'.

Habitat: Grassland, open woodland, and disturbed sites.

Comments: In Philip Munz and David Keck's *California Flora and Supplement*, published in 1968 and for many years the definitive work on California's plants, this annual (then called *Tunica prolifera*) from southern Europe and northern Africa was listed as occasionally present in a few counties. Today it's common in much of northern California except on the Modoc Plateau and occasionally shows up farther south too. In good years the small but vibrantly colored flowers can be abundant enough to put on quite a show. Since Munz and Keck's flora was published, the old *Tunica prolifera* has been split into three species. *Petrorhagia nanteuilii* only has 1–3 dark veins per petal; it occurs in the southern part of the North Coast Ranges. In *Petrorhagia prolifera*, the sheath around the stem formed by the fused petiole bases is about 0.1" long and equally wide, and the petals have squared-off or only slightly notched tips.

SOAPWORT

Family: Caryophyllaceae (pink family)

Also called: Fuller's herb, bouncing Bet, or sweet Betty

Scientific name: *Saponaria officinalis* L.

Height: 1' to more than 3'.

Leaves: Opposite, 1–4" long by 0.2–1.2" wide, sessile, usually hairless, with 3 prominent veins; margins smooth.

Flowers: Roughly 1" wide; sepals 5, fused into a green, cylindrical tube 0.6–1" long; petals 5, white or pink, with a "crown" of slender outgrowths in the center; stamens 10; ovary superior with 2 styles, each stigma just a pinpoint at the tip of the style.

Blooms May through September.

Elevation: Sea level to 6,000'.

Habitat: Riparian areas, woodland, and moist disturbed sites.

Comments: This invasive European herbaceous perennial was introduced to North America as a garden plant. At least in the Sacramento region, though, the plants never seem to produce the abundance of flowers that you find in the eastern and midwestern United States. I sometimes find bitten-off stems, so perhaps some critter eats a lot of the flowers here, or perhaps the plants just don't bloom well in the Sacramento Valley's climate. When crushed in water, the leaves and stems produce a soapy lather that is still used in restoration of old fabrics and tapestries.

SMALL-FLOWERED CATCHFLY

Family: Caryophyllaceae (pink family)

Also called: Windmill pink

Scientific name: *Silene gallica* L.

Height: 4–16".

Leaves: Opposite, 0.4–1.5" long by 0.1–0.2" wide, sessile, with short rough hairs; margins smooth.

Flowers: Borne along one side of the stem with a narrow bract just below each flower; sepals 5, fused into a slightly inflated, hairy tube 0.2–0.4" long with 10 prominent dark veins; petals 5, pale pink or white, with a "crown" of narrow to broad outgrowths in the center; stamens 10; ovary superior with 3 styles; neither stamens nor styles projecting beyond the petals.

Blooms in spring and early summer.

Elevation: Sea level to about 3,000'.

Habitat: Grassland, gravelly or sandy flood plains, and disturbed sites.

Comments: This annual is native to Europe; it occurs in most of northern California except on the Modoc Plateau. Like many of the 30 or so species of *Silene* that occur in California, it's rather inconspicuous; but once your eyes become attuned to it, you'll find that it can be fairly abundant.

CALIFORNIA PINK

Family: Caryophyllaceae (pink family)

Scientific name: *Silene laciniata* Cav. subsp. *californica* (Durand) J. K. Morton

Height: 6" to more than 2'.

Leaves: Opposite, 0.4–4" long by 0.1–1" wide, sessile, hairy; margins smooth.

Flowers: 0.6" to more than 1" wide; sepals 5, fused into a fuzzy cylindrical tube 0.5–1" long; petals 5, bright red, deeply 4- to 6-lobed with a "crown" of wide, toothed or ragged-edged outgrowths in the center; stamens 10, usually projecting beyond the petals, anthers often purplish; ovary superior with 3 styles.

Blooms in spring and summer.

Elevation: Sea level to above 7,000'.

Habitat: Woodland, forest, chaparral, and coastal scrub.

Comments: This eye-catching herbaceous perennial can be found in most of northern California except in the Sacramento Valley and on the Modoc Plateau. Other brightly colored species of *Silene* in the region include the rare Klamath Mountain catchfly (*Silene salmonacea*), which has deeply 4-lobed, apricot to bright salmon-orange petals; serpentine catchfly (*Silene serpentinicola*), also rare, which has 2- or 4-lobed bright red petals; Hooker's catchfly (*Silene hookeri*), with deeply 4-lobed white to pink or purple petals; and San Francisco campion (*Silene verecunda*), with slightly lobed petals that vary from white to deep rose.

NIGHT-FLOWERING CATCHFLY

Family: Caryophyllaceae (pink family)

Scientific name: *Silene noctiflora* L.

Height: 2" to 3'.

Leaves: Opposite, lower leaves 2–6" long by 0.8–2" wide, sessile, hairy; margins smooth; upper leaves smaller.

Flowers: 0.6" to more than 1" wide; sepals 5, fused into a slightly inflated tube 0.5–0.9" long with 10 dark veins that form a net-like pattern near the tip, hairy, sometimes purplish; petals 5, white or pinkish, 2-lobed, a "crown" of wide, ragged outgrowths in the center; stamens 10; ovary superior with 3 styles.

Blooms May through July.

Elevation: Sea level to above 6,000'.

Habitat: Moist woodland and disturbed sites.

Comments: The flowers of this European annual remain closed until late afternoon and wither soon after sunrise. I've hiked a trail in mid-afternoon without noticing anything in bloom, returned for an after-dinner amble and found it full of flowers, and been unable to locate a single photogenic blossom the next morning. The species grows in the Sierra Nevada foothills and Cascades and is easily confused with white campion (*Silene latifolia*), a day-blooming European biennial. In white campion, however, the sepal tube has either 10 or 20 veins that do not anastomose, and the ovary has five styles.

STICKY SAND-SPURREY

Family: Caryophyllaceae (pink family)

Scientific name: *Spergularia macrotheca* (Cham. & Schltdl.) Heyn. var. *macrotheca*

Height: 2–14".

Leaves: Opposite, 0.4–1.5" long, narrow, fleshy, covered with sticky glandular hairs or sometimes hairless.

Flowers: Sepals 5, fused at the base, sticky-haired; petals 5, 0.2–0.3" long, pink or blue; stamens 9 or 10, anthers yellow; ovary superior with 3 styles, each style less than 0.05" (!) long.

Blooms from spring to fall.

Elevation: Sea level to 800'.

Habitat: Dunes, salt marsh, coastal scrub, and rocky outcrops.

Comments: This small but sturdy herbaceous perennial grows along the coast and in the San Francisco Bay region. Sometimes the plants are half-hidden under sand and windblown debris caught on the sticky hairs. Short leafy side branches can make the leaves look clustered. Two other varieties have white flowers and marginally longer styles. Saltmarsh sand-spurrey (*Spergularia marina*) has pink but narrower petals; it's annual, daintier-looking, and lacks clustered leaves. Boccone's sand-spurrey (*Spergularia bocconi*) is an annual from southwestern Europe. It can be hairless or covered with short glandular hairs and has pink or white flowers similar to those of sticky sand-spurrey. All in all, northern California has nine species of *Spergularia*. It helps to have seeds as well as flowers for identification.

COMMON CHICKWEED

Family: Caryophyllaceae (pink family)

Scientific name: *Stellaria media* (L.) Vill.

Height: 2–20".

Leaves: Opposite, the blade 0.3–2" long, oval with an abrupt, tooth-like tip; margins often fringed with hairs near the base of the leaf, otherwise smooth.

Flowers: Sepals 5, less than 0.2" long, hairless or hairy; petals 5, shorter than the sepals, deeply lobed so that they look like 10, white; stamens 5, anthers blue or purplish; ovary superior with 3 styles.

Blooms February through September.

Elevation: Sea level to 5,000'.

Habitat: Woodland, grassland, and disturbed areas.

Comments: If you check out the seeds, about 0.05" in diameter, with a hand lens or microscope, you'll find them covered with round bumps. Greater chickweed (*Stellaria neglecta*) is very similar except that its sepals are at least 0.2" long and its seeds have conical bumps. One or two lines of white hairs run down the stems of both species. I've found plants that had sepals clearly shorter than 0.2" and definitely conical bumps on their seeds—your guess is as good as mine which species they were. Both are weedy annuals from Europe. Northern California also has several native species of *Stellaria*, but they seem less common.

VELEZIA

Family: Caryophyllaceae (pink family)

Scientific name: *Velezia rigida* L.

Height: 2–16".

Leaves: Opposite, 0.2–0.8" long, very narrow with a long-tapered tip, hairy; margins smooth except for a fringe of fine or rough hairs.

Flowers: Sepals fused into a very slender 5-toothed tube 0.5–0.6" long, quite hard at the base, covered with short, sticky glandular hairs; petals 5, slightly longer than the sepals, pink, streaked with darker pink or purple, 2-lobed at the tip; stamens 5, anthers white; ovary superior with 2 styles.

Blooms May through June.

Elevation: Sea level to 2,600'.

Habitat: Flood plains, other open, gravelly sites, and woodland.

Comments: This ultra-inconspicuous annual is from southern Europe; it's the only species in its genus in California. Almost everything about it is rather hard and rigid: stems, leaves, fruit. Its stems can be green or purple and usually fork several times. The cylindrical fruits are only slightly thicker than the stems; when they're mature, four teeth at the top separate from one another to release the tiny seeds inside.

MEXICAN TEA

Family: Chenopodiaceae (goosefoot family)

Also called: American wormseed, yerba de Santa Maria, epazote, and many other names

Scientific name: *Dysphania ambrosioides* (L.) Mosyakin & Clemants

Height: 10" to more than 4'.

Leaves: Alternate, the blade 0.6–4" long, hairless or hairy, dotted with minute, sessile, golden brown resin glands; margins smooth to coarsely toothed.

Flowers: About 0.1" wide; sepals 5, green; no petals; anthers 5, pale yellow; ovary superior, ripening into a fruit about 0.02" (!) wide.

Blooms June through December.

Elevation: Sea level to 4,500'.

Habitat: Disturbed sites.

Comments: Older references call this annual or herbaceous perennial from tropical America *Chenopodium ambrosioides*. "*Ambrosioides*" refers to the plants' superficial resemblance to ragweed (*Ambrosia* spp.), but there's nothing ambrosia-like about their foul, turpentiney smell. Some individuals are sticky with resin, and the stuff doesn't wash off easily. In Latin America, the leaves are used to season food. The oil in the seeds was formerly used to treat intestinal parasites in livestock and humans, but it's a potent neurotoxin with a narrow margin between effective and toxic doses; safer medications are now available. Several other species of *Dysphania* occur in California, all non-native and nondescript in appearance. The related, equally unimpressive-looking genus *Chenopodium* lacks resin glands.

TUMBLEWEED

Family: Chenopodiaceae (goosefoot family)

Also called: Saltwort or Russian thistle

Scientific name: *Salsola tragus* L.

Height: Up to 5'.

Leaves: Lower leaves opposite or alternate; upper leaves alternate, 0.3" to more than 2" long, narrow, sessile, leathery, spine-tipped.

Flowers: Usually 0.2–0.3" wide; sepals 4 or 5, some of them with pink, petal-like wings with translucent margins that persist as the fruit matures; no petals; stamens 5, anthers white; ovary superior with 2 styles.

Blooms July through October.

Elevation: Sea level to above 9,000'.

Habitat: Dry, disturbed sites.

Comments: This extremely variable annual from Eurasia gets its common name from the way the stems break off at the base when the seeds are mature, allowing the entire bushy plant to be blown away by the wind. I once saw a photo of a ploughed field with a bright green line of tumbleweed seedlings meandering across it, showing how effective this method of seed dispersal can be. Tumbleweed is the most widespread of California's seven species of *Salsola*, all non-native and invasive; but it seems to be the only one that routinely breaks off and tumbles across the landscape, sometimes accumulating in huge piles along fence lines and other barriers.

PEAK RUSH-ROSE

Family: Cistaceae (rock-rose family)

Also called: Broom rush-rose, common rush-rose, or common sun-rose

Scientific name: *Crocanthemum scoparium* (Nutt.) Millsp.

Height: 4–18".

Leaves: Deciduous, alternate, 0.2–1.6" long, very narrow, usually sessile; margins smooth.

Flowers: Sepals 5, covered with branched, very short hairs, the 2 outer sepals almost thread-like, the other 3 oval; petals 5, 0.2–0.3" long, lemon-yellow, sometimes crinkled; stamens 10 to many, often swept upwards like a male peacock or turkey fanning out his tail; ovary superior.

Blooms February through September.

Elevation: Sea level to 5,000'.

Habitat: Chaparral and dry, sandy or rocky slopes; often abundant after fire.

Comments: When this herbaceous perennial or subshrub has finished blooming and shed its leaves, the green, stiffly upright branches do look a bit like a clump of rushes or a broom, hence some of its common names. It grows from Mendocino and El Dorado counties to southern California. Until recently it was classified as *Helianthemum scoparium*; now, based on new molecular data, it has been divided into two subspecies plus two additional species of *Crocanthemum*. Visually, the two subspecies differ mainly in the height and overall shape of the plant and can be hard to tell apart. Both of the two new species are 1–3' tall and have petals 0.3–0.5" long; one of them, *Crocanthemum aldersonii*, grows in central and southern California, while the other, *Crocanthemum suffrutescens*, is restricted to a few locations in El Dorado County (where it coexists with *Crocanthemum scoparium*) and Amador and Calaveras counties. So what to call a 1'-tall plant with 0.3"-long petals from the Sierra Nevada foothills (or from the southern California coast)? I'd just call it *Crocanthemum* sp. or, if I *really* needed to know exactly which species or subspecies, consult an expert on the genus.

CHAPARRAL FALSE BINDWEED

Family: Convolvulaceae (morning-glory family)

Scientific name: *Calystegia occidentalis* (A. Gray) Brummitt subsp. *occidentalis*

Height: Stems sprawling to climbing, generally less than 40" long.

Leaves: Alternate, the blade 0.6–1.6" long, usually finely hairy, with 2 basal lobes that can be rounded, almost square, or indented to form 2 smaller lobes each; margins smooth.

Flowers: Sepals 5, overlapping, not hidden by 2 small bracts below the flower; petals 5, fused into a trumpet up to 2" long, white to pale yellow; stamens 5, anthers white; ovary superior with 2 flattened, oblong stigma lobes.

Blooms May through July.

Elevation: Sea level to 4,000'.

Habitat: Chaparral, woodland, and yellow pine forest.

Comments: This widespread herbaceous perennial is one of about nine mostly native species of *Calystegia* in northern California. All are vines that climb by twisting their stems around their support and have a stigma divided into two paddle-like lobes. Beach morning-glory (*Calystegia soldanella*), only found on sandy beaches along the coast, has pink or purple flowers. Purple western morning-glory (*Calystegia purpurata*) has white or cream to purple or purple-striped flowers. The other species are essentially white-flowered. The genus *Convolvulus* is similar except for its very narrow, cylindrical stigma lobes.

FIELD BINDWEED

Family: Convolvulaceae (morning-glory family)

Also called: Orchard morning-glory, European morning-glory, greenvine, lovevine, creeping jenny, or creeping charlie

Scientific name: *Convolvulus arvensis* L.

Height: Stems sprawling to climbing, up to 40" long.

Leaves: Alternate, the blade usually 0.6–1.5" long, usually arrow-shaped with spreading basal lobes, hairless or finely hairy; margins smooth, finely toothed, or slightly wavy.

Flowers: Each flower with 2 very narrow to thread-like bracts 0.4–1" below it; sepals 5, fused into a small cup generally less than 0.2" long; petals 5, fused into a trumpet 0.6–1" long, white, sometimes flushed pink or with dainty pink markings, the outside of the trumpet often with 5 pinkish or purplish stripes; stamens 5, anthers white; ovary superior with 2 thin cylindrical stigma lobes.

Blooms March through October.

Elevation: Sea level to 8,500'.

Habitat: Open, disturbed areas.

Comments: This noxious weed from Europe is widespread throughout California except in the desert. It's a herbaceous perennial with creeping underground stems and roots that can grow 10' deep, making it hard to eradicate, and it can harbor viruses that attack some major crops such as tomatoes and potatoes. Seeds buried in the soil can survive 15–20 years.

VERNAL POOL DODDER

Family: Convolvulaceae (morning-glory family)

Also called: Boggs Lake dodder

Scientific name: *Cuscuta howelliana* P. Rubtzov

Leaves: None.

Flowers: Borne in clusters of 3–30 flowers entangled in the inflorescence of its host plant, each flower 0.1–0.2" wide; sepals usually 4, whitish; petals fused into a membranous, dull orange, usually 4-lobed tube; stamens usually 4, anthers yellow; ovary superior.

Blooms July through September.

Elevation: Sea level to above 5,000'.

Habitat: Vernal pools, often on coyote thistle (*Eryngium*), smooth boisduvalia (*Epilobium campestre*), several species of *Navarettia*, and a handful of other vernal pool plants.

Comments: If you see what looks like a tangle of orange or yellowish string draped over other plants, it's one of California's 18 or so species of dodder (*Cuscuta*); driving by at highway speed, you might even mistake a dodder infestation for a patch of dead plants. All dodders are parasitic; instead of roots anchored in the ground, they grow microscopically thin threads into a host plant, from which they draw all their water and nutrients. Many are not very particular about which plants they attack; others prefer specific hosts. The left-hand photo shows the stems of vernal pool dodder in early June, before they start flowering; they're growing on Great Valley coyote thistle (*Eryngium castrense*), which, incidentally, is not a thistle at all but a member of the Apiaceae (carrot family). The right-hand photo, taken in the same location four weeks later, shows the plants in bloom, entangled in a spiky, gray-green flower head of Great Valley coyote thistle.

CANYON LIVE-FOREVER

Family: Crassulaceae (stonecrop family)

Also called: Canyon dudleya

Scientific name: *Dudleya cymosa* (Lem.) Britton & Rose subsp. *cymosa*

Height: Leaf rosettes a few inches; flowering stems 1–20", sometimes taller.

Leaves: Evergreen, mainly in basal rosettes, 1.2–7" long by 0.4–2.5" wide, fleshy, hairless, often with a waxy bloom; margins smooth; leaves on flowering stems smaller, alternate.

Flowers: Sepals 5, fleshy, often red; petals 0.3–0.6" long, fused into a 5-lobed cylinder or bell, bright yellow, orange, or red; stamens 10; pistils 5, ovaries superior, fused at the base.

Blooms May through July.

Elevation: 300' to almost 9,000'.

Habitat: Cliffs, rocky outcrops, and rocky slopes.

Comments: This herbaceous perennial is the only one of several subspecies of *Dudleya cymosa* that grows in northern California, with the possible exception of *Dudleya cymosa* subsp. *pumila*, which has been reported from Napa County. Northern California is also home to several species of the related genus *Sedum*. The main difference between the two is that in *Dudleya* the flowering stems form among the lower leaves of the basal rosette while in *Sedum* they're a continuation of the short, stubby stem in the rosette and therefore emerge from the center of the leaves.

BLUFF LETTUCE

Family: Crassulaceae (stonecrop family)

Also called: Sea lettuce or powdery live-forever

Scientific name: *Dudleya farinosa* (Lindl.) Britton & Rose

Height: Leaf rosettes a few inches; flowering stems 4–14"

Leaves: Evergreen, mainly in basal rosettes, 1–2.5" long by 0.4–1" wide, fleshy, bright green or covered with a dense, white waxy bloom; margins smooth, often red; leaves on flowering stems smaller, alternate, with small basal lobes that clasp the stem.

Flowers: Often tightly clustered; sepals 5, fleshy, green; petals 0.4–0.6" long, fused into a 5-lobed cylinder or bell, light yellow; stamens 10; pistils 5, ovaries superior, fused at the base.

Blooms May through September.

Elevation: Sea level to about 300'.

Habitat: Coastal scrub, cliffs, and dunes.

Comments: This herbaceous perennial is common along the coast, sometimes easily spotted on rocky outcrops, sometimes hidden by taller vegetation. Researchers suspect that it hybridizes with canyon live-forever (*Dudleya cymosa*). To complicate matters further, these two species, sand lettuce (*Dudleya caespitosa*), and several other species of *Dudleya* represent (to paraphrase the 2012 *Jepson Manual*) a "difficult complex" of several intergrading entities. In short, if you have trouble figuring out the identity of a particular plant, attribute your difficulties to this genetic and taxonomic muddle.

149

DWARF STONECROP

Family: Crassulaceae (stonecrop family)

Scientific name: *Sedella pumila* (Benth.) Britton & Rose

Height: 0.5" to more than 6"

Leaves: Basal leaves opposite; stem leaves alternate, 0.1–0.3" long and less than 0.2" wide, sessile, fleshy, hairless; margins smooth.

Flowers: Sepals 5, very small; petals slightly fused at the base into a 5-pointed star, each petal 0.1–0.2" long, pale to bright yellow; stamens 10, anthers yellow or reddish brown; pistils 5, ovaries superior, fused at the base.

Blooms March through May.

Elevation: 100–5,000'.

Habitat: Open sites that collect water in spring, including rock outcrops and vernal pools.

Comments: Older references call this little annual *Parvisedum pumilum*. In northern California it grows around the perimeter of the Sacramento Valley and in the eastern and southern parts of the North Coast Ranges. Mount Hamilton mock stonecrop (*Sedella pentandra*) is less common, occurring mainly in the eastern part of the North Coast Ranges, the eastern side of the Sacramento Valley, and farther south; it has five stamens and pale yellow petals less than 0.1" long that often have a reddish stripe on the lower side. The rare Lake County stonecrop (*Sedella leiocarpa*) is a diminutive annual with five stamens that has only been found in a few sites in Lake County.

Young male inflorescence, which will soon elongate and have numerous simultaneously open flowers.

Almost mature fruit, about 2" in diameter, not including the stiff spines.

CALIFORNIA MAN-ROOT

Family: Cucurbitaceae (gourd family)

Scientific name: *Marah fabacea* (Naudin) Greene

Height: Stems up to more than 20' long, climbing into trees and shrubs or trailing across the ground.

Leaves: Alternate, the blade 2–4" long and approximately equally wide, palmately 5- to 7-lobed, almost hairless to covered with short hairs.

Flowers: Male and female flowers on the same plant, all without sepals; petals 5, fused at the base, white, cream, or greenish yellow with pale green veins; male flowers in long upright clusters, each flower 0.3–0.5" wide with 3–5 stamens, their anthers twisted together into a roundish knob; female flowers solitary in the angles between the leaves and stem, with a yellow stigma and prickly, spherical, inferior ovary.

Blooms January through May.

Elevation: Sea level to above 5,000'.

Habitat: Riparian areas, coastal scrub, woodland, chaparral, and mixed evergreen forest.

Comments: The new growth of this herbaceous perennial vine often emerges in December or January, then begins climbing into anything tall by means of coiled tendrils. The male inflorescences appear a few weeks later and become increasingly conspicuous as more and more flowers open. The stems and leaves often die back by midsummer, and the plants persist as enormous underground tubers that can weigh 100 pounds. The species is common in northern California except in the northwestern corner of the state and on the Modoc Plateau.

Female flower.

TAW MAN-ROOT

Family: Cucurbitaceae (gourd family)

Scientific name: *Marah watsonii* (Cogn.) Greene

Height: Stems up to 10' long, climbing into trees and shrubs or trailing across the ground.

Leaves: Alternate, the blade 1–3.5" long and more or less equally wide, palmately 5-lobed, often with a waxy bloom, sometimes with scattered short hairs.

Flowers: Male and female flowers on the same plant, all without sepals; petals 5, fused into a cup at the base, white; male flowers 0.2–0.3" wide with 3–5 stamens, their anthers twisted together into a roundish knob; female flowers solitary in the angles between the leaves and stem, each flower 0.3–0.5" wide with an inferior ovary.

Blooms February through May.

Elevation: Sea level to 4,000'.

Habitat: Chaparral, woodland, and sometimes open rocky areas.

Comments: Taw man-root is less widespread than California man-root (*Marah fabacea*), occurring mainly around the perimeter of the Sacramento Valley. Unlike California man-root, in which the male flowers resemble a shallow, wide-rimmed soup plate in profile, the fused lower part of the petals of taw man-root is a rounded cup. The fruit is spherical but only 0.8–1.5" wide and often striped dark green; it varies from completely spine-free to densely covered with flexible, often hooked prickles. Coast man-root (*Marah oregana*) grows in the North Coast Ranges and along the coast; its male flowers are 0.5–0.6" wide, the fused bases of the petals cup-shaped to conical, and its generally spiny fruits more or less football-shaped.

MADRONE

Family: Ericaceae (heath family)

Also called: Pacific madrone

Scientific name: *Arbutus menziesii* Pursh

Height: Usually up to 80', occasionally as much as 130'.

Leaves: Evergreen, alternate, the blade 2–5" long, elongate to oval, leathery, hairless and shiny when fully expanded, upper side dark green, lower side paler; margins smooth or finely toothed.

Flowers: Sepals 5, tiny; petals fused into an urn-like shape, 0.2–0.3" long, with 5 rolled-back lobes around its narrow opening, white, cream-colored, or pale pink; stamens 10, hidden inside the "urn," filaments hairy, 2 horn-like, curved bristles on top of each anther; ovary superior, style white, extending slightly beyond the petals, stigma a green dot.

Blooms March through May.

Elevation: 300–5,000'.

Habitat: Woodland, mixed evergreen forest, and conifer forest.

Comments: Madrone fruits are round, bright red or orange berries less than 0.5" in diameter that ripen in the fall. Band-tailed pigeons and presumably other birds, too, feast on them and disperse the seeds in their droppings. In spring, the pigeons also feed on the flowers. Even when the trees aren't flowering or fruiting, they're easily recognized by their shiny, leathery leaves and colorful peeling bark. The stumps resprout quickly after a forest fire, and the species is common throughout northern California except in the Sacramento Valley and on the Modoc Plateau.

MANZANITA

Flower buds of greenleaf manzanita (*Arctostaphylos patula*) in August of the year before they will bloom.

Flowers of whiteleaf manzanita (*Arctostaphylos viscida*).

Fruit of greenleaf manzanita (*Arctostaphylos patula*).

Pinemat manzanita (*Arctostaphylos nevadensis* subsp. *nevadensis*) with almost ripe fruit, growing espalier-like across a boulder.

154

Family: Ericaceae (heath family)

Scientific name: *Arctostaphylos* spp.

Height: Generally up to 16'; a few species up to 25'.

Leaves: Alternate, evergreen, no more than 2.5" long in most species, generally more or less oval, leathery, often oriented vertically, often gray-green or blue-green, upper and lower sides usually the same color; margins smooth or finely toothed.

Flowers: Sepals generally 5, tiny; petals fused into an urn-like shape, usually less than 0.3" long, with 5 (less often 4) spreading or curled-back lobes around its narrow opening, white or pink; stamens 10 (less often 8), hidden inside the "urn," filaments usually with long hairs, anthers dark red, 2 horn-like, curved bristles on top of each anther; ovary superior.

Blooms from very early spring to summer, depending on the species.

Elevation: Depends on the species.

Habitat: Generally chaparral, rocky slopes and outcrops, and fairly dry woodland and forest.

Comments: Manzanitas can be hard to identify. California has around 50 species, some with multiple sub-species. Many are shrubs, a handful become small trees, and only a few really stand out by some unusual feature. *Arctostaphylos andersonii*, for example, has boat-shaped leaves with two lobes at the base that clasp the stem, but since it only grows in the Santa Cruz Mountains, that's not much help when you're in northern California. Kinnikinnik or bear-berry (*Arctostaphylos uva-ursi*) and pinemat manzanita (*Arctostaphylos nevadensis* subsp. *nevadensis*) are prostrate, their branches hugging the ground; the former grows mainly near the coast, while the latter occurs in the North Coast Ranges, Klamath Ranges, Cascades, Sierra Nevada, and on the Modoc Plateau.

Sometimes location can be helpful. Lassen National Volcanic Park, for example, is home to only two quite different-looking species: pinemat manzanita and greenleaf manzanita (*Arctostaphylos patula*); a third species, whiteleaf manzanita (*Arctostaphylos viscida*) grows just outside the park boundary. To identify many species, though, you need to know whether the shrubs or trees resprout from burls after a forest fire; you may also need old bark, young twigs, young leaves, old leaves, the immature flower buds that start to form in late summer or fall many months before the shrubs bloom (called nascent inflorescences in botanical reference books), open flowers, fruit, and seeds. In short, I'm often happy to let a manzanita simply be a manzanita and just enjoy their reddish, peeling bark, the sometimes bonsai-like forms, and the cute flowers without worrying too much about *exactly* which species I'm looking at.

The flowers produce lots of nectar, which attracts hummingbirds, bees, bumblebees, and probably other insects too. I suspect the hairy filaments work like a sponge to keep the nectar from draining out of the flowers. The hairy petals of snowberry (*Symphoricarpos albus*), which also has nectar-rich flowers that dangle upside down, may serve the same function.

Bark of greenleaf manzanita (*Arctostaphylos patula*).

SALAL

Family: Ericaceae (heath family)

Scientific name: *Gaultheria shallon* Pursh

Height: 8" to more than 6'.

Leaves: Evergreen, alternate, the blade 2" to more than 5" long, oval, leathery, more or less hairless; margins finely toothed.

Flowers: Flower stalks, sepals, and petals covered with stalked glandular hairs; sepals 5, fused, turning blue-black and fleshy as the fruit matures; petals fused into an urn-like shape, 0.3–0.4" long, with 5 curled-back lobes around its narrow opening, white or pink; stamens 10, hidden inside the "urn," each anther with 4 long bristles; ovary superior.

Blooms April through July.

Elevation: Sea level to almost 3,500'.

Habitat: Coastal scrub and forest edges.

Comments: Look for this shrub in relatively moist sites near the coast and in the outer North Coast Ranges and the western part of the Klamath Ranges. Two additional northern California species of *Gaultheria* prefer downright wet forested sites and have leaves less than 2" long, bell-shaped flowers, and red fruit: Alpine wintergreen (*Gaultheria humifusa*), which doesn't get more than 8" tall and has hairless sepals, occurs above 4,500' in the Cascades, Sierra Nevada, and eastern part of the Klamath Ranges. Slender wintergreen (*Gaultheria ovatifolia*) grows at 1,300–6,000' in the same general area; it's up to 15" tall and has hairy sepals.

ONE-SIDED WINTERGREEN

Family: Ericaceae (heath family)

Scientific name: *Orthilia secunda* (L.) House

Height: Less than 8".

Leaves: Mainly clustered near the base of the stem, the blade 0.6–2.5" long, oval, shiny, sometimes leathery; margins smooth or finely scalloped or toothed; upper leaves alternate, smaller.

Flowers: Nodding from short stalks on the lower side of the leaning or arching stem; sepals 5; petals 5, not fused but pinched together at the tip to form a bell- or urn-like silhouette, pale green or creamy white; stamens 10; ovary superior, the style straight and projecting slightly beyond the petals.

Blooms July through September.

Elevation: 3,200' to above 10,000'.

Habitat: Conifer forest, usually but not always in dry locations.

Comments: This herbaceous perennial, which spreads from creeping underground stems, is the only species in its genus. Its flowers produce nectar that attracts pollinators. In northern California, the species grows in the Klamath Ranges, Cascades, and Sierra Nevada. Older texts call it *Pyrola secunda*. Four species still in the genus *Pyrola* also occur in the region; their flowers are evenly distributed around the stem and don't produce nectar. Three of the four further differ from *Orthilia* by their long, markedly curved styles.

PINE DROPS

Family: Ericaceae (heath family)

Scientific name: *Pterospora andromedea* Nutt.

Height: 12" to more than 3'.

Leaves: None except for some reddish scales on the flowering stems.

Flowers: Sepals 5; petals fused into an urn-like shape, 0.2–0.4" long, with 5 curled-back lobes, cream-colored or dingy yellow; stamens 10, hidden inside the petals; ovary superior, style also hidden.

Blooms June through August.

Elevation: 200' to above 12,000'.

Habitat: Conifer forest with a thick layer of humus on the ground.

Comments: This is one of several herbaceous perennials in the Ericaceae that lack chlorophyll, the green pigment that lets plants make sugar from water and carbon dioxide using sunlight to drive the process. Botanists used to think that these species draw nutrients from dead, decaying plants; more recent research indicates they parasitize fungi in the soil. Pine drops grows in most of northern California except in the Sacramento Valley, coastal areas, and the southern end of the North Coast Ranges. Each flower produces a squat, reddish brown seed capsule, roughly 0.5" wide, containing 2,000–4,000 tiny, winged seeds that are dispersed by the wind. The dead stems, still laden with empty seed capsules, often persist until the following summer.

157

CALIFORNIA RHODODENDRON

Family: Ericaceae (heath family)

Also called: Pacific rhododendron or California rose bay

Scientific name: *Rhododendron macrophyllum* G. Don.

Height: Up to more than 12'.

Leaves: Evergreen, alternate, the blade 2.5" to almost 7" long by 1.2–3" wide, leathery, hairless, upper side matte; margins smooth.

Flowers: Up to 1.5" long and 2" wide; sepals 5, tiny; petals 5, fused into a wide funnel, usually pink or rose-purple, the upper 3 with brown speckles, margins wavy; stamens 10, unequal in length, filaments pink, anthers whitish; ovary superior.

Blooms April through July.

Elevation: Sea level to 5,000'.

Habitat: Open areas in conifer forest.

Comments: When in bloom, this is one of California's most spectacular shrubs. In northern California it grows mainly near the coast and in the western part of the Klamath Ranges. As in other *Rhododendron* species, the fruit is a dry, brown capsule that splits open lengthwise to release the seeds. Western Labrador tea (*Rhododendron columbianum*, called *Ledum glandulosum* in older texts) has much less flamyoyant, cream-colored or white flowers only 0.2–0.3" long, but it's more widespread, preferring moist to wet sites such as stream banks and marshy lake shores at elevations from sea level up to 9,000'. The shrubs are generally less than 6' tall, with leaves 0.5–3" long that give off a pleasant spicy scent when rubbed.

WESTERN AZALEA

Family: Ericaceae (heath family)

Also called: California azalea

Scientific name: *Rhododendron occidentale* (Torr. & A. Gray) A. Gray

Height: Usually 3–10', occasionally more than 25'.

Leaves: Deciduous, alternate, the blade 1" to more than 4" long by 0.3–1.5" wide, leathery, hairless or sparsely hairy, upper side somewhat shiny; margins smooth except for a fringe of stiff hairs.

Flowers: Up to 2" long and 1.5" wide; sepals 5, tiny; petals fused into a 5-lobed funnel, white, sometimes with pink streaks, the uppermost petal with a large yellow splotch, margins wavy or ruffled; stamens 5, more or less equal in length, whitish; ovary superior.

Blooms April through August.

Elevation: Sea level to almost 9,000'.

Habitat: Stream banks and moist forested sites.

Comments: The flowers have a sweet scent similar to pinks (several species of *Dianthus* in the Caryophyllaceae, the pink family). This shrub is the most widespread of California's three species of *Rhododendron*. Northern India, western China, and Myanmar have around 700 species, including some that become trees. If you don't want to travel quite that far, the University of California at Berkeley's Botanical Garden is a good place to see examples of tree rhododendrons.

SNOW PLANT

Family: Ericaceae (heath family)

Scientific name: *Sarcodes sanguinea* Torr.

Height: 6–12", occasionally taller.

Leaves: None except for some long, reddish scales on the flowering stems.

Flowers: Sepals 5, red; petals 5, fused into a fairly wide-mouthed urn, bright red; stamens 10, anthers yellow; ovary superior.

Blooms May through July.

Elevation: 2,200' to above 10,000'.

Habitat: Conifer forest with a thick layer of humus on the ground, often in deep shade.

Comments: The brilliant red flower stalks of this parasitic herbaceous perennial emerge soon after the snow has melted. Look for them in the Klamath Ranges, Cascades, Sierra Nevada, the northern part of the North Coast Ranges, and on the Modoc Plateau. The stalks have a woody core but don't remain conspicuous for a long time after flowering like those of pine drops (*Pterospora andromedea*). Molecular studies have shown that snow plant and pine drops are "sister species," yet they depend on different albeit related species of mycorrhizal fungi—that is, soil fungi that obtain at least some of their nutrients from a third species. In other words, the fungus takes nutrients from a green plant, then snow plant and pine drops "steal" from the fungus.

159

EVERGREEN HUCKLEBERRY

Family: Ericaceae (heath family)

Also called: California huckleberry

Scientific name: *Vaccinium ovatum* Pursh

Height: 20" to 10'.

Leaves: Evergreen, alternate, the blade 0.8–2" long, elongate to oval, leathery, upper side shiny, lower side sparsely dark-haired; margins toothed.

Flowers: Loosely clustered; sepals 5, their bases fused, green with pink tips; petals fused into a 5-lobed bell or wide-mouthed urn, 0.2–0.3" long, pink or white; stamens 10; ovary inferior.

Blooms March through May.

Elevation: Sea level to 2,600'.

Habitat: Clearings in conifer forest.

Comments: In northern California, this shrub is common along the coast and in the western part of the North Coast Ranges and Klamath Ranges. Its new foliage is light burgundy, and the flowers attract bees, bumblebees, and hummingbirds. The berries can be glossy black, as shown here, or covered with a waxy bloom that makes them appear as blue as those of western blueberry (*Vaccinium uliginosum* subsp. *occidentale*); black and blue fruits may grow on different branches of the same shrub. Except for cranberry (*Vaccinium macrocarpon*), native to eastern North America but naturalized in a few locations near abandoned gold mines in Nevada County, evergreen huckleberry is California's only evergreen species of *Vaccinium*.

RED HUCKLEBERRY

Family: Ericaceae (heath family)

Scientific name: *Vaccinium parvifolium* Sm.

Height: 3' to more than 12'.

Leaves: Deciduous, alternate, the blade 0.4–1" long, oval, petiole very short; margins smooth or toothed.

Flowers: Usually borne singly, occasionally in pairs; sepals fused at the base, the lobes falling off early; petals 5, fused into a rounded urn roughly 0.2" long, pink, whitish, or greenish; stamens 10; ovary inferior.

Blooms May through June.

Elevation: Sea level to 4,500'.

Habitat: Moist, shady woodland and forest.

Comments: This often rather scraggly-looking shrub can be found along the coast and in the North Coast Ranges, Klamath Ranges, Cascades, and northern Sierra Nevada. Its twigs are green with flattened faces. The berries are bright red, somewhat translucent, and 0.2–0.4" wide, crowned with a low circular ridge left by the fused bases of the sepals. The rare little-leaved huckleberry (*Vaccinium scoparium*), which grows at high elevations in the Klamath Ranges, also has red berries, but they're only about 0.1–0.2" wide; the shrubs themselves rarely get more than 20" tall and spread from creeping underground stems, forming thickets.

WESTERN BLUEBERRY

Family: Ericaceae (heath family)

Also called: Bog bilberry

Scientific name: *Vaccinium uliginosum* L. subsp. *occidentale* (A. Gray) Hultén

Height: Up to 2'.

Leaves: Deciduous, alternate, the blade 0.4–0.8" long, oval, sometimes covered with a waxy bloom, lower side with visible but not prominent veins; margins smooth or toothed.

Flowers: Borne singly or in 2s or 4s; sepals 4 or 5; petals 4 or 5, fused into an egg-shaped to almost spherical urn, 0.2–0.3" long, pink; stamens 8 or 10; ovary inferior.

Blooms June through July.

Elevation: Sea level to above 11,000'.

Habitat: Bogs, wet meadows, and damp forest.

Comments: *Vaccinium*, with about 140 species worldwide, is one of a few genera in the Ericaceae with inferior ovaries. That's especially easy to observe in fruits such as western blueberry, which are crowned by the persistent sepals and often the dry petals as well; in fruit derived from a superior ovary, any remaining sepals, petals, or stamens would be at the stem end of the fruit. Usually western blueberry's fruit is about 0.2" wide; plants with larger fruit and prominent leaf veins, which occur in a few coastal locations, may be a northern European subspecies, *Vaccinium uliginosum* subsp. *uliginosum*.

TURKEY MULLEIN

Family: Euphorbiaceae (spurge family)

Also called: Dove weed or yerba del pescado

Scientific name: *Croton setiger* Hook.

Height: Less than 8".

Leaves: Alternate, the blade 0.4–2.5" long, oval to heart-shaped, blue-green or gray-green, densely covered with fairly short, star-like hairs and longer, stiff, unbranched hairs; margins smooth.

Flowers: Male and female flowers borne on the same plant, small and inconspicuous, nestled among the leaves; male flowers with 5 or 6 hairy sepals, no petals, and 6–10 white-anthered stamens; female flowers consisting simply of 4 or 5 nectar-producing glands and 1 superior ovary.

Blooms May through October.

Elevation: Sea level to 3,200'.

Habitat: Dry, open areas.

Comments: This annual used to be called *Croton setigerus* or *Eremocarpus setigerus*; it occurs throughout California. The plants can grow 2–3' wide, mounding slightly in the center. In late summer and fall, you'll sometimes find smaller plants in the dry beds of vernal pools where, from a distance, they resemble woolly marbles (*Psilocarphus brevissimus*). Doves, quail, other birds, and small mammals feed on the seeds, but the foliage is toxic to livestock and poisonings can occur through contaminated hay. The species' Spanish name refers to a Native American technique of throwing crushed turkey mullein leaves or roots into streams and ponds to stupefy fish and make them float to the surface, where they could easily be gathered. California has two additional native species of *Croton*; both grow farther south, are perennial, and bear male and female flowers on separate plants.

EGGLEAF SPURGE

Family: Euphorbiaceae (spurge family)

Also called: Oblong spurge

Scientific name: *Euphorbia oblongata* Griseb.

Height: 20" to 3'.

Leaves: Alternate, 1.6" to nearly 3" long, sessile, hairless, with a pale midrib; margins finely toothed.

Flowers: Flowers clustered among chartreuse bracts; each cluster composed of 2 or 3 flat, oval, nectar-bearing glands and 20–40 male flowers surrounding 1 female flower; neither type with sepals or petals; each male flower consisting of 1 stamen, each female flower of 1 superior ovary with 3 styles.

Blooms May through August.

Elevation: Sea level to 800'.

Habitat: Woodland and disturbed sites.

Comments: This weedy herbaceous perennial grows from a taproot and has densely hairy stems. Leafy spurge (*Euphorbia virgata*, called *Euphorbia esula* in some texts) spreads by means of deep, creeping roots and is extremely invasive; it has lots of narrow leaves and much more open inflorescences. Petty spurge (*Euphorbia peplus*) is annual, hairless, and no more than 18" tall; it's a common garden weed. All three are from Europe, as are several other weedy spurges, and contain milky sap that can cause mild contact dermatitis. Native species include Chinese caps (*Euphorbia crenulata*), usually an annual, in which the bracts are fused into small green cones.

SPANISH CLOVER

Family: Fabaceae (pea family)

Also called: Spanish lotus, pink lotus, or American bird's-foot trefoil

Scientific name: *Acmispon americanus* (Nutt.) Rydb. var. *americanus*

Height: 2" to 2'.

Leaves: Alternate, undivided or pinnately compound with 3 leaflets, the blade of each leaflet 0.4–0.8" long, oval, usually hairy; margins smooth.

Flowers: Sepals fused into a 5-toothed tube, hairy; petals 5, 0.2–0.4" long, white, cream, or pink, usually pink-veined; stamens 10, 9 with fused filaments, the tenth completely free; ovary superior.

Blooms May through October.

Elevation: Sea level to almost 8,000'.

Habitat: Grassland, chaparral, forest, flood plains, and disturbed areas.

Comments: Despite its common name, Spanish lotus is native to California and occurs in most of the state except the Sonoran Desert. It's annual; nonetheless, it quickly regrows and resumes blooming after grazing or mowing, even in late summer and fall and even in very dry sites such as levees. The stems can be sprawling or upright. At maturity the inch-long seed pods spring open, scattering the seeds away from the parent plant. The species is called *Lotus purshianus* in older texts. Hill lotus (*Acmispon parviflorus*) also has pale pink flowers, but they're only about 0.2" long, and the leaves have 3–5 leaflets.

163

Foothill deervetch (*Acmispon brachycarpus*).

FOOTHILL DEERVETCH

Family: Fabaceae (pea family)

Also called: Short-pod lotus

Scientific name: *Acmispon brachycarpus* (Benth.) D. D. Sokoloff

Height: 2–16".

Leaves: Alternate, usually pinnately compound with 4 leaflets, the blade of each leaflet 0.2–0.5" long, oval, with long, soft, spreading hairs; margins smooth.

Flowers: Borne singly in the angles between the leaves and the stem; sepals fused into a 5-toothed tube, long-haired; petals 5, 0.2–0.4" long, yellow, often turning reddish with age; stamens 10, 9 with fused filaments, 1 completely free; ovary superior. Blooms March through June.

Bishop's lotus (*Acmispon strigosus*).

Elevation: Sea level to 5,500'.

Habitat: Grassland, chaparral, yellow pine forest, flood plains, and disturbed areas.

Comments: This annual, called *Lotus humistratus* in older texts, often grows as a ground-hugging mat and is common throughout northern California except on the Modoc Plateau. Chilean trefoil (*Acmispon wrangelianus*, previously called *Lotus subpinnatus*), another California native, closely resembles foothill deervetch except for marginally smaller flowers and is equally widespread. Red-flowered bird's-foot trefoil (*Acmispon rubriflorus*) is rare, known only from a few locations in Colusa and Tehama counties; it has four shaggy-haired leaflets per leaf, and its bright purplish pink flowers are 0.2–0.3" long and borne singly. Bishop's lotus (*Acmispon strigosus*) bears yellow flowers singly or in pairs. Its flowers are 0.2–0.4" long; but its leaves generally have 4–9 leaflets, and instead of long, soft, spreading hairs it has short, flat-lying, harsh ones. Several other species of *Acmispon* also occur in northern California, but most produce flowers in umbels rather than singly or in pairs and have bright yellow petals.

DEERWEED

Family: Fabaceae (pea family)

Also called: Deervetch or California broom

Scientific name: *Acmispon glaber* (Vogel) Brouillet var. *glaber*

Height: 20" to more than 6'.

Leaves: Deciduous, alternate, pinnately compound with 3–6 leaflets, each leaflet 0.2–0.6" long, oval, hairless or with some hard, flat-lying hairs; margins smooth.

Flowers: In clusters of 2–7, several flowers open simultaneously in each cluster; sepals fused into a 5-toothed tube, hairless; petals 5, 0.3–0.5" long, yellow or reddish; stamens 10, 9 with fused filaments, 1 completely free; ovary superior.

Blooms March through August.

Elevation: Sea level to 5,000'.

Habitat: Flood plains, open areas in woodland, chaparral, and coastal scrub.

Comments: In the Sacramento Valley's dusty fall landscapes, these densely branched, erect or sprawling shrubs or subshrubs, often wider than they're tall, look like dull greenish brown or rust-colored blobs. By early March, the formerly dead-looking branches are covered with fresh foliage, and a little later they burst into bloom. On some plants the clusters of flowers are a lot more closely spaced than shown here. The species also grows along the coast and in the Coast Ranges and Sierra Nevada foothills. In older texts it's called *Lotus scorparius* var. *scorparius*.

SIERRA NEVADA LOTUS

Family: Fabaceae (pea family)

Scientific name: *Acmispon nevadensis* (S. Watson) Brouillet var. *nevadensis*

Height: 2–4".

Leaves: Alternate, pinnately compound with 3–5 leaflets, the blade of each leaflet 0.2–0.5" long, oval, hairy; margins smooth.

Flowers: Usually in clusters of 5–12, several flowers open simultaneously in each cluster; sepals fused into a 5-toothed tube, hairy; petals 5, 0.2–0.4" long, red on the outside as they emerge from the bud, then turning bright yellow; stamens 10, 9 with fused filaments, 1 completely free; ovary superior.

Blooms May through August.

Elevation: 2,800–9,000'.

Habitat: Conifer forest and dry, gravelly flats and slopes.

Comments: This mat-forming herbaceous perennial grows in the Klamath Ranges, Cascades, Sierra Nevada, and the northern part of the North Coast Ranges. In older texts it's called *Lotus nevadensis*. On the basis of molecular research, California natives formerly classified as *Lotus* have been moved into the genera *Acmispon* and *Hosackia*; the genus *Lotus* now just comprises European species such as bird's-foot trefoil (*Lotus corniculatus*), common on disturbed sites in most of northern California. The waterlily-like sacred lotus (*Nelumbo nucifera*), incidentally, important in Buddhism and other religions, belongs to a quite unrelated family.

NUTTALL'S MILKVETCH

Family: Fabaceae (pea family)

Also called: San Francisco rattleweed

Scientific name: *Astragalus nuttallii* (Torr. & A. Gray) J. T. Howell var. *virgatus* (A. Gray) Barneby

Height: 8" to more than 3'.

Leaves: Alternate, 1–7" long, once pinnately compound with 21–43 leaflets per leaf, upper side of each leaflet hairless, lower side hairy; margins smooth except for a fringe of slightly crinkled hairs.

Flowers: Sepals fused into a 5-toothed tube, pale green, hairy; petals 5, creamy white, sometimes tinged lavender; stamens 10, 9 with fused filaments, 1 completely free; ovary superior.

Blooms almost all year long.

Elevation: Sea level to 500'.

Habitat: Sandy soil near the ocean.

Comments: In windswept sites, this strictly coastal herbaceous perennial sprawls in low, tangled mats; in more sheltered places it forms taller, bushy plants. The leaflets of its close relative, ocean bluff milkvetch (*Astragalus nuttallii* var. *nuttallii*), are hairy all over. In both the fruit is an inflated pod with thin, papery walls containing up to 40 seeds that rattle when the wind shakes it. All in all, California has nearly 100 species of *Astragalus*, some with many varieties; you generally need both flowers and fruit for identification.

WESTERN REDBUD

Family: Fabaceae (pea family)

Scientific name: *Cercis occidentalis* A. Gray

Height: Up to more than 20'.

Leaves: Deciduous, alternate, the blade up to 4" long, heart-shaped to almost round, sometimes slightly folded along the midrib, hairless; margins smooth.

Flowers: Mostly opening before the leaves appear; sepals fused into a 5-toothed tube, purple, hairless; petals 5, magenta; stamens 10, filaments all free from one another; ovary superior.

Blooms March through May.

Elevation: Sea level to 5,000'.

Habitat: Riparian areas, chaparral, yellow pine forest, and dry brushy slopes.

Comments: Western redbud can be a shrub or small tree; it grows in most of northern California and is the state's only native species of *Cercis*. Its masses of brilliantly colored flowers, distinctive leaves, and purplish brown seed pods, which often persist until the following spring, make it easy to identify. In late summer and fall, the leaves sometimes but not always turn yellow, pink, or purplish red before dropping off. Eastern redbud (*Cercis canadensis*), which has similar leaves and flowers but grows to 35' tall, is occasionally used in landscaping; it's native from Texas to Wisconsin and farther east but doesn't appear to have become naturalized in California.

CALEY PEA

Family: Fabaceae (pea family)

Also called: Hairy pea

Scientific name: *Lathyrus hirsutus* L.

Height: 6" to more than 3'.

Leaves: Alternate, pinnately compound with 2 leaflets, the tip of each leaf consisting of a branched, coiled tendril instead of additional leaflets; each leaflet 1–2.5" long, narrow to very narrow, more or less hairless; margins smooth.

Flowers: Borne singly or in pairs, rarely in 4s, on long flower stalks; sepals fused into a 5-toothed tube, hairless; petals 5, pink or purple with darker veins, sometimes white in the center; stamens 10, 9 with fused filaments, 1 completely free; ovary superior.

Blooms May through August.

Elevation: Sea level to above 3,000'.

Habitat: Dry or wet grassland and disturbed sites.

Comments: This annual is native to Eurasia but shows up sporadically in northern California. Its name is a bit misleading in that the plants are generally hairless except for the seed pods, which are covered with long, whitish hairs, each hair growing from a small, clear, bulbous base. As in several other members of the genus, two flat wings run lengthwise up the stem.

CALIFORNIA TULE PEA

Family: Fabaceae (pea family)

Scientific name: *Lathyrus jepsonii* Greene var. *californicus* (S. Watson) Hoover

Height: Usually 3–6'.

Leaves: Alternate, pinnately compound with 10–16 leaflets, the tip of each leaf consisting of a branched, coiled tendril instead of another leaflet; each leaflet 1.5" to more than 2" long, oval to narrow, usually finely hairy; margins smooth.

Flowers: Borne in clusters of 6–15; sepals fused into a 5-toothed tube, hairless; petals 5, usually pink with darker pink veins on the uppermost petal; stamens 10, 9 with fused filaments, 1 completely free; ovary superior.

Blooms April through August.

Elevation: Sea level to 5,000'.

Habitat: Riparian areas, stream banks, woodland, and forest.

Comments: This herbaceous perennial vine occurs in most of northern California except along the coast and on the Modoc Plateau. Its pods can be flat like snow peas (albeit narrower), as shown here, or thicker like those of English peas. It's easiest to see the fine hairs on the stems and leaves when backlit by bright light; even then you may need a hand lens. The species is very similar to Pacific pea (*Lupinus vestitus* var. *vestitus*), which grows mainly in chaparral and woodland in coastal areas and the Coast Ranges and has marginally larger flowers, and it's possible that the two hybridize. California tule pea has winged stems with wings that are at least 1 millimeter wide (1 millimeter = 0.04"); Pacific pea's wings are narrower, or its stems may just be angled. The rare Delta tule pea (*Lathyrus jepsonii* var. *jepsonii*) grows in marshes in the Sacramento–San Joaquin River Delta. It tends to be a somewhat bigger, sturdier plant than California tule pea and is hairless. All in all, northern California is home to about 14 native species of *Lathyrus* as well as several non-natives.

EVERLASTING PEA

Family: Fabaceae (pea family)

Also called: Perennial sweet pea

Scientific name: *Lathyrus latifolius* L.

Height: 2' to more than 6'.

Leaves: Alternate, pinnately compound with a winged petiole and 2 leaflets, the tip of each leaf consisting of a branched, coiled tendril instead of additional leaflets; each leaflet 2" to nearly 6" long, fairly narrow to oval, hairless, with 3–5 conspicuous veins fanning out from the base; margins smooth.

Flowers: Borne in clusters of 4–15; sepals fused into a 5-toothed tube, hairless; petals 5, pink, purple, red, or white, the uppermost petal about 1" wide, wider than it's tall, the tip broadly heart-shaped; stamens 10, 9 with fused filaments, 1 completely free; ovary superior.

Blooms April through September.

Elevation: Sea level to 6,500'.

Habitat: Riparian areas and disturbed sites.

Comments: This European herbaceous perennial sometimes blooms in great profusion along northern California's highways—while pretty to look at, it can crowd out native species. The two flat wings running up its hairless stems and petioles can be more than 0.1" wide.

TANGIER PEA

Family: Fabaceae (pea family)

Scientific name: *Lathyrus tingitanus* L.

Height: 2' to more than 6'.

Leaves: Alternate, pinnately compound with 2 leaflets, the tip of each leaf consisting of a branched, coiled tendril instead of additional leaflets; each leaflet 0.8–2.5" long, fairly narrow to broadly oval, hairless; margins smooth.

Flowers: Borne in 2s or 3s; sepals fused into a 5-toothed tube, hairless; petals 5, maroon or rose, the uppermost petal 1–1.2" long, its upper half narrowing to a small notch at the tip; stamens 10, 9 with fused filaments, 1 completely free; ovary superior.

Blooms April through July.

Elevation: Sea level to 1,600', occasionally higher.

Habitat: Disturbed sites.

Comments: This annual, native to Europe and northern Africa, has hairless stems with narrow wings. The two generally leaf-like flaps at the base of the petiole are called stipules and don't count towards the number of leaflets. Tangier pea sometimes blooms in great masses near the coast but also occurs in the North Coast Ranges and around the perimeter of the Sacramento Valley. Another non-native annual, common sweet pea (*Lathyrus odoratus*), has small stipules and rough-haired stems and leaves.

169

Bush lupine (*Lupinus albifrons* var. *albifrons*).

BUSH LUPINE

Family: Fabaceae (pea family)

Also called: Silver lupine

Scientific name: *Lupinus albifrons* Benth. var. *albifrons*

Height: 20" to more than 5'.

Leaves: More or less evergreen, alternate, palmately compound with 6–10 leaflets, each leaflet 0.4–1.5" long by 0.2–0.4" wide, sometimes bright green but often so densely covered with white, silky, flat-lying hair that they look silver; margins smooth.

Yellow bush lupine (*Lupinus arboreus*).

Flowers: Generally not borne in distinct whorls; sepals fused at the base, covered with short, fine hairs; petals 5, blue to lavender, the center of the uppermost petal initially yellow or white, later turning purple; stamens 10, 9 with fused filaments, 1 completely free; ovary superior.

Blooms March through June.

Elevation: Sea level to 5,000'.

Habitat: Gravelly flood plains and river terraces, woodland, and chaparral.

Comments: This shrub, one of four varieties of the species, often forms a distinct although short trunk below its many branches and is usually wider than it's tall. When the pods are ripe, they split lengthwise into two halves that twist into separate spirals. In northern California, silver lupine occurs mainly in the North Coast Ranges and Sierra Nevada foothills. Another shrubby lupine, yellow bush lupine (*Lupinus arboreus*, also called tree lupine) grows in coastal areas; its petals are light yellow or, less often, lavender to purple. Its native range probably only extends from southern California to Sonoma County; where it has been introduced farther north, for example around Humboldt Bay, it has become invasive, displacing native dune vegetation.

SPIDER LUPINE

Family: Fabaceae (pea family)

Scientific name: *Lupinus benthamii* A. Heller

Height: 8" to more than 2'.

Leaves: Alternate, palmately compound with 7–10 leaflets, each leaflet 0.8–2" long by about 0.1" wide, folded lengthwise into a V-shape, upper side hairless, lower side hairy; margins smooth.

Flowers: Sometimes borne in whorls, sometimes not, a slender, long-haired bract 0.4–0.6" long just below each flower bud; sepals fused at the base, long-haired; petals 5, bright blue, the center of the uppermost petal initially yellow or white, later turning magenta; stamens 10, 9 with fused filaments, 1 completely free; ovary superior.

Blooms March through May.

Elevation: Sea level to 5,000'.

Habitat: Well-drained grassland, open sites in woodland, and rocky slopes.

Comments: This annual grows mainly at the southern end of the Sacramento Valley, the Sierra Nevada foothills, and farther south. It's abundant along the Lower American River. All lupines have a bract just below each flower bud, but in spider lupine, they're unusually conspicuous, so that the buds almost look as if they were draped with cobwebs. Then, as the flowers open, the bracts wither and drop off.

MINIATURE LUPINE

Family: Fabaceae (pea family)

Scientific name: *Lupinus bicolor* Lindl.

Height: 4–16".

Leaves: Alternate, palmately compound with 5–7 leaflets, each leaflet 0.4–1.6" long and no more than 0.2" wide, upper side usually hairless; margins smooth.

Flowers: Usually borne in 1–5 whorls; sepals fused at the base, hairy; petals 5, blue, sometimes pink or white, the center of the uppermost petal initially white with purple speckles, later turning magenta; stamens 10, 9 with fused filaments, 1 completely free; ovary superior.

Blooms March through June.

Elevation: Sea level to above 5,000'.

Habitat: Grassland and other open or disturbed sites.

Comments: This annual or occasionally biennial lupine is widespread in northern California but is often inconspicuous, hidden among taller grasses. Very sturdy, large-flowered individuals are easily confused with the equally widespread sky lupine (*Lupinus nanus*) or somewhat less common big-pod lupine (*Lupinus pachylobus*). There are more than 70 species of lupine in California, many with several varieties, many with blue flowers. A few have unusual features, such as hollow stems, that help narrow down the range of possibilities, but in general you need a hand lens to see the small differences in flower structure that characterize different species.

171

CHICK LUPINE

Family: Fabaceae (pea family)

Scientific name: *Lupinus microcarpus* Sims var. *densiflorus* (Benth.) Jeps.

Height: 4" to almost 3'.

Leaves: Alternate, palmately compound usually with 9 but sometimes 5–11 leaflets, each leaflet 0.4–2" long by 0.1–0.5" wide, upper side hairless; margins smooth.

Flowers: Borne in whorls; sepals fused at the base, bright green and fairly conspicuous, covered with short, fine hairs; petals 5, usually white, cream-colored, or bright yellow, the center of the uppermost petal usually with dark purple speckles, petals sometimes flushing pink with age; stamens 10, 9 with fused filaments, 1 completely free; ovary superior.

Blooms March through June.

Elevation: Sea level to above 5,000'.

Habitat: Grassland, open woodland, and disturbed sites.

Comments: This highly variable annual is common from southern California to Mendocino and Tehama counties; it's less frequent farther north. Sometimes it's seeded along highways. The stems vary from sparsely to densely hairy, but at least the lower part is always hollow, which you can sometimes feel by gently squeezing them. Other times, the stems are too sturdy to be compressible. Initially they grow upright, as in the yellow-flowered plant shown here, but they soon start leaning sideways. The rather thick-walled seed pods are less than 1" long, inflated, and all oriented upwards; viewed from above, the pods in each whorl form a star-shaped pattern. Typically each pod only contains two seeds. *Lupinus microcarpus* var. *microcarpus*, common farther south, seems less frequent in northern California; it has pink or purple petals, and its pods symmetrically encircle the stem. The third currently recognized variety occurs only in southern California, but at one time the species was divided into about 24 varieties.

CHAPARRAL PEA

Family: Fabaceae (pea family)

Scientific name: *Pickeringia montana* Nutt. var. *montana*

Height: 3–10'.

Leaves: Evergreen, alternate, sessile or with short petioles, undivided or palmately compound with 2 or 3 leaflets, each leaflet 0.4–0.8" long, oval, hairless or sparsely hairy; margins smooth.

Flowers: About 0.5–0.6" long; sepals fused into a 5-toothed funnel, hairless or sparsely hairy; petals 5, bright pink or purple, a yellow spot in the center of the uppermost petal; stamens 10, all completely free from one another; ovary superior.

Blooms May through August.

Elevation: Usually below 2,200', occasionally as high as 5,000'.

Habitat: Chaparral and sparse woodland.

Comments: This spiny, stiff-branched shrub can be found in the North Coast Ranges, Sierra Nevada foothills, and farther south. A second variety that tends to be woolly-haired occurs only in southern California. Neither variety produces fruit very often. The plants tend to spread by means of creeping underground stems and resprout quickly after fire. *Pickeringia montana* is the only species in its genus.

BLACK LOCUST

Family: Fabaceae (pea family)

Scientific name: *Robinia pseudoacacia* L.

Height: Up to 70'.

Leaves: Deciduous, alternate, once pinnately compound with 7–21 leaflets, each leaflet 0.8–2" long, oval, usually nearly hairless; margins smooth; paired thorns at the base of the petiole.

Flowers: Up to 1" long, fragrant; sepals fused into a 5-toothed tube; petals 5, white, a yellow or greenish spot in the center of the uppermost petal; stamens 10, 9 with fused filaments, 1 completely free; ovary superior.

Blooms May through June.

Elevation: Sea level to above 6,000'.

Habitat: Riparian areas, woodland, and disturbed sites.

Comments: This tree, native to eastern and midwestern North America, has become invasive in California and the Great Basin. It's often grown horticulturally for its magnificent flowers; a cultivated variety with pinkish purple flowers doesn't seem to naturalize as readily as white-flowered trees. The flowers are followed by less attractive, blackish seed pods up to 4" long, which often stay on the tree until the following spring. In fall, the leaflets turn bright yellow. In the past the hard, dense wood was often used for fence posts and tool handles.

174

CALIFORNIA TEA

Family: Fabaceae (pea family)

Also called: Forest scurfpea

Scientific name: *Rupertia physodes* (Douglas) J. W. Grimes

Height: 1–2'.

Leaves: Deciduous, alternate, pinnately compound with 3 leaflets, each leaflet 1.5–3" long, fairly narrow to almost triangular, black-haired to nearly hairless, upper side dotted with yellowish, round, more or less sessile glands that emit a strong herbal odor; margins smooth.

Flowers: Borne in compact clusters; sepals fused into a 5-toothed tube dotted with the same kind of glands as the leaves and covered with short, dark hairs; petals 5, whitish, tinged purple near their tips; stamens 10, 9 with fused filaments, the tenth sometimes free; ovary superior.

Blooms March through September.

Elevation: Sea level to above 8,000'.

Habitat: Open areas in woodland and chaparral.

Comments: This low-growing shrub, called *Psoralea physodes* in older references, grows mainly in the Coast Ranges and Klamath Ranges. It spreads by creeping aboveground stems (called stolons). The leaves look a bit like poison oak (*Toxicodendron diversilobum*) but never have toothed or wavy margins, and the two species have completely different flowers. The rare *Rupertia hallii* only grows in Butte and Tehama counties; it grows to 3' tall and has slightly smaller, hairless leaves.

SPANISH BROOM

Family: Fabaceae (pea family)

Scientific name: *Spartium junceum* L.

Height: Up to 10'.

Leaves: Quickly dropping off the green, upright branches, alternate, less than 1" long, narrow to very narrow, upper side usually hairless, lower side with flat-lying hairs; margins smooth.

Flowers: Fragrant; sepals usually fused into a tube split open on the upper side; petals 5, bright yellow; stamens 10, filaments fused; ovary superior.

Blooms April through June.

Elevation: Sea level to 3,000'.

Habitat: Disturbed sites, flood plains, and woodland.

Comments: This weedy, spine-free shrub is from the Old World's Mediterranean region, where rope, baskets, and paper are made from the stem fibers and a fragrant oil derived from the flowers is used in perfumes. The family includes several other invasive, yellow-flowered shrubs. Gorse (*Ulex europaeus*) is extremely spiny and has proliferated near the coast. French broom (*Genista monspessulana*), Portuguese broom (*Cytisus striatus*), and Scotch or English broom (*Cytisus scoparius*) have three leaflets per leaf. Confusingly, the white-flowered *Cytisus multiflorus* is also called Spanish or Portuguese broom. All produce prodigious quantities of seeds, which can survive in the soil for 30 years or longer. Unfortunately some nurseries continue to sell these species, inadvertently assisting their spread.

HOP CLOVER

Family: Fabaceae (pea family)

Scientific name: *Trifolium campestre* Schreb.

Height: 8–20".

Leaves: Alternate, pinnately compound with 3 leaflets, each leaflet 0.2–0.6" long, oval, finely hairy; margins toothed.

Flowers: Borne in head-like clusters 0.3–0.5" wide of more than 20 flowers; sepals tiny; petals 5, pale to bright yellow, with lengthwise, satiny, tone-on-tone stripes; stamens 10, 9 with fused filaments, 1 completely free; ovary superior.

Blooms April through May.

Elevation: Sea level to 1,000'.

Habitat: Flood plains and disturbed sites.

Comments: The dry seed heads of this European annual look a little like miniature versions of hops inflorescences, used in brewing beer. Most clovers have palmately compound leaves with three leaflets per leaf, but those of hop clover are considered pinnately compound because the center leaflet is borne on a short stalk (that is, on a continuation of the petiole), while the two lateral leaflets are stalkless. Many of California's nearly 60 species of *Trifolium* have pink or red flowers; the few yellow-flowered species include a rare native, Butte County golden clover (*Trifolium jokerstii*), and little hop clover (*Trifolium dubium*), a common, non-native weed that usually only has 5–10 flowers per inflorescence.

COWBAG CLOVER

Family: Fabaceae (pea family)

Also called: Dwarf sack clover

Scientific name: *Trifolium depauperatum* Desv.

Height: 1–5".

Leaves: Alternate, palmately compound with 3 leaflets, each leaflet 0.2–0.8" long, fairly narrow to oval, hairless; margins usually smooth or toothed, occasionally lobed.

Flowers: Borne in heads 0.2–0.4" wide with 3 to many flowers; sepals less than 0.2" long, hairless; petals 5, 0.2–0.4" long, pink or purplish with white tips; stamens 10, 9 with fused filaments, 1 completely free; ovary superior.

Blooms March through June.

Elevation: Sea level to 3,000'.

Habitat: Grassland, often on sites with wet soil in spring.

Comments: In northern California, this diminutive but common annual grows mainly in the Sacramento Valley, North Coast Ranges, and Cascade and Sierra Nevada foothills. It has three subspecies; they differ in size and degree of fusion of the bracts just below each inflorescence, whether the fruit is borne on a short stalk, and other details. In all of them, the uppermost petal turns into a papery, balloon-like hull around the fruit.

LARGE WHITE-TIPPED CLOVER

Family: Fabaceae (pea family)

Also called: Large variegated clover

Scientific name: *Trifolium variegatum* Nutt. var. *major* Lojac.

Height: Usually 4–20".

Leaves: Alternate, palmately compound with 3 leaflets, each leaflet 0.2–0.6" long, oval to narrow, hairless; margins finely toothed.

Flowers: Borne in heads 0.6–1.2" wide of 10 or more flowers, a ring of partly fused bracts just below each head; sepals 5, 0.2–0.4" long; petals 5, 0.4–0.7" long, usually maroon or reddish purple with white tips; stamens 10, 9 with fused filaments, 1 completely free; ovary superior.

Blooms March through July.

Elevation: 160' to above 7,000'.

Habitat: Wet meadows, seeps, and other moist to wet sites.

Comments: In northern California, this generally annual clover grows in the Sacramento Valley, Sierra Nevada and Cascade foothills, North Coast Ranges, and coastal areas. Unlike cowbag clover (*Trifolium depauperatum*), the petals don't inflate as the fruit matures. *Trifolium variegatum* var. *variegatum* only has 5–10 flowers per head, and both the flowers and the heads as a whole are smaller; occasionally the stems lie flat on the ground, forming mats. *Trifolium variegatum* var. *geminiflorum* has heads of no more than five flowers, prefers dry soil, and often grows in mats.

TOMCAT CLOVER

Family: Fabaceae (pea family)

Scientific name: *Trifolium willdenovii* Spreng.

Height: 4–16".

Leaves: Alternate, palmately compound with 3 leaflets, each leaflet 0.4–2" long, often very narrow, hairless; margins sharply toothed.

Flowers: Borne in many-flowered heads 0.6–1.2" wide, a ring of bracts just below each head fused for about half their length into a shallow cone; sepals 0.2–0.4" long, reddish purple; petals 5, 0.3–0.6" long, pink or lavender, usually white-tipped; stamens 10, 9 with fused filaments, 1 completely free; ovary superior.

Blooms March through June.

Elevation: Sea level to above 8,000'.

Habitat: Many habitats, especially grassland.

Comments: This rather variable annual can be found throughout northern California; in older texts it's called *Trifolium tridentatum*. Typically it has very narrow leaflets. It's one of many red- or pink-flowered clovers in the region, among which are two very common European species, red clover (*Trifolium pratense*), which often has pink rather than red flowers, and rose clover (*Trifolium hirtum*). The latter has paler, dusty pink flowers and is often included in erosion-control seed mixes. A third European species, crimson clover (*Trifolium incarnatum*) occurs less frequently. It has cylindrical inflorescences and, for a clover, unusually bright red petals.

177

GIANT VETCH

Family: Fabaceae (pea family)

Scientific name: *Vicia gigantea* Hook.

Height: Up to about 6'.

Leaves: Alternate, once pinnately compound with a coiled, branched tendril at the tip and 16–24 leaflets, each leaflet 0.6–1.5" long, fairly narrow to oval, hairless or sparsely hairy; margins smooth.

Flowers: Crowded together in elongate clusters of 6–15, usually all borne on one side of the flowering stem; sepals fused into an often lopsided tube, reddish; petals 5, 0.5–0.6" long, pink, lavender, or mottled pale yellow; stamens 10, 9 with fused filaments, 1 completely free; ovary superior.

Blooms March through August.

Elevation: Sea level to 1,000'.

Habitat: Chaparral, coastal scrub, and forest.

Comments: This herbaceous perennial vine grows mainly near the coast. Sometimes it's entangled with taller vegetation, sometimes it sprawls across the ground. The stems are exceptionally stout for a *Vicia*. American vetch (*Vicia americana* subsp. *americana*), widespread throughout northern California, is a much daintier plant; it too can have pinkish lavender flowers, but they're borne in more open clusters of three to nine, spaced evenly around the entire circumference of the flowering stem, and 0.6–1" long.

SPRING VETCH

Family: Fabaceae (pea family)

Also called: Narrow-leaved vetch or smaller common vetch

Scientific name: *Vicia sativa* L. subsp. *nigra* (L.) Erhart

Height: 4" to 2'.

Leaves: Alternate, once pinnately compound with a coiled, branched tendril at the tip and 8–14 leaflets, each leaflet 0.6–1.5" long, less than 0.3" wide, hairless or sparsely hairy; margins smooth except for one tooth right at the tip.

Flowers: Borne singly or in 2s or 3s, more or less sessile; sepals fused into a symmetrical tube, greenish; petals 5, 0.5–0.7" long, purplish pink to almost white; stamens 10, 9 with fused filaments, 1 completely free; ovary superior.

Blooms February through June.

Elevation: Sea level to above 5,000'.

Habitat: Grassland, woodland, riparian areas, and disturbed sites.

Comments: In northern California, this annual vine, native to Europe, can be found in the Sacramento Valley, the foothills along its east side, the North Coast Ranges, and coastal areas. Its seed pods are black when fully mature. *Vicia sativa* subsp. *sativa* grows in the same areas. Its leaves can be up to 0.4" wide; its flowers are 0.7–1.2" long and the seed pods brown to black. Both subspecies are often simply called common vetch or garden vetch.

Vicia villosa subsp. *varia.*

Carpenter bee on flowers of *Vicia villosa* subsp. *villosa.*

WINTER VETCH

Family: Fabaceae (pea family)

Also called: Hairy vetch

Scientific name: *Vicia villosa* Roth

Height: Up to about 3'.

Leaves: Alternate, once pinnately compound with a coiled, branched tendril at the tip and 12–18 leaflets, each leaflet 0.4–1" long, fairly narrow to oval, hairless or sparsely hairy; margins smooth except for 1 tooth at the tip.

Flowers: Crowded together in elongate clusters on one side of the flowering stem; sepals fused into a lopsided tube, purple or reddish purple; petals 5; stamens 10, 9 with fused filaments, 1 completely free; ovary superior.

Blooms March through July.

Elevation: Generally sea level to 4,000' for *Vicia villosa* subsp. *varia*, sometimes higher; sea level to almost 7,000' for *Vicia villosa* subsp. *villosa.*

Habitat: Grassland and disturbed sites.

Immature seed pods of *Vicia villosa* subsp. *villosa.*

Comments: Northern California has two subspecies of this annual vine from Europe. *Vicia villosa* subsp. *villosa* grows in most of the region except the Cascades and Modoc Plateau. It has conspicuous, spreading hairs on its leaves and stems, each inflorescence usually consists of 20 or more flowers, and each flower is 0.6–0.7" long. The 2-lobed top petal is bluish purple; the lower petals are lighter in color, sometimes almost white. *Vicia villosa* subsp. *varia* occurs mainly in the Sacramento Valley, the foothills along the east side, and the southern part of the North Coast Ranges. If it has any hairs at all, they're shorter and tend to lie flat. Its inflorescences usually contain only 10–20 flowers, each 0.4–0.6" long, and the petals are reddish purple. In some places the two subspecies grow side by side.

BUSH CHINQUAPIN

Family: Fagaceae (oak family)

Also called: Sierra chinquapin

Scientific name: *Chrysolepis sempervirens* (Kellogg) Hjelmq.

Height: Usually no more than 10'.

Leaves: Evergreen, alternate, the blade 0.8–5" long, oval, leathery, upper side dull olive-green, lower side densely covered with tiny, golden or rust-colored scales, the tip gently pointed or rounded; margins smooth to wavy.

Flowers: Male and female flowers borne on the same plant, both types without petals; male flowers sessile on stiff, upright or spreading stalks with 5 or 6 small sepals and 6–17 stamens per flower; female flowers solitary or in 2s or 3s, each flower with 6 woolly, urn-shaped sepals and an inferior ovary with a 3-armed style and minute stigmas, the whole cluster wrapped in several bur-like bracts and turning into a spiny fruit about 0.8–1.5" wide that takes 2 growing seasons to mature.

Blooms July through August.

Elevation: 2,000' to almost 11,000'.

Habitat: Forest, chaparral, and dry, rocky slopes.

Comments: Look for this smooth-barked shrub in the North Coast Ranges, Klamath Ranges, Cascades, Sierra Nevada, and the western part of the Modoc Plateau. The only other species in the genus has two varieties, both of them found mainly along the coast and in the Klamath Ranges, both with rough, furrowed bark and leaves with a long, tapered tip. Golden chinquapin (*Chrysolepis chrysophylla* var. *minor*) is a shrub or small tree that grows to a height of 16', occasionally more. Its leaves are folded lengthwise so that in cross-section they form a shallow V. Giant chinquapin (*Chrysolepis chrysophylla* var. *chrysophylla*) is a 50–150' forest tree with flat leaves. In older texts the genus is called *Castanopsis*.

TAN OAK

Family: Fagaceae (oak family)

Also called: Tanbark oak

Scientific name: *Notholithocarpus densiflorus* (Hook. & Arn.) Manos et al. var. *densiflorus*

Height: Usually up to 100', occasionally as tall as 150'.

Leaves: Evergreen, alternate, the blade 1.5–6" long, oval, leathery, upper side of young leaves with star-shaped hairs, lower side of young leaves woolly, both sides becoming more or less hairless with age; margins toothed, a prominent vein running straight from the midrib into each tooth.

Flowers: Male and female flowers borne on the same plant, both types without petals; male flowers tightly clustered on stiff, upright or spreading stalks with 5 or 6 minute sepals and 10–12 stamens per flower; female flowers solitary or in small clusters, each flower with numerous bracts surrounding 6 sepals and a 3-styled inferior ovary that will turn into an acorn-like fruit 0.8–1.5" long and requiring 2 growing seasons to mature, the bracts fusing into a shallow cup covered with short, flexible spines.

Blooms June through October.

Elevation: Sea level to 5,000'.

Habitat: Redwood and mixed evergreen forest.

Comments: Tan oak, which older texts call *Lithocarpus densiflora* var. *densiflora*, grows in northwestern California and the Cascades. Brown remnants of the initially silvery white star-shaped hairs may stay on the leaves, petioles, and young twigs for quite some time, making them look as if they had sand stuck to them. In the late 19th and early 20th centuries, innumerable trees were felled for their tannin-rich bark, used by the leather industry. A shrubby variety that grows up to 10' tall and has somewhat smaller leaves, *Lithocarpus densiflora* var. *echinoides*, can be found in forests in the Klamath Ranges, Cascades, and Sierra Nevada at elevations of 2,000–6,500'.

COAST LIVE OAK

Family: Fagaceae (oak family)

Also called: Encina

Scientific name: *Quercus agrifolia* Née var. *agrifolia*

Height: Up to 85'.

Leaves: Evergreen, alternate, the blade usually 1–2.5" long, oval to almost round, leathery, upper side convex and glossy, lower side often hairless except for minute tufts of hairs along the midrib; margins varying from smooth to toothed, often on the same tree.

Flowers and fruit: Flowers similar to those of interior live oak (*Quercus wislizeni*); fruit a slender acorn 1–1.5" long that matures in 1 growing season, the cup covered with thin, flat scales.

Blooms March through April.

Elevation: Sea level to 5,000'.

Habitat: Open valleys and slopes, woodland, and forest.

Comments: Oaks can be hard to identify. Coast live oak is native to the Coast Ranges from Mendocino County southwards but is used extensively in landscaping including, unfortunately, places where it hybridizes with naturally occurring interior live oak, black oak (*Quercus kelloggii*), shreve oak (*Quercus parvula* var. *shrevei*), and probably various non-native oaks in urban and suburban gardens and streetscapes. The flowers are wind-pollinated, and jays, acorn woodpeckers, and squirrels disperse the acorns, all of which, given the genetic compatibility of many oak species, facilitates hybridization.

BLUE OAK

Family: Fagaceae (oak family)

Scientific name: *Quercus douglasii* Hook. & Arn.

Height: Up to 65'.

Leaves: Deciduous, alternate, the blade 1.2–4" long, oval, upper side matte blue-green, lower side paler and finely hairy; margins smooth, wavy, or gently lobed.

Flowers and fruit: Flowers similar to those of interior live oak (*Quercus wislizeni*); fruit an egg-shaped to almost cylindrical acorn 0.8–1.5" long that matures in 1 growing season, the cup covered with rounded bumps.

Blooms April through May.

Elevation: Sea level to 5,200'.

Habitat: Woodland and dry slopes.

Comments: This tree is iconic for the foothills encircling the Central Valley and the slopes around other interior valleys. Although it produces plenty of acorns and the ground can be thick with seedlings in spring, very few of those seedlings survive, and there is concern about the future of California's blue oak woodlands. At higher elevations, blue oak is replaced by California black oak (*Quercus kelloggii*), another deciduous species with lobed, bright green leaves, each lobe tapering to a bristle-tipped point. Blue oak hybridizes with Oregon oak (*Quercus garryana*), valley oak (*Quercus lobata*), and, farther south, Tucker's oak (*Quercus john-tuckeri*).

VALLEY OAK

Family: Fagaceae (oak family)

Also called: Roble

Scientific name: *Quercus lobata* Née

Height: Up to 115'.

Leaves: Deciduous, alternate, the blade 2–5" long, deeply lobed, upper side glossy, lower side usually finely woolly; lobe margins smooth.

Flowers and fruit: Flowers similar to those of interior live oak (*Quercus wislizeni*); fruit a tapered acorn 1.2–2" long that matures in 1 growing season, the cup covered with rounded bumps. Blooms March through April.

Elevation: Generally sea level to 2,000', occasionally up to 6,000'.

Habitat: Riparian areas and valleys with deep, rich soil.

Comments: Broad bands, sometimes several miles wide, of valley oaks once bordered the Sacramento Valley's rivers. Most of these stately riparian forests are gone; Cosumnes River Preserve in Sacramento County is a good place to see remnants. In northern California, valley oak also grows in the North Coast Ranges and Cascade and Sierra Nevada foothills. Unlike some oaks, it doesn't resprout when felled or burned. The species with which it can hybridize include blue oak (*Quercus douglasii*) and Oregon oak (*Quercus garryana*). The latter occurs in the North Coast Ranges, Klamath Ranges, Sierra Nevada, and Cascades; its lobed leaves are 2–6" long, its acorns egg-shaped to spherical.

HUCKLEBERRY OAK

Family: Fagaceae (oak family)

Scientific name: *Quercus vacciniifolia* Kellogg

Height: Up to 5'.

Leaves: Evergreen, alternate, the blade 0.6–1.5" long, oval, leathery, hairless, upper side usually matte olive, lower side paler; margins usually smooth.

Flowers and fruit: Flowers similar to those of interior live oak (*Quercus wislizeni*); fruit an egg-shaped to almost spherical acorn 0.4–0.6" long that takes 2 growing seasons to mature, the cup covered with bumpy or flat scales. Blooms May through July.

Elevation: 500' to almost 10,000'.

Habitat: Conifer forest and rocky slopes.

Comments: This shrub grows in the North Coast Ranges, Klamath Ranges, Cascades, Sierra Nevada, and on the Modoc Plateau. It hybridizes with goldcup oak (*Quercus chrysolepis*), also called maul oak or canyon live oak, another widespread species that can be a picturesque tree up to 65' tall or a much smaller shrub and has unusually shallow acorn cups covered with a dense coat of golden brown hairs. Other shrubby northern California oaks include scrub oak (*Quercus berberidifolia*), leather oak (*Quercus durata*), and deer oak (*Quercus sadleriana*), all of which have leaves with toothed or spiny margins and acorns that mature in 1 growing season.

INTERIOR LIVE OAK

Family: Fagaceae (oak family)

Scientific name: *Quercus wislizeni* A. DC. var. *wislizeni*

Height: Up to 70'.

Leaves: Evergreen, alternate, the blade usually 0.8–2" long, oval, leathery, flat, hairless; margins ranging from smooth to wavy or toothed, often on the same tree.

Flowers and fruit: Male and female flowers borne on the same plant, both types with minute sepals and no petals; male flowers clustered on drooping stalks (called catkins), 5–12 stamens per flower; female flowers solitary, each turning into an egg-shaped to almost cylindrical acorn 0.8–1.6" long that takes 2 growing seasons to mature, the rather deep cup covered with thin, flat scales.

Blooms March through May.

Elevation: Sea level to 5,200'.

Habitat: Foothill woodland and rocky slopes.

Comments: In northern California, these trees grow in the North Coast Ranges, Cascade and Sierra Nevada foothills, and the Sacramento Valley's Sutter Buttes. Many are multi-trunked, a testament to the species' ability to resprout quickly after wildland fire or felling—the wood is too knotty to make good lumber, but the trees were often cut for firewood. The bark can be smooth, scaly, or roughly furrowed. As in many oaks, the leaves come in a bewildering range of shapes, sometimes even on the same twig, but they're always fairly flat, not convex like those of coast live oak (*Quercus agrifolia*), and lack the tiny patches of hair along the midrib often found on the lower side of coast live oak leaves. From a distance, the foliage seems sparser and a slightly lighter, duller green than coast live oak's dense, dark green canopy. The species hybridizes with California black oak (*Quercus kelloggii*) and coast live oak. A shrubby form, *Quercus wislizeni* var. *frutescens*, occurs in chaparral in the same geographic areas as well as in the Klamath Ranges.

SLENDER CENTAURY

Family: Gentianaceae (gentian family)

Scientific name: *Centaurium tenuiflorum* (Hoffmanns. & Link) Janch.

Height: Less than 1" to more than 2'.

Leaves: Opposite, lower leaves not forming an obvious basal rosette, 0.6–1" long, upper stem leaves 0.4–1.2" long, fairly narrow; margins smooth.

Flowers: Sepals fused into a 5-toothed tube; petals 5, fused into a slender tube with a white throat and bright pink lobes, the lobes 0.1–0.2" long; stamens 5, anthers yellow, twisting into spirals after shedding their pollen; ovary superior with 2 oval stigmas on a long style.

Blooms May through August.

Elevation: Sea level to 6,000'.

Habitat: Grassland, riparian areas, and open woodland.

Comments: This widespread annual, native to Eurasia, tolerates a huge range of moisture conditions. In the Sacramento area, I've found it flowering in dry uplands covered with yellow star-thistle (*Centaurea solstitialis*) and fennel (*Foeniculum vulgare*) as well as in shallow water along the Lower American River. Another Eurasian species, *Centaurium erythraea*, grows near the coast; it bears leaves in a basal rosette as well as on its stems and has larger flowers. Several very similar-looking California natives have been moved to the genus *Zeltnera* based on their fan-shaped stigmas.

TIMWORT

Family: Gentianaceae (gentian family)

Scientific name: *Cicendia quadrangularis* (Lam.) Griseb.

Height: Less than 4".

Leaves: Opposite, less than 0.4" long, narrow to oval, hairless; margins smooth.

Flowers: Less than 0.2" wide; sepals 4, fused into a distinctive, boxy, 4-flanged shape, each flange tapering to a point or short horn at the top; petals fused into a 4-lobed tube, yellow, each petal with 2 short, light orange streaks; stamens 4, yellow; ovary superior with a yellow style and 2 yellow stigmas.

Blooms March through May.

Elevation: Sea level to almost 9,000'.

Habitat: Grassland and other open sites.

Comments: In northern California, this diminutive annual grows mainly in the Sacramento Valley, the Cascade and Sierra Nevada foothills, and the southern part of the North Coast Ranges. It seems to prefer locations with moist soil in spring. It's the only species in its genus in the state, and I don't know of any other northern California species with which it's likely to be confused.

WHITESTEM FRASERA

Family: Gentianaceae (gentian family)

Scientific name: *Frasera albicaulis* Griseb. var. *nitida* (Benth.) C. L. Hitchc.

Height: 4" to more than 2'.

Leaves: Those in the basal rosette 1.5–9" long by 0.1–0.5" wide, occasionally wider, hairless, with pointed tips; margins smooth with a narrow white border; stem leaves opposite, smaller, very narrow.

Flowers: Borne in several whorls on a slender stem, upper whorls crowded, the lower ones well separated; sepals 4, fused at the base, very narrow, green; petals 4, 0.2–0.5" long, fused at the base, greenish white to pale blue, often with blue or purple streaks and stipples, an apple-green nectary fringed with white hairs in the center of each petal; stamens 4; ovary superior.

Blooms May through July.

Elevation: 500–6,200'.

Habitat: Chaparral, open woodland, and dry, rocky sites.

Comments: I don't know how this herbaceous perennial got its name: All the plants I've seen had green stems. It's found mainly in the Klamath Ranges, Cascades, and northern Sierra Nevada, less often in the North Coast Ranges. The leaves of *Frasera albicaulis* var. *modocensis*, which grows in the Cascades and on the Modoc Plateau, are hairy on the lower side, and the larger leaves have rounded tips.

MONUMENT PLANT

Family: Gentianaceae (gentian family)

Scientific name: *Frasera speciosa* Griseb.

Height: 2–7'.

Leaves: Those in the basal rosette 3–20" long by 0.4–6" wide, usually finely hairy; margins smooth; stem leaves in whorls of 3–7, smaller, narrow.

Flowers: Borne in many whorls on a thick stem; sepals 4, just barely fused at the base, very narrow, green; petals 4, also fused at the base, pale green with blue or purple dots, 2 elongate nectaries almost completely hidden by a thick fringe of white or lavender hairs in the center of each petal; stamens 4; ovary superior.

Blooms July through August.

Elevation: 5,000–10,000'.

Habitat: Mountain meadows and open forest.

Comments: Look for this hard-to-miss herbaceous perennial in the Klamath Ranges, North Coast Ranges, and Sierra Nevada. In some older references it's called *Swertia radiata*. As the seed capsules develop, the plants look even more massive (above right). A third northern California species in this genus, the rare Umpqua green gentian (*Frasera umpquaensis*), is less conspicuous. It grows up to 5' tall from a basal rosette of hairless, somewhat spoon-shaped leaves up to 1' long and 1–4" wide, but its slender-stemmed inflorescences are much narrower than those of monument plant and have yellowish green flowers. Several additional species of *Frasera* only grow in central and southern California.

ALPINE GENTIAN

Family: Gentianaceae (gentian family)

Scientific name: *Gentiana newberryi* A. Gray var. *tiogana* (A. Heller) J. S. Pringle

Height: Usually 2–4", occasionally taller.

Leaves: Opposite, usually 0.3–2" long by 0.1–1" wide, hairless; margins smooth.

Flowers: Sepals fused into a tube 0.5" to more than 1" long; petals fused into a 5-lobed, trumpet-shaped tube, white or pale blue with light green speckles on the inside and 5 bold, purplish brown stripes on the outside; stamens 5; ovary superior.

Blooms July through September.

Elevation: 5,000–13,000'.

Habitat: Stream banks, wet mountain meadows, and moist sites in open conifer forest.

Comments: This herbaceous perennial is restricted to the Cascades and Sierra Nevada. It stands out among northern California's gentians by its pale flowers—most other species have medium or deep blue flowers, including king's scepter gentian (*Gentiana sceptrum*) and Oregon gentian (*Gentiana affinis* var. *ovata*), both of which are coastal species. A second variety of alpine gentian, *Gentiana newberryi* var. *newberryi*, lacks the dark stripes on the outside of its petals, which usually are medium to dark blue, only rarely pale blue to white, and occurs in the Klamath Ranges, Cascades, and Sierra Nevada.

BROADLEAF FILAREE

Family: Geraniaceae (geranium family)

Also called: Long-beaked stork's bill

Scientific name: *Erodium botrys* (Cav.) Bertol.

Height: 4" to 3'.

Leaves: Opposite, the blade of the lower leaves 1.2–6" long, shallowly to deeply pinnately lobed, hairless to sparsely hairy, especially along the veins; margins toothed.

Flowers: Sepals 5, 0.4–0.5" long, tips bristly; petals 5, about 0.6" long, pink to lavender, with conspicuously darker veins; stamens 5; ovary superior, deeply 5-lobed and as a fruit splitting into 5 segments, each segment containing 1 seed and topped with a long spike, 2–5" long, that dries into a spiral, corkscrewing itself into the ground or your socks.

Blooms March through July.

Elevation: Sea level to above 3,000'.

Habitat: Grassland and disturbed sites.

Comments: California has several species of *Erodium*, all but one European or Eurasian, distinguished from one another largely by minute differences in their fruits. The non-natives were probably intentionally or unintentionally introduced by the Spaniards. Some have flowers that are fairly flat in profile, like a wide-rimmed soup plate, but broadleaf filaree has strongly cupped sepals so that in profile, the overall length (or depth) of the flower more or less equals its overall width.

REDSTEM FILAREE

Family: Geraniaceae (geranium family)

Also called: Common stork's bill or redstem stork's bill

Scientific name: *Erodium cicutarium* (L.) Aiton

Height: 4–20".

Leaves: Opposite, the blade of the lower leaves 1.2–4" long, once pinnately compound with 9–13 leaflets, each leaflet deeply pinnately lobed, sparsely hairy.

Flowers: Sepals 5, 0.1–0.2" long, tips bristly; petals 5, 0.2–0.3" long, pink to lavender, with 3 slightly darker veins; stamens 5; ovary superior, deeply 5-lobed and maturing into a fruit similar to that of broadleaf filaree (*Erodium botrys*) except that the spike on each fruit segment is only 1–2" long.

Blooms February through September.

Elevation: Sea level to 6,500'.

Habitat: Grassland and disturbed sites.

Comments: This weedy Eurasian annual or biennial is common throughout northern California. As its common names indicate, its stems are reddish. Whitestem filaree (*Erodium moschatum*, also called greenstem filaree or musky stork's bill) has pale green stems; the leaflets of its pinnately compound leaves are slightly to moderately lobed. Short-fruited filaree (*Erodium brachycarpum*) has lobed but not compound leaves; it doesn't seem well named in that the spikes on its fruit segments, at 2" to more than 3" long, exceed those of redstem and whitestem filaree.

CAROLINA CRANE'S BILL

Family: Geraniaceae (geranium family)

Also called: Carolina geranium

Scientific name: *Geranium carolinianum* L.

Height: 4–28".

Leaves: Alternate or opposite, the blade 1–3.5" wide, nearly round, deeply palmately lobed into 5–7 segments, soft-haired; margins of each segment smooth except for a few small pinnate lobes.

Flowers: Sepals 5, roughly 0.2" long; petals 5, as long as the sepals, heart-shaped, white to deep pink; stamens 10; ovary superior, deeply 5-lobed and as a fruit splitting into 5 segments, each segment containing 1 seed and topped with a spike or "beak" 0.6–0.8" long that dries into a flat spiral.

Blooms February through August.

Elevation: Sea level to 5,500'.

Habitat: Grassland, chaparral, woodland, and forest.

Comments: Despite its restrictive-sounding common names, this inconspicuous but widespread annual is native from California to the East Coast. It's similar to the non-native cutleaf geranium (*Geranium dissectum*), but the hairs on its flower stalks are non-glandular, while cutleaf geranium has both glandular and non-glandular hairs. Northern California's other native geraniums, Oregon geranium (*Geranium oreganum*) and sticky geranium (*Geranium viscosissimum*), are a lot showier. Incidentally, the geraniums that are sold as houseplants belong to the genus *Pelargonium* and are mostly native to southern Africa.

DOVEFOOT GERANIUM

Family: Geraniaceae (geranium family)

Scientific name: *Geranium molle* L.

Height: 4–18".

Leaves: Alternate or opposite, the blade 0.3" to more than 2" wide, round, palmately lobed with 5–9 wide lobes, soft-haired; lobe margins scalloped.

Flowers: Sepals 5; petals 5, 0.1–0.4" long, heart-shaped, bright purplish pink; stamens 10; ovary superior, deeply 5-lobed and as a fruit splitting into 5 segments, each segment containing 1 seed and topped with a spike or "beak" 0.2–0.4" long that dries into a flat spiral.

Blooms February through August.

Elevation: Sea level to 1,600'.

Habitat: Woodland and disturbed sites.

Comments: Both dovefoot geranium and cutleaf geranium (*Geranium dissectum*) are annuals native to Eurasia, northern Africa, and western Asia. Here they sometimes grow side by side. Their flowers are similar, but the leaves of cutleaf geranium are palmately divided into 5–7 very narrow segments, each segment further lobed. They're two of about 10 non-native geraniums found in northern California, some annual or biennial, others herbaceous perennials. *Geranium potentilloides* and *Geranium solanderi* are unusual in having white to light pastel petals; in all the other non-natives, they're intensely pink. You need underground parts and fruit as well as flowers to identify them all.

WAX CURRANT

Family: Grossulariaceae (gooseberry family)

Scientific name: *Ribes cereum* Douglas var. *cereum*

Height: Up to 5'.

Leaves: Deciduous, alternate, the blade 0.4–1.5" wide, round to kidney-shaped, hairless to densely covered with glandular hairs, palmately lobed; lobe margins toothed.

Flowers: Borne in drooping clusters of 3–7; the bases of the sepals, petals, and filaments fused into a fairly slender tube, 0.2–0.3" long, that sits on top of the inferior ovary; sepals 5, the free part less than 0.1" long, petal-like, curled back, white to pink; petals 5, smaller than the sepals, white to pale pink; stamens 5.

Blooms June through July.

Elevation: 2,800–8,000'.

Habitat: Dry, rocky slopes and open forest.

Comments: This spine-free shrub with red berries grows in the Klamath Ranges, Cascades, and Sierra Nevada. It's one of more than 20 species of *Ribes* found in northern California. Trailing gooseberry (*Ribes binominatum*), white-stemmed gooseberry (*Ribes inerme*), and the rare Victor's gooseberry (*Ribes victoris*) can be white-flowered too but have spiny branches. Sticky currant (*Ribes viscosissimum*) lacks spines, but its pink or white flowers are wider in proportion to their length, the sepals more than 0.2" long, and the berries black with a waxy bloom.

CHAPARRAL CURRANT

Family: Grossulariaceae (gooseberry family)

Scientific name: *Ribes malvaceum* Sm. var. *malvaceum*

Height: Up to 7'.

Leaves: Deciduous, alternate, the blade 0.8–2" long and equally wide with 3–5 shallow palmate lobes, densely covered with glandular hairs; margins toothed.

Flowers: Borne in drooping clusters of 10–25; the lower part of the sepals, petals, and filaments fused into a fairly slender tube, 0.2–0.3" long, that sits on top of the inferior ovary; sepals 5, the free part about 0.2" long, petal-like, spreading, bright pink; petals 5, smaller than the sepals, pink to white; stamens 5; style forked at the tip, hairy at its base.

Blooms October through April.

Elevation: Sea level to 4,000'.

Habitat: Chaparral and woodland.

Comments: In northern California, this bristly-haired but spine-free shrub grows in the eastern part of the North Coast Ranges and the Sierra Nevada foothills. Red-flowered currant (*Ribes sanguineum*) looks similar but has hairless styles and white to deep pink or red flowers; it occurs mainly in coastal areas, the Klamath Ranges, and the western part of the North Coast Ranges. In mountain pink currant (*Ribes nevadense*), the cup- to bell-shaped flowers are tightly packed together in clusters of 8–20.

CANYON GOOSEBERRY

Family: Grossulariaceae (gooseberry family)

Scientific name: *Ribes menziesii* Pursh var. *menziesii*

Height: Up to 10'.

Leaves: Deciduous, alternate, the blade 0.6–1.5" long with 3–5 shallow palmate lobes, lower side with glandular hairs; margins toothed.

Flowers: Borne singly or in 2s or 3s; the lower part of the sepals, petals, and filaments fused into a tube 0.1" long that sits on top of the inferior ovary; sepals 5, the free part 0.2–0.4" long, dark red or purple, swept upwards; petals 5, 0.1–0.2" long, white; stamens 5, projecting beyond the petals, anthers whitish; style hairless, forked near the tip, longer than the anthers.

Blooms February through April.

Elevation: Sea level to 6,000'.

Habitat: Chaparral and open areas in forest.

Comments: You'll find three spines at the base of each leaf of this mainly coastal shrub and lots of harsh bristles on the branches. Gummy gooseberry (*Ribes lobbii*), found in the North Coast Ranges and Klamath Ranges, has similar flowers; its branches have spines but lack bristles. In Sierra gooseberry (*Ribes roezlii*), common in much of northern California, not just the Sierra Nevada, the anthers are dark red; in California gooseberry (*Ribes californicum*), they're pale yellow.

WESTERN PRICKLY GOOSEBERRY

Family: Grossulariaceae (gooseberry family)

Also called: Alpine prickly currant

Scientific name: *Ribes montigenum* McClatchie

Height: Up to 3'.

Leaves: Deciduous, alternate, the blade 0.4–1" long, round, usually deeply palmately 5-lobed, both sides covered with glandular hairs; margins toothed.

Flowers: Borne in clusters of 5 or more; the lower part of the sepals, petals, and filaments fused into a shallow saucer that sits on top of the inferior ovary; sepals 5, the free part 0.1–0.2" long, petal-like, usually greenish or pale yellow, less often pink or reddish; petals 5, small, red, fan-shaped; stamens 5; style forked almost to its base.

Blooms June through July.

Elevation: 2,600' to above 13,000'.

Habitat: Conifer forest and dry rocky places.

Comments: This scraggly shrub grows in the Klamath Ranges, Cascades, and Sierra Nevada. The dull red sepals of the flowers shown here are a bit unusual—most often they're greenish yellow. The branches bear 1–5 spines at the base of each leaf. In general, species of *Ribes* are called gooseberries if the branches are spiny and currants if they lack spines, and so the common name "alpine prickly currant" seems an oxymoron.

WILD MOCK ORANGE

Family: Hydrangeaceae (hydrangea family)

Scientific name: *Philadelphus lewisii* Pursh

Height: Up to 10'.

Leaves: Deciduous, opposite, the blade 1–3" long by 0.8–1.6" wide, oval, upper side more or less hairless, lower side usually with some hard, flat-lying hairs; margin smooth or toothed.

Flowers: Fragrant; sepals 4 or 5, 0.2–0.3" long, green; petals 4 or 5, 0.3–0.6" long, white; stamens 20 or more, anthers yellow; ovary half-inferior to completely inferior.

Blooms April through July.

Elevation: Sea level to 8,000'.

Habitat: Woodland, chaparral, and forest.

Comments: This graceful shrub occurs in most of northern California except on the Modoc Plateau, although it's uncommon in the Sacramento Valley and the southern part of the North Coast Ranges. The lower portion of the sepals, petals, and stamens can fuse with the ovary partway up the ovary wall, making the ovary half-inferior, or all the way to the top of the ovary, making the ovary fully inferior. The sepals persist as the fruit matures into a dry capsule, giving it a star shape. Native Americans made everything from snowshoes and digging sticks to pipe stems and arrow shafts from the wood; some tribes also used the leaves or bark to make a soap-like lather for washing hands, faces, and hair. The state's only other species of *Philadelphus* grows in desert mountain ranges from southern California to Texas. Older texts include the genus in the Saxifragaceae (saxifrage family).

MODESTY

Family: Hydrangeaceae (hydrangea family)

Also called: Whipplevine, western whipplea, or yerba de selva

Scientific name: *Whipplea modesta* Torr.

Height: Up to 15", with stems up to 30" long trailing across the ground.

Leaves: Deciduous, opposite, the blade 0.6–1.6" long by 0.4–1.2" wide, hairy, each hair growing from a bulb-shaped base; margins toothed.

Flowers: Sepals 4–6, less than 0.1" long; petals 4–6, 0.1–0.3" long, white; stamens 8–12, anthers white; ovary half-inferior.

Blooms March through July.

Elevation: 150–5,000'.

Habitat: Stream banks and shady slopes in chaparral, coastal scrub, and forest.

Comments: The trailing stems of this little subshrub root where they touch the ground, while the shorter flowering stems grow straight upright. The leaves are shaped rather like those of yerba buena (*Clinopodium douglasii*), which sometimes grows in the same places, but lack yerba buena's minty scent. The fruit is a small, spherical capsule containing only four or five seeds, unlike the many-seeded capsules of wild mock orange (*Philadelphus lewisii*). Modesty occurs mainly in the Coast Ranges, from Monterey County northwards to Washington, and in the Klamath Ranges. Older texts include it in the Saxifragaceae (saxifrage family).

TINKER'S PENNY

Family: Hypericaceae (St. John's wort family)

Also called: Creeping St. John's wort

Scientific name: *Hypericum anagalloides* Cham. & Schltdl.

Height: 1–12".

Leaves: Opposite, those below the flowering branches 0.2–0.6" long, oval to almost round, sessile, hairless, with smooth margins; upper leaves smaller and narrower.

Flowers: Sepals 5, less than 0.2" long, green; petals 5, less than 0.2" long, golden yellow to salmon-colored; stamens 15–25; ovary superior.

Blooms May through September.

Elevation: Sea level to 10,500'.

Habitat: Wet meadows, stream banks, lake shores, marshes, and other damp sites.

Comments: This annual or herbaceous perennial has creeping aboveground stems and can form mats several feet wide. Its flowers often don't open until mid-morning. It occurs in most of northern California except in the southern half of the Sacramento Valley. Aaron's beard (*Hypericum calycinum*) is a Turkish species that has escaped from cultivation in some places. It too is a creeping groundcover but has woody stems, evergreen leaves, and grows up to 2' tall. Its flowers are much showier than those of tinker's penny, 2" to more than 3" wide, and have reddish anthers. Some references place the genus *Hypericum* in the Clusiaceae (mangosteen family), which includes many tropical plants.

DWARF ST. JOHN'S WORT

Family: Hypericaceae (St. John's wort family)

Scientific name: *Hypericum mutilum* L. subsp. *mutilum*

Height: 8" to 2'.

Leaves: Opposite, those below the flowering branches 0.4–1" long, fairly narrow to oval, sessile, hairless, with smooth margins; upper leaves smaller and narrower.

Flowers: Sepals 5, about 0.1" long; petals 5, also about 0.1" long, yellow; stamens 6–20 or more; ovary superior.

Blooms June through October.

Elevation: Sea level to 1,000'.

Habitat: Stream banks and riparian woodland.

Comments: This annual or herbaceous perennial is native to eastern North America. In northern California it grows in the Sacramento Valley and adjacent Sierra Nevada foothills. Along the Lower American River, it's common in shallow flowing water among sedges and rushes as well as on the flood plain. As the summer gets hotter, its leaves sometimes turn a bright rose color, starting at the bottom of the stem, that can be more conspicuous than the small flowers. *Hypericum scouleri* is a California native that also likes moist to wet habitats, but its flowers are 0.6–1" wide, and its stamens and pale to bright yellow petals are edged with tiny black dots.

KLAMATH WEED

Family: Hypericaceae (St. John's wort family)

Scientific name: *Hypericum perforatum* L. subsp. *perforatum*

Height: 1–4'.

Leaves: Opposite, 0.6–1" long, fairly narrow, sessile, hairless, lower side sprinkled with small clear dots, leaf tip rounded; margins edged with small back dots and rolled under.

Flowers: Sepals 5; petals 5, 0.3–0.5" long, yellow, edged with many small black dots, turning brown and twisting with age; stamens numerous, each anther topped with a black dot; ovary superior.

Blooms April through September.

Elevation: Sea level to 6,500'.

Habitat: Disturbed sites.

Comments: This noxious weed from Europe occurs throughout northern California. It's a herbaceous perennial that spreads by means of creeping underground stems; it also reproduces prolifically by seed. To see the clear dots on the leaves, hold a leaf up to a bright light. The black dots are oil glands that produce a compound toxic to livestock. The dry petals look a bit like short pieces of brown string. Gold-wire (*Hypericum concinnum*), a fairly widespread native species found on dry brushy slopes, resembles Klamath weed in that it too has black-dotted yellow petals and foliage, but its pointy-tipped leaves are much narrower and creased lengthwise into a V-shape.

195

NORTHERN CALIFORNIA BLACK WALNUT

Family: Juglandaceae (walnut family)

Scientific name: *Juglans hindsii* R. E. Sm.

Height: Up to 75'.

Leaves: Deciduous, alternate, once pinnately compound with 13–21 leaflets per leaf, each leaflet roughly 3–5" long with tiny tufts of hairs along the veins on the lower side; margins toothed.

Flowers: Male and female flowers borne on the same tree; male flowers in long, drooping inflorescences called catkins, each flower consisting of a few small sepals and 15–40 stamens; female flowers in small clusters, each flower just an inferior ovary topped by 4 sepals and 2 feathery stigmas.

Blooms April through May.

Elevation: Sea level to 1,000'.

Habitat: Riparian areas, roadsides, and disturbed sites.

Comments: In its genetically pure form, this tree is said to grow only in a few locations near the Sacramento–San Joaquin River Delta and around Native American village sites. It's resistant to several soil-borne diseases that attack the commercially valuable, non-native English walnut (*Juglans regia*); hence it's commonly used as rootstock for the latter—the bottoms of the trunk of these grafted trees have the rough, dark gray trunk characteristic of the native tree, while above the graft union the bark abruptly becomes much smoother and lighter gray. The two species hybridize freely, and most black walnut–like trees probably carry some English walnut genes. Jay, crows, and squirrels help disperse the nuts, and so *Juglans hindsii* hybrids are common in the Sacramento Valley and the southern end of the North Coast Ranges. Southern California black walnut (*Juglans californica*) has slightly narrower leaflets; it's native from Monterey County southwards.

YERBA BUENA

Family: Lamiaceae (mint family)

Scientific name: *Clinopodium douglasii* (Benth.) Kuntze

Height: A few inches, with trailing stems up to 2' long.

Leaves: Opposite, the blade 0.4–1.5" long by 0.2–1" wide, oval to almost round, sparsely hairy; margins scalloped or toothed.

Flowers: 0.1–0.3" long; sepals fused into a 5-lobed tube; petals fused into a 2-lipped tube, upper lip 2-lobed and white to lavender, lower lip larger, 3-lobed, and usually white; stamens 4; ovary superior.

Blooms April through September.

Elevation: Sea level to 3,000'.

Habitat: Forest, woodland, and shady sites in chaparral.

Comments: This little perennial lacks the square stems found in most members of the mint family, but its leaves have an unmistakably minty scent when crushed. The slender, slightly woody stems creep across the ground and root where they touch it, sometimes forming mats several feet wide. It grows mainly in the Coast Ranges from southern California to British Columbia and in the Klamath Ranges and is called *Satureja douglasii* in older references. Modesty (*Whipplea modesta*), in the Hydrangeaceae, has somewhat similar opposite leaves but lacks the minty smell.

HENBIT

Family: Lamiaceae (mint family)

Also called: Bee nettle or dead nettle

Scientific name: *Lamium amplexicaule* L.

Height: 4–16".

Leaves: Opposite, the blade 0.4–1" long, oval or heart-shaped to almost round, hairy; margins scalloped or slightly lobed; upper leaves sessile.

Flowers: 0.4–0.7" long; sepals fused into a 5-lobed tube; petals fused into a slender 2-lipped tube, the inside of the tube hairless, upper lip hood-like, lower lip larger with a small lobe on each side and a big central lobe that is further divided into 2 lobes, pink to bright lavender with magenta spots on the lower lip; stamens 4; ovary superior.

Blooms February through September.

Elevation: Sea level to 2,600'.

Habitat: Disturbed areas.

Comments: This Eurasian annual, widespread throughout California except in the desert, is often one of the first plants to bloom in spring. Purple dead nettle (*Lamium purpureum*), another non-native, is less common, occurring mainly near the coast. All its leaves have petioles 0.4–0.8" long, the flowers "peek out" from among slightly drooping leaves, and the inside of the petal tube is hairy. The leaves of both species lack a minty fragrance; as in most members of the family, though, the stems are square in cross-section.

PITCHER SAGE

Family: Lamiaceae (mint family)

Also called: White pitcher sage or woodbalm

Scientific name: *Lepechinia calycina* (Benth.) Munz

Height: Usually 1–4', occasionally up to 7'.

Leaves: Deciduous, opposite, the blade 1.5–5" long, fairly narrow to oval, long-haired, sometimes with additional shorter glandular hairs or sessile glands; margins smooth, scalloped, or toothed.

Flowers: 1–1.2" long; sepals fused into a 5-lobed, yellowish green, hairy tube with conspicuous raised veins, inflating into a brown or reddish, more or less spherical, longitudinally pleated "balloon" up to 1.2" long as the fruit matures; petals fused into a 2-lipped tube, upper lip 4-lobed, lower lip a bit longer and only slightly lobed, white or pale lavender; stamens 4; ovary superior.

Blooms April through June.

Elevation: 500–3,000'.

Habitat: Chaparral and woodland.

Comments: This shrub grows in the Coast Ranges from Mendocino and Lake counties southwards and in the Cascade and Sierra Nevada foothills. The genus includes about 55 species, but this is the only northern California representative. Confusingly, a red-flowered member of the mint family, *Salvia spathacea*, is also called pitcher sage by some authors.

198

BUGLEWEED

Family: Lamiaceae (mint family)

Also called: American water-horehound

Scientific name: *Lycopus americanus* W. P. C. Barton

Height: 8–32".

Leaves: Opposite, the blade 1–4" long, deeply pinnately lobed with very narrow lobes, slightly hairy along the veins to completely hairless, petioles short.

Flowers: About 0.1" long; sepals fused into a 5-lobed tube, each lobe tapered to a long point; petals fused into a usually 4-lobed bell, the lobes slightly unequal in size, white; functional stamens 2, often with 2 additional, minute, club-shaped, sterile stamens (called staminodes); ovary superior.

Blooms June through September.

Elevation: Sea level to 3,000'.

Habitat: Stream banks and marshy areas.

Comments: This inconspicuous herbaceous perennial grows mainly in the Sacramento Valley, Cascades, and northwards to British Columbia. As in most mints, the stems are square, but the plants lack a minty odor. Northern bugleweed (*Lycopus uniflorus*), found in the Klamath Ranges and Cascades, is rare; it has fairly narrow to oval leaves with short petioles and toothed but not lobed margins. Its specific epithet *uniflorus* seems a bit of a misnomer in that its flowers are borne in clusters along the stem just like those of *Lycopus americanus*. Rough bugleweed (*Lycopus asper*) has toothed, sessile leaves.

HOREHOUND

Family: Lamiaceae (mint family)

Also called: White horehound, common horehound, or houndsbane

Scientific name: *Marrubium vulgare* L.

Height: 4" to 2'.

Leaves: Opposite, the blade 0.6" to more than 2" long, oval to almost round, upper side gray-green with veins so deeply depressed that the leaves look crinkled, lower side densely covered with woolly white hairs; margins scalloped.

Flowers: About 0.2" long; sepals fused into a 10-lobed tube; petals fused into a 2-lipped tube, white, upper lip narrow and unlobed to deeply 2-lobed, lower lip 3-lobed; stamens 4; ovary superior.

Blooms March through November.

Elevation: Sea level to 2,000'.

Habitat: Woodland and disturbed sites such as overgrazed pastures.

Comments: This weedy herbaceous perennial is from Europe but common throughout northern California. Its stems are so densely covered with woolly hairs that they look white, and even in winter the plants are easily recognized by the pompom-like blackened remnants of the whorls of flowers along the stems. The species used to be cultivated for medicinal uses and as a flavoring for candy.

PENNYROYAL

Family: Lamiaceae (mint family)

Scientific name: *Mentha pulegium* L.

Height: 4–12".

Leaves: Opposite, the blade 0.2–1" long, oval, hairy, lower leaves with short petioles, upper leaves usually sessile; margins smooth or finely toothed.

Flowers: 0.2–0.3" long; sepals fused into a 5-lobed tube; petals fused into a 2-lipped funnel, lavender, upper lip narrow and 2-lobed, lower lip 3-lobed; stamens 4; ovary superior.

Blooms June through October.

Elevation: Sea level to 4,500'.

Habitat: Moist to wet sites.

Comments: The genus *Mentha* includes several species popular in teas and flavorings, such as spearmint (*Mentha spicata*) and peppermint (a hybrid of two mint species). Pennyroyal, though, is highly toxic; in fact the oil extracted from its leaves is used as an insect repellent and can be fatal to humans. Some people get contact dermatitis just from handling the plants. The species is native to Europe but widespread in northern California. It's a herbaceous perennial that spreads from creeping underground stems and can be invasive. Unlike northern California's eight other mints, all but one non-native, it has a ring of hairs inside the fused sepals; you need a hand lens, though, to see it.

MUSTANG MINT

Family: Lamiaceae (mint family)

Scientific name: *Monardella breweri* A. Gray subsp. *lanceolata* (A. Gray) A. C. Sanders & Elvin

Height: 4" to more than 2'.

Leaves: Opposite, the blade 0.6–2.5" long by 0.2–0.5" wide, with a pleasant minty smell when bruised, upper side covered with short hairs; margins smooth or toothed.

Flowers: Each cluster of flowers cupped by a cluster of bracts, all bracts with prominent longitudinal veins connected by smaller cross veins almost at right angles to the main veins, outer bracts with green or purple tips, inner bracts sometimes papery in texture, each group of flowers 0.2" to more than 1" wide, individual flowers 0.5–0.6" long; sepals fused into a 5-lobed tube; petals fused into a 5-lobed funnel, purple; stamens 4; ovary superior.

Blooms May through October.

Elevation: Sea level to above 11,000'.

Habitat: Open, dry, grassy or rocky sites in chaparral, woodland, and forest.

Comments: In northern California, this annual grows in the Klamath Ranges, Cascades, and Sierra Nevada. It's one of about 10 species of *Monardella* in the region, several of them rare. Central and southern California have many additional species.

COYOTE MINT

Family: Lamiaceae (mint family)

Scientific name: *Monardella villosa* Benth. subsp. *villosa*

Height: Up to 20".

Leaves: Opposite, the blade 0.4–1" long, narrow to oval, with a minty scent when bruised, upper side gray-green to fairly dark green and sparsely hairy, lower side paler and sparsely hairy to densely woolly; margins usually toothed or scalloped, occasionally smooth.

Flowers: Perched on a whorl of bracts, each cluster of flowers 0.4" to more than 1" wide; sepals fused into a 5-lobed tube; petals fused into a 5-lobed funnel 0.4–0.8" long, pink to purple; stamens 4; ovary superior.

Blooms May through August.

Elevation: Sea level to above 4,000'.

Habitat: Woodland, chaparral, ephemeral drainages, and rocky or gravelly sites.

Comments: Look for this rather variable subshrub in the Coast Ranges between San Luis Obispo and Humboldt counties and in the Klamath Ranges. It also grows along the eastern edge of the Sacramento Valley and in the adjacent foothills. On some plants the hairs on the leaves are obvious; on others they're so short that you need a hand lens to see them. Tiny glands on the leaves, sepals, and petals contain the oils that give the plants their fragrance; they look like glistening beads when magnified. The nectar-rich flowers attract numerous butterflies, bees, bumblebees, and other insects.

SACRAMENTO BEARDSTYLE

Family: Lamiaceae (mint family)

Scientific name: *Pogogyne zizyphoroides* Benth.

Height: 2–12".

Leaves: Opposite, the blade 0.1–0.6" long, oval to narrow, with a pleasant minty smell when bruised; margins usually smooth.

Flowers: Borne in compact, egg-shaped to cylindrical clusters, individual flowers peeking out from among numerous hairy bracts; sepals fused into a 5-lobed tube; petals fused into a 2-lipped tube 0.2–0.3" long, lavender to purple; stamens 2 or 4; ovary superior.

Blooms March through June.

Elevation: Sea level to 1,300'.

Habitat: Vernal pools and moist depressions.

Comments: This rather stout-stemmed annual grows in the Central Valley, Cascade and Sierra Nevada foothills, and North Coast Ranges. In early summer the plants sometimes turn a rusty color, darker than the predominantly tawny color of the surrounding grasslands. Douglas' beardstyle (*Pogogyne douglasii*), another vernal pool annual, has larger flowers with lavender petals 0.4–0.8" long and yellow or purple speckles on the lower lip. Thymeleaf beardstyle (*Pogogyne serpylloides*, also called thymeleaf mesa mint) occurs in moist grassy or brushy places. Its slender stems often sprawl across the ground, and its flowers are borne singly or clustered in small, inconspicuous heads. *Pogogyne floribunda* is restricted to the Modoc Plateau.

SONOMA SAGE

Family: Lamiaceae (mint family)

Also called: Creeping sage

Scientific name: *Salvia sonomensis* Greene

Height: Up to 16".

Leaves: Opposite, the blade 1.5–2.5" long by 0.2–0.6" wide, wrinkled-looking, with a pleasant minty smell when bruised, lower side densely covered with white hairs, the tip rounded; margins finely scalloped or toothed.

Flowers: Sepals fused into a 5-lobed tube, the upper 3 tiny; petals fused into a 2-lipped tube 0.2–0.6" long, whitish, lavender, blue, or purple, upper lip 2-lobed and smooth-margined, lower lip bigger, 3-lobed, the large center lobe with ruffled margins; stamens 4, longer than the petals; ovary superior.

Blooms March through July.

Elevation: Sea level to 6,500'.

Habitat: Chaparral, woodland, and yellow pine forest.

Comments: This low-growing subshrub or herbaceous perennial can form big mats. It occurs in the North Coast Ranges, Klamath Ranges, and Cascade and Sierra Nevada foothills. Wand or meadow sage (*Salvia virgata*) is a blue- or purple-flowered European herbaceous perennial sometimes planted as an ornamental, but it becomes invasive when it escapes from cultivation. It grows to more than 3' tall, the upper lip of the petals is arched and longer than the lower, the lower isn't ruffled, and the stamens are usually hidden.

PITCHER SAGE

Family: Lamiaceae (mint family)

Also called: California hummingbird sage

Scientific name: *Salvia spathacea* Greene

Height: 1–2', occasionally up to more than 3'.

Leaves: Opposite, the blade of the lower leaves 3–8" long, shaped like a narrow arrowhead, wrinkled-looking, with a sweet minty smell when bruised, sticky, upper side sparsely long-haired, lower side densely hairy; margins scalloped; upper leaves smaller.

Flowers: Sepals fused into a tube; petals fused into a 2-lipped tube 1–1.5" long, salmon to dark red, upper lip slightly 2-lobed, lower lip larger and 3-lobed; stamens 4, longer than the petals; ovary superior.

Blooms March through May.

Elevation: Sea level to 2,600'.

Habitat: Shady slopes in chaparral and woodland.

Comments: This herbaceous perennial grows in Solano County and farther south. Its stems tend to sprawl, although their upper ends, where the flowers are, usually are fairly upright. The plants often grow under taller shrubs, where they can be hard for human eyes to spot in the dappled light, but hummingbirds don't seem to have any trouble finding them. About 16 additional species of *Salvia* occur in central and southern California. Sagebrush, incidentally, refers to a number of species of *Artemisia* in the Asteraceae (sunflower family).

HEDGE-NETTLE

Family: Lamiaceae (mint family)

Also called: Rough hedge-nettle

Scientific name: *Stachys rigida* Benth. var. *quercetorum* (A. Heller) G. A. Mulligan & D. B. Munro

Height: 2' to more than 3'.

Leaves: Opposite, the blade 2" to nearly 4" long, oval, with a minty smell when bruised, hairless to soft-haired; margins scalloped.

Flowers: Sepals fused into a 5-lobed tube; petals fused into a narrow 2-lipped tube 0.2–0.4" long and with a small pouch or bulge on the lower side, light pink or lavender speckled or striped with purple, upper lip unlobed, lower lip larger and 3-lobed; stamens 4; ovary superior.

Blooms March through October.

Elevation: Sea level to above 8,000'.

Habitat: Moist or dry sites in coastal scrub, woodland, and forest.

Comments: This herbaceous perennial grows mainly in the North Coast Ranges, Klamath Ranges, and coastal areas. It's one of eight species of *Stachys* that occur in northern California. Whitestem hedge-nettle (*Stachys albens*) is notable for the dense, cobwebby white hairs on its stems, sepals, and the lower side of its leaves; it has white to pink, purple-veined petals. *Stachys bergii*, found only in Del Norte County, has dense but woolly silvery hairs and pink petals.

VINEGAR WEED

Family: Lamiaceae (mint family)

Scientific name: *Trichostema lanceolatum* Benth.

Height: 4" to about 3'.

Leaves: Opposite, 0.8–3" long, sessile or with a short petiole, narrow to narrowly oval with a long, tapered tip that makes the plants look spikey, with a vinegary-turpentiney stench, hairy; margins smooth.

Flowers: Sepals fused into a 5-lobed tube 0.1–0.2" long; petals fused into a narrow 5-lobed tube 0.2–0.4" long and abruptly bent upwards about halfway along its length, medium blue; stamens 4, blue to lavender, filaments arched backwards and much longer than the petals; ovary superior.

Blooms June through November.

Elevation: Sea level to above 7,000'.

Habitat: Dry, open, disturbed sites.

Comments: This widespread annual is one of those plants you're likely to smell, if you happen to step on it, before you see it. The flowers, though, attract bees and other insects. In turpentine weed (*Trichostema laxum*), found mainly in the North Coast Ranges, the flowers are borne on short side branches instead of the main stem; the narrow leaves have petioles 0.2–0.6" long. In *Trichostema oblongum*, *Trichostema simulatum*, and the rare Napa bluecurls (*Trichostema ruygtii*), the stamens are far less prominent than in vinegar weed.

CALIFORNIA BAY

Family: Lauraceae (laurel family)

Also called: California laurel, Oregon myrtle, or pepperwood

Scientific name: *Umbellularia californica* (Hook. & Arn.) Nutt.

Height: Up to 150'.

Leaves: Evergreen, alternate, the blade 1.5–4" long, narrow, leathery, medium green with a yellowish cast, often glossy, hairless to slightly hairy, intensely but rather harshly fragrant when bruised; margins smooth.

Flowers: Borne in clusters of 5–10; sepals and petals alike, in 2 whorls of 3, each up to 0.2" long, pale yellow; fertile stamens 9 plus an additional 3 infertile stamens (called staminodes); ovary superior, turning into an olive-like fruit 0.8–1" long.

Blooms November through May.

Elevation: Sea level to above 5,000'.

Habitat: Riparian areas, canyons, and chaparral.

Comments: This tree grows in coastal areas, the Coast Ranges, Klamath Ranges, Cascade and Sierra Nevada foothills, and the Sacramento Valley's Sutter Buttes. On drier sites it may just become a large shrub. The only similar species in the region is sweet bay (*Laurus nobilis*) from the Old World's Mediterranean areas, which has naturalized here and there in northern California. Its leaves are wider than those of California bay, dark green without the yellowish cast, and have a sweeter aroma.

MEADOWFOAM

Family: Limnanthaceae (meadowfoam family)

Scientific name: *Limnanthes douglasii* R. Br. subsp. *nivea* (C. T. Mason) C. T. Mason

Height: Usually 1–14", occasionally up to 3'.

Leaves: Alternate, 1–10" long, once pinnately compound with 5–13 leaflets, hairless; leaflets narrow to oval with smooth to deeply lobed margins.

Flowers: Sepals 5; petals 5, 0.4–0.7" long, slightly heart-shaped, white with translucent or purplish veins; stamens usually 10, anthers cream-colored to yellow; ovary superior, deeply 4- or 5-lobed.

Blooms March through May.

Elevation: Sea level to above 3,000'.

Habitat: Vernal pools, wet meadows, and banks of ephemeral streams.

Comments: This annual grows in the Sacramento Valley and the North Coast Ranges. It's one of five subspecies of *Limnanthes douglasii* found in northern California, along with several other members of the genus. Some have widely accepted common names, such as Butte County meadowfoam (*Limnanthes floccosa* subsp. *californica*) and Sebastopol meadowfoam (*Limnanthes vinculans*), both of which are rare; but judging by the plethora of common names for others, I suspect that many people just make up their own common names for the various meadowfoams, sometimes based on where they happen to have found the plants.

PALE FLAX

Family: Linaceae (flax family)

Scientific name: *Linum bienne* Mill.

Height: 2" to 2'.

Leaves: Alternate, 0.2–1" long, sessile, very narrow, oriented almost parallel to the stem, hairless; margins smooth.

Flowers: 0.5–0.8" wide; sepals 5; petals 5, pale blue with darker veins; stamens 5, anthers blue; ovary superior, yellowish green, styles 5, each style tipped with a linear to club-shaped stigma.

Blooms March through July.

Elevation: Sea level to above 3,000'.

Habitat: Grassland, woodland, and disturbed areas.

Comments: This biennial or short-lived herbaceous perennial, native to Eurasia, is fairly common in coastal grassland; it also occurs in the North Coast Ranges and along the eastern side of the Sacramento Valley. The native and much showier Lewis' flax (*Linum lewisii* var. *lewisii*) grows mainly in the Cascades, Sierra Nevada, and on the Modoc Plateau, sometimes as high as 12,000'; its flowers are bright blue with knob-like stigmas and can be up to 1.2" wide. Common flax (*Linum usitatissimum*), another Eurasian species from which linen has been made since ancient times, sometimes escapes from cultivation, especially near the coast; it resembles Lewis' flax but has slender to club-shaped stigmas. *Linum grandiflorum* originated in northern Africa; it has red petals.

SMOOTH-STEM BLAZING STAR

Family: Loasaceae (loasa family)

Also called: Giant blazing star

Scientific name: *Mentzelia laevicaulis* (Hook.) Torr. & A. Gray

Height: 9" to more than 3'.

Leaves: Basal leaves in a rosette, their blades up to 10" long, narrow, blue-green to gray-green, with pinnately lobed, sometimes wavy margins; stem leaves 0.8–4" long, sessile, covered with short rough hairs, margins smooth or toothed.

Flowers: Sepals 5, narrow, tapered to a long point and persisting on the fruit; petals 5, 1.6" to more than 3" long, narrow, upper side yellow, lower side cream-colored; stamens too many to count, filaments 0.6" to more than 2" long, anthers tiny; ovary inferior, hairy, the style 1–3" long, also persisting on the fruit.

Blooms May through October.

Elevation: Sea level to 9,500'.

Habitat: Flood plains and dry, sandy or rocky sites.

Comments: This biennial or herbaceous perennial grows throughout northern California and as far north and east as British Columbia, Montana, and Wyoming. Its stems and branches are very pale, almost white, and the upper parts are densely stiff-haired. Typically the plants grow fairly upright; once in a while you may find one sprawling. Four other species of *Mentzelia* occur in northern California, but their yellow flowers are much smaller, with petals no more than 0.3" long. Numerous additional species with yellow, whitish, or orange flowers can be found in central and especially southern California; all are native to the state.

FLANNELBUSH

Family: Malvaceae (mallow family)

Scientific name: *Fremontodendron californicum* (Torr.) Coville

Height: 5–16'.

Leaves: Evergreen, alternate, the blade 0.4" to almost 3" long, usually palmately lobed, hairy, especially on the lower side, the hairs branched in a star-like pattern; margins smooth.

Flowers: 1–3" wide; sepals 5, petal-like, upper side shiny and bright yellow, lower side hairy and often rust-colored; no petals; stamens 5, yellow, anthers contorted; ovary superior but hidden by the partly fused filaments that form a kind of cap over it.

Blooms February through July.

Elevation: 500' to above 7,500'.

Habitat: Chaparral and woodland.

Comments: Look for this handsome shrub in the North Coast Ranges and the foothills surrounding the Sacramento Valley. Occasionally it's planted in the Valley in places like freeway interchanges. The genus only has two other species, both of them rare. Mexican flannelbush (*Fremontodendron mexicanum*) grows farther south, while Pine Hill flannelbush (*Fremontodendron decumbens*) is restricted to a few sites with unusual soil chemistry in El Dorado County. The genus was formerly called *Fremontia* and placed in the predominantly tropical family Sterculiaceae, which includes the West African genus *Cola*, extracts of which used to be a key ingredient in cola drinks.

CALIFORNIA HIBISCUS

Family: Malvaceae (mallow family)

Also called: Woolly rose-mallow

Scientific name: *Hibiscus lasiocarpos* Cav. var. *occidentalis* (Torr.) A. Gray

Height: 3' to nearly 7'.

Leaves: Alternate, the blade 2.5–4" long, heart-shaped or 3–5 lobed, hairy, the hairs branched in a star-like pattern; margins toothed.

Flowers: 10 very narrow, hairy bracts just below each flower; sepals fused into a 5-lobed bell, hairy; petals 5, 2.5–4" long, the base deep red, the rest white; stamens numerous, white, filaments fused into a tube that hides the superior ovary and single style, which is topped by 10–15 knob-like, creamy white stigmas.

Blooms July through November.

Elevation: Sea level to about 300'.

Habitat: Freshwater marshes and damp river banks.

Comments: This rare herbaceous perennial or subshrub only grows from the Sacramento–San Joaquin River Delta to Butte County. Its habitat has been largely eliminated by levee construction and other riverside development, and I confess that I photographed the plant shown here in the visitor parking lot at Cosumnes River Preserve in Sacramento County, where it has been planted right next to the restrooms. It does grow wild along some channels in the preserve but is much harder to get close to.

BRISTLY MALLOW

Family: Malvaceae (mallow family)

Also called: Carolina bristle-mallow

Scientific name: *Modiola caroliniana* (L.) G. Don.

Height: Up to 20".

Leaves: Alternate, the blade 0.8" to more than 3" long, kidney-shaped, round, or lobed, usually sparsely hairy; margins toothed.

Flowers: 3 narrow bracts just below each flower; sepals fused into a shallow, 5-lobed bowl, hairy; petals 5, 0.1–0.3" long, dull orange to dull red; stamens numerous, yellow, filaments fused into a tube that hides the superior ovary; styles 15–25, red, each topped by a pinhead-like maroon stigma. Blooms March through November.

Elevation: Sea level to 1,300'.

Habitat: Grassland and disturbed sites.

Comments: Botanists aren't sure where this widespread annual or herbaceous perennial originated; possibly it's from South America. The stems often sprawl across the ground, rooting wherever they touch it. At maturity the round, rather flat fruits (shown here while still green) turn dark brown, then split into 15–25 narrow, bristly wedges, each wedge containing two seeds. It's the only species in its genus. Several weedy species of the related genus *Malva* have somewhat similar-looking flowers and fruit, but their petals are white to pale pink or lavender.

VERNAL POOL CHECKERBLOOM

Family: Malvaceae (mallow family)

Also called: Hogwallow checkerbloom

Scientific name: *Sidalcea calycosa* M. E. Jones subsp. *calycosa*

Height: 1–3'.

Leaves: Blades of basal leaves usually 0.8–2" wide, more or less round, usually hairless, with scalloped but not lobed margins; stem leaves alternate, smaller, deeply 5- to 11-lobed, each lobe narrow to very narrow with smooth or toothed margins.

Flowers: 2 small bracts below each flower; sepals 5, fused at the base, very hairy, often reddish; petals 5, 0.4–0.8" long, white, lavender, or pink; stamens numerous, white, filaments fused into a tube that hides the superior ovary; style splitting into 5 branches, each branch with a slender white stigma along one side. Blooms March through June.

Elevation: Sea level to 4,000'.

Habitat: Vernal pools and moist, open sites in woodland and chaparral.

Comments: Vernal pool checkerbloom is a taprooted annual that grows mainly in the Sacramento Valley, the adjacent foothills, and the western part of the North Coast Ranges. Point Reyes checkerbloom (*Sidalcea calycosa* subsp. *rhizomata*), found at elevations below 100' in Marin, Sonoma, and Mendocino counties, is perennial and has creeping underground stems. More than 15 other species of *Sidalcea* occur in northern California.

CARPET-WEED

Family: Molluginaceae (carpet-weed family)

Also called: Green carpet-weed, whorled chickweed, or devil's grip

Scientific name: *Mollugo verticillata* L.

Height: 1–2".

Leaves: In whorls of 3–8 leaves, each leaf 0.2" to more than 1.5" long, very narrow to oval or spoon-shaped, more or less sessile, hairless; margins smooth.

Flowers: Sepals 5, petal-like, about 0.1" long, the upper side white or greenish with 3 pale green veins, the sparsely hairy lower side greenish brown with a pale margin; no petals; stamens usually 3, less often 4 or 5, white, their filaments pressed against the superior, yellowish green ovary, which is topped by 3 fuzzy, white stigmas.

Blooms May through November.

Elevation: Sea level to above 3,000'.

Habitat: River banks, flood plains, wetland margins, and other moist, disturbed sites.

Comments: This widespread, taprooted little annual is native to the American tropics, including the southern United States. The stems usually lie flat on the ground and can form mats up to 20" wide. Most of the 90 or so species in the Molluginaceae are tropical and somewhat weedy. They have sometimes been included in the Aizoaceae (iceplant family) or Phytolaccaceae (pokeweed family) but are now considered to constitute a separate family based on the chemistry of some of their pigments. Northern California's only other representatives of the carpet-weed family are lotus sweetjuice (*Glinus lotoides*), which grows in the Sacramento Valley and eastern part of the North Coast Ranges and has nearly round, gray-green, crinkled-looking leaves, and the fairly uncommon shining damascisa (*Glinus radiatus*), which has oval leaves. Both are hairy, rather nondescript in appearance, and grow on the margins of seasonal wetlands.

RED MAIDS

Family: Montiaceae (miner's lettuce family)

Scientific name: *Calandrinia menziesii* (Hook.) Torr. & A. Gray

Height: Up to 12", with spreading stems up to 18" long.

Leaves: Alternate, the blade narrow to spoon-shaped, 0.4–4" long, hairless except for a fringe of fine hairs along the margins.

Flowers: Sepals 2, green; petals 5, 0.2–0.6" long, the base white, the rest bright magenta; stamens 3–15, anthers yellow or orange; ovary superior, style 3-branched.

Blooms February through June.

Elevation: Sea level to above 7,000'.

Habitat: Grassland and open disturbed areas.

Comments: This slightly succulent annual used to be included in the Portulacaceae (purslane family) and called *Calandrinia ciliata*. It's widespread throughout northern California and sometimes abundant enough in orchards and agricultural fields to carpet the ground with its magenta flowers. Each seed capsule is only slightly longer than the sepals, which stay on the plant as the fruit matures, and the seed surface has a net-like pattern. The rare Brewer's redmaids (*Calandrinia breweri*) grows mainly in the Coast Ranges; its petals don't exceed 0.2" in length, it only has 3–6 stamens, the seed capsules are about twice as long as the sepals, and the seeds are covered with tiny bumps.

NARROW-LEAVED MINER'S LETTUCE

Family: Montiaceae (miner's lettuce family)

Scientific name: *Claytonia parviflora* Hook. subsp. *parviflora*

Height: 0.5–12".

Leaves: Those in the basal rosette 0.4–7" long, very narrow, hairless, slightly fleshy, margins smooth; stem leaves much wider, opposite, fused around the stem into a disk up to 2" wide.

Flowers: Sepals 2, green; petals 5, 0.1" to about 0.2" long, light pink or white; stamens 5, anthers bright pink; ovary superior with 3 stigmas on an unbranched style.

Blooms February through June.

Elevation: Sea level to 7,500'.

Habitat: Moist woodland and disturbed sites.

Comments: The plant shown here just started blooming, and the flowers are still nestled against the upper leaves; later the stem will become much longer. It's the most widespread of four subspecies of *Claytonia parviflora*, all annual. The other three generally grow farther south, but they intergrade and it can be hard to figure out exactly which one you're looking at. A further complication is that they also hybridize with three subspecies of *Claytonia perfoliata* and two subspecies of *Claytonia rubra*, all of which occur in northern California. Long story short: The extremes are easy to tell apart, but the intermediates can be a mystery.

MINER'S LETTUCE

Family: Montiaceae (miner's lettuce family)

Scientific name: *Claytonia perfoliata* Willd. subsp. *perfoliata*

Height: 0.5–16".

Leaves: Those in the basal rosette with blades up to 1.5" long, oval to triangular or kidney-shaped, hairless, slightly fleshy, petioles 2–8" long; margins smooth; stem leaves opposite, sessile, fused around the stem into a disk up to 4" wide.

Flowers: Sepals 2, greenish; petals 5, 0.1" to about 0.2" long, light pink or white; stamens 5, anthers pink or white; ovary superior, style 3-branched.

Blooms January through May.

Elevation: Sea level to above 3,000'.

Habitat: Moist woodland and disturbed sites.

Comments: The plant shown here has just started blooming, with the flowers tightly clustered in the shallow cone formed by the fused uppermost pair of leaves. As the season progresses, the flowering part of the stem elongates considerably and the flowers and fruit become widely spaced. This subspecies of miner's lettuce is common throughout northern California except on the Modoc Plateau, but as described under narrow-leaved miner's lettuce (*Claytonia parviflora* subsp. *parviflora*), it hybridizes with several other species and subspecies and so its appearance can vary a lot. Some older texts call it *Montia perfoliata*.

CANDY FLOWER

Family: Montiaceae (miner's lettuce family)

Scientific name: *Claytonia sibirica* L.

Height: 2" to 2'.

Leaves: Those in the basal rosette with blades 0.4" to more than 3" long, narrow to almost triangular, hairless, petioles 0.5–8" long; margins smooth; stem leaves opposite, narrow to oval, sessile but not fused around the stem.

Flowers: Sepals 2, green; petals 5, 0.2–0.5" long, striped purplish pink and white, sometimes with a row of small yellow dots near the base; stamens 5, anthers pink or white; ovary superior, style 3-branched.

Blooms February through August.

Elevation: Sea level to above 4,000'.

Habitat: Stream banks, marshes, and moist, shady woodland and forest.

Comments: Usually candy flower is a herbaceous perennial with a short, upright underground stem up to 0.4" thick called a caudex; it also produces creeping underground stems. Occasionally it's annual. It's native from the San Francisco Bay region to Montana, Alaska, and Siberia. Some older texts call it *Montia sibirica*. The flowers are easily confused with western spring beauty (*Claytonia lanceolata*). The caudex of western spring beauty, though, is much thicker than that of candy flower, and each plant only has one or two basal leaves or sometimes none at all.

Nevada bitter-root (*Lewisia nevadensis*).

NEVADA BITTER-ROOT

Family: Montiaceae (miner's lettuce family)

Scientific name: *Lewisia nevadensis* (A. Gray) B. L. Rob.

Height: 1–2".

Leaves: All in a basal rosette, each leaf 1.5" to more than 5" long, thread-like to narrow, hairless, somewhat fleshy; margins smooth.

Flowers: Usually borne singly on a stem that's leafless except for 2 bracts somewhere on its lower half; sepals 2, green; petals 5–10, 0.4–0.8" long, the base often yellowish green, the rest white or pale pink; stamens 6–15, anthers white, pollen yellow; ovary superior with 3–6 stigmas.

Blooms May through August.

Elevation: 4,000–10,000'.

Habitat: Damp meadows, moist gravel, and open areas in forest.

Comments: This herbaceous perennial grows from a thick taproot; in northern California it occurs in the North Coast Ranges, Klamath Ranges, Cascades, Sierra Nevada, and on the Modoc Plateau. Three-leaved lewisia (*Lewisia triphylla*) has a similar range, and sometimes the two hybridize. Three-leaved lewisia, however, is a much daintier perennial with white or pale pink petals less than 0.4" long and only 3–5 stamens per flower. Its basal leaves wither quickly, and by the time you notice the flowers, only the very narrow stem leaves are left, either one pair of opposite leaves or one whorl of 3–5 leaves. (It's one of those cases where you shouldn't take the common name and specific epithet, *triphylla*, too literally.)

Three-leaved lewisia (*Lewisia triphylla*).

213

BITTER-ROOT
Family: Montiaceae (miner's lettuce family)

Scientific name: *Lewisia rediviva* Pursh var. *rediviva*

Height: 1–2".

Leaves: The numerous leaves all in a basal rosette, each leaf 0.2–2" long, very narrow, hairless, fleshy, often almost round in cross-section.

Flowers: Sepals 4–9, darker pink than the petals, papery; petals 10–19, 0.7–1.5" long, occasionally white but usually pink or lavender with a paler base; stamens 30–50, anthers generally pink to light purple, pollen yellow; ovary superior with 4–9 slender white stigmas.

Blooms March through June.

Elevation: 200' to above 6,000'.

Habitat: Open, rocky or sandy sites.

Comments: This herbaceous perennial, one of the showiest of northern California's dozen species of *Lewisia*, grows in most of the region except in the Sacramento Valley and along the coast. The sturdy taproots were an important food for Native Americans, and dried roots were a valuable trade item for some tribes, often exchanged for salmon. Large patches of bitter-root and other species with nutritious roots, corms, or bulbs, carefully tended for centuries or perhaps millennia by Native American women, undoubtedly contributed to the gorgeous displays of spring wildflowers that amazed John Muir and other early naturalists. Sadly, ploughing, disturbance caused by introduced livestock, and competition by non-native weeds have decimated the majority of California's Native American garden plots; others were destroyed by highway construction and urban development.

OSAGE ORANGE

Family: Moraceae (mulberry family)

Scientific name: *Maclura pomifera* (Raf.) C. K. Schneid.

Height: Up to 65' but usually much less.

Leaves: Deciduous, alternate, the blade 1–6" long, oval with a long, drawn-out tip, sparsely soft-haired; margins smooth.

Flowers: Male and female flowers borne in umbels on separate trees; each male flower with 4 small sepals and 4 stamens; each female flower consisting of 4 sepals and a superior ovary with a single style, all female flowers in one umbel coalescing into one tennisball-sized, stringy-fleshed, yellowish green fruit.

Blooms April through June.

Elevation: Sea level to almost 1,500'.

Habitat: Stream banks and disturbed areas.

Comments: This tree or big shrub, native to Missouri, Arkansas, Oklahoma, and Texas, bears lots of inch-long thorns, especially while young. Several Native American tribes prized the hard but flexible wood for making bows. The wood contains a chemical toxic to many wood-decaying fungi, and so European settlers used it for fence posts, tool handles, and the wheels of horse-drawn vehicles, later for mine timbers and railroad ties. Before barbed wire became widely available, hedges of osage orange were often planted to enclose livestock pastures—one 19th-century writer described it as "horse high, bull strong, and pig tight." It was also useful as a windbreak. Squirrels seem to be the only animals that appreciate the fruit, which they tear apart to get at the seeds; perhaps that's how the species spreads naturally. From a distance, the trees resemble white mulberry (*Morus alba*), which, like osage orange, occasionally escapes from cultivation into California's riparian areas; up close, though, you'll see that mulberry lacks thorns and has toothed, sometimes deeply lobed leaf margins. The leaves of both turn a clear yellow in fall.

SCARLET PIMPERNEL

Family: Myrsinaceae (myrsine family)

Also called: Shepherd's clock or poison chickweed

Scientific name: *Lysimachia arvensis* (L.) U. Manns & Anderb.

Height: 2–16".

Leaves: Opposite or whorled, 0.2–0.8" long, sessile, oval, generally hairless; margins smooth.

Flowers: Borne singly on stalks 0.4–1.5" long that curve down as the fruit matures; sepals 5, green; petals 5, 0.2–0.3" long, longer than the sepals, the base banded bright purple and red, the rest usually salmon-orange, fringed with tiny hairs; stamens 5, filaments red, anthers yellow; ovary superior. Blooms March through September.

Elevation: Sea level to above 3,000'.

Habitat: Disturbed sites.

Comments: Occasionally this widespread, weedy European annual has deep blue, brick-red, or whitish petals. Its often sprawling, 4-angled stems don't root where they touch the ground. Seeds buried in the ground can remain viable for about 70 years. Chaffweed (*Lysimachia minima*), also annual, is native to California; its inconspicuous flowers are borne directly on the stem, and its white or pale pink petals are shorter than the sepals. The genus used to be called *Anagallis* and included in the primrose family (Primulaceae). The leaves of common chickweed (*Stellaria media*) resemble scarlet pimpernel, but the stems are round in cross-section.

SAND VERBENA

Family: Nyctaginaceae (four o'clock family)

Also called: Yellow sand verbena

Scientific name: *Abronia latifolia* Eschsch.

Height: A few inches, with sprawling stems up to more than 6' long.

Leaves: Opposite, the blade 0.8–2" long, broadly oval to round or kidney-shaped, fleshy, ranging from almost hairless to densely covered with sticky glandular hairs; margins smooth.

Flowers: Borne in umbels of 17–34 flowers, each flower 0.3–0.5" wide; no sepals; petals fused into a 4- or 5-lobed trumpet, each main lobe often divided into 2 smaller lobes, bright yellow; stamens 4 or 5; ovary superior. Blooms May through October.

Elevation: Sea level to 300'.

Habitat: Sandy beaches, dunes, and coastal scrub.

Comments: This common herbaceous perennial can be found along the Pacific coast from Santa Barbara County to British Columbia. The rare pink sand verbena (*Abronia umbellata* var. *breviflora*) grows in similar habitats from Marin County to southern Oregon, while *Abronia umbellata* var. *umbellata*, also pink-flowered, occurs only in Sonoma County and south of the Golden Gate. The two subspecies differ in the number of flowers in each umbel and some details in the structure of the fruit. Farther south you may find several more species of *Abronia*.

Clusters of young male flowers.

Fruit.

OREGON ASH

Family: Oleaceae (olive family)

Scientific name: *Fraxinus latifolia* Benth.

Height: Up to about 80'.

Leaves: Deciduous, alternate, once pinnately compound, usually with 5–7 leaflets per leaf, rarely 3 or 9, most leaflets 1.5–6" long by 1–3" wide, the leaflet at the end often larger, hairless or hairy; margins smooth or toothed.

Flowers: Male and female flowers borne in compact clusters on separate trees; each male flower with 4 minute sepals, 2 stamens, and a vestigial pistil, all yellowish to somewhat rust-colored; each female flower with 4 minute sepals and a superior ovary that matures into a narrow, 1-winged fruit 1–2" long.

Blooms March through May.

Elevation: Sea level to 5,500'.

Habitat: Riparian areas and moist woodland.

Comments: This tree is widespread throughout northern California. Its lightweight fruits are wind-dispersed; on male trees the dried-up, blackened remains of the flowers often persist until fall. California ash (*Fraxinus dipetala*, also called flowering ash) is a shrub or small tree usually no more than 10' tall that grows in chaparral and woodland, mainly at elevations of 300–4,000' in the mountains bordering the Sacramento Valley. Each of its flowers has both male and female parts as well as two white or cream-colored petals that can be more than 0.2" long. These two are northern California's only native ashes. Several non-native species of *Fraxinus* are often used in landscaping but don't seem to hybridize with the natives.

CONTORTED SUN CUP

Family: Onagraceae (evening-primrose family)

Scientific name: *Camissonia contorta* (Douglas) Kearney

Height: 1–12".

Leaves: Alternate, 0.4–1.5" long, sessile, usually very narrow, often covered with short, soft hairs; margins smooth or slightly toothed.

Flowers: Sepals 4 but fused so that they look like 1 or 2, often red; petals 4, 0.1–0.2" long, yellow but turning orange or reddish with age, sometimes with 2 tiny red spots near the base of each petal; stamens 8; ovary inferior, very slender, the style topped with a knob-like yellow stigma.

Blooms March through June.

Elevation: Sea level to 7,500'.

Habitat: Open sites with sandy soil in grassland, chaparral, and pinyon-juniper woodland.

Comments: I'm not sure how this widespread, wiry-stemmed little annual got its name: Neither the plants as a whole nor their long, skinny, straight to curved fruits seem contorted. In good years, the small flowers can be abundant enough to make the ground look as if it were sprinkled with yellow dots. Grassland sun cup (*Camissonia lacustris*) is similar but has slightly bigger flowers, with petals up to 0.3" long; in northern California it only grows in Lake County and northwestern Napa County.

BEACH EVENING-PRIMROSE

Family: Onagraceae (evening-primrose family)

Scientific name: *Camissoniopsis cheiranthifolia* (Spreng.) W. L. Wagner & Hoch subsp. *cheiranthifolia*

Height: A few inches, with sprawling stems usually no more than 2' long.

Leaves: Those in the basal rosette with blades 0.4–3" long, oval, tapering to the petiole, hairless to densely hairy; margins minutely toothed; stem leaves alternate, smaller, sometimes sessile.

Flowers: Sepals 4 but fused so that they look like 1 or 2; petals 4, 0.2–0.5" long, yellow but turning reddish with age, often with 1 or 2 red spots near the base of each petal; stamens 8; ovary inferior, slender, the style topped with a knob-like yellow stigma.

Blooms April through September.

Elevation: Sea level to 300'.

Habitat: Dunes and open, sandy areas.

Comments: This herbaceous perennial, the most common of northern California's four species of *Camissoniopsis*, is a strictly coastal species. Its reddish stems form rosettes of leaves at their tips that will root and grow into new plants. *Camissoniopsis*'s seed capsules are 4-sided when dry, filled with matte, flattened seeds; *Camissonia* is similar but has cylindrical fruit and glossy seeds that are triangular in cross-section. Both genera are better represented farther south.

FIREWEED

Family: Onagraceae (evening-primrose family)

Scientific name: *Chamerion angustifolium* (L.) Holub subsp. *circumvagum* (Mosquin) Hoch

Height: Up to 10'.

Leaves: Alternate, 0.6–8" long, narrow, sessile or with a short petiole, upper side hairless, lower side often with hard, flat-lying hairs along the midrib; margins smooth or finely toothed.

Flowers: Sepals 4, narrow, pink, spreading; petals 4, 0.4–1" long, magenta; stamens 8, anthers pink, dull orange, or red, pollen usually blue-gray; ovary inferior, very slender, pale green, stigma 4-lobed, white.

Blooms July through September.

Elevation: Sea level to almost 11,000'.

Habitat: Moist, open or rocky areas, and lodgepole pine forest.

Comments: As in many species of Onagraceae, the inferior ovaries and later the seed capsules of this herbaceous perennial almost look like flower stalks or segments of stem. If you split one open, though, you'll find it full of tiny ovules or seeds, each topped with a tuft of long white hairs. Fireweed is common throughout the colder parts of the northern hemisphere, spreads by means of creeping underground stems, and often forms big, colorful stands. Older texts call it *Epilobium angustifolium*. Dwarf fireweed (*Chamerion latifolium*) is much less common in northern California, occurring only in the Sierra Nevada at elevations of 8,200–10,000'; it doesn't get much more than 2' tall but has slightly bigger flowers, with petals 0.5–1.3" long.

GLANDULAR CLARKIA

Family: Onagraceae (evening-primrose family)

Also called: Glandular fairyfan

Scientific name: *Clarkia arcuata* (Kellogg) A. Nelson & J. F. Macbr.

Height: 4–32".

Leaves: Alternate, 0.6–2.5" long, very narrow to narrow, sessile, hairless or with short, spreading hairs; margins smooth.

Flowers: Flower buds nodding; sepals 4, greenish or pink, with short glandular hairs, fused and pushed to one side by the unfolding petals; petals 4, 0.4–1.5" long, fan-shaped, deep pink or lavender to almost white; stamens 8, anthers purple or white; ovary inferior, very slender, 8-grooved, stigma 4-lobed, usually light yellow.

Blooms April through June.

Elevation: Sea level to 5,500'.

Habitat: Grassland and open grassy areas in woodland, forest, or chaparral.

Comments: This annual grows mainly in the Cascade foothills and the Sierra Nevada. It's one of nearly 20 species of *Clarkia* in northern California, many of them with showy flowers. Red ribbons (*Clarkia concinna* subsp. *concinna*), primarily found in the North Coast Ranges and Cascade foothills, is unusual in having only four stamens. Features to look for in identifying the others include whether the flower buds are upright or nodding, the exact shape and color of the petals, and whether the ovary and fruit are 4- or 8-grooved.

FOUR SPOT

Family: Onagraceae (evening-primrose family)

Also called: Winecup clarkia or winecup fairyfan

Scientific name: *Clarkia purpurea* (Curtis) A. Nelson and J. F. Macbr. subsp. *quadrivulnera* (Lindl.) H. Lewis & M. Lewis

Height: Usually 4–20", occasionally taller.

Leaves: Alternate, 0.6–2" long, very narrow to narrow, sessile, hairless or sparsely hairy; margins smooth.

Flowers: Flower buds upright; sepals 4, green, fused but split apart by the unfolding petals; petals 4, 0.2–0.6" long, diamond-shaped to fan-shaped, usually pink to lavender with a relatively large darker area at or near the margin, sometimes solid wine-red or purple; stamens 8, anthers white; ovary inferior, very slender, 8-grooved, stigma 4-lobed, purple.

Blooms April through August.

Elevation: Sea level to 5,000'.

Habitat: Grassland and other dry, open areas.

Comments: This widespread annual is among our least showy species of *Clarkia* but can be quite abundant. It often doesn't start blooming until nearby annual grasses are drying out. *Clarkia purpurea* subsp. *purpurea* is less common; it has wider leaves and petals 0.4–1" long. *Clarkia purpurea* subsp. *viminea* also has petals up to 1" long, but its leaves are very narrow.

ELEGANT CLARKIA

Family: Onagraceae (evening-primrose family)

Scientific name: *Clarkia unguiculata* Lindl.

Height: Up to 40".

Leaves: Alternate, the blade 0.4–2.5" long, narrow to oval, sessile or with a petiole up to 0.4" long, hairless, often with a waxy bloom; margins smooth.

Flowers: Flower buds nodding; sepals 4, green or red, often hairy, fused but pushed aside by the unfolding petals; petals 4, 0.4–1" long, the bottom half a narrow ribbon, the upper half a broad fan, pink, lavender, or less frequently salmon, dark reddish purple, or white; stamens 8, 4 fairly large with bright rose anthers, 4 smaller with whitish anthers; ovary inferior, very slender, 8-grooved, hairy, stigma white, initially knob-like but then unfolding into 4 lobes.

Blooms April through September.

Elevation: Sea level to 5,000'.

Habitat: Grassland, woodland, and flood plains.

Comments: This annual is widespread from Mendocino and Tehama counties southwards. In the Sacramento region, its seedlings start growing in January or February. They have bright green leaves with maroon staining along the main veins, and for a while they add small but bold splashes of color to the wintry landscape. Initially the leaves are opposite; as the plants grow taller, their arrangement transitions to alternate.

TALL ANNUAL WILLOWHERB

Family: Onagraceae (evening-primrose family)

Also called: Panicled willowweed

Scientific name: *Epilobium brachycarpum* C. Presl

Height: 8" to more than 6'.

Leaves: Lower leaves opposite, upper leaves alternate, 0.4" to more than 2" long, very narrow to narrowly oval, often folded into a V-shape along the midrib, nearly hairless; margins smooth or with a few small teeth.

Flowers: Sepals 4, green; petals 4, 0.1–0.8" long, so deeply lobed that they almost look like 8 petals, white to rose with darker veins; stamens 8; ovary inferior, slender.

Blooms June through September.

Elevation: Sea level to above 10,000'.

Habitat: Dry, open grassland, woodland, forest, and disturbed sites.

Comments: This inconspicuous annual grows throughout northern California. The leaves drop early, and by the time the fruit is mature, the stems are often leafless. The narrow greenish structures in the photo are immature seed capsules, not leaves. Fringed willowherb (*Epilobium ciliatum*, also called northern willowherb) looks similar but is perennial, has wider leaves, and prefers much moister sites such as stream banks, wet meadows, and shady riparian areas. All in all, northern California is home to 25 or more species of *Epilobium*, most with white, pink, or pinkish purple flowers.

221

CALIFORNIA FUCHSIA

Family: Onagraceae (evening-primrose family)

Scientific name: *Epilobium canum* (Greene) P. H. Raven subsp. *canum*

Height: 8" to 4'.

Leaves: Alternate, with very short, leafy side branches that make the leaves look clustered; 0.3" to almost 3" long, narrow, generally sessile, gray or gray-green, hairy; margins smooth or slightly toothed.

Flowers: Sepals and petals fused for most of their length into a slender scarlet funnel, topped by 4 fairly narrow sepals and 4 wider, 2-lobed petals; stamens 8, red, pollen white; ovary inferior, slender and easily mistaken for a flower stalk, stigma 4-lobed.

Blooms June through December.

Elevation: Sea level to almost 7,000'.

Habitat: Gravelly flats and other dry sites.

Comments: This widespread subshrub or herbaceous perennial is one of the few species of *Epilobium* that don't have white or pink flowers. It's a good hummingbird plant for gardens but can get weedy, spreading by creeping underground stems and copious amounts of seeds. *Epilobium canum* subsp. *latifolium* has opposite, wider, non-clustered leaves and only gets 4–20" tall. The rare Humboldt County fuchsia (*Epilobium septentrionale*), also red-flowered, forms mats 2–12" tall; its leaves are covered with short, dense, white hair. Older texts place all three in the genus *Zauschneria*.

URUGUAYAN WATER-PRIMROSE

Family: Onagraceae (evening-primrose family)

Scientific name: *Ludwigia hexapetala* (Hook. & Arn.) Zardini et al.

Height: 1' to more than 6'.

Leaves: Alternate, the blade 1–6" long, narrow to oval, usually hairless; margins smooth.

Flowers: 1 fairly narrow bract below each flower; sepals usually 5; petals usually 5, less often 6 (despite the species' scientific name!), 0.7–1.2" long, bright yellow; stamens usually 10; ovary inferior, slender, maturing into a fruit covered with long, spreading hairs.

Blooms May through December.

Elevation: Sea level to 1,000'.

Habitat: Wetlands, shallow slow-moving waters, and moist soil along their shores.

Comments: This invasive herbaceous perennial or subshrub can form big floating mats or grow entangled with riparian vegetation near the water's edge. It's widespread in the Sacramento Valley and the southern part of the North Coast Ranges. *Ludwigia grandiflora* is very similar but has slightly *smaller* flowers and hairless fruit. In *Ludwigia peploides*, which has two subspecies, the bract below each flower is triangular. Older texts place all three species in the genus *Jussiaea*; none is native to California. *Ludwigia palustris*, native from South America to British Columbia, has opposite leaves and inconspicuous, sessile flowers with four small sepals and no petals.

COMMON EVENING-PRIMROSE

Family: Onagraceae (evening-primrose family)

Scientific name: *Oenothera biennis* L.

Height: 1' to more than 6'.

Leaves: Basal leaves in a broad rosette; stem leaves alternate, 2–8" long, fairly narrow to oval, hairy, usually sessile; margins usually smooth or toothed, sometimes slightly lobed near the base.

Flowers: Densely clustered, each flower with a narrow, green, hairy bract below the stem-like inferior ovary; the lower part of the sepals, petals, and filaments fused into a slender tube 0.8" to more than 1.5" long above the ovary; sepals 4, usually green or yellow, sometimes reddish; petals 4, usually 0.4–1" long, lemon-yellow, often turning dull orange with age; stamens 8, yellow; stigma 4-lobed, greenish yellow, not projecting beyond the anthers.

Blooms June through October.

Elevation: Sea level to 1,000'.

Habitat: Disturbed sites.

Comments: This biennial is native to central and eastern North America; in California it grows mainly in the northwestern part of the state and the southern end of the Sacramento Valley. Its seed capsules are 0.8–1.6" long, relatively wide, and held close to the stem. The genus *Oenothera* is well represented in central and southern California, especially in the desert. Northern California's relatively few species include hairy evening-primrose (*Oenothera villosa* subsp. *strigosa*), a California native found mainly in western Tehama County, the Klamath Ranges, Cascades, and on the Modoc Plateau, which resembles common evening-primrose except for its less compact inflorescences and hairs that sprout from red, blister-like bases.

HOOKER'S EVENING-PRIMROSE

Family: Onagraceae (evening-primrose family)

Scientific name: *Oenothera elata* Kunth subsp. *hirsutissima* (S. Watson) W. Dietr.

Height: 3' to more than 8'.

Leaves: Alternate, 1.5–10" long, usually narrow, sessile, covered with short, dense hairs plus some longer ones; margins smooth or toothed.

Flowers: Each flower with a leaf-like bract just below the narrow inferior ovary; the lower part of the sepals, petals, and filaments fused into a slender tube 0.8" to more than 2" long above the ovary; sepals 4, green or reddish; petals 4, 1–2" long, often heart-shaped, lemon-yellow, turning orange with age; stamens 8, yellow; style longer than the stamens, stigma 4-lobed, yellow.

Blooms June through October.

Elevation: Sea level to above 9,000'.

Habitat: Stream banks and other moist sites.

Comments: This biennial, widespread in the western United States, is considered a subspecies of *Oenothera hookeri* in some older texts. The rare Wolf's evening-primrose (*Oenothera wolfii*) is similar except that its petals are 0.5–1" long and the style is about the same length as the anthers. It only grows near the coast from Mendocino County to Oregon and in the Klamath Ranges. *Oenothera glazioviana*, a European species, has leaves with ruffled edges and reddish sepals.

JOHNNY-NIP

Family: Orobanchaceae (broomrape family)

Scientific name: *Castilleja ambigua* Hook. & Arn. subsp. *ambigua*

Height: 4–12"

Leaves: Alternate, 0.4–2" long, narrow, hairy; margins smooth or with up to 5 narrow lobes.

Flowers: Borne in dense, upright clusters 1–5" long, a hairy, 3- to 9-lobed, green or purplish bract just below each flower, the tips of the lobes white, cream, yellow, or purplish pink; sepals fused into a 4-lobed tube; petals typically light yellow, sometimes pink, fused into a 2-lipped tube, the upper lip ending in a pointed "beak," the lower lip ballooning into 3 elongated pouches topped by 3 small teeth; stamens 4, hidden; ovary superior, the pinhead-like, reddish, fuzzy stigma just barely protruding from the upper petal lip.

Blooms May through August.

Elevation: Sea level to 1,600'.

Habitat: Coastal scrub and grassland.

Comments: This mainly coastal annual is uncommon, but where it does occur, it can be abundant. It's possible that some plants hybridize with purple owl's clover (*Castilleja exserta* subsp. *exserta*), which may explain the many variations in color. The rare Humboldt Bay owl's clover (*Castilleja ambigua* subsp. *humboldtiensis*) tends to be fleshy; it only grows in salt marshes right at sea level from Marin County to Humboldt County.

VALLEY TASSELS

Family: Orobanchaceae (broomrape family)

Scientific name: *Castilleja attenuata* (A. Gray) T. I. Chuang & Heckard

Height: 4–20".

Leaves: Alternate, 0.8" to more than 3" long, very narrow, hairy; margins smooth or with a few lobes.

Flowers: Borne in dense, upright clusters 1–12" long but only 0.4–0.8" wide, a hairy, 3-lobed, green bract just below each flower, the tips of the lobes white or pale yellow; sepals green, white-tipped, fused into a slender 4-lobed tube; petals fused into a 2-lipped tube, white except for a yellow area and a few purple dots on the lower lip, which balloons into 3 narrow pouches before terminating in 3 small teeth, the upper lip ending in a pointed "beak"; stamens 4, hidden; ovary superior.

Blooms March through May.

Elevation: Sea level to 5,200'.

Habitat: Grassland.

Comments: In older texts, this annual is called *Orthocarpus attenuatus*. It's widespread throughout northern California except on the Modoc Plateau. Pale owl's clover (*Castilleja lineariloba*), another grassland species that grows in the Sierra Nevada foothills, is similar, but its bracts have 5–7 lobes and its inflorescences are twice as wide as those of valley tassels, making them a bit less inconspicuous.

FIELD OWL'S CLOVER

Family: Orobanchaceae (broomrape family)

Scientific name: *Castilleja campestris* (Benth.) T. I. Chuang & Heckard subsp. *campestris*

Height: 4–12"

Leaves: Alternate, 0.6–1.5" long, very narrow, more or less hairless; margins smooth.

Flowers: Borne in dense, upright clusters 1–6" long, an unlobed green bract just below each flower; sepals green, hairy, fused into a slender 4-lobed tube; petals fused into a 2-lipped tube, yellow, usually fading to white with age, the upper lip short, the lower lip ballooning into 3 spreading, sometimes heart-shaped pouches; stamens 4, hidden; ovary superior, the pinhead-like, greenish, fuzzy stigma just barely protruding from the petals.

Blooms April through July.

Elevation: Sea level to almost 7,000'.

Habitat: Vernal pools and other moist, open sites.

Comments: Older texts call this annual *Orthocarpus campestris*. It grows mainly in the Sacramento Valley, Cascades, southern part of the North Coast Ranges, and on the Modoc Plateau. As in the majority of flowering plants, each anther consists of two pollen-producing pouches (called anther sacs by botanists). Butter-and-eggs (*Triphysaria eriantha*) superficially resembles field owl's clover except that the plants usually have a purple tinge, their leaves are lobed and hairy, and each anther consists of a single pollen sac.

225

PURPLE OWL'S CLOVER

Family: Orobanchaceae (broomrape family)

Scientific name: *Castilleja exserta* (A. Heller) T. I. Chuang & Heckard subsp. *exserta*

Height: 4–18".

Leaves: Alternate, 0.4–2" long, with 5–9 thread-like lobes, covered with short stiff hairs.

Flowers: Borne in dense, upright clusters 1–8" long, a hairy 5- to 9-lobed whitish to purple bract just below each flower, the tips of the lobes white, pale yellow, bright pink, or purple; sepals colored like the bracts, hairy, fused into a slender 4-lobed tube; petals fused into a 2-lipped tube, usually purple and white, the very hairy upper lip forming a short "beak," the lower lip ballooning into 3 pouches; stamens 4, hidden; ovary superior, the knob-like, purple, fuzzy stigma just barely protruding from the upper petal lip.

Blooms March through May.

Elevation: Sea level to 5,200'.

Habitat: Grassland.

Comments: Older texts call this annual *Orthocarpus purpurascens.* Like many members of its family, it's a hemiparasite: It has green foliage and so it can make its own carbohydrates, but its roots "steal" water and nutrients from the roots of nearby vegetation. Greenhouse experiments have shown that although it can grow and flower without a host, it grows far more vigorously with a host, while the host's growth is drastically diminished. Purple owl's clover occurs from Humboldt, Trinity, and Tehama counties southwards.

In coastal dunes and grassland, you may come across *Castilleja exserta* subsp. *latifolia,* in which the bracts below each flower have lavender tips and the inflorescence as a whole appears encircled by alternating pale and dark bands. *Castilleja densiflora* subsp. *densiflora,* which grows mainly in the Coast Ranges and Sierra Nevada foothills, resembles *Castilleja exserta* subsp. *exserta* but is hairless. Three rare species of *Castilleja* can also have purple flowers. Humboldt Bay owl's clover (*Castilleja ambigua* subsp. *humboldtiensis*) tends to be fleshy; it only grows in coastal salt marshes. Siskiyou paintbrush (*Castilleja miniata* subsp. *elata*) mainly grows in bogs in Del Norte County and can have bright purplish pink or yellowish orange flowers. And lastly, split-hair Indian paintbrush (*Castilleja schizotricha*) is densely covered with woolly, white, branched hairs and has pastel pink or lavender flowers; it's only found on decomposed granite or marble at elevations above 5,000' in the Klamath Ranges.

WOOLLY PAINTBRUSH

Family: Orobanchaceae (broomrape family)

Scientific name: *Castilleja foliolosa* Hook. & Arn.

Height: 1–2'.

Leaves: Alternate, 0.4–2" long, very narrow, densely covered with white, branched, woolly hairs, upper leaves sometimes 3- or 5-lobed; margins smooth.

Flowers: Borne in upright clusters 1–8" long, an unlobed to 5-lobed, typically orange-red, sometimes greenish yellow, hairy bract just below each flower; sepals green with red tips, hairy, fused into a tube; petals fused into a narrow 2-lipped tube, yellowish green; stamens 4, hidden; ovary superior, the small green or yellow stigma just barely protruding from the petals.

Blooms March through June.

Elevation: Sea level to 6,000'.

Habitat: Chaparral and dry, open, often rocky sites.

Comments: This herbaceous perennial or subshrub tends to be heavily branched. In northern California it occurs in the Coast Ranges and Sierra Nevada foothills. It's one of about 15 perennial species of *Castilleja* that typically have red, less often yellow or orange flowers. Frosted paintbrush (*Castilleja pruinosa*) has grayish hairs; sometimes there's a yellowish band between the red and green portions of its bracts. Wavy-leaf paintbrush (*Castilleja applegatei*), with four subspecies, has ruffle-edged leaves and is densely covered with sticky glandular hairs. The narrow leaves of Wyoming paintbrush (*Castilleja linariifolia*) are folded upwards into a V-shape. Giant paintbrush (*Castilleja miniata* subsp. *miniata*), 16" to 3' tall, grows on wet soils at elevations above 5,000'.

LEMMON'S PAINTBRUSH

Family: Orobanchaceae (broomrape family)

Scientific name: *Castilleja lemmonii* A. Gray

Height: 4–8".

Leaves: Alternate, 0.8–1.5" long, very narrow to narrow, unlobed or 3-lobed, usually with both non-glandular and glandular hairs; margins smooth.

Flowers: Borne in upright clusters 1–5" long, a 3- to 5-lobed, purplish red, hairy bract just below each flower; sepals purplish red, hairy, fused into a tube; petals fused into a narrow 2-lipped tube, the upper lip extended into a white, pale yellow, or green "beak," the lower lip mainly greenish yellow; stamens 4, hidden; ovary superior, the small greenish yellow stigma just barely protruding from the "beak."

Blooms July through August.

Elevation: 5,000' to above 12,000'.

Habitat: Moist meadows.

Comments: This herbaceous perennial grows in the Cascades and Sierra Nevada. Unlike many species of *Castilleja*, its stems tend to be unbranched. There aren't many purple-flowered species of *Castilleja*, and its mountain meadow habitat and lack of branching make Lemmon's paintbrush pretty distinctive.

FROSTED PAINTBRUSH

Family: Orobanchaceae (broomrape family)

Scientific name: *Castilleja pruinosa* Fernald

Height: 12–32".

Leaves: Alternate, 0.8" to more than 3" long, narrow, unlobed or with up to 5 lobes, usually covered with dense, short, grayish hairs; margins smooth.

Flowers: Borne in upright clusters 1–8" long, an unlobed or 3- to 5-lobed bract just below each flower, usually red-tipped; sepals fused into a 4-lobed tube, the lobes red, sometimes with a band of yellow below; petals fused into a narrow 2-lipped tube, usually red and green, the upper lip about twice as long as the tube and tapering to a point, the lower lip much shorter and inconspicuous; stamens 4, hidden; ovary superior, the style and small stigma clearly protruding from the upper lip.

Blooms April through August.

Elevation: Sea level to 8,500'.

Habitat: Forest edges and dry, open areas.

Comments: Frosted paintbrush can be a herbaceous perennial or a subshrub; in northern California it grows mainly in the Klamath Ranges, Cascades, Sierra Nevada, the northern end of the North Coast Ranges, and on the Modoc Plateau. The common name refers to the dense cover of velvety hairs found on many but not all members of the species.

WIGHT'S PAINTBRUSH

Family: Orobanchaceae (broomrape family)

Scientific name: *Castilleja wightii* Elmer

Height: 12–32".

Leaves: Alternate, 0.8–2.5" long, narrow to oval, unlobed or 3-lobed, usually with both long, bristly, non-glandular hairs and shorter, sticky, glandular hairs; margins smooth.

Flowers: Borne in upright clusters 2–8" long, a 3-lobed bract just below each flower, the lobes red to yellow; sepals the same color as the tips of the bracts, hairy, fused into a tube; petals fused into a narrow 2-lipped tube, mainly greenish, the margins of the lips often red or yellow; stamens 4, hidden; ovary superior, the small green stigma just barely protruding from the petals.

Blooms March through September.

Elevation: Sea level to 1,000'.

Habitat: Coastal scrub and dunes.

Comments: This heavily branched herbaceous perennial is one of five or so red-flowered species of *Castilleja* that grow along northern California's coast; because of the sticky glandular hairs, the plants are sometimes coated with sand and other windblown debris. Seashore Indian paintbrush (*Castilleja affinis* subsp. *litoralis*) is hairless to sparsely hairy, not sticky, and has relatively wide, unlobed leaves. The rare Mendocino paintbrush (*Castilleja mendocinensis*) has wide, unlobed or 3-lobed, rather fleshy leaves.

SLENDER BIRD'S BEAK

Family: Orobanchaceae (broomrape family)

Scientific name: *Cordylanthus tenuis* A. Gray subsp. *tenuis*

Height: 8" to 4'.

Leaves: Alternate, 0.4–2.5" long, very narrow, hairless or soft-haired, often with sticky glandular hairs; margins smooth.

Flowers: Usually 0.4–0.8" long, each flower with 1–4 very narrow, unlobed, green or purplish, 0.2–0.8"-long outer bracts plus one wider inner bract at its base; sepals fused, partly wrapped around the petals, often purplish; petals fused into a short tube, then ballooning into 2 maroon-and-white lips that taper into a narrow yellow tip; stamens 4; ovary superior.

Blooms July through September.

Elevation: 1,000–8,500'.

Habitat: Foothill woodland and dry, open conifer forest.

Comments: This annual grows in the Klamath Ranges, Cascades, and Sierra Nevada. Even when the plants are a few feet tall and quite bushy, their thin stems and branches, narrow leaves, and generally drab color make them rather inconspicuous. Close up, the flowers are intriguing: Gently pinch their sides, and the petals will gape like baby birds demanding to be fed. Four other subspecies of slender bird's beak can be found in northern California, three of them rare, as well as four more species of *Cordylanthus*.

CALIFORNIA BROOMRAPE

Family: Orobanchaceae (broomrape family)

Scientific name: *Orobanche californica* Cham. & Schltdl. subsp. *californica*

Height: 2" to nearly 1'.

Leaves: None other than fairly narrow, somewhat fleshy, drab pink or purplish bracts.

Flowers: Generally densely crowded, often forming more or less spherical clusters up to about 3" in diameter; sepals fused into a funnel with 5 narrow lobes, typically dingy pink or grayish brown; petals fused into a 5-lobed funnel, whitish to dull pink, drab maroon, or reddish purple with darker veins and 2 fat, usually yellow ridges between the lower 3 petals that are easy to mistake for stamens; stamens 4; ovary superior, stigma 2-lobed, white.

Blooms June through August.

Elevation: Sea level to 500'.

Habitat: Coastal bluffs.

Comments: This uncommon annual or herbaceous perennial only grows along the coast, where it parasitizes the roots of beach gumweed (*Grindelia stricta*) and perhaps a few other species. On the Mendocino Headlands, you may find some plants with dingy yellow petals growing side by side with the more typical maroon- or purple-flowered form. *Orobanche californica* subsp. *grayana* and subsp. *jepsonii* occur farther inland and parasitize other members of the sunflower family. A total of nine species of *Orobanche* occur in northern California, all native except for branched broomrape (*Orobanche ramosa*), which is an invasive European species. It differs from the natives by having only four sepals, not five, and occurs mainly in the Sacramento–San Joaquin River Delta and farther south. The stems are yellowish, the petals whitish to light blue. Heavy infestations can significantly reduce the crop in tomato fields; it also attacks native plants such as cocklebur (*Xanthium strumarium*).

NAKED BROOMRAPE

Family: Orobanchaceae (broomrape family)

Scientific name: *Orobanche uniflora* L.

Height: Stems 0.2–2" tall, topped by a flower 0.5–1.5" long.

Leaves: None except for 2–6 crowded bracts near the base of the stem.

Flowers: Usually borne singly at the tip of the stem, occasionally in 2s or 3s; sepals 5, 0.2–0.3" long, very narrow, fused near the base, yellowish to tan or purplish gray; petals fused into a curved tube with 5 rounded lobes, blue, purple, or white with 2 bright yellow area ridges on the lower side of the tube; stamens 4; ovary superior.

Blooms April through July.

Elevation: Sea level to above 10,000'.

Habitat: Relatively moist sites.

Comments: This diminutive parasite is widespread throughout northern California except in the Sacramento Valley, where it seems to have been reported only from the Sutter Buttes and one location on the Lower American River. It attacks species of stonecrop (*Sedum* spp.) and members of the Saxifragaceae (saxifrage family) and Asteraceae (sunflower family). Usually the entire plant is hairy. It's by far the smallest of California's 11 species of *Orobanche*, all of which are parasitic on other plants.

SHORT-FLOWERED OWL'S CLOVER

Family: Orobanchaceae (broomrape family)

Scientific name: *Orthocarpus cuspidatus* Greene subsp. *cryptanthus* (Piper) T. I. Chuang & Heckard

Height: 4–16".

Leaves: Alternate, 0.4–2" long, narrow sessile, finely hairy, lower leaves unlobed with smooth margins, upper leaves often deeply 3-lobed.

Flowers: Borne in dense clusters 0.8–4" long, a wide bract just below each flower, the tips of the upper bracts purplish pink; sepals fused into a 4-lobed tube; petals 0.3–0.5" long, fused into a narrow 2-lipped tube, purplish pink, the upper lip tapering into a straight "beak," the lower shorter and ballooning into 3 small, narrow, white or pink pouches; stamens 4; ovary superior.

Blooms June through August.

Elevation: 5,000' to above 10,000'.

Habitat: Sagebrush scrub and fairly dry meadows.

Comments: This annual grows in the Cascades and Sierra Nevada and has petals just barely visible among the colorful bracts. In Copeland's owl's clover (*Orthocarpus cuspidatus* subsp. *copelandii*), which is more widely distributed in northern California's mountains, the petals protrude a lot farther from the bracts, and the pouches on the lower petal lip are more conspicuous. The two subspecies can intergrade. The rare Siskiyou Mountains owl's clover (*Orthocarpus cuspidatus* subsp. *cuspidatus*) has petals 0.6–1" long.

231

YELLOW GLANDWEED

Family: Orobanchaceae (broomrape family)

Scientific name: *Parentucellia viscosa* (L.) Caruel

Height: Up to 20".

Leaves: Opposite, 0.8–1.5" long, fairly narrow, sessile, covered with sticky glandular hairs; margins boldly toothed.

Flowers: Densely clustered, a green, leaf-like bract just below each flower; sepals fused into a 4-lobed funnel, green; petals fused into a narrower, 2-lipped funnel 0.6–0.8" long, yellow, the upper lip hood-like, the lower lip larger with 3 wide lobes; stamens 4, hidden inside the "hood"; ovary superior, the small, knob-like stigma just barely protruding.

Blooms April through July.

Elevation: Sea level to above 2,000'.

Habitat: Moist grassland and coastal wetlands.

Comments: Older references call this European annual *Bellardia viscosa* or *Bartsia viscosa*. It occurs near the coast, in the North Coast Ranges and Cascades, and on the eastern side of the Sacramento Valley and can get quite invasive in coastal wetlands. You might say the plants have a hybrid lifestyle: Although they're green and therefore can make their own food via photosynthesis, they also parasitize the roots of nearby plants. Broadleaf glandweed (*Parentucellia latifolia*) is a daintier-looking species, also from Europe, with smaller leaves, less dense inflorescences, and reddish purple flowers only 0.3–0.4" long.

LITTLE ELEPHANT'S HEAD

Family: Orobanchaceae (broomrape family)

Scientific name: *Pedicularis attollens* A. Gray

Height: 2" to 2'.

Leaves: Basal leaves 1–8" long, pinnately divided into 17–41 very narrow segments with toothed margins; stem leaves alternate, smaller.

Flowers: Borne in crowded, upright, densely shaggy-haired clusters 0.8–12" long; sepals 5, fused at the base; petals 2-lipped, the upper lip forming an upwards-curved "trunk" about 0.2" long, the lower lip 3-lobed, the center lobe smaller than those at the sides, light pink to magenta with some darker streaks; stamens 4; ovary superior, the small stigma just barely protruding from the tip of the trunk.

Blooms June through September.

Elevation: 4,000' to above 13,000'.

Habitat: Wet meadows, stream banks, and bogs.

Comments: All of northern California's eight species of *Pedicularis* are herbaceous perennial hemiparasites; that is, they parasitize the roots of other plants but also make some of their own food via photosynthesis. Of the eight, only elephant's head (*Pedicularis groenlandica*) resembles little elephant's head, but the plants are hairless, 3–32" tall with more numerous flowers in each inflorescence, and the "trunks" are 0.2–0.5" long. Both species occur in the Klamath Ranges, Cascades, and Sierra Nevada.

WARRIOR'S PLUME

Family: Orobanchaceae (broomrape family)

Also called: Indian warrior

Scientific name: *Pedicularis densiflora* Hook.

Height: 2" to almost 2'.

Leaves: Basal leaves 2–12" long, pinnately divided into 13–41 segments, each segment very narrow to oval, its margins lobed or double-toothed; stem leaves alternate, only slightly smaller.

Flowers: Borne in upright clusters 1.5–5" long; sepals 5, fused about half their length, reddish; petals fused into a straight 2-lipped tube 1–1.5" long, the upper lip shaped a bit like a hotdog bun, usually dark red or purple, occasionally yellow or dull orange, the lower lip much shorter with 3 small lobes, often pink to almost white; stamens 4; ovary superior.

Blooms March through May.

Elevation: Sea level to almost 7,000'.

Habitat: Chaparral, dry woodland, and yellow pine forest.

Comments: This rather dark-colored herbaceous perennial is widespread in most of northern California except in the Sacramento Valley but can be hard to spot in the dappled shade where it often grows. Dwarf lousewort (*Pedicularis semibarbata*), generally found above 5,000', has similar, very dark green or purplish foliage; it only grows a few inches tall and has dingy yellow flowers more or less hidden by the leaves.

BUTTER-AND-EGGS

Family: Orobanchaceae (broomrape family)

Also called: Johnny-tuck

Scientific name: *Triphysaria eriantha* (Benth.) T. I. Chuang & Heckard subsp. *eriantha*

Height: 4–14".

Leaves: Alternate, 0.4–2" long, pinnately divided into 3–7 very narrow segments, sessile, hairy, often tinged purple; margins smooth.

Flowers: Borne in dense upright clusters 1–6" long with a hairy, 3- to 5-lobed, purple-tinged bract just below each flower; sepals fused into a 5-lobed tube, often purplish; petals fused into a 2-lipped tube, mainly yellow, the upper lip ending in a short, dark purple "beak," the lower lip much showier, ballooning into 3 wedge-shaped pouches; stamens 4, each with 1 pollen-producing sac; ovary superior.

Blooms March through May.

Elevation: Sea level to 5,200'.

Habitat: Grassland and margins of vernal pools.

Comments: Older texts call this little annual *Orthocarpus erianthus*. It's widespread in most of northern California except in the Klamath Ranges. On coastal bluffs, you may find *Triphysaria eriantha* subsp. *rosea*, which has white petals that turn purplish pink with age. *Triphysaria versicolor* subsp. *versicolor* resembles butter-and-eggs except that it lacks any purplish coloration. There are also several yellow-flowered species of *Castilleja* somewhat similar to butter-and-eggs, but they all have two pollen-producing sacs per anther.

233

CREEPING WOOD-SORREL

Family: Oxalidaceae (oxalis family)

Also called: Creeping lady's-sorrel

Scientific name: *Oxalis corniculata* L.

Height: Often less than 1", but creeping stems up to 20" long occasionally climb upwards.

Leaves: Alternate, palmately compound with 3 heart-shaped leaflets per leaf, each leaflet up to 0.8" long but often much less, sometimes reddish or purplish, upper side hairless, lower side sparsely hairy; margins usually smooth, occasionally fringed with fine hairs.

Flowers: Sepals 5; petals 5, no more than 0.3" long and often much smaller, lemon-yellow; stamens 10, 5 of them longer than the other 5; ovary superior, the tip of the style divided into 5 branches, each branch ending in a small, fuzzy, green stigma.

Blooms almost all year.

Elevation: Sea level to above 6,000'.

Habitat: Disturbed sites.

Comments: This annoying, hard-to-get-rid-of herbaceous perennial weed probably came from Mediterranean Europe. In northern California, it's most abundant in coastal areas and the North Coast Ranges, Sacramento Valley, and Sierra Nevada foothills. At maturity, the slender seed capsules, 0.2–1" long, pop open abruptly, flinging out the tiny seeds several inches to several feet; the seeds readily cling to shoes and paws and so are spread even farther to new sites.

DWARF WOOD-SORREL

Family: Oxalidaceae (oxalis family)

Scientific name: *Oxalis micrantha* Colla

Height: Up to 8".

Leaves: Alternate, palmately compound with 3 heart-shaped leaflets per leaf, each leaflet up to 0.5" long, sparsely hairy on both sides; margins smooth.

Flowers: Sepals 5; petals 5, less than 0.5" long, light lemon-yellow; stamens 10, 5 of them longer than the other 5; ovary superior, the tip of the style divided into 5 branches, each branch ending in a small, fuzzy, yellow stigma.

Blooms February through May.

Elevation: Sea level to above 3,000'.

Habitat: Woodland, rocky outcrops, and disturbed sites.

Comments: This annual, native to Chile, grows in small upright tufts that often stand out by their rather light green color. In the morning, the leaflets spread to catch as much light as possible; then, if the light gets too intense, they fold down. The seed capsules, about 0.2" wide, are egg-shaped to spherical. In northern California, the species occurs mainly in the Sacramento Valley, Sierra Nevada foothills, and southern end of the North Coast Ranges. Hairy wood-sorrel (*Oxalis pilosa*) is somewhat similar, but it's perennial, growing from a relatively sturdy taproot, and its petals are narrower and more tapered.

REDWOOD SORREL

Family: Oxalidaceae (oxalis family)

Scientific name: *Oxalis oregana* Nutt.

Height: Up to 8".

Leaves: Produced in small clusters, each leaf palmately compound with 3 heart-shaped leaflets, each leaflet up to 1.5" long with a pale green midrib, upper side hairless, lower side hairy and often intensely purple; margins smooth except for a fringe of fine hairs.

Flowers: Borne singly on stalks up to 6" long; sepals 5; petals 5, up to 1" long, white to lavender or deep pink except for a yellow spot near the base, veins darker; stamens 10, 5 of them longer than the other 5; ovary superior, style 5-branched.

Blooms February through August.

Elevation: Sea level to above 3,000'.

Habitat: Moist conifer forest.

Comments: This herbaceous perennial grows in coastal areas, the North Coast Ranges, and Klamath Ranges. It has creeping underground stems and often blankets the forest floor with its leaves. In dense conifer forest in northwestern California, you may also find *Oxalis trilliifolia*; its white or pale pink flowers are borne in umbel-like clusters of three to nine. Windowbox wood-sorrel (*Oxalis articulata* subsp. *rubra*), native to Brazil but naturalized near the coast, has white to deep purplish pink flowers.

BERMUDA BUTTERCUP

Family: Oxalidaceae (oxalis family)

Also called: Buttercup oxalis, Cape sorrel, Cape cowslip, or sourgrass

Scientific name: *Oxalis pes-caprae* L.

Height: Up to 12".

Leaves: Produced in clusters of up to 40, each leaf palmately compound with 3 heart-shaped leaflets, each leaflet up to 1.5" long, upper side hairless and often brown- or purple-spotted, lower side hairy; margins smooth.

Flowers: Borne in umbel-like clusters of up to 20; sepals 5; petals 5, up to 1" long, lemon-yellow with greenish veins; stamens 10, 5 of them longer than the other 5, anthers orange-yellow; ovary superior with a 5-branched style.

Blooms January through May.

Elevation: Sea level to 2,600'.

Habitat: Disturbed places, riparian areas, grassland, and dunes.

Comments: This herbaceous perennial is native not to Bermuda but to southern Africa. There it readily reseeds itself, but in California it never seems to set seed. Instead, its creeping underground stems produce numerous inch-long, white or brown bulbs, which probably get pushed around by gophers and other burrowing animals. The upshot is that the plants often form big patches wherever they occur in the Sacramento Valley, Sierra Nevada foothills, southern part of the North Coast Ranges, and coastal areas.

235

WESTERN PEONY

Family: Paeoniaceae (peony family)

Also called: Mountain peony

Scientific name: *Paeonia brownii* Douglas

Height: 8–16".

Leaves: Alternate, once or twice pinnately compound with 3 main divisions and deeply lobed leaflets, somewhat fleshy, hairless, blue-green with a waxy bloom.

Flowers: Sepals 5, leathery; petals 5–10, 0.3–0.5" long, slightly shorter than the inner sepals, maroon to brown with yellowish or greenish margins; stamens numerous, anthers yellowish; pistils 2–5, superior, green, the stigmas attached more or less directly on top of the ovary.

Blooms April through July.

Elevation: 600–10,000'.

Habitat: Dry, open forest, chaparral, sagebrush scrub, and dry sites above timberline.

Comments: Look for this herbaceous perennial in northern California's mountains. The flower stalks curve down, and the flowers are often partly hidden by leaves. In southern and central California's coastal areas and nearby mountain ranges, it's replaced by California peony (*Paeonia californica*), which has dark red petals that are slightly longer than the inner sepals and have pink or red margins. These are California's only two members of the family, which is better represented in southern Europe and eastern Asia.

BUSH POPPY

Family: Papaveraceae (poppy family)

Also called: Tree poppy

Scientific name: *Dendromecon rigida* Benth.

Height: 3–10'.

Leaves: Alternate, the blade 1–4" long by 0.3–1" wide, leathery, blue-green or gray-green; margins minutely toothed.

Flowers: Sepals 2, shed as the flowers open; petals 4, 0.8–1.5" long, yellow; stamens numerous; ovary superior, with a 2-lobed stigma directly on top of it.

Blooms January through June.

Elevation: Sea level to above 6,000'.

Habitat: Chaparral and dry slopes.

Comments: In northern California, this shrub or small tree occurs in the southern part of the North Coast Ranges and the Cascade and Sierra Nevada foothills, where it can thrive on some ultra-dry sites such as south-facing cliffs. Except for its wider, smooth-margined leaves, *Dendromecon harfordii* looks very similar, but it's restricted to the Channel Islands of southern California and Baja California. California's only other woody members of the poppy family are two species of matilija poppy (*Romneya coulteri* and *Romneya trichocalyx*), native to southern California, which are occasionally planted in northern California for their spectacular, white, crinkly-petalled flowers.

CALIFORNIA POPPY

Family: Papaveraceae (poppy family)

Scientific name: *Eschscholzia californica* Cham.

Height: 2" to 2'.

Leaves: Basal leaves several times pinnately divided with 3 main divisions, hairless, sometimes with a waxy bloom; stem leaves alternate, smaller.

Flowers: Flower buds upright; sepals fused into a narrow cap that is pushed off as the petals expand; petals 4, 0.8–2.5" long, orange to yellow; stamens numerous; ovary superior.

Blooms February through October.

Elevation: Sea level to above 8,000'.

Habitat: Grassland, dunes, and other open areas.

Comments: This is one of three species of *Eschscholzia* in northern California; it occurs throughout the region. The plants can be annual or perennial, upright or sprawling, the leaves bright green to intensely blue-green. The first flowers to bloom are solid orange; as the seasons progress, the petals become more and more yellow, and late summer flowers may be solid yellow. Because the species is so variable, some botanists have divided it into different subspecies, collectively ending up with more than 90 groupings of characteristics. What all California poppies have in common is a pronounced red or pink rim under each flower, a bit like a small saucer under a big cup, which is more or less lacking in other species of *Eschscholzia*. The slender seed capsules explode into two halves at maturity, flinging the small black seeds several feet.

FRYING PANS

Family: Papaveraceae (poppy family)

Scientific name: *Eschscholzia lobbii* Greene

Height: 2–6".

Leaves: All basal, twice pinnately divided with 3 main divisions, hairless.

Flowers: Flower buds upright; sepals fused into a narrow cap that is pushed off as the petals expand; petals 4, 0.3–0.5" long, yellow, the sides meeting at a wide angle at the tip so that the flowers often look somewhat square or diamond-shaped from above; stamens numerous; ovary superior.

Blooms February through April.

Elevation: Sea level to 2,600'.

Habitat: Grassland.

Comments: The stems of this small annual are completely leafless. It grows in the Sacramento Valley and Cascade and Sierra Nevada foothills. Tufted poppy (*Eschscholzia caespitosa*) has a few leaves on its stems and slightly deeper yellow flowers that look round from above; its petals are 0.4–1" long. The two sometimes grow side by side. In older references the genus is spelled *Eschscholtzia*—it's named for J. F. G. von Eschscholtz, the surgeon and botanist on the Russian ship *Rurik*, which in the early 1800s made a voyage of discovery along North America's Pacific coast. Why the "t" has been dropped, I don't know.

CARNIVAL POPPY

Family: Papaveraceae (poppy family)

Scientific name: *Hesperomecon linearis* (Benth.) Greene

Height: 1–16".

Leaves: In a basal rosette, 0.2–3.5" long, very narrow, with rather sparse, long, spreading, slightly wavy hairs; margins smooth.

Flowers: Flower buds nodding; sepals 3, brownish, dropping off as the petals unfold; petals 6, 0.1–0.8" long, 3 white petals with a yellow base alternating with 3 all-yellow ones; more than 12 stamens, anthers yellow; ovary superior with 3 narrowly triangular stigmas.

Blooms March through June.

Elevation: Sea level to above 3,000'.

Habitat: Grassland, washes, and dunes.

Comments: This annual, the only species in its genus, used to be called *Meconella linearis.* Its fruit is a slender capsule that splits open lengthwise to release the shiny black seeds. Occasionally you may find plants with all-white or cream-colored petals and stamens. The species grows mainly in central and southern California but does put in an appearance in the dunes at Sonoma County's Bodega Bay. Cream cups (*Platystemon californicus*), which is similar to the all-white form of carnival poppy, grows nearby on Bodega Head. Its flowers have six or more stigmas, and its fruits break apart into small, 1-seeded segments.

CREAM CUPS

Family: Papaveraceae (poppy family)

Scientific name: *Platystemon californicus* Benth.

Height: 1–12".

Leaves: Some in a basal rosette, others alternate or whorled on the stem; 0.4" to almost 4" long, very narrow to narrow, covered with stiff, spreading hairs; margins smooth.

Flowers: Flower buds nodding; sepals 3, hairy; petals 6, 0.2–0.8" long, usually cream-colored, often with yellow markings at the tip or base or both, occasionally all-yellow; stamens numerous, anthers white; pistils 6–25 (usually 9–18), fused to each other but with the corresponding number of stigmas.

Blooms March through May.

Elevation: Sea level to 3,000'.

Habitat: Grassland, especially areas with sandy or clayey soil.

Comments: This highly variable annual is widespread in most of northern California except on the Modoc Plateau; it's also common farther south. It can be abundant in recently burned areas. Although some plants have as few as 13 stamens, most have so many that they resemble a small pompom on top of the petals. When the seeds are mature, the pistils break apart into 1-seeded segments. Cream cups is the only species in its genus. California fairy poppy (*Meconella californica*), which grows in the Cascade and Sierra Nevada foothills, and the rare white fairy poppy (*Meconella oregana*), found only in the San Francisco Bay region, Oregon, and Washington, also have six white petals but only one pistil.

GRASS-OF-PARNASSUS

Family: Parnassiaceae (grass-of-Parnassus family)

Also called: Marsh grass-of-Parnassus

Scientific name: *Parnassia palustris* L.

Height: 6–20".

Leaves: Mostly in a basal rosette, the blade 0.8–2" long, oval, hairless; margins smooth; a single, much smaller leaf on each flowering stem.

Flowers: Sepals 5, green; petals 5, 0.3–0.8" long, white with prominent translucent veins; 5 fertile stamens with yellow or white anthers alternating with 5 sterile stamens (called staminodes) that are divided into 7–27 long, thread-like, yellow-tipped lobes; ovary superior.

Blooms July through October.

Elevation: Sea level to above 11,000'.

Habitat: Stream banks, lake shores, and wet meadows.

Comments: In northern California, this herbaceous perennial can be found in the North Coast Ranges, Klamath Ranges, Cascades, and Sierra Nevada; some older texts call it *Parnassia californica* and include it in the Saxifragaceae (saxifrage family). The rare Cascade grass-of-Parnassus (*Parnassia cirrata* var. *intermedia*), which grows in the Klamath Ranges and Cascades, has narrower petals that are heavily fringed at the base. Fringed grass-of-Parnassus (*Parnassia fimbriata*) occurs in the Klamath Ranges, Sierra Nevada, and the Modoc Plateau's Warner Mountains; it too has fringed petals, but its staminodes are yellowish green with very short lobes, looking a bit like a small, broad hand with up to eight stumpy, upwards-curled fingers.

PANSY MONKEYFLOWER

Family: Phrymaceae (lopseed family)

Scientific name: *Mimulus angustatus* (A. Gray) A. Gray

Height: Stem less than 0.5" tall, topped by flowers 1–2.5" long.

Leaves: In a basal rosette, 0.2–1.5" long, very narrow, upper and lower sides hairless; margins smooth except for a fringe of fine hairs, at least on the lower half of each leaf.

Flowers: Sepals fused into a 5-lobed tube; petals fused into a 5-lobed tube 0.8–2.5" long, the lower part of the tube very slender, then becoming trumpet-like, the upper 2 petal lobes bigger than the lower 3, magenta with purple, yellow, and white marking on the lower lobes; stamens 4; ovary superior with a 2-lobed, magenta stigma.

Blooms March through June.

Elevation: 800–4,000'.

Habitat: Sites with moist soil in spring.

Comments: This annual grows in the North Coast Ranges and the foothills of the Cascades and Sierra Nevada. It's one of more than 15 species of *Mimulus* that occur in northern California and have pink to deep magenta petals, generally with some yellow markings. Bolander's monkeyflower (*Mimulus bolanderi*), another annual found mainly in the North Coast Ranges and Sierra Nevada, is unusual in that its magenta petals only have white markings.

BUSH MONKEYFLOWER

Family: Phrymaceae (lopseed family)

Scientific name: *Mimulus aurantiacus* Curtis var. *aurantiacus*

Height: Usually 2–5'.

Leaves: Opposite, 0.4–3.5" long, very narrow to oval, sessile, upper surface hairless, lower surface sticky and slightly to densely hairy; margins smooth or toothed, often rolled downwards.

Flowers: Borne in 2s or 4s; sepals fused into a 5-lobed tube; petals fused into a 5-lobed tube 1–1.5" long, the upper 2 petal lobes bigger than the lower 3, lobes sometimes heart-shaped, orange; stamens 4, anthers slightly darker orange than the petals; ovary superior, with a 2-lobed, white stigma.

Blooms March through June.

Elevation: Sea level to 2,600'.

Habitat: Open woodland, chaparral, coastal scrub, and disturbed sites.

Comments: This shrub or subshrub is the only species of *Mimulus* with bright orange flowers. It's common in the Coast Ranges and Sierra Nevada foothills. *Mimulus aurantiacus* var. *grandiflorus* (called *Mimulus bifidus* in older texts), found on rocky hillsides in the Cascades and Sierra Nevada foothills, has pale orange or pale yellow flowers that can be more than 2" long; its petals are always 2-lobed or heart-shaped. Other varieties that grow farther south have deep orange to bright red flowers and are occasionally planted as ornamentals.

YELLOW AND WHITE MONKEY-FLOWER

Family: Phrymaceae (lopseed family)

Scientific name: *Mimulus bicolor* Benth.

Height: 2–12".

Leaves: Opposite, 0.1–1.2" long, very narrow to fairly narrow, sessile, densely covered with short hairs; margins toothed, the teeth sometimes very small.

Flowers: Sepals fused into a 5-lobed tube, usually green with red or purple speckles; petals fused into a 5-lobed tube 0.4–0.8" long, all lobes slightly heart-shaped, the upper 2 lobes white, the lower 3 yellow with red speckles; stamens 4; ovary superior, with a 2-lobed, white or pale yellow stigma.

Blooms April through July.

Elevation: 1,000' to almost 7,000'.

Habitat: Moist open areas, drainages, volcanic outcrops, and small moist pockets on bedrock or among boulders.

Comments: This annual grows in the Klamath Ranges, Cascades, and Sierra Nevada. In some individuals, all five petals are yellow. The sepals persist as the fruit develops and tend to become corky, which helps distinguish plants without white petals from northern California's nearly 20 other yellow-flowered species of monkeyflower.

PURPLE MOUSE-EARS

Family: Phrymaceae (lopseed family)

Scientific name: *Mimulus douglasii* (Benth.) A. Gray

Height: Up to 2".

Leaves: Opposite, the blade 0.2–1.2" long, oval, hairy, upper side glossy; margins scalloped or slightly lobed.

Flowers: Sepals fused into a 5-lobed tube; petals fused into a 5-lobed tube 0.8" to more than 1.5" long, the lower part of the tube very slender, the upper end abruptly widening into a bell with irregular purple and yellow stripes on the inside, the bell topped with 2 large upright lobes and 3 small lower lobes, all lobes bright magenta; stamens 4; ovary superior.

Blooms February through April.

Elevation: 150–4,000'.

Habitat: Banks of small creeks and open, rocky or gravelly sites that are moist in spring.

Comments: In northern California, this annual can be found in the North Coast Ranges, Klamath Ranges, and the foothills of the Cascades and Sierra Nevada. Its "Mickey Mouse" ears distinguish it from other purple or magenta monkeyflowers. The fruit is an asymmetrical capsule less than 0.3" long and about half as wide. Kellogg's monkeyflower (*Mimulus kelloggii*), which sometimes grows in the same locations, has much better developed lower petal lobes and 0.2–0.5" long, slender, often slightly curved seed capsules.

SEEP-SPRING MONKEYFLOWER

Seep-spring monkeyflower (*Mimulus guttatus*) on a cobble-strewn flood plain.

Seep-spring monkeyflower (*Mimulus guttatus*).

The inflated sepals of seep-spring monkeyflower (*Mimulus guttatus*) enclose its fruit, which is a small, dry seed capsule.

244

Family: Phrymaceae (lopseed family)

Also called: Seep monkeyflower or common monkeyflower

Scientific name: *Mimulus guttatus* DC.

Height: 1" to 5'.

Leaves: Opposite, the blade 0.2–5" long, oval to round, hairless or hairy, with or without a petiole; margins usually scalloped with some irregular lobes near the base.

Flowers: Usually at least 5 flowers per stem; sepals fused into a 5-lobed tube that expands into a 5-ribbed, asymmetrical balloon around the fruit; petals 5, their bases fused into a tube 0.1" to more than 1.5" long, yellow, the 3 lower petals with or without red spots; stamens 4; ovary superior.

Blooms March through August.

Elevation: Sea level to above 8,000'.

Habitat: A wide range of sunny, moist to wet locations, usually terrestrial.

Comments: This extremely variable species, common throughout northern California, can be annual or perennial. In spring it often forms a colorful border along freshwater creeks and roadside ditches, and occasionally it grows in shallow water or even forms floating mats. It also tolerates saline conditions: I've found towering individuals in brackish marsh in the San Joaquin–Sacramento River Delta and diminutive plants on salt-encrusted soil right next to some of Yellowstone National Park's hot springs. Even at the same location, the plants can vary considerably: One individual may be several times taller, with much larger leaves and flowers, than a daintier-looking neighbor; one may have red-spotted petals, another may lack spots, and so on. If you don't see five or more flowers per stem, check for unopened flower buds or maturing fruit.

Many-flowered monkeyflower (*Mimulus floribundus*), also widespread, sometimes grows in the same area as seep-spring monkeyflower but prefers moist, shady sites such as crevices in north-facing cliffs. The plants are hairy and feel a bit slimy. In shield-bracted monkeyflower (*Mimulus glaucescens*), found in the Cascade and Sierra Nevada foothills, the leaves are hairless and covered with a waxy bloom that gives them a blue-green cast; the uppermost pairs of leaves are completely fused into a round disk with the stem passing through its center.

Many-flowered monkeyflower (*Mimulus floribundus*) on a north-facing basalt cliff.

KELLOGG'S MONKEYFLOWER

Family: Phrymaceae (lopseed family)

Scientific name: *Mimulus kelloggii* (Greene) A. Gray

Height: 0.5–12".

Leaves: Opposite, the blade 0.2" to more than 1.5" long, oval, usually sparsely hairy, lower side often purplish; margins smooth or toothed.

Flowers: Sepals fused into a 5-lobed tube; petals fused into a 5-lobed tube 0.8–2" long, the lower part of the tube very slender, the upper end widening into a bell topped with 2 upper lobes and 3 slightly smaller lower lobes, all lobes deep to bright magenta with 2 parallel yellow stripes or oblong spots in the center lower lobe; stamens 4, anthers bright yellow; ovary superior.

Blooms March through June.

Elevation: 160–5,000'.

Habitat: Sparse grassland, open areas with thin or rocky soil, and disturbed sites.

Comments: This annual grows in the North Coast Ranges, Klamath Ranges, and Cascade and Sierra Nevada foothills, sometimes in great profusion. It's thought that the yellow stripes help guide pollinating insects to the nectar inside the petal tube.

LEWIS'S MONKEYFLOWER

Family: Phrymaceae (lopseed family)

Scientific name: *Mimulus lewisii* Pursh

Height: 10–32".

Leaves: Opposite, 0.8–3" long, narrow to oval, sessile, the leaf bases often clasping the stem, hairy; margins smooth or toothed.

Flowers: Sepals fused into a 5-lobed tube, hairy; petals also noticeably hairy and fused into a slender 5-lobed funnel 1.2–2" long, each lobe slightly notched at the tip with a lengthwise crease leading up to the notch, light pink to bright purplish pink with 2 parallel yellow ridges that start in the flower's "throat" and extend out into the middle of the center lower petal; stamens 4; ovary superior.

Blooms June through August.

Elevation: 4,000' to above 10,000'.

Habitat: Stream banks, springs, and seeps.

Comments: This herbaceous perennial spreads by creeping underground stems, sometimes forming good-sized patches. It's the only northern California monkeyflower that has such large pink flowers *and* grows in very moist, typically partly shaded sites; it occurs in the Klamath Ranges, Cascades, and Sierra Nevada as well as farther north and east.

MUSK MONKEYFLOWER

Family: Phrymaceae (lopseed family)

Scientific name: *Mimulus moschatus* Lindl.

Height: 2–12".

Leaves: Opposite, the blade 0.4–2.5" long, oval, more or less hairless to densely hairy and slimy-feeling, with or without a petiole; margins smooth or toothed.

Flowers: Sepals fused into a 5-lobed tube; petals fused into a slender 5-lobed funnel 0.6–1" long, yellow, usually with small red speckles and fine red or brown lines on the 3 lower lobes; stamens 4; ovary superior.

Blooms June through August.

Elevation: Sea level to 9,500'.

Habitat: Stream banks, seeps, and forest with moist soil.

Comments: This widespread herbaceous perennial grows in most of northern California except in the Sacramento Valley. Like many-flowered monkey-flower (*Mimulus floribundus*), it likes shady sites and tends to feel rather slimy, but the plants as a whole look "stockier" and the flowers are roughly twice as big as those of *Mimulus floribundus*.

PRIMROSE MONKEYFLOWER

Family: Phrymaceae (lopseed family)

Scientific name: *Mimulus primuloides* Benth. var. *primuloides*

Height: Stems 0.2–1.6" tall, topped by flowers borne on thin, wiry stalks 0.4–5" long.

Leaves: Opposite but so closely packed that they seem to be in rosettes, each leaf 0.3–1.5" long, oval, more or less sessile, upper surface densely long-haired or sometimes almost hairless; margins smooth or toothed.

Flowers: Borne singly; sepals fused into a 5-lobed tube, hairless; petals fused into a slender 5-lobed funnel 0.3–0.8" long, yellow, each lobe heart-shaped, usually with red spots on the 3 lower lobes; stamens 4; ovary superior.

Blooms June through September.

Elevation: 2,000' to above 11,000'.

Habitat: Wet meadows, stream banks, and seeps.

Comments: This dainty herbaceous perennial, common in northern California's mountains, spreads by creeping underground or aboveground stems and often forms big mats. It's easy to distinguish from other yellow-flowered monkey-flowers by its rosettes of exceptionally long-haired leaves and upright, hairless, ultra-slender flower stalks. *Mimulus primuloides* var. *linearifolius* has very narrow leaves; it mainly grows in the Klamath Ranges at elevations of 2,000–7,200'.

POKEWEED

Family: Phytolaccaceae (pokeweed family)

Scientific name: *Phytolacca americana* L. var. *americana*

Height: Usually up to 10', sometimes taller.

Leaves: Alternate, the blade 3–14" long by 1–7" wide, more or less hairless; margins smooth.

Flowers: Borne in 4–12"-long, often drooping clusters; sepals 5, white, pink, or magenta, resembling small petals; no petals; stamens 10; ovary superior.

Blooms in summer and fall.

Elevation: Sea level to above 3,000'.

Habitat: Disturbed sites, usually in partial shade.

Comments: This weedy herbaceous perennial is native to the eastern and midwestern United States. Occasionally it's planted as an ornamental for its red stems and handsome clusters of purple-black fruit. My next-door neighbor had one for a while, and I'm still pulling pokeweed seedlings 15 years later. Birds relish the berries, but all parts of the plant can be deadly poisonous to humans and livestock if eaten raw. The berries and very young leaves are said to be edible when cooked correctly, but the complicated process for removing the toxins hardly seems worth the potentially fatal consequences of any error. Early colonists in eastern North America used the juice of the berries as ink and dye and to "improve" cheap wine.

SYRIAN SNAPDRAGON

Family: Plantaginaceae (plantain family)

Scientific name: *Antirrhinum orontium* L.

Height: Up to 12".

Leaves: Lower leaves opposite, upper leaves alternate, very narrow, upper side deeply "creased" along the midrib, hairless or hairy; margins smooth.

Flowers: Sepals 5, very narrow, hairy, just barely fused at the base; petals fused into a wide 2-lipped tube, bright pink and white with darker pink veins, the upper lip 2-lobed, the lower lip 3-lobed and swollen so that it blocks the mouth of the tube; stamens 4; ovary superior.

Blooms March through May.

Elevation: Sea level to 3,000'.

Habitat: Flood plains and other disturbed areas.

Comments: This annual, native to the Old World's Mediterranean regions, is uncommon in northern California, but when and where it does occur, it can be quite abundant. In 2016 I found lots of it on a gravelly flood plain along the Lower American River; the following spring, after prolonged high flows, I didn't find a single plant. Spurred snapdragon (*Antirrhinum cornutum*) is one of five native species of *Antirrhinum* in northern California. It too is fairly uncommon, occurring mainly in the northern Sacramento Valley and nearby foothills; it has somewhat wider leaves and light pink petals.

GIANT BLUE-EYED MARY

Family: Plantaginaceae (plantain family)

Scientific name: *Collinsia grandiflora* Lindl.

Height: 2–14".

Leaves: Opposite or whorled in 3s or 4s, the blade 1–1.5" long, narrow, lower leaves with petioles, upper leaves sessile; usually covered with fine, very short hairs; margins smooth or slightly scalloped.

Flowers: Borne in several whorls, each flower with a small leaf-like bract just below the flower stalk; sepals 5, fused at the base; petals fused into a 2-lipped tube, the lower lip predominantly blue and 3-lobed with the middle lobe almost hidden by the lateral lobes, the 2-lobed upper lip mainly white with purplish speckles; stamens 4; ovary superior.

Blooms April through July.

Elevation: 1,000' to above 5,000'.

Habitat: Grassland, open woodland, and open, gravelly sites.

Comments: This annual, one of 10 species of *Collinsia* found in northern California, sometimes blooms in great profusion, especially in recently burned areas. It grows in the North Coast Ranges and Klamath Ranges and as far north as British Columbia.

CHINESE HOUSES

Family: Plantaginaceae (plantain family)

Scientific name: *Collinsia heterophylla* Graham var. *heterophylla*

Height: 4–20".

Leaves: Opposite, the blade 0.4–3" long, narrow or narrowly triangular, usually hairless, lower leaves with short petioles, upper leaves sessile; margins toothed.

Flowers: Borne in whorls; sepals 5, fused at the base; petals fused into a 2-lipped tube, the lower lip usually reddish purple and 3-lobed with the middle lobe almost hidden by the lateral lobes, the 2-lobed upper lip burgundy at the base, white with red or purple speckles in the middle, and solid white, pale lavender, or deep purple at the tip; stamens 4; ovary superior.

Blooms March through June.

Elevation: Sea level to above 4,000'.

Habitat: Woodland and shady spots in chaparral.

Comments: This annual grows in the North Coast Ranges, the Cascade and Sierra Nevada foothills, the Sacramento Valley's Sutter Buttes, and farther south. The seedlings usually have deeply lobed leaves, quite different from those formed later, hence the scientific name. Sticky Chinese houses (*Collinsia tinctoria*) is a sturdy plant up to 2' tall covered with glandular hairs; it too has whorled flowers, but generally the petals are white, pale yellow, or pale lavender with dainty purple markings.

NARROW-LEAVED BLUE-EYED MARY

Family: Plantaginaceae (plantain family)

Scientific name: *Collinsia linearis* A. Gray

Height: 4–16".

Leaves: Opposite, the blade 0.4–2" long, narrow, hairy, lower leaves with short petioles, upper leaves sessile; margins smooth.

Flowers: Borne on slender stalks in 2s, 3s, or 4s; sepals 5, fused at the base; petals fused into a bent 2-lipped tube 0.3–0.6" long with a conspicuous "hump" on the upper side, the lower lip white to bluish purple and 3-lobed with the middle lobe almost hidden by the lateral lobes, the 2-lobed upper lip white with purple speckles and two small bulges projecting into the flower's "throat"; stamens 4; ovary superior.

Blooms April through July.

Elevation: 600–6,500'.

Habitat: Woodland and open conifer forest.

Comments: In northern California, this dainty annual grows mainly in the Klamath Ranges and northern North Coast Ranges. Sticky blue-eyed Mary (*Collinsia rattanii*) has flowers only half as big; the petal tube is almost straight, its "hump" more or less hidden by the sepals. It occurs in the Cascades as well as the Klamath and North Coast Ranges. Both species have conspicuous glandular hairs on the sepals, flower stalks, and the slender bracts just below the flower stalks.

WRIGHT'S BLUE-EYED MARY

Family: Plantaginaceae (plantain family)

Scientific name: *Collinsia torreyi* A. Gray var. *wrightii* (S. Watson) I. M. Johnst.

Height: Usually 2–4", occasionally up to 10".

Leaves: Opposite, 0.6–1.5" long, narrow, usually sessile, hairy; margins smooth.

Flowers: Borne in pairs; sepals 5, fused at the base; petals fused into a wide 2-lipped tube 0.2–0.4" long, the lower lip mainly blue, lavender, or purple and 3-lobed with the middle lobe almost hidden by the lateral lobes, the 2-lobed upper lip white or pale lavender; stamens 4; ovary superior.

Blooms May through August;

Elevation: 2,500–13,000'.

Habitat: Subalpine areas and openings in conifer forest, often on sandy, granitic soil.

Comments: This diminutive annual often carpets the ground for a short time after the snow melts; a few weeks later, you won't find any trace of it. The plants are covered with dark-tipped glandular hairs. Broad-leafed blue-eyed Mary (*Collinsia torreyi* var. *latifolia*) has oval leaves. Both varieties grow in the North Coast Ranges, Klamath Ranges, and Cascades. Wright's blue-eyed Mary also occurs in the Sierra Nevada along with two more varieties of the species. Other very small species of *Collinsia* include maiden blue-eyed Mary (*Collinsia parviflora*) and spinster's blue-eyed Mary (*Collinsia sparsiflora*).

BRACTLESS HEDGE-HYSSOP

Family: Plantaginaceae (plantain family)

Scientific name: *Gratiola ebracteata* A. DC.

Height: 2–8".

Leaves: Opposite, 6–12 pairs of leaves per stem, each leaf 0.3–1" long, narrow to oval, sessile, the base often clasping the stem, upper leaves with short velvety hairs, lower leaves hairless; margins more or less smooth.

Flowers: Sepals 5; petals fused into a rather wide 5-lobed tube 0.2–0.3" long, tube, yellow to greenish white with purplish veins, lobes white, sometimes tinged pink; fertile stamens 2; ovary superior.

Blooms April through June.

Elevation: Sea level to almost 8,000'.

Habitat: Vernal pools and wet, muddy areas.

Comments: The common name of this annual is confusing because two of northern California's three species of *Gratiola* are bractless: Neither this species nor the rare Bogg's Lake hedge-hyssop (*Gratiola heterosepala*) have bracts below their flowers. The latter has four to seven pairs of leaves per stem, and two of its five petal lobes are light yellow; also, the tips of its leaves and sepals are rounded or notched, not pointed. Only clammy hedge-hyssop (*Gratiola neglecta*) has bracts; they're small and sepal-like, and each flower has two of them. Unlike most species of Scrophulariaceae, all the hedge-hyssops have completely free sepals.

GAPING BEARDTONGUE

Family: Plantaginaceae (plantain family)

Scientific name: *Keckiella breviflora* (Lindl.) Straw var. *breviflora*

Height: 20" to 7'.

Leaves: Deciduous, opposite, 0.4–1.5" long, narrow, almost sessile; margins generally toothed.

Flowers: Sepals 5, fused at the base, covered with long, spreading hairs; petals fused into a 2-lipped tube, white, cream-colored, or rose, the narrow, 2-lobed upper lip arching forwards and very hairy on its upper side, the 3-lobed lower lip with magenta stripes; fertile stamens 4 along with 1 sterile stamen (called a staminode); ovary superior.

Blooms May through July.

Elevation: Sea level to 6,500'.

Habitat: Chaparral, woodland, and dry rocky slopes.

Comments: In northern California, this shrub, called *Penstemon breviflorus* in older texts, occurs mainly in the Cascades and Sierra Nevada, including their foothills; it's more common farther south. Before the flowers open, the outside of the petals is rusty yellow. In late summer, the leaves often turn purplish brown before dropping off. *Keckiella breviflora* var. *glabrisepala* is very similar but has hairless sepals; it grows in the North Coast Ranges, Sacramento Valley, Cascades, and Sierra Nevada. Red beardtongue (*Keckiella corymbosa*) has scarlet petals; those of Lemmon's beardtongue (*Keckiella lemmonii*) are yellow striped with brownish purple.

SHARP-LEAVED FLUELLIN

Family: Plantaginaceae (plantain family)

Scientific name: *Kickxia elatine* (L.) Dumort.

Height: Usually a few inches, with leaning or sprawling stems forming mats that can be more than 3' wide.

Leaves: Alternate, the blade 0.4–1.5" long by 0.4–1" wide, oval to arrowhead-shaped, covered with long, soft hairs, petiole short; margins smooth.

Flowers: Borne singly on very slender flower stalks; sepals 5, fairly narrow, fused at the base, not enlarging as the fruit matures; petals fused into a 2-lipped tube with a long spur at its base, the 2-lobed upper lip velvety dark purple, the 3-lobed lower lip butter-yellow; stamens 4; ovary superior.

Blooms April through October.

Elevation: Sea level to 3,000'.

Habitat: Disturbed areas.

Comments: This annual, native to Europe, is widespread in the Sacramento Valley, the foothills to the east, and the North Coast Ranges. Round-leaved fluellin (*Kickxia spuria*) is very similar except for its oval to almost round leaves and relatively wide sepal lobes, which enlarge slightly as the fruit matures; it's less common in northern California. The two species can hybridize, and perhaps that accounts for the presence of both arrow-shaped and widely oval leaves on some plants in Sacramento County.

FALSE PIMPERNEL

Family: Plantaginaceae (plantain family)

Scientific name: *Lindernia dubia* (L.) Pennell

Height: A few inches, sometimes with leaning or sprawling stems up to 15" long.

Leaves: Opposite, 0.1–1.5" long, narrow to oval, sessile, usually hairless; margins smooth or toothed.

Flowers: Sepals 5, fused only at the base; petals fused into a 2-lipped tube 0.2–0.4" long, 2 hairy yellow ridges inside the "throat" of the tube, the 2-lobed upper lip pointing forwards; the larger, 3-lobed lower lip spreading, all 5 lobes white to pale lavender or blue, often edged with a slightly darker shade; stamens 2; ovary superior.

Blooms June through September.

Elevation: Sea level to 5,500'.

Habitat: Stream banks, flood plains, and wet meadows.

Comments: Although this little annual seems utterly inconspicuous to human eyes, it can be quite abundant, and herbivores don't seem to have any trouble locating it: I often find plants with their tops bitten off and new growth resprouting from lower down on the stem. The slender seed capsules are generally 0.3–0.4" long, and the seeds are yellow or golden yellow. The species grows in most of northern California except along the coast and on the Modoc Plateau.

PURDY'S FOOTHILL PENSTEMON

Family: Plantaginaceae (plantain family)

Scientific name: *Penstemon heterophyllus* Lindl. var. *purdyi* (D. D. Keck) McMinn

Height: Usually 10–30", occasionally up to 5'.

Leaves: Opposite, 0.8" to nearly 4" long by 0.1–0.3" wide, sessile, usually covered with short hairs; margins more or less smooth.

Flowers: Sepals fused into a 5-lobed tube, hairless; petals fused into a 2-lipped tube 1–1.5" long that narrows rather abruptly near its base, also hairless, yellow while the flower buds are expanding, then turning bright blue or sometimes pinkish purple, upper lip 2-lobed, lower lip 3-lobed; fertile stamens 4 along with 1 hairless sterile stamen (called a staminode); ovary superior.

Blooms May through June.

Elevation: Sea level to above 6,000'.

Habitat: Grassland, chaparral, and open areas in forest.

Comments: This herbaceous perennial or subshrub grows in the Sacramento Valley as well as the North Coast Ranges, Cascades, and Sierra Nevada. *Penstemon heterophyllus* var. *heterophyllus*, which occurs in the North and South Coast Ranges, is very similar except that its leaves are generally hairless and it produces very short, leafy side branches so that the leaves look as if they grew in small bundles. About eight additional species of *Penstemon* with showy blue flowers an inch or more in length can be found in northern California's foothills and mountains. They differ in details such as the shape of the petals, exactly how the anthers open to release their pollen, whether the stamens or staminode are smooth or hairy, and so on.

MEADOW PENSTEMON

Family: Plantaginaceae (plantain family)

Scientific name: *Penstemon rydbergii* A. Nelson var. *oreocharis* (Greene) N. H. Holmgren

Height: 8" to 2'.

Leaves: Opposite, 1–3" long, narrow, sessile, usually hairless; margins smooth.

Flowers: Usually borne in several fairly distinct whorls; sepals 5, narrow, fused only at the base; petals fused into a 2-lipped tube 0.3–0.6" long, blue to purple, the lower side of the "throat" of the petal tube densely hairy, upper lip 2-lobed, lower lip 3-lobed; fertile stamens 4 along with 1 sterile stamen (called a staminode), its tip covered with fairly long, golden yellow or brownish hairs; ovary superior.

Blooms May through August.

Elevation: 3,000' to above 11,000'.

Habitat: Wet to fairly dry meadows, stream banks, and sagebrush scrub.

Comments: This herbaceous perennial grows in the Cascades and Sierra Nevada as well as in Oregon and Nevada. When viewed from directly in front, each flower is wider than it's tall. Northern California has about 10 more species of *Penstemon* with relatively small blue flowers, as well as some pink-, white-, or purplish red-flowered species.

DWARF PLANTAIN

Family: Plantaginaceae (plantain family)

Scientific name: *Plantago erecta* E. Morris

Height: 1–12".

Leaves: In a basal rosette, 1" to more than 5" long, thread-like to narrow, sessile, usually with scattered silky hairs; margins smooth or with a few small teeth.

Flowers: Densely clustered, each flower roughly 0.2" wide; sepals 4, fused at the base, hairy, green; petals 4, fused at the base, translucent, papery, spreading or folded back, white or beige; stamens 4; ovary superior.

Blooms March through May.

Elevation: Sea level to above 2,000'.

Habitat: Dry grassland and woodland.

Comments: This little annual, called *Plantago hookeriana* var. *californica* in older references, is widespread from Baja California to Oregon and often quite abundant. The bract just below each flower is green, inconspicuous, and shorter than the sepals. Two non-native species look somewhat similar: In *Plantago aristata*, though, the bracts are 3–12 times as long as the sepals, very narrow, and spread outwards, making the inflorescence look bristly; in *Plantago pusilla*, which only grows 0.2–3" tall and generally is hairless, the flowers are less than 0.1" wide and slightly separated so that a bit of stem is visible between most of them.

ENGLISH PLANTAIN

Family: Plantaginaceae (plantain family)

Also called: Narrow-leaved plantain, ribgrass, or ribwort

Scientific name: *Plantago lanceolata* L.

Height: 8" to nearly 3'.

Leaves: In a basal rosette, the blade 2–10" long, narrow, the base tapered to the petiole, usually covered with short hairs, with several conspicuous parallel veins running the length of the leaf; margins usually finely toothed.

Flowers: Densely clustered, each flower roughly 0.2" wide; sepals 4, fused at the base, green; petals 4, fused at the base, translucent, papery, spreading, beige; stamens 4, with long thread-like filaments and white anthers; ovary superior.

Blooms April through August.

Elevation: Sea level to above 5,000'.

Habitat: Disturbed sites.

Comments: This widespread, weedy herbaceous perennial is native to Europe. Each initially egg-shaped inflorescence starts blooming at the bottom; as time goes on the inflorescence elongates into a slender cylinder with a steadily increasing number of brown, spent flowers at the bottom, a ring of open flowers with showy anthers in the middle, and a decreasing number of unopened flower buds at the top, each bud tucked under a green bract. Common plantain (*Plantago major*), another European species, also has ribbed leaves, but they're broadly oval, and most of the flowers in its pencil-thin inflorescences open at about the same time. Several additional species of *Plantago* grow in northern California, some native, some not, but none of them has inflorescences quite like those of English plantain, with a narrow but conspicuous ring of long-stamened flowers that slowly "travels upwards."

SEASIDE PLANTAIN
Family: Plantaginaceae (plantain family)

Scientific name: *Plantago maritima* L.

Height: 3–12".

Leaves: In a basal rosette, the blade 1–6" long, very narrow to narrow, the base tapered to a short winged petiole, fleshy, hairless; margins smooth or with a few small teeth.

Flowers: Densely clustered, each flower less than 0.1" wide; sepals 4, fused at the base, green; petals 4, fused at the base, translucent, papery, white, inconspicuous; stamens 4, with fairly short filaments and pale yellow anthers that turn dull orange or brown with age; ovary superior.

Blooms May through September.

Elevation: Sea level to 500'.

Habitat: Coastal bluffs and rocky outcrops.

Comments: This strictly coastal herbaceous perennial grows from a long taproot but also spreads by creeping aboveground stems that produce new rosettes of leaves at their tips. It can be found from southern California to Alaska and also along the Atlantic coast. It's northern California's only species of *Plantago* with succulent leaves.

WATER SPEEDWELL
Family: Plantaginaceae (plantain family)

Scientific name: *Veronica anagallis-aquatica* L.

Height: Usually 4" to 2', occasionally taller.

Leaves: Opposite, 0.8" to more than 3" long, fairly narrow to oval, usually sessile with 2 rounded lobes at the base clasping the stem, generally hairless; margins smooth or toothed.

Flowers: 0.2–0.4" wide; sepals 4, green; petals 4, fused at the base to form a very short tube, light blue or lavender with purple streaks; stamens 2, anthers blue; ovary superior.

Blooms March through September.

Elevation: Sea level to almost 10,000'.

Habitat: Slow-moving water, stream banks, and wet meadows.

Comments: This European herbaceous perennial is widely naturalized in northern California. Several other herbaceous perennial species of *Veronica*, though, are native to the region. They include American brooklime (*Veronica americana*), which occurs in most of the state; its leaves are always toothed, with a short petiole, and its flowers are medium blue. Marsh speedwell (*Veronica scutellata*) has sessile but very narrow leaves; it grows mainly along the coast and in the North Coast Ranges, Cascades, and Sierra Nevada. *Veronica wormskjoldii* can be found at elevations of 5,000–11,500'; its flowers are deep blue. All prefer very moist or wet habitats.

PURSLANE SPEEDWELL

Family: Plantaginaceae (plantain family)

Also called: Western speedwell, hairy purslane speedwell, or neckweed

Scientific name: *Veronica peregrina* L. subsp. *xalapensis* (Kunth) Pennell

Height: 2–12".

Leaves: Lower leaves opposite, 0.2–1" long, fairly narrow to spoon-shaped, more or less sessile, often slightly fleshy, sparsely hairy, some of the hairs glandular; margins smooth, wavy, toothed, or slightly scalloped; upper leaves alternate and smaller.

Flowers: Roughly 0.1" wide; sepals 4 or occasionally 5, green, nearly hairless to sparsely hairy; petals 4, fused at the base to form a very short tube, white, sometimes streaked with lavender; stamens 2, anthers white; ovary superior.

Blooms April through August.

Elevation: Sea level to above 10,000'.

Habitat: Riparian areas and other moist sites.

Comments: This annual is native from South America through Mexico to western Canada and occurs throughout northern California. The fruits are less than 0.2" long, heart-shaped, and full of minute seeds. Corn speedwell (*Veronica arvensis*), native to Europe, has wider leaves, hairy sepals, and equally tiny but bright to dark blue flowers; it's a common weed in lawns.

PERSIAN SPEEDWELL

Family: Plantaginaceae (plantain family)

Scientific name: *Veronica persica* Poir.

Height: Usually 1–2", with sprawling stems up to 2' long.

Leaves: Opposite, the blade 0.2–1" long, broadly oval to almost round, usually sparsely hairy, petioles short; margins scalloped, coarsely toothed, or lobed.

Flowers: 0.3–0.5" wide; sepals 4, green, hairy; petals 4, fused at the base to form a very short tube, the opening of the tube greenish yellow ringed with white, the rest of each petal bright blue with darker streaks; stamens 2, anthers blue; ovary superior.

Blooms January through May.

Elevation: Sea level to 3,600'.

Habitat: Moist, disturbed sites.

Comments: This widespread annual from western Asia is a common weed in lawns; it grows from a taproot. Chain speedwell (*Veronica catenata*) came here from Europe; it's a herbaceous perennial with creeping underground stems, has pink flowers 0.1–0.2" in diameter, and is often found in wet meadows and along slow-moving streams. A total of 11 species of *Veronica* grow in northern California, most of them in moist to wet habitats.

WESTERN SYCAMORE

Three female inflorescences.

Five male inflorescences.

Foliage in fall.

Bark.

Family: Platanaceae (sycamore family)

Scientific name: *Platanus racemosa* Nutt.

Height: Typically 30–50', although some trees exceed 100'.

Leaves: Deciduous, alternate, the blade 4–10" long and about equally wide, palmately 3- to 7-lobed, upper surface hairless to moderately hairy, lower surface densely covered with short woolly hairs; margins smooth to slightly toothed.

Flowers: Male and female flowers borne in separate spherical heads on the same tree, with 2–7 heads widely spaced on a long, dangling stalk; male flowers lacking sepals but with 3–6 tiny petals and 3–8 yellowish to greenish brown stamens; female flowers with 3–6 sepals and 3–6 petals, all tiny, and a superior ovary with a hairless maroon stigma.

Blooms February through April.

Elevation: Sea level to 6,500'.

Habitat: Riparian areas and canyon bottoms.

Comments: Western sycamore is common in the Sacramento Valley, Cascade and Sierra Nevada foothills, and farther south. The trunks, up to 5–6' in diameter but relatively short, often lean or even sprawl on the ground, sending up massive branches from the upper side "like a horse scratching his back on the ground and kicking up his legs," as D. C. Peattie put it in his *Natural History of Western Trees*. Other trees fork into two or more trunks. The wood is rather brittle (although when dry it's hard to split), and the ground under old trees is often littered with broken-off branches. Very young leaves are almost furry on both sides, but the upper side sheds most or all of its hairs as the leaves expand. The trees resprout quickly from the base of the trunk after wildland fire.

Two related species not native to California are often planted in urban areas: London plane (called *Platanus* x. *hispanica* by botanists and *Platanus acerifolia* in gardening books and the nursery trade) and American sycamore (*Platanus occidentalis*). London plane is a hybrid of American sycamore and Oriental plane (*Platanus orientalis*) that appeared in Oxford, England, around 1670 or possibly even earlier, presumably as a spontaneous crossing of two trees planted near each other. It's exceptionally tolerant of polluted air, but its shallow roots tend to heave nearby paving. The female inflorescences and seed balls are usually borne in pairs on a single stalk and have brown, densely hairy stigmas. The trees can hybridize with western sycamore. American sycamore, which is native to the eastern and central United States, produces its seed balls singly, not in short chains. In both species, the leaves tend to be less deeply lobed than in California sycamore.

Sweet gum (*Liquidambar styraciflua*), another native of eastern North America, also has palmately lobed leaves. Its bark, though, is rather ordinary-looking—gray and roughly furrowed, not peeling in colorful irregular plates like *Platanus*—and its hard, spiny, spherical fruits stay intact at maturity. See Plate 1 in the introduction for photos. It's widely planted in northern California, and you'll sometimes find it naturalized in riparian areas.

Each of these inch-wide balls developed from one female inflorescence. At maturity, they'll disintegrate into numerous bristly, 1-seeded fruits that can be dispersed by wind, water, or birds.

THRIFT

Family: Plumbaginaceae (leadwort family)

Also called: Sea pink

Scientific name: *Armeria maritima* (Mill.) Willd. subsp. *californica* (Boiss.) A. E. Porsild

Height: Up to 2'.

Leaves: All in a basal rosette, 2.5–5" long by no more than 0.1" wide, hairless; margins smooth.

Flowers: Borne on leafless stems in a compact, rounded cluster up to 0.8" wide; sepals fused into a pinkish, translucent, papery, 5-lobed cone; petals 5, bright pink; stamens 5; ovary superior.

Blooms February through September.

Elevation: Sea level to 800'.

Habitat: Coastal grasslands and bluffs.

Comments: This herbaceous perennial grows in coastal areas from the Channel Islands and central California to British Columbia; other subspecies occur farther north and in northern Europe. It spreads by creeping underground stems and is often used horticulturally in rock gardens. From a distance, coastal onion (*Allium dichlamydeum*), which often occurs in the same habitats, looks a bit similar. Its flowers, though, are slightly deeper purplish pink, and their three sepals look just like the three petals. Also, its leaves and flower stalks smell distinctly onion-like when bruised.

LARGE-FLOWERED COLLOMIA

Family: Polemoniaceae (phlox family)

Also called: Mountain collomia

Scientific name: *Collomia grandiflora* Lindl.

Height: 4" to more than 3'.

Leaves: Alternate, 1–2" long, narrow to very narrow, sessile, hairless or hairy; margins smooth.

Flowers: Borne in compact clusters at the top of the stem, sometimes with a few additional flowers farther down; sepals fused into a green, hairy, 5-lobed cone; petals fused into a narrow, 5-lobed trumpet 0.6–1.2" long, soft orange fading to almost white with age; stamens 5, anthers and pollen usually blue; ovary superior

Blooms April through June

Elevation: 400–10,000'.

Habitat: Fairly dry, open areas.

Comments: This annual with its rather unusual pastel orange flowers is widespread in most of northern California except in the Sacramento Valley. The region's six other species of *Collomia* all have smaller, pink, lavender, purple, or occasionally white flowers, some with a white or yellow center. The leaves of staining collomia (*Collomia tinctoria*) will turn your fingers yellow if you crush them. Talus collomia (*Collomia larsenii*) is the only perennial in the group; it's a rare, small, mounded plant with blue-green foliage and purple flowers that grows in the Cascades at elevations above 7,000' among volcanic boulders.

BLUEHEAD GILIA

Family: Polemoniaceae (phlox family)

Scientific name: *Gilia capitata* Sims subsp. *pedemontana* V. E. Grant

Height: 1–3'.

Leaves: Alternate, lower leaves 1–5" long, once or twice pinnately lobed, each lobe very narrow, hairless or sticky-haired; margins smooth; upper leaves smaller.

Flowers: Borne in tight spherical clusters at the tips of long flower stalks, the base of each cluster densely woolly; sepals fused into a 5-lobed tube; petals fused into a 5-lobed funnel, 0.3–0.5" long, light blue or violet; stamens 5, anthers blue; ovary superior.

Blooms April through June.

Elevation: 200–6,500'.

Habitat: Rocky slopes and open areas in conifer forest.

Comments: This annual grows in the Cascades, Sierra Nevada, their foothills, and the Sacramento Valley's Sutter Buttes. Several other subspecies occur elsewhere in the region; they differ in hairiness, the length and shape of the petals, and similar details. Blue coast gilia (*Gilia capitata* subsp. *chamissonis*) stands out by its bright purplish blue petals and skunky odor; it's uncommon and only grows in sandy areas near the ocean. California gilia (*Gilia achilleifolia* subsp. *achilleifolia*) has medium blue flowers clustered in domes in which you can easily see the attachment of the lower flowers to the stem.

BIRD'S-EYE GILIA

Family: Polemoniaceae (phlox family)

Scientific name: *Gilia tricolor* Benth. subsp. *tricolor*

Height: 4–15".

Leaves: Alternate, lower leaves 0.4–1.5" long, once or twice pinnately lobed, each lobe very narrow, upper side hairy; margins smooth; upper leaves smaller, usually palmately lobed.

Flowers: Mostly borne in fairly dense clusters of 2–5; sepals fused into a 5-lobed tube; petals fused into a 5-lobed funnel, 0.4–0.8" long, with a dark purple ring or spots inside the funnel and a yellow ring around its opening, the lobes light to medium blue or lavender; stamens 5, anthers blue or white; ovary superior.

Blooms February through May.

Elevation: Sea level to 4,000'.

Habitat: Grassland.

Comments: All of California's many species of *Gilia* are annual, generally with blue or violet petals. Most are restricted to central and southern California; the north only has six, of which bird's-eye gilia is the most common. It grows in the Cascade and Sierra Nevada foothills and the North Coast Ranges and can be exceptionally showy in a good year. *Gilia tricolor* subsp. *diffusa* has somewhat smaller, loosely clustered flowers. In drought years *Gilia tricolor* subsp. *tricolor* may only produce a few flowers and look very much like subspecies *diffusa*.

SCARLET GILIA

Family: Polemoniaceae (phlox family)

Scientific name: *Ipomopsis aggregata* (Pursh) V. E. Grant subsp. *aggregata*

Height: 1' to nearly 3'.

Leaves: Alternate, lower leaves 1–2" long, once pinnately lobed with 9–11 lobes, each lobe narrow with a pointed tip, hairless or hairy; margins smooth; upper leaves smaller.

Flowers: Borne all along the stem in clusters of 3–7; sepals fused into a short 5-lobed tube; petals fused into a 5-lobed tube, 0.8–1.2" long, bright red with white or pale yellow speckles; stamens 5, anthers projecting from the petal tube, pollen yellow, white, or blue; ovary superior.

Blooms June through September.

Elevation: 3,600' to above 8,000'.

Habitat: Open areas in forest or woodland.

Comments: This short-lived herbaceous perennial grows in the Klamath Ranges, Cascades, Sierra Nevada, and the northern part of the North Cast Ranges; usually the plants flower only once. The photo shows just one of the many clusters of flowers each plant produces; clusters can droop or angle upwards. In *Ipomopsis aggregata* subsp. *bridgesii*, found at elevations above 6,000' in the Sierra Nevada, the tips of the leaf lobes are blunt or rounded; the plants bloom more than once and usually have blue pollen.

SLENDER-FLOWERED SKYROCKET

Family: Polemoniaceae (phlox family)

Also called: Lavender gilia

Scientific name: *Ipomopsis tenuituba* (Rydb.) V. E. Grant

Height: Usually 8–16".

Leaves: Alternate, lower leaves 1–2.5" long, once pinnately lobed, hairless or hairy; margins smooth; upper leaves smaller.

Flowers: Borne all along the stem in clusters of 3–7; buds sometimes orange; sepals 5, fused at the base; petals fused into a very slender 5-lobed tube, 1–2" long, pink to lavender with white speckles; stamens 5, anthers barely projecting from the petal tube if at all, pollen usually yellow or white, sometimes blue-gray; ovary superior.

Blooms June through September.

Elevation: 7,800–10,000'.

Habitat: Sagebrush scrub and open, rocky or gravelly sites.

Comments: This short-lived herbaceous perennial usually blooms only once before dying; it grows in the Cascades and Sierra Nevada as well as on the Modoc Plateau and eastwards to the Rocky Mountains. It can hybridize with *Ipomopsis aggregata* and in some older references is considered a subspecies, *Ipomopsis aggregata* subsp. *attenuata*. As in several other members of this family, the common name reflects earlier classifications: There has been a lot of reshuffling of species of *Gilia*, *Ipomopsis*, *Leptosiphon*, *Linanthus*, and *Navarretia*, but the older common names are still widely used.

TRUE BABY STARS

Family: Polemoniaceae (phlox family)

Scientific name: *Leptosiphon bicolor* Nutt.

Height: 1–8".

Leaves: Opposite, palmately lobed with 3–7 narrow lobes, each lobe 0.1–0.5" long, rough-haired; margins smooth.

Flowers: Flower buds borne at the tip of the stem in tight clusters, each bud with a leaf-like bract just below it, usually only 1 flower open at a time; sepals 5, fused at the base; petals fused into an extremely slender 5-lobed tube, 0.5–1.5" long, the opening of the tube bright yellow, the petal lobes pink, pale yellow, or white; stamens 5, anthers yellow; ovary superior.

Blooms March through June.

Elevation: Sea level to 5,500'.

Habitat: Open areas in grassland, chaparral, and woodland.

Comments: This small annual is common in the North Coast Ranges and Cascade and Sierra Nevada foothills. Plants with different petal colors often grow intermingled. The flowers open mid-morning and close early in the evening. In older texts the species is called *Linanthus bicolor*. Viewed from above, the small flowers of thread linanthus (*Leptosiphon filipes*) look a bit similar, but in profile they're quite different, each on a 0.2–0.5"-long flower stalk with a short, funnel-shaped petal tube.

WHISKER BRUSH

Family: Polemoniaceae (phlox family)

Scientific name: *Leptosiphon ciliatus* (Benth.) Jeps.

Height: 1–12".

Leaves: Opposite, palmately lobed with 5–11 narrow lobes, each lobe 0.2–0.8" long, rough-haired; margins smooth.

Flowers: Flower buds borne at the tip of the stem in tight clusters, each bud with a leaf-like bract just below it, each bract fringed with stiff white hairs, usually only 1 to a few flowers open simultaneously; sepals 5, fused at the base; petals fused into a slender 5-lobed tube, 0.4–1" long, the opening of the tube bright yellow, the base of the petal lobes white and yellow with a dark pink or maroon spot, the rest of each lobe bright pink; stamens 5, anthers yellow; ovary superior.

Blooms March through July.

Elevation: Sea level to almost 10,000'.

Habitat: Dry, open or wooded sites.

Comments: Older texts call this annual *Linanthus ciliatus*; it sometimes blooms in great profusion and is common in most of northern California except near the coast. Nearly 20 species of *Leptosiphon* grow in the region, most with pink or white petals, but only whisker brush has such an intricate, colorful pattern on each petal lobe.

NARROW-LEAVED FLAXFLOWER

Family: Polemoniaceae (phlox family)

Scientific name: *Leptosiphon liniflorus* (Benth.) J. M. Porter and L. A. Johnson

Height: 4–20".

Leaves: Opposite, palmately lobed with 3–9 very narrow lobes, each lobe 0.4–1.5" long, hairless or hairy; margins smooth.

Flowers: Borne singly on long, very thin, dark reddish brown flower stalks; sepals fused into a narrow 5-lobed funnel, hairy; petals fused into a short, yellow, 5-lobed funnel, each petal lobe 0.3–0.4" long, white with lavender or purple streaks; stamens 5, anthers bright yellow; ovary superior.

Blooms April through June.

Elevation: Sea level to 5,500'.

Habitat: Dry, open areas and sparse woodland.

Comments: Older texts call this annual *Linanthus liniflorus*. It can grow in dense patches and may actually do better in drought years when there's less competition from annual grasses. As in some other species of *Linanthus*, each pair of leaves is so deeply lobed that at first glance you might mistake it for a whorl of almost needle-like leaves encircling the stem. Narrow-leaved flaxflower occurs from the western Mojave Desert through northern California up into Washington.

THIN-STEMMED NAVARRETIA

Family: Polemoniaceae (phlox family)

Scientific name: *Navarretia filicaulis* (A. Gray) Greene

Height: 3–8".

Leaves: Alternate, 0.4–1.5" long, with 2–6 pinnate lobes near the base, the center or main lobe by far the longest, each lobe very narrow and ending in a prickly point, usually sparsely hairy, sometimes sticky; margins smooth.

Flowers: Borne in many small clusters, each flower with a leaf-like bract just below it; sepals fused into a 5-lobed tube; petals fused into a narrow, yellow, 5-lobed funnel, 0.2–0.3" long, the petal lobes bright purple; stamens 5, anthers blue; ovary superior, style longer than the petals and tipped with 2 minute stigmas.

Blooms June through July.

Elevation: 1,000–4,000'.

Habitat: Chaparral and open areas in woodland and forest.

Comments: Like California's more than 30 other members of this genus, thin-stemmed navarretia is annual. It grows in the Cascades, Sierra Nevada, and on the Modoc Plateau. The thin, wiry stems are heavily branched and bloom profusely, and so for a short time in early summer the ground may seem carpeted purple. Bur navarretia (*Navarretia prolifera* subsp. *prolifera*), found only in the Sierra Nevada, also has intensely purple flowers, but they're tightly clustered in almost spherical heads.

BRIDGE'S GILIA

Family: Polemoniaceae (phlox family)

Scientific name: *Navarretia leptalea* (A. Gray) L. A. Johnson subsp. *leptalea*

Height: 3–15".

Leaves: Alternate, 0.4–2" long, very narrow, generally *not* lobed except for a few pinnately lobed leaves near the base of the stem, usually covered with small glandular hairs; margins smooth.

Flowers: Borne singly or in pairs on long, thin flower stalks; sepals fused into a 5-lobed tube; petals fused into a 5-lobed funnel, yellow at the base, its opening marked with long purple streaks, each petal lobe 0.1–0.2" long, bright pink; stamens 5, anthers blue; ovary superior.

Blooms June through September.

Elevation: 3,000' to almost 7,000'.

Habitat: Open, rocky sites.

Comments: Older texts call this dainty annual *Gilia leptalea* subsp. *leptalea*. In northern California it mainly grows in the Cascades, Sierra Nevada, and on the Modoc Plateau and, despite the wispy look of its stems and leaves, can carpet the ground with colorful flowers. Unlike many species of *Navarretia*, the plants don't feel the least bit prickly. Occasionally you may find a plant in which all leaves are pinnately lobed. In *Navarretia leptalea* subsp. *bicolor*, the opening of the petal tube (or "throat") ranges from yellow to almost white.

WHITE-HEADED NAVARRETIA

Family: Polemoniaceae (phlox family)

Scientific name: *Navarretia leucocephala* Benth. subsp. *leucocephala*

Height: 1–9".

Leaves: Alternate, 0.4" to more than 3" long, once or twice pinnately lobed, each lobe very narrow and ending in a prickly point, lower leaves hairless, upper leaves hairy at their bases; margins smooth.

Flowers: Borne in tight clusters, each flower with a leaf-like bract just below it; sepals fused into a 5-lobed tube, the lobes hairless; petals fused into a 5-lobed funnel that's longer than the sepals, the petal lobes narrowly oval, white; stamens 5, anthers white; ovary superior.

Blooms April through May.

Elevation: Sea level to almost 7,000'.

Habitat: Vernal pools.

Comments: This annual is one of a group—five subspecies of *Navarretia leucocephala*, two subspecies each of *Navarretia intertexta* and *Navarretia myersi*, and *Navarretia heterandra*—that grow in northern California's vernal pools and have white to light blue flowers. They differ in features such as whether the sepals are hairy, the length of the petal tube, the shape of the petal lobes, and exactly where the filaments are attached to the petals. Several members of the group are legally protected, and it can take a specialist to tell them apart.

DOWNY PINCUSHION

Family: Polemoniaceae (phlox family)

Scientific name: *Navarretia pubescens* (Benth.) Hook. & Arn.

Height: 5–13".

Leaves: Alternate, 0.6–2" long, once or twice pinnately lobed, each lobe very narrow and ending in a prickly point, lower leaves hairless, upper leaves hairy; margins toothed.

Flowers: Borne in dense spherical clusters, each flower with a leaf-like bract just below it, a few to many flowers open at the same time; sepals fused into a narrow funnel with 5 long, sharply pointed lobes; petals fused into a narrow 5-lobed tube, 0.4–0.6" long, the wider "throat" of the tube maroon or reddish purple, the lobes bright blue with purple veins; stamens 5, filaments purple, anthers cream-colored or white; ovary superior, style projecting well beyond the petals and ending in 2 small purple stigmas.

Blooms May through July.

Elevation: Sea level to 6,000'.

Habitat: Dry, open areas, especially those with gravelly or clayey soil.

Comments: In northern California, this tan- to reddish brown-stemmed annual can be found in the Sacramento Valley, North Coast Ranges, Klamath Ranges, Cascades, and Sierra Nevada. A few plants have flowers with a mainly white, purple-rimmed throat.

SKUNKWEED

Family: Polemoniaceae (phlox family)

Scientific name: *Navarretia squarrosa* (Eschsch.) Hook. & Arn.

Height: 4" to 2'.

Leaves: Alternate, 0.6–2" long, once or twice pinnately lobed, each narrow lobe ending in a hard, sharp point, often with some lobes on the lower side of the leaf making the leaves 3-dimensional, covered with long-stalked glandular hairs; margins smooth.

Flowers: Borne in dense spherical clusters, each flower with a leaf-like bract just below it, usually with relatively few flowers open at the same time; sepals fused into a narrow funnel with 5 long, sharply pointed lobes; petals fused into a narrow 5-lobed tube, 0.4–0.5" long, medium blue; stamens 5; ovary superior, stigmas 3.

Blooms June through August.

Elevation: Sea level to 3,600'.

Habitat: Open areas ranging from wet to dry.

Comments: This annual is aptly named: Its stench makes it easy to distinguish from California's numerous other species of *Navarretia*. It's most common in the North Coast Ranges, Klamath Ranges, and coastal areas but also occurs in the Sacramento Valley and Cascade and Sierra Nevada foothills. Unlike downy pincushion (*Navarretia pubescens*), skunkweed has solid blue petals and its stamens, style, and stigmas are hidden inside the petal tube.

MARIGOLD PINCUSHION

Family: Polemoniaceae (phlox family)

Scientific name: *Navarretia tagetina* Greene

Height: 3–12".

Leaves: Alternate, 0.8–2" long, twice or occasionally 3-times pinnately lobed, each very narrow lobe ending in a needle-sharp point, hairy near the base; margins smooth or toothed.

Flowers: Borne in dense spherical clusters, each flower with a leaf-like bract just below it; sepals fused into a narrow funnel with 5 toothed lobes; petals fused into a 5-lobed funnel about 0.4" long, pale to light blue; stamens 5, anthers yellow; ovary superior, style shorter than the stamens and topped with a 3-lobed stigma.

Blooms April through June.

Elevation: Sea level to above 5,000'.

Habitat: Vernal pools and open grassy areas.

Comments: A total of about 23 species of *Navarretia*, not counting subspecies, occur in northern California; several are rare. Marigold pincushion, however, is widespread throughout the region except along the coast. It can tolerate a wide range of moisture regimes, ranging from vernal pools to dry uplands. In eastern Sacramento County, it grows together with downy pincushion (*Navarretia pubescens*) in small clearings in blue oak woodland.

SPREADING PHLOX

Family: Polemoniaceae (phlox family)

Scientific name: *Phlox diffusa* Benth.

Height: A few inches, with creeping stems up to 12" long.

Leaves: Opposite, 0.4–0.6" long, sessile, very narrow but not spine-tipped, usually hairless except for some woolly white hairs at the base; margins smooth.

Flowers: Sepals fused into a 5-lobed tube; petals 5, fused at the base into a tube 0.4–0.5" long, pink, lilac, or white; stamens 5, anthers yellow; ovary superior.

Blooms May through August.

Elevation: 3,600' to above 11,000'.

Habitat: Sparse conifer forest near timberline and dry, open areas.

Comments: This mat-forming subshrub is common in northern California's mountains. Sometimes it's so abundant that, when white-flowered, it looks like small drifts of snow. A few other low-growing species of *Phlox* occur in the region but are less widespread, such as stiff or Douglas' phlox (*Phlox douglasii*). It grows mainly in sagebrush scrub and pinyon-juniper woodland at elevations above 5,000' and tends to form mounded cushions rather than flat mats; its leaves are sharp-tipped and covered with short glandular hairs. Most species of *Phlox* have petals with rounded or gently pointed tips, but showy phlox (*Phlox speciosa*), which has upright stems 8–16" tall, has white to bright pink petals that are heart-shaped to deeply two-lobed. You'll generally find it above 5,000'.

JACOB'S LADDER

Family: Polemoniaceae (phlox family)

Scientific name: *Polemonium californicum* Eastw.

Height: 5–10".

Leaves: Alternate, up to 6" long, once pinnately compound with 9–25 leaflets, leaflets narrow to oval, the leaflet at the end partly fused to its 2 neighbors, covered with soft glandular hairs; margins smooth.

Flowers: 0.3–0.6" wide; sepals 5, fused at the base, hairy; petals 5, fused at the base into a short tube, each petal light to dark blue or purple except for its bright yellow base and a narrow white band between the 2 other colors; stamens 5, anthers white; ovary superior.

Blooms June through August.

Elevation: 5,000' to above 10,000'.

Habitat: Dry, shady or open areas.

Comments: This herbaceous perennial grows in the Klamath Ranges, Cascades, and Sierra Nevada. *Polemonium pulcherrimum* var. *pulcherrimum* looks similar but grows primarily on talus (boulder fields) above 7,500'. It's sometimes called sky pilot, but the same common name is also used for a very different-looking alpine species in the Sierra Nevada, *Polemonium eximium*. Western Jacob's ladder (*Polemonium occidentale*) has yellow anthers but no yellow on its petals; it spans the same geographic range as *Polemonium californicum* but prefers moist habitats such as stream banks.

CALIFORNIA MILKWORT

Family: Polygalaceae (milkwort family)

Scientific name: *Polygala californica* Nutt.

Height: 2–14".

Leaves: Alternate, the blade 0.3–2.5" long, narrow to oval, sparsely hairy along the veins, petiole short; margins smooth.

Flowers: 0.3–0.6" long; sepals 5, 3 of them rather ordinary, 2 much larger, pink, petal-like; petals 3, fused at the base, narrow, purplish pink, the far end of 1 petal ballooning into a pouch that encloses the stamens and style and ends in a curved white "beak"; stamens usually 8; ovary superior.

Blooms April through July.

Elevation: Sea level to 4,500'.

Habitat: Coastal forest and chaparral.

Comments: This herbaceous perennial grows in the North Coast Ranges, Klamath Ranges, and coastal areas. In addition to the typical flowers described above, it often produces small bud-like flowers, 0.1–0.2" long, that never open and are self-fertilized. Sierra milkwort (*Polygala cornuta* var. *cornuta*) is a subshrub found in the Klamath Ranges, Cascades, and Sierra Nevada; all its flowers open, and the beak on its third petal is straight, thin, and greenish or dark pink. In eastern Lassen County, you may come across spiny milkwort (*Polygala subspinosa*). *Polygala* is California's sole representative of this small family, which has about 1,000 species worldwide.

WESTERN BISTORT

Family: Polygonaceae (buckwheat family)

Scientific name: *Bistorta bistortoides* (Pursh) Small

Height: 8–28", occasionally shorter.

Leaves: Mostly basal, the blade 1.5–12" long by 0.4–2" wide, often with a waxy bloom, upper side hairless, lower side hairless to somewhat hairy, petiole 0.4–2" long; margins smooth; stem leaves smaller, the uppermost ones sessile.

Flowers: In dense clusters that typically are 0.8–2" long by 0.4–1" wide; individual flowers about 0.2" wide; sepals and petals not differentiated, 5, fused near the base, white or pale pink; stamens 5–8, anthers yellow; ovary superior.

Blooms July through September.

Elevation: Sea level to 10,000'.

Habitat: Wet meadows, stream banks, and fresh-water marshes.

Comments: This herbaceous perennial grows from a thick, creeping underground stem. You'll find it mainly above 5,000' in the North Coast Ranges, Klamath Ranges, Cascades, Sierra Nevada, and the Modoc Plateau's Warner Mountains, but it also occurs in coastal freshwater marshes. The inflorescences can be fairly short, as shown here, or up to about twice as long as they are wide. Older texts call the species *Polygonum bistortoides*.

PINK SPINEFLOWER

Family: Polygonaceae (buckwheat family)

Scientific name: *Chorizanthe membranacea* Benth.

Height: Usually 4" to 2', occasionally taller.

Leaves: Alternate, 0.4–2.5" long, roughly 0.1" wide, sessile, woolly-haired; margins smooth.

Flowers: Borne in dense round clusters, each cluster with 2–5 leaf-like bracts just below it; each flower set in a wide-rimmed "urn" of 6 fused, hairy bracts with translucent, white or pale pink margins, the stout pink or red vein in the center of each bract ending in a hooked spine; sepals and petals 3 each, similar in appearance, tiny, white to rose; stamens 9, anthers red; ovary superior but hidden inside the wide part of the urn formed by the bracts.

Blooms April through July.

Elevation: Sea level to 4,500'.

Habitat: Dry, rocky, gravelly, or sandy areas.

Comments: This annual, common in northern California, is one of those confusing plants where not everything is what it seems at first glance. The bracts with their Velcro-like hooks stay wrapped around the fruit, and the seed heads readily break apart and cling to anything that brushes against them. Shown here are several seed heads; they're similar in size and overall appearance to the flower heads except for their pinkish tan color.

COAST BUCKWHEAT

Family: Polygonaceae (buckwheat family)

Also called: Seaside wild buckwheat

Scientific name: *Eriogonum latifolium* Sm.

Height: 8–28".

Leaves: Mainly clustered near the base of the stems, the blade usually 1–2" long by 0.6–1.5" wide, blue-gray, usually woolly on both sides, upper side occasionally hairless; margins smooth.

Flowers: Borne in dense round heads; sepals and petals 3 each, similar in appearance, white or pink with a darker pink vein down the center; stamens 9, anthers red; ovary superior.

Blooms throughout the year.

Elevation: Sea level to 250'.

Habitat: Coastal scrub, grassland, and bluffs.

Comments: This subshrub or herbaceous perennial is common on sandy soils along the coast from southern California's Channel Islands to Oregon. Sometimes the stems stand upright by themselves or clamber up into taller vegetation; other times they sprawl across the ground, forming mats that can be more than 6' wide. As in other members of this genus, there's a cone or tube of fused bracts below each flower that is often important in identifying species, but it's inconspicuous—what you first notice when you look at an intact inflorescence are the look-alike sepals and petals and the stamens. *Eriogonum* has about 250 species worldwide, nearly 120 of which (not counting the multiple varieties of many species) occur in California. Almost all have white, pink, or lemon-yellow flowers.

FREMONT'S WILD BUCKWHEAT

Family: Polygonaceae (buckwheat family)

Also called: Hairy-flowered buckwheat

Scientific name: *Eriogonum nudum* Benth. var. *pubiflorum* Benth.

Height: 1' to more than 4'.

Leaves: Mostly clustered at the base of the stems, the blade usually 0.4–3" long by 0.2–1.5" wide, upper side hairless or cobwebby to sparsely woolly, lower side densely white-woolly, petiole often longer than the blade; sometimes with a whorl of smaller, sessile leaves partway up each stem; margins smooth or wavy.

Flowers: Borne mainly at the tips of the branches in dense round heads; sepals and petals 3 each, similar in appearance, fused into a single 6-lobed funnel, hairy on the outside, white, cream-colored, or yellow; stamens 9; ovary superior.

Blooms June through October.

Elevation: Sea level to above 7,000'.

Habitat: Open, sandy or gravelly areas.

Comments: This herbaceous perennial occurs in most of northern California except near the coast. On a breezy day in late summer the small, pompom-like flower heads seem to dance a few feet above the ground. It's one of 14 currently recognized varieties of *Eriogonum nudum*; they all have rather stiff, upright stems but differ in features such as which parts of the plant are hairy or hairless, the size of the leaves, and whether the flowers are white, yellow, or pink.

Upper and lower sides of basal leaves.

WAND WILD BUCKWHEAT

Family: Polygonaceae (buckwheat family)

Scientific name: *Eriogonum roseum* Durand & Hilg.

Height: 4–16".

Leaves: Some clustered near the base of the plant, others alternate on the stems, the blade 0.2–2" long by 0.1–0.8" wide, usually woolly; margins smooth or wavy.

Flowers: Borne in dense round heads, several widely spaced heads per stem; sepals and petals 3 each, similar in appearance, fused into a single hairless 6-lobed tube, usually pink with a darker vein in the center of each lobe; stamens 9, filaments white, anthers pink; ovary superior.

Blooms May through November.

Elevation: Sea level to above 7,000'.

Habitat: Open, sandy or gravelly areas.

Comments: This annual is more common farther south but does occasionally appear in the Sacramento Valley, Cascade and Sierra Nevada foothills, Klamath Ranges, and North Coast Ranges. The stems are covered with long, flat-lying, silky hairs, and the multiple small flower heads strung out along each stem, resembling widely spaced beads, help distinguish it from other species of *Eriogonum*. In Sacramento County it sometimes grows together with Fremont's wild buckwheat (*Eriogonum nudum* var. *pubiflorum*).

LADY'S THUMB

Family: Polygonaceae (buckwheat family)

Also called: Spotted smartweed or red shanks

Scientific name: *Persicaria maculosa* Gray

Height: Generally 4–28", occasionally more than 4'.

Leaves: Alternate, the blade usually 2–4" long, occasionally significantly longer or shorter, fairly narrow, gradually tapered to the tip, hairless or bearing short, flat-lying hairs, sometimes with a dark purplish green blotch in the center; margins smooth.

Flowers: Borne in narrow, dense clusters; sepals and petals not differentiated, fused into a 4- or 5-lobed bell, deep pink to almost white; stamens 4–8, anthers pink or yellow; ovary superior.

Blooms June through November.

Elevation: Sea level to 5,000'.

Habitat: Margins of creeks and lakes and moist, disturbed sites.

Comments: This annual, native to Eurasia and formerly called *Polygonum persicaria*, is widespread throughout northern California. The stems can be upright or sprawling, but the flower clusters are always oriented more or less upright. It sometimes hybridizes with a native species, pale smartweed (*Persicaria lapathifolia*), which has greenish white to pale pink flowers borne in long, drooping clusters. False waterpepper (*Persicaria hydropiperoides*), some forms of water smartweed (*Persicaria amphibia*), and the non-native pinkweed (*Persicaria pensylvanica*) have pink flowers similar to lady's thumb but differ in various details.

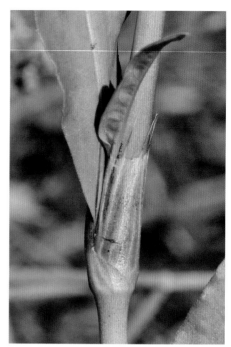

DOTTED SMARTWEED

Family: Polygonaceae (buckwheat family)

Scientific name: *Persicaria punctata* (Elliott) Small

Height: 6" to more than 3'.

Leaves: Alternate, the blade 2–6" long by 0.2–1" wide, gradually tapered to the tip, hairless or with short, flat-lying hairs mainly along the midrib, dotted with little round glands embedded in the leaf surface; margins smooth.

Flowers: Borne in narrow clusters; sepals and petals not differentiated, fused into a 5-lobed bell, white except for the greenish, gland-dotted base; stamens 6–8, anthers red, pink, or white; ovary superior.

Blooms June through November.

Elevation: Sea level to 5,000'.

Habitat: Shallow freshwater, river banks, flood plains, and marshes.

Comments: Older references call this annual *Polygonum punctatum*. In northern California it occurs mainly in the Sacramento Valley and the southern part of the North Coast Ranges, often in big patches. You may need a hand lens to see the small glands that help characterize the species. The flower clusters may grow upright or droop at the tip. In fall, the lower leaves wither, some stems turn reddish, and the plants start to look rather bedraggled, but they keep on flowering until late in the season. The shiny black or dark brown fruits, roughly 0.1" wide, can be flat like lentils or 3-sided like buckwheat kernels; they're an important food for many species of waterfowl, songbirds, and mammals, as are the equally small, seed-like fruits of northern California's other eight species of *Persicaria*. In each species, a delicate membrane (called an ocrea) wraps around the stem at the base of the leaf stalks; in dotted smartweed, it's edged with thin bristles 0.1–0.5" long.

SHASTA KNOTWEED

Family: Polygonaceae (buckwheat family)

Scientific name: *Polygonum shastense* W. H. Brewer

Height: 2–16".

Leaves: Alternate, the blade 0.2–1" long by 0.1–0.2" wide, hairless, leathery, with or without a short petiole; margins smooth and rolled under.

Flowers: Sepals and petals not differentiated, fused into a 5-lobed bell, 0.2–0.4" long, pink or white with darker veins; stamens 8, anthers red or pink; ovary superior.

Blooms July through September.

Elevation: 6,800' to above 11,000'.

Habitat: Rocky or gravelly areas.

Comments: In northern California, this gnarled, very low-growing shrub can be found in the Cascades and Sierra Nevada. It's one of more than 15 species of *Polygonum* that occur in the region; they range from annuals to herbaceous perennials to shrubs, and from rare to weedy. As in *Persicaria* and *Rumex*, there's a delicate membranous sleeve (called an ocrea) around the stem at the base of each petiole that is useful in identifying some species of *Polygonum*. Beach or dune knotweed (*Polygonum paronychia*) closely resembles Shasta knotweed but only grows near the ocean at elevations below 200'. Common knotweed or knotgrass (*Polygonum aviculare*), native to Europe, is a common annual weed in lawns, fields, and other disturbed places.

SHEEP SORREL

Family: Polygonaceae (buckwheat family)

Also called: Red-top sorrel, red-weed, field sorrel, sour dock, or sour grass

Scientific name: *Rumex acetosella* L.

Height: Usually less than 16".

Leaves: Sometimes all in a basal rosette, sometimes alternate on the stem, the blade 0.8–2.5" long, typically fairly narrow and arrowhead-shaped, the basal lobes often spreading, hairless; margins smooth.

Flowers: Male and female flowers borne on separate plants; both types nodding, less than 0.1" long, their 6 sepals and petals not differentiated, initially yellowish green but turning reddish with age; male flowers with 6 stamens; female flowers with a superior ovary topped by 3 stigmas.

Blooms March through November.

Elevation: Sea level to 10,000'.

Habitat: Grassland and disturbed areas.

Comments: This weedy, widespread, highly variable herbaceous perennial is native to Eurasia. Its creeping underground stems can form large stands of slender aboveground stems with fairly upright branches, and the plants tend to stand out by their reddish flowers and tiny, egg-shaped, reddish brown fruit. Confusingly, the common name sour dock is sometimes applied to curly dock (*Rumex crispus*). Red dock or fiddleleaf dock (*Rumex pulcher*) has more wide-spreading branches, narrow leaves with heart-shaped bases, and small, winged fruit with spine-like teeth.

CURLY DOCK

Family: Polygonaceae (buckwheat family)

Also called: Curly-leaved dock, sour dock, yellow dock, or narrow-leaved dock

Scientific name: *Rumex crispus* L.

Height: Usually 16–40", occasionally up to 5'.

Leaves: Alternate, the blade 6–14" long by 0.8–2.5" wide, hairless, lower leaves with petioles, upper leaves sessile; margins heavily ruffled, especially near the base of the leaf.

Flowers: Sepals 3, greenish to reddish; petals 3, green, often with pink edges, each with a whitish bump (resembling a short, fat maggot) enlarging and hardening around the developing fruit; stamens 6; ovary superior with 3 feathery stigmas.

Can bloom almost any time of year, depending on local weather conditions.

Elevation: Sea level to almost 9,000'.

Habitat: Disturbed areas.

Comments: This taprooted herbaceous perennial or sometimes biennial native of Eurasia is a common weed throughout California and tolerates a wide range of conditions. You're more likely to notice the tall, rusty brown fruiting stems than the greenish flowering ones. Bitter or broadleaf dock (*Rumex obtusifolius*), another Eurasian species, is less common in northern California; its leaves are 4–6" wide and up to 30" long and have smooth to finely ruffled margins. A total of about 20 species of *Rumex* occur in the region; they can be hard to identify, and to make things even harder, some of them hybridize. The visible distinctions between species focus largely on differences in the shape and color of their petals. Many botanical references lump the sepals and petals in this genus together as "perianth parts" or call them all sepals, but then they differentiate again between an inner and an outer set; for simplicity, I've retained the terms *sepals* and *petals*.

276

COMMON PURSLANE

Family: Portulacaceae (purslane family)

Also called: Pursley, pussley, pigweed, or little hogweed

Scientific name: *Portulaca oleracea* L.

Height: Usually 1–2", with sprawling, often reddish stems up to 16" long.

Leaves: Nearly opposite to clearly alternate, 0.1–1.2" long, oval to spoon-shaped with a rounded tip, more or less sessile, fleshy, hairless; margins smooth.

Flowers: 0.2–0.4" wide; sepals 2, fused at the base, green or reddish; petals 5, fused at the base, each petal heart-shaped or 2-lobed, bright yellow; stamens 5–20, anthers yellow; ovary half-inferior. Blooms April through October.

Elevation: Sea level to almost 7,000'.

Habitat: Disturbed areas.

Comments: This weedy, drought-tolerant annual may be native to Europe or northern Africa but now occurs almost worldwide; evidence from old sediments in lakebeds suggests that it may have arrived in California before the Spanish. Perhaps it was carried here by birds: Some of the tiny black seeds do survive ingestion. California's only other representative of the genus, desert portulaca (*Portulaca halimoides*), has finger-like, fleshy leaves 0.1–0.6" long and is native from southern California to Texas and Mexico; back in 1928 it also grew in Yolo County but apparently hasn't been found again in northern California.

PADRE'S SHOOTING STAR

Family: Primulaceae (primrose family)

Scientific name: *Primula clevelandii* (Greene) Mast & Reveal var. *patula* (Kuntze) Mast & Reveal

Height: 2–18".

Leaves: In a basal rosette, the blade 0.4–7" long, narrow to oval, typically with short glandular hairs; margins more or less smooth to toothed.

Flowers: Similar to those of mosquito bills (*Primula hendersonii*, described on the next page), but with 5 petal lobes 0.2–1" long, frequently with a conspicuous twist and often white or cream-colored, sometimes pink; stamens purple and yellow; stigma at most marginally wider than the style but never pinhead-like. Blooms March through May.

Elevation: Sea level to 2,000'.

Habitat: Grassland and other open areas with moist soil in spring.

Comments: Until recently, this herbaceous perennial was classified as *Dodecatheon clevelandii* subsp. *patulum*. It occurs in the Sacramento Valley and the Cascade and Sierra Nevada foothills and can tolerate alkaline conditions. As the fruit starts to develop, the flower stalks straighten and the small seed capsules are held upright. Five other species of shooting star also grow in northern California, all with short, wide filaments; the details of the filaments' color, surface texture, and whether they're free or fused are important in identification.

277

MOSQUITO BILLS

Family: Primulaceae (primrose family)

Also called: Sailors' caps

Scientific name: *Primula hendersonii* (A. Gray) Mast & Reveal

Height: 5–18".

Leaves: In a basal rosette, the blade 1–7" long, oval, hairless or hairy; margins smooth to toothed.

Flowers: Borne in nodding umbels of 3–17 flowers; sepals 4 or 5, fused at the base, bent back so that they're parallel to the flower stalk, green; petals 4 or 5, also fused at the base and swept back so that they point upwards, the lobes 0.2–1" long, their bases banded black (or dark maroon), then yellow, then white, the rest usually lavender to magenta, occasionally white; stamens 4 or 5, pointing to the ground, dark maroon to black; ovary superior, the stigma no wider than the style.

Blooms March through July.

Elevation: Sea level to above 6,000'.

Habitat: Woodland and other shady sites.

Comments: Until recently, this rather variable herbaceous perennial was classified as *Dodecatheon hendersonii*. Possibly it hybridizes with *Primula clevelandii*. It's widespread throughout northern California except on the Modoc Plateau. Even on the same plant, some flowers may have all their parts in fours, others all in fives.

SIERRA SHOOTING STAR

Family: Primulaceae (primrose family)

Scientific name: *Primula jeffreyi* (Van Houtte) Mast & Reveal

Height: 4" to 2'.

Leaves: In a basal rosette, the blade 4–20" long, narrow, hairless; margins smooth to scalloped.

Flowers: Similar to those of mosquito bills (*Primula hendersonii*) except for 0.4–1"-long petal lobes, dark purple stamens, and a pinhead-like stigma.

Blooms June through August.

Elevation: 2,000–10,000'.

Habitat: Stream banks and moist to dry meadows.

Comments: This hairy-stemmed herbaceous perennial, formerly classified as *Dodecatheon jeffreyi*, occurs in the North Coast Ranges, Klamath Ranges, Cascades, and Sierra Nevada as well as on the Modoc Plateau. Although the flowers hang upside down, the flower stalk straightens as the fruit ripens so that the mature seed capsules point straight up. Alpine shooting star (*Primula tetrandra*, formerly *Dodecatheon alpinum*) grows in wet meadows and along streams above 5,500'; it has hairless stems, often very narrow leaves 1–8" long with smooth margins, and flowers with their parts always in fours. In both species, the stigma looks like a miniature pinhead. Northern California has a few other species of *Primula* with nodding flowers, but their stigmas are at most marginally wider than the style.

MONKSHOOD

Family: Ranunculaceae (buttercup family)

Scientific name: *Aconitum columbianum* Nutt. subsp. *viviparum* (Greene) Brink

Height: Usually 1–5', occasionally up to 7'.

Leaves: Alternate, lower leaves 2–6" wide, palmately divided into 3–5 wedge- or diamond-shaped segments, hairless or finely hairy; margins irregularly toothed or lobed; upper leaves smaller.

Flowers: Sepals 5, petal-like, hairy, usually light to dark blue, sometimes dingy yellowish green, the upper arched into a helmet or hood 0.6–1" tall, the 2 at the sides round to kidney-shaped, the lower 2 narrower and smaller; petals 2, small, blue or whitish, tucked inside the "helmet"; stamens 20–50; pistils 3–5, ovaries superior.

Blooms July through September.

Elevation: 3,000' to above 8,000'.

Habitat: Stream banks and other moist areas in forest or meadows.

Comments: This herbaceous perennial grows in the Klamath Ranges, Cascades, and Sierra Nevada. The subspecies gets its name from small, pale outgrowths at the base of the petioles and flower stalks; these little lumps, called bulblets, break off and grow into new plants genetically identical to their parent. *Aconitum columbianum* subsp. *columbianum* is very similar except for not producing bulblets; it grows at elevations of 1,000' to above 11,000'. Both are deadly poisonous to livestock and humans.

WESTERN COLUMBINE

Family: Ranunculaceae (buttercup family)

Scientific name: *Aquilegia formosa* DC.

Height: Usually 8" to 3', occasionally up to 5'.

Leaves: Basal leaves usually divided into 3s, then divided into 3s again, leaflets typically 0.3–2" long, hairless; upper leaves smaller, unlobed to deeply 3-lobed.

Flowers: Nodding; sepals 5, petal-like, spreading, red; petals 5, each forming a long, narrow cone (called a spur) 0.5–1" long, the closed end red, the open end yellow, the opening itself usually not visible when you look at the flower in profile; stamens numerous, anthers yellow; pistils usually 5, ovaries superior.

Blooms April through September.

Elevation: Sea level to almost 11,000'.

Habitat: Stream banks, forest, woodland, and chaparral.

Comments: This herbaceous perennial grows throughout northern California except in the Sacramento Valley. In sticky columbine (*Aquilegia eximia*), found in the North Coast Ranges, the openings of the petals generally slant out and are more easily visible in the dangling flowers, and the plants are covered with sticky glandular hairs. Both are pollinated by hummingbirds that brush against the anthers and stigmas as they probe for nectar. *Aquilegia pubescens*, a Sierra Nevadan species, has white, cream, or pale pink flowers that are pollinated by night-flying hawkmoths.

MARSH MARIGOLD

Family: Ranunculaceae (buttercup family)

Scientific name: *Caltha leptosepala* DC.

Height: 3–20".

Leaves: Mostly basal with no more than 1 leaf on the stem, the blade 0.8" to almost 4" wide, round to kidney- or heart-shaped, hairless, petiole 1–10" long; margins smooth to scalloped.

Flowers: Sepals 5–11, 0.3–0.8" long, petal-like, white to pale yellow; no petals; stamens numerous, anthers bright yellow; pistils 5 to many, ovaries superior, each turning into a small, dry fruit.

Blooms May through July.

Elevation: 3,000' to almost 11,000'.

Habitat: Marshes, wet meadows, stream banks, and shallow, gently flowing or standing water.

Comments: Some older texts call this herbaceous perennial *Caltha howellii*. In northern California it grows in the Klamath Ranges, Cascades, Sierra Nevada, and on the Modoc Plateau. The flowers start opening soon after the snow melts, and if you find them at that time, they may be all you may see—the leaves emerge more slowly. Yellow marsh marigold (*Caltha palustris*), which has become naturalized in some wetlands in coastal areas and the North Coast Ranges, has more than one leaf per stem and bright yellow flowers that resemble big buttercups (*Ranunculus* spp.); it's native from Alaska to Nebraska, Tennessee, and Newfoundland. Some species of *Anemone* have flowers somewhat similar to marsh marigold, but the plants have compound leaves and grow in drier habitats.

CHAPARRAL CLEMATIS

Family: Ranunculaceae (buttercup family)

Also called: Pipestem clematis

Scientific name: *Clematis lasiantha* Nutt.

Height: Up to 16'.

Leaves: Deciduous, opposite, once pinnately compound with 3–5 leaflets per leaf, hairy, the largest leaflet 0.8–2.5" long; leaflet margins 3-lobed or coarsely toothed.

Flowers: Male and female flowers usually borne on the same plant; both types with 4 sepals per flower and no petals, each sepal 0.4–0.9" long, creamy white, and hairy on both sides; male flowers with 50–100 stamens, quite a bit shorter than the sepals, white to yellow, filaments usually flattened like paper matches; female flowers with 75–100 pistils, ovaries superior, each pistil maturing into a small, hard fruit with a long, feathery, white "tail."

Blooms January through June.

Elevation: Sea level to 6,500'.

Habitat: Chaparral and open woodland.

Comments: This woody vine grows in fairly dry places in the Klamath Ranges, the Cascade and Sierra Nevada foothills, the Sacramento Valley's Sutter Buttes, and the eastern part of the North Coast Ranges. Northern California's only other species in the genus is western virgin's bower (*Clematis liguisticifolia*), which grows along streams and in other wet areas. It has 5–15 leaflets per leaf and flowers with sepals only 0.2–0.4" long; its male flowers have 25–50 stamens equal to the sepals in length, while the female flowers have 25–65 pistils. The state's third species of *Clematis*, in which the upper side of the sepals is hairless, is restricted to southern California.

HANSEN'S LARKSPUR

Family: Ranunculaceae (buttercup family)

Scientific name: *Delphinium hansenii* (Greene) Greene subsp. *hansenii*

Height: 16" to 6'.

Leaves: Basal leaves 1.5" to nearly 4" wide, palmately 3- to 15-lobed, hairy, usually withered by the time the plants bloom; stem leaves alternate, smaller.

Flowers: Borne in narrow clusters with 12 or more flowers per stem, individual flowers borne on finely hairy stalks that are usually, although by no means always, less than 0.4" apart; sepals 5, petal-like, often dark blue, occasionally white or pink, with a grayish or dull greenish blotch at the tip of each, the uppermost sepal drawn into a slender cone called the spur that points back towards the stem; petals 4, each petal 2-lobed, much smaller than the sepals, purplish blue to white, the ends of the upper 2 petals tucked into the spurred sepal, the lower 2 petals hairy; stamens many, anthers yellow or greenish; pistils 3, ovaries superior, each pistil maturing into a thin-walled fruit that splits open along one side to release numerous small, grayish brown seeds.

Blooms March through July.

Elevation: Sea level to 10,000'.

Habitat: Grassland and oak woodland.

Comments: This herbaceous perennial grows in the Sacramento Valley, the Cascade and Sierra Nevada foothills, and the eastern part of the North Coast Ranges. Neighboring plants can vary a lot: One may have densely crowded flowers, another may have flowers spaced widely enough for the long spurs extending past its stem to be clearly visible, falsely giving the stem a zigzag look. What they all have in common are the seeds. Many of California's 27 or so species of *Delphinium* have winged seeds, but in Hansen's larkspur they're wingless and oddly shaped, a bit as if you cut a few inches off the end of a cucumber, covered the stub with short, dense bristles, and then miniaturized the whole thing. Royal larkspur (*Delphinium variegatum* subsp. *variegatum*) has winged seeds and usually fewer than 10 flowers per stem; it sometimes grows near Hansen's larkspur, and the two can hybridize.

Two of northern California's larkspurs stand out by their color: The relatively common red larkspur (*Delphinium nudicaule*) has bright red or once in a while light yellow sepals, while the rare golden larkspur (*Delphinium luteum*), restricted to coastal areas in Marin and Sonoma counties, always has yellow sepals. To identify many of northern California's nearly 20 species of *Delphinium*, though, you need the entire plant, including roots and seeds.

What looks like a single seed capsule is actually a cluster of three separate fruits, each derived from one of the three pistils in each flower.

SPREADING LARKSPUR

Family: Ranunculaceae (buttercup family)

Also called: Zigzag larkspur

Scientific name: *Delphinium patens* Benth. subsp. *patens*

Height: 4" to 3'.

Leaves: Mainly on the lower third of the stem, alternate, the blade 1.5" to nearly 4" wide, deeply palmately 3- to 5-lobed, each lobe generally less than 0.6" wide, more or less hairless.

Flowers: See Hansen's larkspur (*Delphinium hansenii* subsp. *hansenii*) for a general description of larkspur flowers. Spreading larkspur differs in usually having fewer than 12 flowers per stem; individual flower stalks generally are hairless, more than 0.4" apart, almost at right angles to the stem, and long enough to hold the sepal spur away from the stem. The sepals range from bright blue to dark purplish blue; some or all of the petals can be pale and streaked with purple.

Blooms March through June.

Elevation: 250–3,600'.

Habitat: Grassland and open woodland.

Comments: This hollow-stemmed herbaceous perennial grows in the Sacramento Valley, Cascade and Sierra Nevada foothills, and southern part of the North Coast Ranges. Its shiny seeds have a raised rim or "collar" at one end and two narrow wings. Like most species of *Delphinium*, it's seriously toxic to livestock.

ROYAL LARKSPUR

Family: Ranunculaceae (buttercup family)

Scientific name: *Delphinium variegatum* Torr. & A. Gray subsp. *variegatum*

Height: Usually less than 20".

Leaves: Mainly on the lower third of the stem or clustered near the base, alternate, the blade 1.5" to nearly 4" wide, palmately 3- to 15-lobed, the lobes often overlapping, hairy.

Flowers: See Hansen's larkspur (*Delphinium hansenii* subsp. *hansenii*) for a general description of larkspur flowers. Royal larkspur differs in usually having 2–10 flowers per stem; individual flower stalks are finely hairy and 0.4–1" apart. The sepals usually are rather wide, slightly overlapping, and dark purplish blue. Occasionally they're light blue or even white. The spur is 0.4–0.8" long and tends to be straight or curve downwards.

Blooms March through May.

Elevation: 60' to above 2,500'

Habitat: Grassland and open oak woodland.

Comments: In northern California, this herbaceous perennial grows along the coast and in the North Coast Ranges, Sacramento Valley, Cascades, and Sierra Nevada foothills. The flowers on each plant can be widely spaced, as shown here, or moderately clustered. Royal larkspur hybridizes with four other species, including Hansen's larkspur (*Delphinium hansenii* subsp. *hansenii*).

PLANTAIN-LEAVED BUTTERCUP

Family: Ranunculaceae (buttercup family)

Also called: Water plantain buttercup

Scientific name: *Ranunculus alismifolius* Benth. var. *hartwegii* (Greene) Jeps.

Height: 4–12".

Leaves: Mainly basal, the blade 1.5–4" long by about 0.4" wide, the base gradually tapered into the petiole, hairless; margins smooth or gently wavy; stem leaves (if any) smaller and sessile.

Flowers: Sepals 5, greenish; petals typically 4–6, sometimes 7 or 8, each petal 0.2–0.3" long, bright yellow, the lower part exceptionally shiny; stamens many, yellow; pistils many, ovaries superior, greenish yellow, each pistil ripening into a small, hard, 1-seeded fruit.

Blooms April through August.

Elevation: 4,000–7,000'.

Habitat: Meadows and open lodgepole pine forest.

Comments: This herbaceous perennial starts blooming soon after the snow melts. It grows in the North Coast Ranges, Sierra Nevada, on the Modoc Plateau, and as far north as Washington and Wyoming. *Ranunculus alismifolius* var. *alismifolius* has leaves 2.5–6" long and 0.4–1.2" wide with minutely toothed margins; its petals are 0.3–0.5" long, and it prefers sites that stay wet for a longer time such as wet meadows, bogs, and shallow streams. *Ranunculus alismifolius* var. *alismellus* also likes damp to wet sites; its leaves are oval, 1–2" long, and have smooth margins. *Ranunculus alismifolius* var. *lemmonii* has the largest flowers, with petals 0.4–0.6" long, and occurs in meadows on the Modoc Plateau and in the Sierra Nevada. In none of these four varieties do the stems take root if they touch the ground. The leaves and flowers of greater creeping spearwort (*Ranunculus flammula*) resemble those of plantain-leaved buttercup, but like strawberry (*Fragaria* spp.), the plants produce runners that root and develop new plantlets as they cross the pond margins and other muddy sites where this species is most often found.

Ranunculus aquatilis var. *diffusus*.

Ranunculus aquatilis var. *diffusus*.

WHITE WATER CROWFOOT

Family: Ranunculaceae (buttercup family)

Scientific name: *Ranunculus aquatilis* L. var. *diffusus* With.

Height: 2–32".

Leaves: Alternate, the blade of both floating and underwater leaves divided 3–6 times into thread-like segments.

Flowers: Sepals 5, greenish; petals 5, 0.2–0.3" long, solid white or white with a yellow base; stamens many, yellow; pistils 15 or more, ovaries superior, greenish yellow.

Blooms March through September.

Elevation: Sea level to above 10,000'.

Habitat: Marshes, streams, ponds, lakes, and relatively deep vernal pools.

Comments: This widespread herbaceous perennial typically grows in fairly shallow water but can also be found sprawled across muddy ground, the stems rooting where they touch it. *Ranunculus aquatilis* var. *aquatilis* differs in having two kinds of leaves: Those submersed in water are as described above, while those floating on the surface have 3- to 5-lobed blades 0.3–1" wide; it too occurs throughout northern California. The rare Lobb's aquatic buttercup (*Ranunculus lobbii*) is annual. It occurs mainly in the southern part of the North Coast Ranges and the San Francisco Bay region; its small floating leaves, 0.3–0.6" wide, are deeply 3-lobed, the two lateral lobes heart-shaped, and its flowers only have 5–15 stamens and 2–6 pistils. Waterfall buttercup (*Ranunculus hystriculus*), another white-flowered species, can be found in wet, rocky spots along streams in the Sierra Nevada and southern Cascades; all its leaves are roundish and shallowly palmately lobed.

Ranunculus aquatilis var. *aquatilis*.

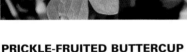

PRICKLE-FRUITED BUTTERCUP

Family: Ranunculaceae (buttercup family)

Also called: Spiny buttercup or rough-seeded buttercup

Scientific name: *Ranunculus muricatus* L.

Height: 2–20".

Leaves: Mainly in a loose basal rosette, the blade 0.8–2" long by 1.2" to almost 3" wide, usually palmately 3-lobed, each lobe coarsely scalloped or with a few smaller lobes, hairless or sparsely hairy, upper side rather shiny.

Flowers: Sepals 5, greenish; petals 5, 0.2–0.3" long, bright yellow; stamens usually 10, yellow; pistils 10–20, ovaries superior, more conspicuous than the stamens, greenish yellow, each pistil ripening into a flat fruit about 0.2" long studded on both sides with short, thick, curved spines.

Blooms April through June.

Elevation: Sea level to above 2,000'.

Habitat: Grassland, stream banks, and oak woodland.

Comments: This annual or biennial, native to Eurasia, is widespread in the Sacramento Valley, Sierra Nevada foothills, North Coast Ranges, and coastal areas. It's a common weed in lawns and can invade vernal pools. California has several other low-growing, weedy species of *Ranunculus*; you generally need fruit as well as flowers and leaves to identify them.

WESTERN BUTTERCUP

Family: Ranunculaceae (buttercup family)

Scientific name: *Ranunculus occidentalis* Nutt. var. *occidentalis*

Height: 4" to 2'.

Leaves: Lower leaves alternate, the blade 0.6" to more than 2" long by 1–3.5" wide, deeply palmately lobed to once palmately compound with 3 main lobes or leaflets, each further lobed or coarsely toothed, usually bearing short, hard, flat-lying hairs; upper leaves smaller.

Flowers: Sepals 5, greenish yellow, falling off soon after the flowers open; petals 5–6, 0.2–0.4" long, bright yellow, the lower part exceptionally shiny; stamens 25–50, yellow; pistils usually 8–15, yellow, ovaries superior, each pistil ripening into a flat, hairless to bristly, 1-seeded fruit less than 0.2" long with a pointed, curved tip.

Blooms March through July.

Elevation: Sea level to 5,000'.

Habitat: Grassland and woodland with moist soil in spring.

Comments: This herbaceous perennial, which grows in most of northern California except in the Sacramento Valley, is the most common of four varieties of *Ranunculus occidentalis* and is typical of the region's dozen or so species of relatively tall, upright-growing, terrestrial buttercups. As with most species of *Ranunculus*, it helps to have fruit as well as flowers and leaves for identification.

BUCKBRUSH

Family: Rhamnaceae (buckthorn family)

Scientific name: *Ceanothus cuneatus* Nutt. var. *cuneatus*

Height: Up to 10'.

Leaves: Evergreen, opposite, the blade 0.5–1.2" long, fairly narrow to oval, leathery, upper side glossy and hairless, lower side hairless or with short, flat-lying hairs; margins usually smooth.

Flowers: Sepals 5, spreading, petal-like, usually white; petals 5, spoon-shaped with a long narrow base, smaller than the showy sepals, usually white; stamens 5, anthers yellow; ovary partly inferior with the bases of the sepals and petals fused to its lower half, surrounded by a yellowish nectar-secreting disk, stigmas 3.

Blooms February through May.

Elevation: Sea level to 7,000'.

Habitat: Chaparral and other open, dry, often sandy or rocky sites.

Comments: This shrub is widespread in most of northern California except in the Central Valley, where it has been reported only from the Sutter Buttes. Each flower bud is protected by a hairy purplish scale that drops off as the sepals and petals expand; the flowers themselves can be so profuse that the entire bush looks white. The fruit is a dry capsule, about 0.2" wide and topped with three small bumps, that splits open to release its three, shiny black seeds. Even when not blooming, the species is relatively easy to recognize by its pale grayish brown, very stiff but not spiny twigs and small, thick, smooth-margined leaves. Mountain whitethorn (*Ceanothus cordulatus*) also has white flowers but spiny, light gray twigs and matte, gray-green leaves; it's usually less than 5' tall and grows at elevations of 1,100–11,000'. Tobacco brush (*Ceanothus velutinus*), another white-flowered species common in northern California, has oval, sometimes sticky leaves 1.5–3" long with very finely toothed margins and three prominent veins fanning out from the base of each leaf. All in all, northern California is home to about 30 species of *Ceanothus*, some quite rare, many evergreen, all with white or blue flowers.

DEERBRUSH

Family: Rhamnaceae (buckthorn family)

Scientific name: *Ceanothus integerrimus* Hook. & Arn. var. *macrothyrsus* (Torr.) G. T. Benson

Height: Up to 13'.

Leaves: Deciduous, alternate, 0.6" to more than 2" long, oval, hairless to sparsely short-haired, generally with 3 prominent veins fanning out from the base; margins usually smooth.

Flowers: Borne in elongated clusters 1.5–8" long; sepals 5, petal-like but curled towards the center of the flower, usually white; petals 5, spoon-shaped with a long narrow base, radiating out from among the sepals, usually white; stamens 5, anthers yellow; ovary partly inferior with the bases of the sepals and petals fused to its lower half, surrounded by a yellowish nectar-secreting disk, stigmas 3.

Blooms May through July.

Elevation: 200–8,500'.

Habitat: Chaparral, woodland, and conifer forest.

Comments: This shrub has unusually large, thin leaves for a *Ceanothus* as well as quite large clusters of flowers. Some individuals have pale blue or pink flowers, and a few become tree-like. The species is common in most of northern California except in the Sacramento Valley and along the coast and occurs from Arizona to Washington. Tobacco brush (*Ceanothus velutinus*) also has large, three-veined leaves, but they're evergreen, somewhat leathery, and often a bit sticky; its white flowers grow in clusters 1–4" long. Blue blossom (*Ceanothus thyrsiflorus* var. *thyrsiflorus*), another species with large, prominently three-veined but fairly thin leaves that's common near the coast, has bright green twigs and light to dark blue flowers.

LEMMON'S CEANOTHUS

Family: Rhamnaceae (buckthorn family)

Scientific name: *Ceanothus lemmonii* Parry

Height: 20–40".

Leaves: Evergreen, alternate, the blade 0.5–1.5" long, oval; upper side bright green and hairless to covered with short, more or less flat-lying hairs; lower side paler and densely short-haired; margins finely toothed, each tooth tipped with a small, egg-shaped or spherical gland.

Flowers: Sepals 5, petal-like but curled towards the center of the flower, blue; petals 5, spoon-shaped with a long narrow base, blue; stamens 5, anthers pale yellow; ovary partly inferior with the bases of the sepals and petals fused to its lower half, surrounded by a dark gray-green nectar-secreting disk, stigmas 3.

Blooms April through May.

Elevation: 500' to almost 5,500'.

Habitat: Open, rocky areas.

Comments: This shrub often develops into a mounded heap instead of a more upright form; it grows in the eastern part of the North Coast Ranges as well as the Klamath Ranges, Cascades, and Sierra Nevada. Its flexible, thornless twigs and gland-edged but flat leaf margins help distinguish it from other blue-flowered species of *Ceanothus.* For example, in dwarf ceanothus (*Ceanothus dentatus*), which grows in the San Francisco Bay region, the leaf margins bear glands but curl down.

MAHALA MAT

Family: Rhamnaceae (buckthorn family)

Scientific name: *Ceanothus prostratus* Benth. var. *prostratus*

Height: Usually 1–2".

Leaves: Evergreen, opposite, the blade 0.3–1.2" long, oval, leathery, more or less hairless; margins flat and with 3–7 sharply pointed teeth near the tip.

Flowers: Sepals 5, petal-like but curled towards the center of the flower, light to dark blue or purple; petals 5, spoon-shaped with a long narrow base, the same color as the sepals; stamens 5, anthers pale yellow; ovary partly inferior with the bases of the sepals and petals fused to its lower half, surrounded by a grayish nectar-secreting disk, stigmas 3.

Blooms April through June.

Elevation: 2,600' to almost 9,000'.

Habitat: Conifer forest.

Comments: This variety of *Ceanothus prostratus*, while technically a shrub, spreads carpet-like across the forest floor. It's common in the Klamath Ranges, Cascades, and Sierra Nevada, on the Modoc Plateau, and at the northern end of the North Coast Ranges. Farther south in the North Coast Ranges it's replaced by *Ceanothus prostratus* var. *occidentalis*, which grows in mounds up to a foot high. The leaves of this second variety tend to be folded lengthwise and usually have somewhat wavy margins.

CALIFORNIA COFFEE BERRY

Family: Rhamnaceae (buckthorn family)

Also called: Hoary coffee berry or pigeon berry

Scientific name: *Frangula californica* (Eschsch.) A. Gray subsp. *tomentella* (Benth.) Kartesz & Gandhi

Height: Usually 4–10', sometimes up to 16'.

Leaves: Usually evergreen, alternate, the blade 1.2" to almost 3" long, narrow to oval, dull olive to blue-green or gray-green, upper side hairless to short-haired or white-woolly, lower side with prominent pinnate veins and dense silvery or short velvety hairs; margins usually smooth.

Flowers: Roughly 0.1" long; sepals 5, light yellowish green, fleshy, lower side hairy, upper side hairless with a low ridge in the center; petals 5, tiny (smaller than the already small sepals), whitish, spoon-shaped with the "bowl" of the spoon arched over the stamens; stamens 5; ovary more or less inferior.

Blooms January through June and sometimes again in the fall.

Elevation: Sea level to above 7,000'.

Habitat: Chaparral and woodland.

Comments: This shrub, called *Rhamnus californica* subsp. *tomentella* or *Rhamnus tomentella* subsp. *tomentella* in some older references, is common in the North Coast Ranges, Klamath Ranges, and the foothills of the Cascades and Sierra Nevada. Occasionally you'll find flowers with only four sepals, petals, and stamens. The small fleshy fruits first turn bright red, then black as they ripen; they contain two seeds, each encased in a stony layer like a cherry pit. Five other subspecies of *Frangula californica* grow in the state. They differ in the exact shape of the leaves, whether the leaves are hairless, velvety, or silvery, whether the fruit is 2- or 3-seeded, and similar details. The subspecies do intergrade, however, which can make identification difficult. The region's two other species of *Frangula*, cascara (*Frangula purshiana*) and Sierra coffee berry (*Frangula rubra*), both with several subspecies, generally have deciduous leaves.

CASCARA

Family: Rhamnaceae (buckthorn family)

Also called: Cascara sagrada or chittimwood

Scientific name: *Frangula purshiana* (DC.) J. G. Cooper subsp. *purshiana*

Height: Up to 40'.

Leaves: Deciduous, alternate, the blade 2–6" long, oval, hairless to sparsely hairy; margins smooth to toothed.

Flowers: Roughly 0.2" long; sepals 5, light yellow-ish green, fleshy, hairless with a small ridge on the upper side; petals 5, tiny, pale green, notched at the tip and arched over the stamens like a hawk mantling its prey with its wings; stamens 5; ovary partly inferior with the bases of the sepals and petals fused to its lower half, surrounded by a reddish nectar-secreting disk.

Blooms February through July.

Elevation: Sea level to 6,500'.

Habitat: Conifer forest and coastal scrub.

Comments: This shrub or small tree grows in coastal areas, the Klamath Ranges, the western part of the North Coast Ranges, and as far north as British Columbia. Its twigs are gray or reddish, and its round, black, berry-like fruits, 0.1–0.2" wide, typically contain three seeds. In older texts it's called *Rhamnus purshiana* subsp. *purshiana*. *Frangula purshiana* subsp. *annonifolia* has leaves with tapered rather than rounded bases; *Frangula purshiana* subsp. *ultramafica*, only found in Plumas County, is evergreen.

HOLLYLEAF REDBERRY

Family: Rhamnaceae (buckthorn family)

Scientific name: *Rhamnus ilicifolia* Kellogg

Height: Up to 13'.

Leaves: Evergreen, alternate, the blade 0.8" to more than 1.5" long, oval, leathery, hairless or hairy; margins smooth or edged with spine-tipped teeth.

Flowers: Borne singly or in small clusters of up to 6, male and female flowers generally on different plants, both types with 4 greenish sepals without a thickened ridge on the upper side and lacking petals; male flowers with 4 stamens; female flowers with a superior or partly inferior ovary.

Blooms March through June.

Elevation: Sea level to above 3,500'.

Habitat: Woodland, chaparral, and forest.

Comments: The main branches of this spine-free shrub angle upwards, and its bark is gray. It grows in most of northern California except on the Modoc Plateau. Spiny redberry (*Rhamnus crocea*) can be found in the Klamath Ranges, North Coast Ranges, and Sierra Nevada. Its main branches spread widely; its red or purplish twigs are spiny, its leaves only 0.4–0.6" long. Both species produce small, inconspicuous flowers and red, berry-like fruits roughly 0.2–03" wide and containing two seeds, each seed enclosed in a hard casing like a tiny cherry pit.

CHAMISE

Family: Rosaceae (rose family)

Also called: Greasewood

Scientific name: *Adenostoma fasciculatum* Hook. & Arn. var. *fasciculatum*

Height: Up to 13'.

Leaves: Evergreen, alternate, the blade 0.2–0.5" long, usually very narrow, stiff, usually hairless, petiole very short; margins smooth.

Flowers: Borne in feathery sprays; sepals 5, greenish; petals 5, up to 0.1" long, white or cream-colored; stamens 10 or 15 in 5 groups of 2 or 3, anthers light yellow; ovary superior, set into the bottom of an open cone formed by the fused bases of the sepals, petals, and filaments.

Blooms May through June.

Elevation: Sea level to 6,000'.

Habitat: Chaparral and dry, open areas.

Comments: This shrub is northern California's only species of *Adenostoma*. It's common in the North Coast Ranges and the foothills of the Cascades and Sierra Nevada and even more so farther south. The leaves look clustered because at the base of each petiole there's a very short side branch bearing a few additional leaves. Mature shrubs are extremely flammable but resprout readily after a fire from woody burls at their base. Deer relish the new growth, stripping the leaves off between their incisors and leaving just the bare twigs—chamise has been described as a "bread and butter plant" for deer.

BIRCH-LEAF MOUNTAIN MAHOGANY

Family: Rosaceae (rose family)

Scientific name: *Cercocarpus betuloides* Nutt. var. *betuloides*

Height: Usually up to 10', sometimes taller.

Leaves: Evergreen, alternate, the blade 0.4–1" long (rarely up to 1.6" long), oval to almost round, usually with 3–6 veins on each side of the midrib, lower side sparsely hairy; margins toothed.

Flowers: Usually borne singly or in clusters of 2–6, sometimes in larger clusters; the bases of the sepals, petals, and filaments fused into a slender cylinder that flares into a roughly 0.2"-wide bowl at the top; sepals 5, broadly triangular but curled back, pale greenish yellow; no petals; stamens 25–45, anthers hairy; ovary superior.

Blooms March through May.

Elevation: Sea level to above 8,000'.

Habitat: Chaparral and dry, rocky sites.

Comments: This shrub or small tree occurs in much of northern California except near the coast and in the Sacramento Valley. Far more conspicuous than its flowers are its fruits, each bearing a dainty white plume that can be anywhere from 2–5" long. *Cercocarpus betuloides* var. *macrourus* grows in yellow pine forest in the Klamath Ranges, Cascades, and on the Modoc Plateau. Its leaves are 1–3" long and more than 0.6" wide; they have 5–10 veins on each side of the midrib. The leaves of curl-leaf mountain mahogany (*Cercocarpus ledifolius*), which in northern California grows mainly above 3,000', have smooth margins that curl downwards, sometimes almost to the midrib, and its anthers are hairless.

MOUNTAIN MISERY

Family: Rosaceae (rose family)

Scientific name: *Chamaebatia foliolosa* Benth.

Height: 8" to 2'.

Leaves: Evergreen, alternate,1–4" long, usually 3-times pinnately compound, covered with glandular hairs that produce a sticky resin with a strong, harshly herbal smell.

Flowers: Borne singly or in clusters of 2–10; sepals 5, green, densely covered with glandular hairs; petals 5, 0.2–0.4" long, white; stamens 35–65, anthers bright yellow; ovary superior, set into the bottom of a shallow bowl formed by the fused bases of the sepals, petals, and filaments. Blooms May through July.

Elevation: 2,000' to almost 8,000'.

Habitat: Conifer forest.

Comments: This low-growing shrub is common in the Cascades and Sierra Nevada, where it sometimes seems to cover acres of forest floor. The only somewhat similar plant in northern California is the equally strong-smelling fern bush (*Chamaebatiaria millefolium*), which grows 2' to more than 6' tall and has once or twice pinnately compound leaves. Its flowers grow in fairly narrow, upright clusters with 20 to several hundred flowers per cluster, and each flower has four or five pistils. Look for it in sagebrush scrub, pinyon-juniper woodland, and pine forest in the Klamath Ranges, Cascades, and on the Modoc Plateau.

AUSTIN'S WOODBEAUTY

Family: Rosaceae (rose family)

Scientific name: *Drymocallis lactea* (Greene) Rydb. var. *austiniae* (Jeps.) Ertter

Height: 4" to 2'.

Leaves: Basal leaves 2–8" long, once pinnately compound, 7 or 9 leaflets per leaf, hairs glandular; margins toothed; stem leaves alternate, smaller, sessile, often deeply 3-lobed rather than compound.

Flowers: Sepals 5, green, covered with glandular hairs, with 5 smaller, sepal-like bracts just below them; petals 5, 0.2–0.3" long, light yellow; stamens 20–25, yellow; pistils many, yellow, mounded on a small saucer formed by the fused bases of the sepals, petals, and filaments. Blooms May through September.

Elevation: 3,000–8,500'.

Habitat: Moist, often rocky sites.

Comments: This herbaceous perennial grows in the Klamath Ranges, Cascades, Sierra Nevada, the northern part of the North Coast Ranges, and on the Modoc Plateau. It used to be included in *Potentilla glandulosa* subsp. *nevadensis*, but the genus has undergone a lot of revision in recent years. Northern California still has more than a dozen species of *Potentilla*, but Austin's woodbeauty is now one of five species of *Drymocallis* in the region. Most have creamy white to yellow petals. Shrub cinquefoil (*Dasiphora fruticosa*, formerly *Potentilla fruticosa*) is the only shrub in the group.

295

BEACH STRAWBERRY

Family: Rosaceae (rose family)

Scientific name: *Fragaria chiloensis* (L.) Mill.

Height: 2–8".

Leaves: All basal, once compound with 3 leaflets per leaf, each leaflet 0.4–2.5" long, oval, leathery, upper side dark green and shiny, lower side densely hairy; margins toothed, the tooth right at the tip of each leaflet noticeably smaller than its neighbors.

Flowers: Sepals 5, green, with 5 smaller, sepal-like bracts just below them; petals 5, 0.3–0.7" long, white; stamens 20–35, yellow; pistils many, yellow, mounded onto a small plate formed by the fused bases of the sepals, petals, and filaments.

Blooms February through November.

Elevation: Sea level to 650'.

Habitat: Coastal dunes, beaches, and grassland.

Comments: This herbaceous perennial grows along the coast from central California to Alaska. It spreads by creeping, leafless, aboveground stems called runners; when the runners have grown some distance away from the parent, their tips take root and produce a new plant. Although all the flowers look similar, some can be functionally male, others functionally female, and the two types are often produced on different plants. The sepal-like bracts are easily visible after the petals have dropped off. As in cultivated strawberries, each pistil ripens into a small, hard, seed-like fruit perched on a fleshy and delicious red center. Northern California's two other wild strawberries have thin, not leathery leaves. In wood strawberry (*Fragaria vesca*), each leaflet has 12–21 teeth, the central tooth is at least as big as the adjacent teeth, and the moderately shiny upper side is sparsely hairy; the species grows in lightly shaded forest at elevations up to 6,500'. Mountain strawberry (*Fragaria virginiana*), found in forests and meadows at elevations from 4,000' to almost 11,000', only has 7–13 teeth per leaflet with a central tooth that is smaller than its neighbors; the leaflets' upper side is matte and generally hairless.

TOYON

Family: Rosaceae (rose family)

Also called: Christmas berry or California holly

Scientific name: *Heteromeles arbutifolia* (Lindl.) M. Roem.

Height: Up to about 30'.

Leaves: Evergreen, alternate, the blade 2–4" long, narrow to oval, leathery, hairless or sparsely hairy; margins toothed with a vein running into each tooth.

Flowers: Sepals 5, green, triangular, very small but persisting and turning red as the fruit ripens; petals 5, less than 0.2" long, white; stamens usually 10, anthers cream-colored; ovary inferior.

Blooms May through August.

Elevation: Sea level to above 4,000'.

Habitat: Chaparral, woodland, and forest.

Comments: This shrub or small tree is the only species in its genus. It's common in the North Coast Ranges, Klamath Ranges, the foothills of the Cascades and Sierra Nevada, and the Sacramento Valley's Sutter Buttes, but it's also frequently used in landscaping and habitat restoration, and so you may see it in other locations as well. Apparently mature leaves are too leathery to interest deer, but the plants resprout vigorously after a fire, and the tender new growth is much more palatable to browsing animals. The fruit, roughly 0.2–0.4" in diameter, looks a bit like a miniature apple but has relatively little flesh enclosing two or three brown seeds; usually it's bright red, less often a deep golden yellow. It's eaten by many species of birds and some mammals, and in late fall and winter you may find animal scat full of undigested toyon seeds.

THREE-TOOTHED HORKELIA

Family: Rosaceae (rose family)

Scientific name: *Horkelia tridentata* Torr. var. *tridentata*

Height: Up to 18".

Leaves: Mainly basal, 1–5" long, once pinnately compound, 5–11 leaflets per leaf, each leaflet oval, gray-green, usually densely hairy at least on the lower side, 3-toothed at the tip.

Flowers: Borne in tight round clusters with 3–40 flowers per cluster; sepals 5, pale green, triangular, with 5 short, very narrow bracts just below them; petals 5, very narrow, white; stamens 10, anthers dull purplish pink; pistils 5–15, ovaries superior, set in a hairless bowl formed by the fused bases of the sepals, petals, and filaments.

Blooms April through August.

Elevation: 1,000' to above 8,000'.

Habitat: Conifer forest.

Comments: This herbaceous perennial grows in the Cascades, Sierra Nevada, and on the Modoc Plateau. *Horkelia tridentata* var. *flavescens*, which occurs in the North Coast Ranges, Klamath Ranges, and northern Sierra Nevada, has somewhat wider but shorter petals, and the inside of the "bowl" in which the ovary sits is usually hairy. The two varieties represent one of about a dozen species of *Horkelia* found in northern California, all herbaceous perennials, most with fairly inconspicuous flowers, some quite rare.

PACIFIC SILVERWEED

Family: Rosaceae (rose family)

Scientific name: *Potentilla anserina* L. subsp. *pacifica* (Howell) Rousi

Height: Usually a few inches.

Leaves: All basal, generally 1–20" long, rarely up to 30" long, once pinnately compound with 11–21 or more closely spaced leaflets per leaf, each leaflet oval to fairly narrow, upper side more or less hairless, lower side densely covered with white, silky or woolly hairs; margins sharply toothed.

Flowers: Borne singly; sepals 5, green, with 5 sepal-like bracts just below them that often exceed the sepals in length; petals usually 5, 0.3–0.8" long, bright yellow; stamens 20–25, yellow; pistils 20–200, yellow, mounded in the bottom of a small saucer formed by the fused bases of the sepals, petals, and filaments.

Blooms March through October.

Elevation: Sea level to 500'.

Habitat: Coastal wetlands.

Comments: This herbaceous perennial, which spreads by creeping aboveground stems (called stolons or runners) like strawberry (*Fragaria* spp.), can tolerate brackish water and grows along the coast from southern California to Alaska. Northern California has quite a few other yellow-flowered species of *Potentilla* and related genera, but the habitat and distinctive leaves of Pacific silverweed make it easy to recognize.

298

BITTER CHERRY

Family: Rosaceae (rose family)

Also called: Bird cherry

Scientific name: *Prunus emarginata* (Douglas) Eaton

Height: Usually 3–20', sometimes up to 50'.

Leaves: Deciduous, alternate, the blade usually 0.6–2.5" long, oval, hairless or slightly hairy; margins toothed or scalloped.

Flowers: Borne in flat-topped to domed clusters of 3–12; sepals 5, green; petals 5, 0.1–0.3" long, white; stamens typically 10–30, filaments white, anthers yellow; ovary superior, set in the bottom of a deep cup formed by the fused bases of the sepals, petals, and filaments.

Blooms April through June.

Elevation: Sea level to 10,000'.

Habitat: Chaparral, sagebrush scrub, and open areas in forest, often on rocky sites.

Comments: This thornless shrub or small tree often forms big thickets. In the fall of a good year, the bushes almost glow with innumerable small red fruits that taste atrociously bitter to humans but are relished by many small rodents, other mammals, and birds. Pacific, Klamath, or Sierra plum (*Prunus subcordata*) also is a small tree or thicket-forming shrub but has stiff, crooked, thorny branches, oval to almost round leaves, and yellow to dark red, plum-like fruit 0.6–1" in diameter. The slender, 2–5"-long inflorescences of western choke cherry (*Prunus virginiana* var. *demissa*) often droop or dangle and typically consist of 18 or more flowers; the fruit is small, red or black, berry-like, and very astringent. All three are widespread in northern California except in the Sacramento Valley.

BITTERBRUSH

Family: Rosaceae (rose family)

Also called: Antelope bush

Scientific name: *Purshia tridentata* (Pursh) DC. var. *tridentata*

Height: Usually 8" to 8', sometimes up to 13'.

Leaves: Evergreen or deciduous, alternate, the blade 0.2–1.2" long, wedge-shaped, the tip usually 3-lobed, rarely 5-lobed, upper side moderately to densely hairy, lower side woolly-haired; margins typically curled downwards.

Flowers: Sepals 5, small, light green; petals 5, 0.2–0.3" long, pale yellow; stamens typically about 25, anthers yellow; pistils 1 or 2, their ovaries superior, set in the bottom of a narrow funnel formed by the fused bases of the sepals, petals, and filaments, the outside of the funnel studded with short hairs topped with round, yellowish glands.

Blooms March through July.

Elevation: 3,000' to above 11,000'.

Habitat: Well-drained sites in sagebrush scrub, pinyon-juniper woodland, and conifer forest.

Comments: This shrub, an important food for deer and pronghorn antelope, is northern California's only species of *Purshia*. It occurs in the North Coast Ranges, Klamath Ranges, and Cascades as well as on the Modoc Plateau and the eastern slope of the Sierra Nevada. It may retain its leaves all year or shed them when conditions get too dry. The mature fruit consists of a leathery husk, about 0.6" long, half as wide, enclosing a single seed. After a wildland fire, bitterbrush seems to regrow mainly from seed, although a few burned plants may resprout; seedling mortality is high, but those shrubs that do make it can reach an age of 160 years or older.

CALIFORNIA ROSE

Family: Rosaceae (rose family)

Scientific name: *Rosa californica* Cham. & Schltdl.

Height: 30" to 8'.

Leaves: Deciduous, alternate, once pinnately compound, usually with 5–7 leaflets per leaf, leaflets oval, hairless to somewhat hairy, the largest 0.6–1.5" long; margins toothed, occasionally double-toothed.

Flowers: Borne singly or in clusters of 3–30 or more; sepals 5, narrow and tapered to a long point, green, drying to tan as the fruit matures but not falling off; petals 5, 0.6–1" long, pink; stamens numerous; pistils 20–40, ovaries superior, set in the bottom of a narrow-necked "vase" formed by the fused bases of the sepals, petals, and filaments.

Blooms February through November.

Elevation: Sea level to 6,000'.

Habitat: Stream banks and other moist sites.

Comments: This rather variable shrub is widespread throughout northern California. Its branches are studded with fairly thick, straight or curved thorns borne singly or in pairs. The bright orange-red, fleshy fruit, called a hip, develops from the fused bases of the sepals, petals, and stamens; the pistils ripen into small, hard, seed-like fruits inside the hip. Rose hips are a favorite fall food for many animals, and I've seen coyote scat full of the distinctive "seeds." Northern California has several other pink-flowered species of *Rosa*; they differ in features such as the exact shape of the leaflets, whether the thorns are straight or curved like claws, slender or stout, single or paired, whether the sepals have smooth or pinnately lobed margins, and whether the dried-out brown sepals persist on the fruit or drop off as it matures.

WOOD ROSE

Family: Rosaceae (rose family)

Scientific name: *Rosa gymnocarpa* Nutt. var. *gymnocarpa*

Height: Usually no more than 3' but sometimes up to 7'.

Leaves: Deciduous, alternate, once pinnately compound, usually with 7–9 leaflets per leaf, leaflets oval to almost round, hairless, terminal leaflet 0.4–1.2" long; margins usually double-toothed, each tooth tipped with a small gland.

Flowers: Often borne singly, sometimes in 2s or 3s; sepals 5, narrow and tapered to a long point, green, dropping off the fruit as it matures; petals 5, 0.3–0.5" long, pink to red with a lighter-colored base; stamens numerous; pistils 5–10, ovaries superior, set in the bottom of a narrow-necked "vase" formed by the fused bases of the sepals, petals, and filaments.

Blooms April through June

Elevation: 100–6,500'.

Habitat: Forest and other shady sites.

Comments: This is one of those instances when common names can be really confusing. Wood rose grows mainly in coastal areas and the Coast Ranges and Klamath Ranges; it seems to be less frequent in the Cascades, Sierra Nevada, and on the Modoc Plateau. It's a loose shrub with slender stems and bright green foliage; its thorns are small, slender, straight, and usually not paired; and the sepals are shed as the egg-shaped to almost spherical fruits mature. *Rosa woodsii* var. *ultramontana*, on the other hand, sometimes called Woods' rose, grows at elevations of 3,200–9,000' in the Cascades, Sierra Nevada, and on the Modoc Plateau; it has stout stems, rather stout curved or straight thorns, blue-green leaves, and fruit crowned with the dry but persistent sepals. Other sources call it mountain rose or interior rose.

RAMBLER ROSE

Family: Rosaceae (rose family)

Also called: Multiflora rose

Scientific name: *Rosa multiflora* Thunb.

Height: Usually 5–10', occasionally climbing much higher.

Leaves: Deciduous, alternate, once pinnately compound, usually with 7–9 leaflets per leaf, leaflets oval, hairless or sparsely hairy, terminal leaflet 0.4" to nearly 2" long; margins toothed.

Flowers: Borne in clusters of 5–30; sepals 5, with toothed lobes, green; petals 5, 0.3–0.6" long, white; stamens numerous; pistils usually fewer than 10, ovaries superior, set in the bottom of a narrow-necked "vase" formed by the fused bases of the sepals, petals, and filaments.

Blooms April through June.

Elevation: 50' to above 2,000'.

Habitat: Disturbed sites.

Comments: Occasionally this thicket-forming shrub with stout, curved thorns turns into a woody vine. It's native to eastern Asia but has become naturalized in the Sacramento Valley, Cascades, and North Coast Ranges; sometimes it's planted to provide food and shelter for game birds and other wildlife. Dog rose (*Rosa canina*), native to Eurasia, can also have white petals, but they're 0.6–1.5" long and the flowers are borne singly or in twos to fives. In both species, the sepals curl back as the fruit matures, and some are shed while others stay in place.

NOOTKA ROSE

Family: Rosaceae (rose family)

Scientific name: *Rosa nutkana* C. Presl. var. *nutkana*

Height: 20" to more than 6'.

Leaves: Deciduous, alternate, once pinnately compound, usually with 5–7 leaflets per leaf, leaflets oval, sparsely hairy, terminal leaflet 0.6–2.5" long; margins double-toothed, the secondary teeth very small.

Flowers: Borne singly or in clusters of up to 6; sepals 5, green, their tips long, narrow, and toothed, staying in place as the fruit ripens; petals 5, 0.6–1" long, wide enough to overlap each other, pink; stamens numerous; pistils usually 30–60, ovaries superior, set in the bottom of a narrow-necked "vase" formed by the fused bases of the sepals, petals, and filaments.

Blooms May through July.

Elevation: Sea level to above 2,000'.

Habitat: Moist, flat sites in forest or coastal scrub.

Comments: This densely branched, very thorny, thicket-forming shrub occurs from coastal central California and the western side of the North Coast Ranges all the way to Alaska. *Rosa nutkana* var. *macdougalii*, which grows from the North Coast Ranges, Klamath Ranges, and Cascades to British Columbia, is a more open shrub with few thorns and single-toothed leaf margins. Both varieties produce more or less spherical fruit with persistent sepals.

THIMBLEBERRY

Family: Rosaceae (rose family)

Scientific name: *Rubus parviflorus* Nutt.

Height: 1' to more than 8'.

Leaves: Deciduous, alternate, the blade 4–6" wide, typically palmately 5-lobed, less frequently 3-lobed, upper side almost hairless to moderately hairy, lower side often densely covered with soft hairs; margins irregularly toothed.

Flowers: Borne in clusters of 3–15; sepals 5, green, sometimes with a pink tinge, their bases just barely fused with each other and the bases of the petals; petals 5, 0.4–1.5" long, white, crinkled; stamens many; more than 30 pistils, ovaries superior, densely hairy.

Blooms March through August.

Elevation: Sea level to above 8,000'.

Habitat: Moist, lightly shaded areas in woodland and forest.

Comments: This thornless shrub grows in most of northern California except in the Sacramento Valley, sometimes in big, dense patches. Each pistil ripens into a small, fleshy fruit that adheres to its neighbors; the result resembles a 0.4–0.6"-wide, shallowly bowl-shaped raspberry. I suspect that the fruit attracts all kinds of animals, from bears to small rodents, because, although unripe fruits are often abundant, it can be hard to find a single ripe one.

SALMONBERRY

Family: Rosaceae (rose family)

Scientific name: *Rubus spectabilis* Pursh

Height: 6' to more than 12'.

Leaves: Deciduous, alternate, the blade usually compound with 3 often slightly lobed leaflets, the center leaflet 1.5–4" long, oval, upper side usually with short fine hairs, lower side hairless to densely hairy; margins double-toothed.

Flowers: Borne singly or in pairs; sepals 5, green, hairy, forming a cup in profile but free from one another except right at the base, where they and the bases of the petals are fused into a small plate; petals 5, 0.6" to more than 1" long, magenta, crinkled; stamens many; more than 30 pistils, ovaries superior, hairless.

Blooms March through June.

Elevation: Sea level to 1,600'.

Habitat: Stream banks and moist, lightly shaded sites.

Comments: Compared to most blackberries and raspberries (all of which are other species of *Rubus*), the woody canes of salmonberry aren't very thorny. The species grows mainly near the coast from Santa Cruz County northwards to Alaska and is the region's only *Rubus* with magenta petals. Each pistil ripens into a small, fleshy fruit that adheres to its neighbors but not to the central core to which all the pistils were attached, resulting in a shiny fruit very similar in shape and size to a raspberry but yellow, orange, or bright red when ripe. The fruit looks appealing but is mealy to mushy in texture and bland in flavor.

Male flowers.

Female flowers.

CALIFORNIA BLACKBERRY

Family: Rosaceae (rose family)

Scientific name: *Rubus ursinus* Cham. & Schltdl.

Height: A few feet.

Leaves: Deciduous, alternate, the blade usually 3-lobed to compound with 3 leaflets, occasionally 5-lobed or with 5 leaflets, the center leaflet 2–5" long and often nearly as wide, sparsely to densely hairy; margins irregularly toothed.

Flowers: Male and female flowers often borne on different plants, both types singly or in clusters of 2–5; male flowers with 5 green sepals, 5 narrow white petals 0.4–0.7" long, and numerous stamens, their anthers initially cream-colored, turning tan after the pollen has been shed; female flowers with 5 green sepals, 5 white petals 0.2–0.4" long and slightly wider than those of the male flowers, a ring of nonfunctional stamens often represented just by their filaments, and 30 or more pistils with superior, pale green ovaries and creamy white styles and stigmas.

Blooms March through July.

Elevation: Sea level to 5,000'.

Habitat: Sparse woodland and open, disturbed sites

Comments: This thorny, woody species is common in most of northern California. The canes, which are round in cross-section and covered with a waxy bloom, usually just live two years; they sprawl in low mounds or lean against whatever else is growing nearby but don't form impenetrable thickets like the notoriously invasive, ferociously thorny, and even more common Himalaya blackberry (*Rubus armeniacus*, called *Rubus discolor* or *Rubus procerus* in many older references). The latter, native to Eurasia, has stems that are 5-sided in cross-section and produces loose clusters of numerous bisexual flowers with white or pale pink petals. In both species each pistil turns into a small, black, fleshy fruit that adheres to its neighbors as well as a fleshy core at the center, resulting in the familiar blackberry type of fruit. Northern California has several additional white-flowered species of *Rubus*, but they don't seem to occur quite as frequently; it helps to have second-year stems, leaves, flowers, and fruit for identification.

DOUGLAS' SPIRAEA

Family: Rosaceae (rose family)

Also called: Hardhack

Scientific name: *Spiraea douglasii* Hook.

Height: 3' to more than 6'.

Leaves: Deciduous, alternate, the blade 1.2" to nearly 4" long, oval, upper side often hairless, lower side densely hairy, petiole up to 0.4" long; margins toothed.

Flowers: Borne in dense elongate clusters 4–6" long; sepals 5, very small, pinkish, bent downwards; petals 5, less than 0.1" long, bright pink; stamens 15 or more, pink; pistils usually 5, ovaries superior, set into the bottom of a cup or bowl formed by the fused bases of the sepals, petals, and filaments.

Blooms June through September.

Elevation: Sea level to almost 7,000'.

Habitat: Moist sites in conifer forest.

Comments: In northern California, this shrub grows in the Klamath Ranges, Cascades, northern North Coast Ranges, northern Sierra Nevada, and on the Modoc Plateau. Each pistil develops into a small dry fruit, about 0.1" long, that splits open on one side to release the two or more seeds inside. Some Native American tribes made brooms from the twigs; others used the branches as racks for drying or smoking salmon.

ROSE-COLORED MEADOW-SWEET

Family: Rosaceae (rose family)

Also called: Pink spiraea or mountain spiraea

Scientific name: *Spiraea splendens* K. Koch

Height: 8" to 3'.

Leaves: Deciduous, alternate, the blade 0.4" to almost 3" long, oval, hairless to sparsely hairy, nearly sessile or with a very short petiole; margins toothed or scalloped.

Flowers: Borne in dense, flat-topped to slightly domed clusters 1–2" wide; sepals 5, very small, pale green; petals 5, less than 0.1" long, bright pink; stamens 15 or more, pink; pistils usually 5, ovaries superior, set into the bottom of a cup or bowl formed by the fused bases of the sepals, petals, and filaments.

Blooms June through September.

Elevation: 1,800–11,000'.

Habitat: Moist sites in conifer forest and moist rocky areas.

Comments: This shrub, called *Spiraea densiflora* in older texts, grows in the Klamath Ranges, Cascades, Sierra Nevada, and as far north as British Columbia. I prefer to avoid the common name "rose spiraea" used by some authors because occasionally it's also applied to Douglas' spiraea (*Spiraea douglasii*). The plants can form extensive thickets, and the flowers attract many butterflies, bees, and bumblebees. The fruit resembles that of Douglas' spiraea.

307

BUTTON WILLOW

Family: Rubiceae (madder family)

Also called: Button bush

Scientific name: *Cephalanthus occidentalis* L.

Height: 5–30'.

Leaves: Deciduous, opposite or in whorls of 3, the blade 3–8" long, narrow to oval, older leaves more or less hairless; margins smooth.

Flowers: Borne in dense, spherical heads 0.4–1" in diameter; sepals fused into a greenish 4-lobed tube; petals 4, fused into a slender tube that widens abruptly near the top, creamy white; stamens 4; ovary inferior with a very long, white style and small, pale yellow stigma.

Blooms May through September, occasionally even later.

Elevation: Sea level to above 3,000'.

Habitat: Stream banks, lake shores, and flood plains.

Comments: In California, this shrub or small tree grows mainly in the Central Valley, Sierra Nevada foothills, eastern part of the North Coast Ranges, and southeastern part of the Klamath Ranges. It also occurs in other parts of North and Central America; the jury still seems to be out as to whether California's button willows should be considered a distinct variety. Bobelaine Audubon Sanctuary (south of Yuba City) and Cosumnes River Preserve (south of Sacramento) have some exceptionally big specimens. The pompom-like flower heads make the plants fairly noticeable from a distance and attract lots of butterflies and other insects. The ovary and persistent sepals sometimes turn reddish after pollination and fertilization, and eventually each small fruit disintegrates into two to four dry, 1-seeded segments. Button willow is one of several kinds of shrubs that Native Americans used to burn in the fall. The following year, they harvested the straight, unbranched new growth to make arrow shafts; three years after burning, the shoots were suitable for spear shafts and fish harpoons.

Despite its common name, this species most definitely does not belong to the willow family (Salicaceae), which is characterized by alternate leaves, flowers that lack sepals and petals, and seed capsules that split open to release numerous wind-dispersed seeds.

Western tiger swallowtail (*Pterourus rutulus*) on button willow.

Skippers are a group of small, stocky butterflies called the Hesperioidea; many rest with their wings folded at different angles, like paper airplanes.

GOOSE GRASS

Family: Rubiceae (madder family)

Also called: Common bedstraw, cleavers, cleaverwort, barweed, stick-a-back, or stickywilly

Scientific name: *Galium aparine* L.

Height: Usually a few inches to about 3', occasionally up to 5'.

Leaves: In whorls of 5–8, 0.5" to almost 1.5" long, very narrow, sessile, tipped with a small straight spine, upper side with scattered hard hairs; margin edged with hard hooked hairs.

Flowers: Generally less than 0.1" wide; no sepals; petals 4, white; stamens 4; ovary inferior, 2-lobed. Blooms March through July.

Elevation: Sea level to 5,000'.

Habitat: Open woodland and other partly shaded sites.

Comments: Occasionally this weak-stemmed annual just trails across the ground, but when next to taller vegetation it may climb several feet, its tiny, downward-pointing prickles, rather like the rough part of Velcro, helping it cling to its support. Sometimes it even climbs up on itself. Each lobe of the ovary develops into a dry, nearly spherical fruit, 0.1–0.2" in diameter, that's also covered with hooked hairs. Goose grass is widespread from southern California to Alaska and also occurs in eastern North America and Europe. More than 20 species of *Galium* can be found in northern California, some rare, all with tiny flowers and stems that are square in cross-section. Yellow bedstraw (*Galium verum*), a herbaceous perennial that's native to Eurasia but has become weedy in the San Francisco Bay region, is less inconspicuous than most because its small, bright yellow flowers grow in compact clusters of hundreds of flowers. Worldwide, the genus has over 650 species. Other members of the family include coffee, quinine, and *Gardenia*.

CLIMBING BEDSTRAW

Family: Rubiceae (madder family)

Scientific name: *Galium porrigens* Dempster var. *porrigens*

Height: Climbing to about 5'.

Leaves: In whorls of 4, 0.1–0.7" long, narrowly oval, sessile, sometimes with short bristly hairs, tip rounded or gently pointed; margin edged with hard, backward-pointing hairs.

Flowers: Male and female flowers borne on different plants, both types about 0.05" wide, without sepals, and with 4 pale yellow or reddish petals; male flowers with 4 stamens; female flowers with an inferior ovary.

Blooms February through August.

Elevation: Sea level to 7,000'.

Habitat: Woodland, chaparral, and forest.

Comments: Older texts call this climbing species *Galium nuttallii* var. *ovalifolium* or *Galium suffruticosum*. It has perennial woody main branches that often grow entangled in other woody vegetation and, in early spring, produce clumps of soft-stemmed, leafy shoots that become more diffuse as the new growth elongates. At least in the Sacramento area, these soft shoots die back by early summer. The fruit is said to be a translucent white berry, but despite persistent searching I've not found one yet. Climbing bedstraw grows in the North Coast Ranges, Klamath Ranges, Sacramento Valley, and Sierra Nevada foothills. Another variety, *Galium porrigens* var. *tenue*, grows in the North Coast Ranges, Klamath Ranges, and Cascade and Sierra Nevada foothills; its leaves are very narrow, no more than 0.3" long, and tend to have more sharply pointed tips.

CALIFORNIA HOP TREE

Family: Rutaceae (rue family)

Scientific name: *Ptelea crenulata* Greene

Height: Up to 16'.

Leaves: Deciduous, alternate, palmately compound with 3 leaflets per leaf, each leaflet 0.8–3" long, oval, upper side hairless and shiny, lower side somewhat hairy; margins slightly toothed or scalloped.

Flowers: Sepals tiny; petals 4 or 5, about 0.2" long, white, greenish, or cream-colored; stamens 4 or 5; ovary superior.

Blooms March through May.

Elevation: Sea level to 3,500'.

Habitat: Woodland and yellow pine forest.

Comments: On some of these big shrubs or small trees, all the flowers are bisexual, meaning they have functional stamens and pistils; on others, all are female. Both types have a sweet fragrance that reminds me of cloves and carnations, and I've sometimes smelled the flowers before I saw the trees. The fruit is a thin flat disk, 0.4–0.8" wide, with a bulge in the center that contains the seed; once in a while you'll find a 3-winged fruit. Interestingly, all-female plants sometimes seem to fruit more abundantly than bisexual individuals. The surface of the fruit is speckled with tiny embedded glands, which are characteristic of other members of the Rutaceae too, such as lemons, limes, and oranges. California hop tree grows mainly in the Sacramento Valley, the Cascade and Sierra Nevada foothills, and the eastern part of the Coast Ranges.

Expanding male catkins.

Immature seed capsules.

FREMONT'S COTTONWOOD

Family: Salicaceae (willow family)

Also called: Alamo

Scientific name: *Populus fremontii* S. Watson subsp. *fremontii*

Height: Usually up to 65', sometimes taller.

Leaves: Deciduous, alternate, the blade 1.5–3" long and sometimes even wider, roughly triangular, hairless to hairy, petioles flattened; margins coarsely scalloped.

Flowers: Male and female flowers borne on separate trees, both types in dangling catkins 1–4" long, sepals and petals fused into a small unlobed saucer; male flowers with 6–80 initially reddish stamens; female flowers with 1 pistil with a superior ovary and several greenish yellow, flattened, wavy-margined stigma lobes that at first glance resemble minute petals.

Fully ripe, open seed capsules and seeds.

Blooms February through April.

Elevation: Sea level to 6,500'.

Habitat: Stream banks and flood plains.

Comments: This tree is widespread from northern Mexico to northern California and eastwards to the Rocky Mountains. Beavers relish the leaves and the softer tissues under the gray, roughly furrowed outer bark and will fell even large old trees to get at these favorite foods. The fruit is a small tan capsule that splits apart to release the fluffy seeds, which in late spring can be so abundant that they carpet the ground wherever the wind has blown them. The seeds only live a month or so, and to germinate they need to land on very wet soil that dries slowly as summer approaches; if the soil dries too quickly, the seedlings' roots can't keep up with the receding water table; if it stays wet too long, the seedlings are susceptible to attack by fungi. Spring floods used to provide the right conditions every few years; now that most of western North America's rivers are controlled by dams or restricted by levees, such floods are even less frequent, and as a result, natural regeneration of Fremont's cottonwood is a rare event. Black cottonwood (*Populus trichocarpa*, called *Populus balsamifera* subsp. *trichocarpa* in older texts) has narrower leaves with finely scalloped margins.

QUAKING ASPEN

Family: Salicaceae (willow family)

Scientific name: *Populus tremuloides* Michx.

Height: Usually less than 50', occasionally up to 90'.

Leaves: Deciduous, alternate, the blade usually 1–2" long, broadly oval to almost round, hairless, petioles flattened, allowing the leaves to flutter in the slightest breeze; margins finely scalloped or toothed to nearly smooth.

Flowers: Male and female flowers borne on separate trees, both types in dangling catkins 1.5–3" long, their sepals and petals fused into a small unlobed saucer; male flowers with 6–12 stamens; female flowers with 1 pistil with a superior ovary and a reddish, 2-lobed stigma.

Blooms April through June.

Elevation: 3,000' to above 10,000'.

Habitat: Stream banks, open areas in forest, and moist sites in sagebrush scrub.

Comments: In northern California, these trees grow mainly in the Klamath Ranges, Cascades, Sierra Nevada, and on the Modoc Plateau. Their spreading root systems produce numerous upright suckers that grow into groves of genetically identical new trees. In spring, genetic differences make some groves leaf out earlier than others; in fall, one grove may still have bright green foliage while its neighbors on the same hillside have already turned bright gold or orange or shed all their leaves. The bark is distinctive: smooth and nearly white with rough black marks around the scars of old, broken-off branches and other places where it has been stressed or damaged, for example, where bears climbing the trees have scratched it with their claws. Beavers like aspen even better than cottonwood, willow, and alder; and grouse, black bears, deer, elk, snowshoe hares, and porcupines also feed extensively on aspen leaves, buds, and bark. The bases of the trunks shown here have been wrapped with wire mesh to protect them from beavers, but that hasn't kept bears from climbing the trees. Narrow-leaved cottonwood (*Populus angustifolia*), very rare in California although more common elsewhere west of the Rockies, also has smooth, pale bark, but it lacks aspen's bold black markings, and its leaves are much narrower. White polar (*Populus alba*), a European species sometimes found near homesites, has wide, slightly lobed leaves that are dark glossy green on the upper side but densely white-woolly underneath.

Male catkins.

Female catkins.

HIND'S WILLOW

Family: Salicaceae (willow family)

Also called: Sandbar willow or coyote willow

Scientific name: *Salix exigua* Nutt. var. *hindsiana* (Benth.) Dorn

Height: Up to 16'.

Leaves: Deciduous, alternate, the blade 1.2–6" long, very narrow, gray-green, usually both sides covered with long, soft, silky or wavy hairs, lower side occasionally hairless; margins smooth or finely toothed.

Flowers: Male and female flowers borne on separate plants, both types in elongate clusters called catkins that bloom after the leaves emerge, their sepals and petals reduced to 2 minute, stubby, nectar-producing structures (called nectaries); male flowers with 2 stamens; female flowers with 1 superior, hairy ovary topped by a small, 4-lobed stigma.

Blooms April through May.

Elevation: Sea level to about 2,000'.

Habitat: Flood plains and sandy or gravelly shores.

Comments: Willows can be hard to figure out. Most of California's 30-odd species are shrubs that visually differ from one another in features like the color of the twigs, whether the margins of the scale that protects immature leaf buds are free or fused, the shape and hairiness of the leaves, whether the plants bloom before or after the leaves emerge, and how many nectaries and stamens each flower has; you need a microscope to see some of these details. Sandbar willow, common in much of northern California, often forms dense stands and is one of the easier species to recognize because of its soft-haired, gray-green leaves. Like many other species of willow, it's widely used in Native American basketry. Relatively few native willows become trees; they include black willow (*Salix gooddingii*), which occurs mainly in the Sacramento Valley and the surrounding foothills and sometimes reaches a height of 100', and the more widespread red willow (*Salix laevigata*), which can grow 50' tall.

Male catkins.

Female catkins.

ARROYO WILLOW

Family: Salicaceae (willow family)

Also called: White willow

Scientific name: *Salix lasiolepis* Benth.

Height: Up to more than 30'.

Leaves: Deciduous, alternate, the blade 1.5–5" long by 0.4–0.8" wide, upper side dark green and hairless, lower side paler and usually covered with woolly or silky hairs; margins smooth to irregularly toothed and sometimes rolled downwards.

Flowers: Male and female flowers borne on separate plants, both types in elongate clusters called catkins that start blooming before the leaves emerge, their sepals and petals reduced to 1 minute, stubby, nectar-producing structure (called a nectary); male flowers with 2 stamens; female flowers with 1 flask-shaped superior, hairless ovary and a small, 4-lobed, pale yellow stigma.

Blooms January through June.

Elevation: Sea level to above 9,000'.

Habitat: Marshes, stream banks, and other moist to wet sites.

The tips of arroyo willow's stipules are often pointed, but occasionally, as shown here, they can be rounded.

Comments: This large shrub or small tree, widespread throughout northern California, is one of the willows that begin flowering before the leaves have fully emerged. It's highly variable and probably hybridizes with at least two other species of *Salix*. All species in this genus have a small bract beneath each flower; in arroyo willow the bract is very dark, almost black, which makes it relatively conspicuous. Also typical of the genus are pairs of small, ear-shaped to leaf-like structures called stipules at the base of the petioles of leaves produced in summer. Leaves produced earlier in the growing season often lack stipules.

BOX ELDER

Family: Sapindaceae (soapberry family)

Scientific name: *Acer negundo* L.

Height: Up to 65'.

Leaves: Deciduous, opposite, pinnately compound with 3 or less often up to 9 leaflets, the terminal leaflet 1.5–5" long by 1.2" to nearly 4" wide, lower side sparsely hairy to densely covered with felted hairs; margins toothed and somewhat lobed.

Flowers: Male and female flowers borne on different trees in drooping clusters of 10–250, both types with 5 minute sepals per flower and no petals, flower stalks often tinged pink; male flowers with 4–5 stamens, anthers sometimes reddish; female flowers with a superior ovary and 2 long stigmas.

Blooms February through April.

Elevation: Sea level to 6,000'.

Habitat: Riparian forest and stream banks.

Comments: This tree can be found in most of northern California, although it seems to be rare on the Modoc Plateau. Leaves with three leaflets are the most common type and look a bit like poison oak (*Toxicodendron diversilobum*), but poison oak's leaves are always alternate, never opposite. In some years, box elder's leaves turn a soft tawny yellow in early fall; in others they just go straight to brown. The 2-winged fruit, often called a key or samara, is dry and dispersed by wind. The wood is soft and brittle, completely different from the dense, hard wood of some eastern maples that's prized by cabinetmakers. Mountain maple (*Acer glabrum*) is a shrub or small tree less than 20' tall that grows at elevations of 5,000–10,000'; its leaves can be palmately 3-lobed or compound with three leaflets. California's other species of *Acer*— two native, one from the East Coast—all have palmately lobed leaves.

CALIFORNIA BUCKEYE

Family: Sapindaceae (soapberry family)

Scientific name: *Aesculus californica* (Spach) Nutt.

Height: 12–40'.

Leaves: Deciduous, opposite, palmately compound with 5–7 leaflets, each leaflet 2.5" to almost 7" long by 1.5–2" wide, almost hairless to covered with short fine hairs; margins finely toothed.

Flowers: In dense, elongate, spreading to almost upright clusters; sepals fused into a usually 2-lobed tube; petals 4 or occasionally 5, 0.5–0.7" long, white to pale pink; stamens 5–7, filaments white, anthers soft orange; ovary superior.

Blooms April through June.

Elevation: Sea level to 5,500'.

Habitat: Woodland, stream banks, and dry, open slopes.

Comments: In northern California, this small tree is most common around the perimeter of the Sacramento Valley and in the North Coast Ranges, Klamath Ranges, and Cascade and Sierra Nevada foothills. The flowers attract pipevine swallowtails and other butterflies, but the nectar and pollen are poisonous to honeybees. Of the many flowers in each inflorescence, generally only a few near the tip produce fruit. The leaves die when the weather gets hot and dry, and by late June the branches of some trees may be completely bare except for the 2–3"-wide fruits; other trees don't shed their dead leaves until fall. Each fruit consists of a thin leathery husk that splits open to release one big, glossy, orange-brown or mahogany-colored seed. Unlike most species, the seeds don't need to be buried to germinate; when the rainy season returns, they quickly send out a sturdy whitish root that is soon followed by an upright green shoot. Native Americans used crushed seeds to stupefy fish and make them float to the surface where they could easily be netted or gathered by hand.

Germinating seeds.

CALIFORNIA PITCHER-PLANT

Family: Sarraceniaceae (pitcher-plant family)

Scientific name: *Darlingtonia californica* Torr.

Height: Flowering stems up to about 3' tall.

Leaves: In basal rosettes, each leaf a narrow, upright hooded cone 4" to 2' tall, occasionally taller, yellowish green to dark red, with a handlebar mustache–like appendage dangling from under the hood and numerous small translucent "windows" on the hood's upper side.

Flowers: Nodding, borne singly; sepals 5, 1.5–2.5" long, narrow, greenish or yellowish, sometimes tinged with purple; petals 5, dark red or purple to yellowish green; stamens 12–15; ovary superior.

Blooms April through June.

Elevation: 200' to above 7,000'.

Habitat: Bogs with gently flowing water.

Comments: This rare herbaceous perennial spreads by creeping aboveground and underground stems and can form big colonies. The bogs where it grows tend to be poor in nitrogen, and like other insectivorous plants it "has solved" the problem by trapping insects. Many insects that enter a leaf end up drowning in a pool of water inside the leaf where they are digested by bacteria and other small resident organisms; the nitrogen that's released is then absorbed by the plant. The odd-looking flowers are pollinated by a native species of bee and possibly spiders. California pitcher-plant occurs in the Klamath Ranges, the northern Sierra Nevada, and western Oregon and is the only species in its genus.

BOLANDER'S WOODLAND STAR

Family: Saxifragaceae (saxifrage family)

Scientific name: *Lithophragma bolanderi* A. Gray

Height: 8–32".

Leaves: Basal leaves palmately 3- to 5-lobed, the indentations between lobes less than half the distance from margin to petiole, lobe margins with teeth like small gothic arches; stem leaves alternate, smaller, more deeply lobed.

Flowers: The bases of the sepals and petals fused into a round-bottomed cup; sepals 5, greenish; petals 5, 0.2–0.3" long, white, unlobed or with 5 or more lobes; stamens 10; ovary partly inferior.

Blooms February through July.

Elevation: Sea level to 6,500'.

Habitat: Woodland, lightly shaded grassland, and riparian areas.

Comments: In northern California, this herbaceous perennial grows mainly in the North Coast Ranges, Cascades, and Sierra Nevada. Plants with completely unlobed and 5-lobed petals may grow side by side. Hillside woodland star (*Lithophragma heterophyllum*) is very similar; it's more common in the Coast Ranges than east of the Sacramento Valley. The base of each flower is abruptly squared off, its petals are generally 3-lobed, and its ovary is superior. Five other species of *Lithophragma* grow in the region, all with white or pink flowers; they differ in small details in the structure of their flowers and basal leaves.

FRINGE CUPS

Family: Saxifragaceae (saxifrage family)

Scientific name: *Tellima grandiflora* (Pursh) Lindl.

Height: 20" to more than 3'.

Leaves: Basal leaves 0.8–4" long and equally wide, the blade slightly palmately lobed, lobe margins toothed; stem leaves alternate, smaller, sessile.

Flowers: The bases of the sepals and petals fused into a bell or urn shape; sepals 5, green; petals 5, 0.1–0.3" long, greenish white, cream-colored, or purplish red, with 5–7 finger-like lobes; stamens 10; ovary half-inferior with a 2-lobed purple stigma.

Blooms April through July.

Elevation: Sea level to 6,500'.

Habitat: Moist shady areas.

Comments: This herbaceous perennial with conspicuously hairy stems, the only species in its genus, grows along the coast and in the North Coast Ranges, Klamath Ranges, Cascades, and Sierra Nevada. Like most species of Saxifragaceae, each plant produces many small, often rather widely spaced flowers. A few other northern California representatives of the family, namely three species of *Pectiantia* and the rare leafy-stemmed mitrewort (*Mitellastra caulescens*), also have white to greenish petals with finger-like lobes, but in all of these the lobes jut out more or less at right angles to the petal's main axis.

CALIFORNIA BEE-PLANT

Family: Scrophulariaceae (figwort family)

Also called: California figwort

Scientific name: *Scrophularia californica* Cham. & Schltdl.

Height: 30" to 4'.

Leaves: Opposite, the blade of the largest leaves 2–7" long by 1–3" wide, narrow to oval or somewhat triangular, veins deeply indented on the upper side, the base usually heart-shaped or rounded; margins toothed or double-toothed.

Flowers: Sepals 5, small, mainly green, fused at the base; petals fused into a 5-lobed cup, the 2 upper lobes the largest and usually red or maroon, the 2 at the sides shading from red to cream or pink, and the bottom lobe cream-colored; fertile stamens 4 plus a sterile stamen (called a staminode) with a slightly widened tip; ovary superior.

Blooms March through July.

Elevation: Sea level to above 8,000'.

Habitat: Damp sites in woodland, chaparral, and coastal scrub.

Comments: This common but inconspicuous herbaceous perennial occurs from southern California and Arizona to British Columbia. The stems are square in cross-section, and occasionally the flowers are greenish yellow. Mountain figwort (*Scrophularia lanceolata*) is very similar, but the tip of its staminode is fan-shaped; it grows in the Klamath Ranges, Cascades, and on the Modoc Plateau. A third northern California species, desert figwort (*Scrophularia desertorum*), can be found on the Modoc Plateau and the eastern side of the Cascades and Sierra Nevada; its leaves are wedge-shaped at the base, tapering towards the petiole.

MOTH MULLEIN

Family: Scrophulariaceae (figwort family)

Scientific name: *Verbascum blattaria* L.

Height: 1–4'.

Leaves: Basal leaves with blades 1.5–10" long and short petioles, narrow to oval, typically hairless; margins scalloped or irregularly toothed; stem leaves alternate, smaller, sessile, often with basal lobes that clasp the stem.

Flowers: 1" to more than 1.5" wide; sepals 5, fused at the base, narrow, green or purplish; petals 5, fused at the base, usually white or yellow, rarely purple; stamens 5, filaments purple and very hairy, anthers light yellow to orange; ovary superior with a small green stigma on a long purplish style.

Blooms May through August.

Elevation: Sea level to 5,500'.

Habitat: Disturbed areas, flood plains, stream banks, chaparral, woodland, and yellow pine forest.

Comments: This Eurasian biennial is widespread through-out northern California; occasionally it's an annual or short-lived perennial. Typically the stems are unbranched. Each flower opens for just one day; if not pollinated by an insect during that time, it pollinates itself as it closes. The resulting seeds can remain viable for 90 years. Wand mullein (*Verbascum virgatum*), also native to Eurasia, is less common in northern California; its yellow flowers are crowded together, and its leaves are bristly-haired.

WOOLLY MULLEIN

Family: Scrophulariaceae (figwort family)

Also called: Common mullein

Scientific name: *Verbascum thapsus* L.

Height: 1" to nearly 7'.

Leaves: Basal leaves with blades 3–20" long and short petioles, fairly narrow to oval and densely covered with woolly, many-branched hairs; margins usually smooth; stem leaves alternate, 2–12" long, sessile.

Flowers: 0.6" to more than 1" wide; sepals 5, fused at the base, narrow, woolly-haired like the leaves; petals 5, fused at the base, lemon-yellow; stamens 5 with yellow filaments and orange anthers, 3 of the filaments very hairy, the other 2 hairless or sparsely hairy; ovary superior with a small green stigma on a long greenish style.

Blooms May through September.

Elevation: Sea level to above 8,000'.

Habitat: Flood plains and other disturbed areas.

Comments: Woolly mullein, another Eurasian biennial, is common in most of California and can be invasive. In their first growing season, the plants just produce big rosettes of soft, fuzzy, blue-gray to blue-green leaves; the flowering stems that appear the second year can be unbranched or branched and candelabra-like. The plants die after flowering, but the dead stems sometimes persist for another year; the seeds may remain viable in the soil for more than 35 years.

TREE-OF-HEAVEN

Family: Simaroubaceae (quassia family)

Also called: Copal tree or varnish tree

Scientific name: *Ailanthus altissima* (Mill.) Swingle

Height: Up to 65'.

Leaves: Deciduous, alternate, 1–3' long, once pinnately compound with 6–22 pairs of opposite leaflets plus 1 terminal leaflet, each leaflet 3" to almost 6" long; narrow, young leaves with short velvety hairs, mature leaves hairless; margins smooth except for a few teeth near the base; odor of bruised leaves rancid.

Flowers: Male and female flowers usually borne on separate trees in large branched clusters; both types with 5–6 tiny, partly fused sepals and 5–6 spreading white petals about 0.1" long; male flowers with 10–15 stamens with long white filaments and cream-colored anthers; female flowers usually with 2–5 pistils with flattened ovaries, their styles twisted together.

Blooms May through July.

Elevation: Sea level to above 6,000'.

Habitat: Riparian areas, grassland, oak woodland, and disturbed sites.

Comments: I'm not sure how this fast-growing, notoriously invasive tree, native to China, got its most common English name, tree-of-heaven. Its roots send up numerous suckers, forming thickets that displace native vegetation, and a single tree can produce well over 300,000 of the curiously asymmetrical, winged, 1-seeded fruits every year. Some people get contact dermatitis from handling the leaves, others get allergies from the pollen. The foamy flowers have an odd scent, rather like that of *Ceanothus*, that I find unpleasant. The species is now established in most of California, including some desert locations and cracked paving in urban areas, and unfortunately is probably here to stay. The leaves of northern California black walnut (*Juglans hindsii*) look somewhat similar but have finely toothed margins and give off a pleasant herbal aroma when bruised.

JIMSON WEED

Family: Solanaceae (nightshade family)

Also called: Sacred thorn-apple, hairy thorn-apple, Indian apple, moon lily, or tolguacha

Scientific name: *Datura wrightii* Regel

Height: 20" to 5'.

Leaves: Alternate, the blade 3–8" long, oval, covered with velvety gray or white hairs; margins smooth, coarsely toothed, or slightly lobed; odor foul.

Flowers: Sepals fused into a ribbed tube 3–5" long, green; petals 5, fused into a wide-flaring funnel 6–8" long, white; stamens 5; ovary superior.

Blooms April through October.

Elevation: Sea level to above 7,000'.

Habitat: Open areas with sandy or gravelly soil.

Comments: This annual or herbaceous perennial smells really bad—you get the stench on your fingers just touching a plant. It reminds me of the fug on city buses in winter when I was a child in England: unwashed bodies, damp woolen clothing, cigarette smoke, the pervasive smell of soot and burning coal. . . . Luckily, jimson weed's smell dissipates quickly, but some people get contact dermatitis from handling the plants. The flowers point upwards, but the painfully spiny fruits always grow downwards, with remnants of the sepals forming a "skirt" at their base; the seeds are tan. The species grows in the Sacramento Valley, Sierra Nevada foothills, and eastern part of the North Coast Ranges; it's widespread farther south. Two other species of *Datura* found in northern California have smaller flowers and white to lavender petals; their seed capsules grow upright, and their seeds are black. Thorn-apple (*Datura stramonium*), native to Mexico and eastern North America, has fairly narrow flowers. The seed capsules of Chinese thorn-apple (*Datura ferox*) have fewer but larger, even more ferocious spines than *Datura wrightii*; despite its common name, it's native to Mexico and South America. All species of *Datura* are extremely poisonous. The name jimson weed is often applied to the entire genus.

Unfurling petals of jimson weed (*Datura wrightii*).

Fruit and seeds of thorn-apple (*Datura stramonium*).

327

MANY-FLOWERED TOBACCO

Family: Solanaceae (nightshade family)

Scientific name: *Nicotiana acuminata* (Graham) Hook. var. *multiflora* (Phil.) Reiche

Height: 20" to 5'.

Leaves: Basal leaves with blades 2–10" long, oval, covered with sticky glandular hairs; margins smooth; stem leaves alternate, smaller, often very narrow, with short petioles; odor musty.

Flowers: Sepals 0.6–0.8" long, fused into a tube with 5 long narrow lobes, light green with darker green stripes, densely sticky-haired; petals fused into an abruptly flaring 5-lobed tube 1.2–2" long, the outside of the tube light green, the lobes white or greenish white and slightly notched or crimped at the tip; stamens 5; ovary superior.

Blooms May through November.

Elevation: Sea level to above 5,000'.

Habitat: Open areas with sandy or gravelly soil.

Comments: This annual is native to South America but widespread in northern California. The plants are very sticky and have an unpleasant smell, a bit like stale cigarette butts. The flowers close up during the day, and so the best time to look for this species is early morning or late afternoon. Indian tobacco (*Nicotiana quadrivalvis*), which is native to the western and central United States, looks similar, but its stem leaves are sessile. Its flowers are a bit bigger than those of many-flowered tobacco, can be white, greenish, or tinged violet, and have pointed lobes, making each flower look like a five-pointed star when viewed from above. In coyote tobacco (*Nicotiana attenuata*), another California native, the sepal tube is hairless to sparsely hairy with short triangular lobes, while the petal tube is tinged pink.

TREE TOBACCO

Family: Solanaceae (nightshade family)

Scientific name: *Nicotiana glauca* Graham

Height: Up to 25'.

Leaves: Evergreen, alternate, the blade 2–8" long, oval, hairless, covered with a waxy bloom; margins smooth; odor musty.

Flowers: Sepals fused into a wide tube about 0.4" long, greenish yellow, hairless; petals fused into a tube about 1.5" long, the open end of the tube first slightly swollen, then constricted, then flaring into 5 short lobes, yellow to greenish yellow; stamens 5; ovary superior with a bright green stigma.

Blooms almost all year.

Elevation: Sea level to 3,600'.

Habitat: Riparian areas and disturbed sites.

Comments: This small, invasive tree, native to South America, is the only woody species of *Nicotiana* in California. It grows in the Sacramento Valley and the eastern part of the North Coast Ranges and is common farther south. All parts of the plant contain the alkaloid anabasine, as well as nicotine, and are highly toxic to humans and livestock. The waxy bloom on the leaves disappears if you rub it because you're smoothing out the microscopic flakes of wax.

DOUGLAS' NIGHTSHADE

Family: Solanaceae (nightshade family)

Also called: Greenspot nightshade

Scientific name: *Solanum douglasii* Dunal

Height: Up to nearly 7'.

Leaves: Alternate, the blade 0.4–4" long, oval, slightly hairy to nearly hairless; margins smooth to irregularly toothed.

Flowers: About 0.4" wide; sepals small, green; petals fused into a short tube with 5 long narrow lobes, the base of each lobe apple-green, the rest white to lavender; stamens 5, anthers 0.1–0.2" long, bright yellow; ovary superior.

Blooms almost all year.

Elevation: Sea level to 3,200'.

Habitat: Woodland, chaparral, and dry coastal scrub.

Comments: This mainly coastal, typically heavily branched herbaceous perennial or subshrub is common south of San Francisco Bay but does put in an occasional appearance along California's north coast. The fruit is a black, round berry 0.2–0.4" wide. American nightshade (*Solanum americanum*) is similar but not restricted to the coast. Its petals lack a green spot, and its anthers are less than 0.1" long; it sometimes hybridizes with Douglas' nightshade, but the offspring are sterile. A total of about 15 species of *Solanum* occur in northern California, several of them non-native and weedy. The genus is easy to recognize, but it can be hard to identify species.

CHAPARRAL NIGHTSHADE

Family: Solanaceae (nightshade family)

Also called: Purple nightshade

Scientific name: *Solanum xanti* A. Gray.

Height: 16" to 3'.

Leaves: Alternate, the blade 0.8–3" long, narrow to oval, usually with short spiky hairs that make the leaves feel rough; margins smooth or lobed at the base of the blade.

Flowers: 0.6–1.2" wide; sepals 5, fused into a small 5-lobed bell, green; petals 5, fused into an umbrella-like shape, lavender to purple with 2 green spots near the base of each petal; stamens 5, anthers about 0.2" long, bright yellow; ovary superior.

Blooms February through June.

Elevation: Sea level to almost 9,000'.

Habitat: Chaparral, woodland, and conifer forest.

Comments: This rather variable herbaceous perennial or subshrub grows along the coast and in the North Coast Ranges, Klamath Ranges, and Sierra Nevada; it's also common farther south. The fruit is a greenish berry 0.4–0.6" wide. The species probably hybridizes with Parish's nightshade (*Solanum parishii*) and blue witch nightshade (*Solanum umbelliferum*), both of which look rather similar to chaparral nightshade and are widespread in most of northern California. Interestingly, the genus *Solanum* also includes potatoes and eggplant, but all wild members of the group should be considered highly toxic.

SNOWDROP BUSH

Family: Styracaceae (storax family)

Scientific name: *Styrax redivivus* (Torr.) L. C. Wheeler

Height: 3–15'.

Leaves: Deciduous, alternate, the blade 0.8" to more than 3" long, oval to nearly round, upper side hairless, lower side with small branched hairs; margins smooth.

Flowers: Dangling, borne singly or in clusters of 2–6; sepals fused into a 6- to 9-toothed cone, pale green, hairy; petals 5 or occasionally 10, 0.5–1" long, fused at the base, white, gently flaring; stamens usually 10, filaments white, fused at the base, anthers yellow; ovary more or less superior, stigma only marginally wider than the long white style.

Blooms April through June.

Elevation: Sea level to 5,000'.

Habitat: Woodland and chaparral.

Comments: Most of the year this often wispy shrub or small understory tree is easy to miss, but during the two to three weeks that it's in bloom it's simply spectacular. The flowers are followed by round fruits 0.4–0.5" wide, each fruit consisting of a thin husk enclosing one large, caramel-colored seed or less often two or three seeds; the long "tail" on the fruit is the remnant of the style and stigma. In northern California, snowdrop bush grows mainly around the perimeter of the Sacramento Valley. It's the only Californian representative of its family; older texts call it *Styrax officinalis* var. *californicus*.

SEA BLUSH

Family: Valerianaceae (valerian family)

Scientific name: *Plectritis congesta* (Lindl.) DC. subsp. *congesta*

Height: 1–18".

Leaves: Basal leaves 0.4–2" long, spoon-shaped, hairless; margins mostly smooth; stem leaves opposite, oval, sessile.

Flowers: Densely clustered, a deeply palmately 3- to 5-lobed bract below each flower; no sepals; petals fused into a 2-lipped tube 0.2–0.4" long with a short extension called a spur pointing back towards the stem, pale to bright pink, upper lip 2-lobed, lower lip 3-lobed; stamens 3; ovary inferior.

Blooms March through June.

Elevation: Sea level to 5,500'.

Habitat: Coastal bluffs and open to partly shaded slopes in woodland, chaparral, and yellow pine forest.

Comments: In northern California, this annual grows in the North Coast Ranges, Klamath Ranges, Sierra Nevada, Sacramento Valley, and coastal areas; in good years it can bloom profusely. *Plectritis congesta* subsp. *brachystemon* has smaller, paler flowers that sometimes lack a spur. The name "sea blush" is misleading since both subspecies grow far inland. Two additional species occur in northern California. Long-spurred plectritis (*Plectritis ciliosa*) has long, slender, conspicuous spurs. In *Plectritis macrocera* the petals are white to pale pink, less than 0.2" long, and only very slightly two-lipped; the spur is rather thick.

LAMB LETTUCE

Family: Valerianaceae (valerian family)

Also called: Common corn salad

Scientific name: *Valerianella locusta* (L.) Betcke

Height: 4–18".

Leaves: Opposite, the blade 0.2–1.5" long, narrow to oval, hairless to sparsely hairy, often slightly succulent, lower leaves with petioles, upper leaves sessile; margins fringed with short, fine hairs, otherwise smooth or with a few large teeth.

Flowers: Borne in clusters set in a ruff of leaf-like bracts; no sepals; petals fused into a 5-lobed funnel less than 0.1" long, white, the lobes sometimes tinged blue; stamens 3; ovary inferior.

Blooms April through June.

Elevation: Sea level to 4,500'.

Habitat: Moist, shady sites.

Comments: In northern California, this annual occurs in the Sacramento Valley, North Coast Ranges, Klamath Ranges, and northern Sierra Nevada. The stems are hollow, more or less hexagonal in cross-section, and branch into equal forks. The species is native to Europe, where it's cultivated as a salad green. It used to be a common weed in wheat fields (called corn in Britain), hence the name "corn salad." In some texts it's called *Valerianella olitoria*. Keel-fruited corn salad (*Valerianella carinata*) is similar except for the shape of its fruits, which are small and seed-like in both species.

COMMON LIPPIA

Family: Verbenaceae (vervain family)

Also called: Turkey-tangle fogfruit

Scientific name: *Phyla nodiflora* (L.) Greene

Height: Usually 1–2", with branches up to 6" long lying flat on the ground.

Leaves: Opposite, the blade 0.2–1.2" long, oval, gray-green to blue-green, with short flat-lying forked hairs; margins smooth or with a few large teeth.

Flowers: Borne in dense, initially fairly flat clusters that elongate as the older flowers start setting fruit, an oval purple bract just below each flower; sepals fused, tiny; petals fused into a 2-lipped tube, white to pink or lavender, upper lip 2-lobed, lower lip 3-lobed with a yellow spot in the center that turns purple as the flower ages; stamens 4; ovary superior.

Blooms May through November.

Elevation: Sea level to 1,300'.

Habitat: Stream banks and other open sites with moist, disturbed soil.

Comments: This variable, mat-forming herbaceous perennial grows in the Sacramento Valley, North Coast Ranges, and coastal areas; it's also common farther south and sometimes planted as a ground cover. Opinions differ about whether the species is native to California or South America. In older texts it's called *Lippia nodiflora*. In frog fruit or lanceleaf fogfruit (*Phyla lanceolata*), the leaves have 11–21 teeth.

TALL VERVAIN

Family: Verbenaceae (vervain family)

Scientific name: *Verbena bonariensis* L.

Height: 20" to more than 5'.

Leaves: Opposite, 3–6" long, narrow, sessile, covered with short stiff hairs, bases tapered but clasping the stem slightly; margins toothed.

Flowers: Borne in narrow, dense clusters, 3–17 clusters loosely grouped into an inflorescence; sepals fused into a 5-toothed tube, purplish; petals fused into a 5-lobed tube, blue, lavender, or occasionally white; stamens 4; ovary superior.

Blooms April through November.

Elevation: Sea level to about 600'.

Habitat: Disturbed sites ranging from wet to very dry.

Comments: In California this South American annual or biennial grows mainly in the Central Valley and San Francisco Bay area. Usually its stems are rather leggy, square in cross-section, and feel rough. You have to look closely to see the clasping leaf bases. The flowers are tightly packed together and the inflorescences don't elongate after flowering, and so the mature fruits overlap each other. Seashore vervain (*Verbena litoralis*), another South American species, occurs mainly in the Central Valley and Sierra Nevada foothills despite its common name; its tapered leaves don't clasp the stem. The leaves of blue vervain (*Verbena hastata*) have petioles 0.4–1" long.

333

WESTERN VERVAIN

Family: Verbenaceae (vervain family)

Scientific name: *Verbena lasiostachys* Link var. *scabrida* Moldenke

Height: 12–32".

Leaves: Opposite, the blade 1.5–4" long, overall shape oval with several wide pinnate lobes, upper side fairly bright green and covered with stiff hairs; margins coarsely toothed.

Flowers: Borne in long, narrow clusters; sepals fused into a 5-ribbed tube, green except for the purplish ribs and 5 purplish teeth, bristly; petals fused into a 5-lobed tube, blue to purple; stamens 4; ovary superior.

Blooms May through September.

Elevation: Sea level to 7,500'.

Habitat: Open or lightly shaded, dry to wet sites.

Comments: In northern California, this bristly-stemmed, sometimes sprawling, sometimes upright herbaceous perennial grows in the North Coast Ranges, Klamath Ranges, Sierra Nevada foothills, and Sacramento Valley. The petal lobes can be evenly distributed around the lip of the petal tube or slightly two-lipped, with two lobes on the upper side and three on the lower. The stem elongates after flowering, separating the fruits enough for them not to overlap. As in other species of *Verbena*, each fruit splits into four 1-seeded "nutlets" cupped by the persistent sepals. *Verbena lasiostachys* var. *lasiostachys*, also widespread, has soft-haired, more grayish green leaves.

WESTERN DOG VIOLET

Family: Violaceae (violet family)

Also called: Early blue violet

Scientific name: *Viola adunca* Sm. subsp. *adunca*

Height: 1.5" to more than 12".

Leaves: Basal leaves with blades 0.2" to more than 2.5" long, oval to triangular, hairless to hairy; margins smooth or scalloped; stem leaves alternate, smaller.

Flowers: Sepals 5, narrow; petals 5, medium blue to deep violet, the base of the lower 3 white with purple veins, the base of the bottom petal drawn out into a conspicuous sock-like spur 0.1–0.3" long that points back towards the stem; stamens 5; ovary superior.

Blooms April through August.

Elevation: Sea level to above 11,000'.

Habitat: Stream banks, moist banks around the edges of meadows, and grassy openings in conifer forest.

Comments: The northwestern corner of California abounds with blue- or purple-flowered species of *Viola*; they're less frequent in other parts of the state. Western dog violet, a herbaceous perennial, is widespread in California's mountains, and along the north coast it descends to sea level. Its stems can be upright or sprawling, and their bases often become woody with age. The caterpillars of three federally protected species of butterfly feed on western dog violet.

334

BAKER'S VIOLET

Family: Violaceae (violet family)

Scientific name: *Viola bakeri* Greene

Height: 1–12".

Leaves: Basal leaves with blades 0.7–3.5" long by 0.3–1.5" wide, narrow to oval, nearly hairless to hairy; margins usually smooth; stem leaves alternate, smaller.

Flowers: Sepals 5, narrow; petals 5, yellow, the base of the lower 3 with purplish brown veins, the base of the bottom petal forming a very short spur hidden by the sepals, the back of the 2 upper petals often maroon or brown; stamens 5; ovary superior.

Blooms May through July.

Elevation: 3,000-12,500'.

Habitat: Moist open sites surrounded by conifer forest.

Comments: This herbaceous perennial grows from a deep, woody taproot. It occurs in the Klamath Ranges, Cascades, Sierra Nevada, and the highest parts of the North Coast Ranges as well as on the Modoc Plateau and farther north. Astoria violet (*Viola praemorsa*, with two subspecies in California) is similar, but its leaves have toothed, scalloped, or wavy margins. Stream violet (*Viola glabella*), also yellow-flowered, has two to six basal leaves, but the upright flowering stem is leafless until just below the flowers, where you'll find a few large, oval to heart- or kidney-shaped leaves.

DOUGLAS' VIOLET

Family: Violaceae (violet family)

Also called: Golden violet

Scientific name: *Viola douglasii* Steud.

Height: 1–8".

Leaves: Basal leaves with blades 0.5–2" long, twice pinnately compound, leaflets narrow to very narrow, sparsely hairy; margins smooth except for a fringe of short hairs; stem leaves alternate, similar.

Flowers: Sepals 5, narrow, fringed with short hairs; petals 5, yellow, the base of the lower 3 with dark brown veins, the base of the bottom petal forming a very short spur hidden by the sepals, the back of the 2 upper petals maroon to almost black; stamens 5; ovary superior.

Blooms February through July.

Elevation: 60–7,500'.

Habitat: Grassland.

Comments: This herbaceous perennial is one of our first spring wildflowers, blooming before nearby grasses get tall enough to hide it. It grows in most of northern California except along the coast and on the Modoc Plateau. The orange-yellow, partly closed flower in the lower right quadrant of the photo is frying pans (*Eschscholzia lobbii*), which doesn't open until mid-morning. Johnny-jump-up or California golden violet (*Viola pedunculata*) also grows in grasslands (as well as sunny spots in chaparral and woodland) and looks similar but has oval to heart-shaped leaves with toothed or scalloped margins.

PINE VIOLET

Family: Violaceae (violet family)

Also called: Yellow wood violet or moose-horn violet

Scientific name: *Viola lobata* Benth. subsp. *lobata*

Height: 2–18".

Leaves: Alternate, the blade 0.6–3.5" long, wider than long, deeply palmately divided into 3–12 finger-like segments, hairless or slightly hairy along the veins on the lower side; margins smooth to coarsely toothed.

Flowers: Sepals 5, narrow, usually fringed with short hairs; petals 5, yellow, the base of the lower 3 (and sometimes all 5 petals) with purplish brown veins, the base of the bottom petal forming a short wide spur that protrudes slightly from among the sepals, the backs of the 2 upper petals (and sometimes the 2 at the side) maroon; stamens 5; ovary superior.

Blooms April through August.

Elevation: 150–7,500'.

Habitat: Dry sites in forest, woodland, and chaparral.

Comments: This herbaceous perennial is easy to recognize by its distinctive leaves. It grows in the North Coast Ranges, Klamath Ranges, Cascades, and Sierra Nevada as well as southwestern Oregon; to the south, it occurs only in San Diego County and Baja California. Once in a while you'll find it in moist places. *Viola lobata* subsp. *integrifolia* is less common; its leaves are longer than wide, not lobed, and have irregularly scalloped or toothed margins.

WESTERN HEART'S EASE

Family: Violaceae (violet family)

Also called: Two-eyed violet or pinto violet

Scientific name: *Viola ocellata* Torr. & A. Gray

Height: 1–15".

Leaves: Basal leaves with blades 0.4–2.5" long, oval to triangular or kidney-shaped, not shiny, hairless or covered with short hairs; margins toothed or scalloped; stem leaves similar.

Flowers: Sepals 5, narrow, usually fringed with short hairs; petals 5, white with yellow bases, the 2 at the sides with a bold purple blotch, the base of the bottom petal with purple veins and a short spur almost hidden by the sepals, the backs of the 2 upper petals reddish or purple; stamens 5; ovary superior.

Blooms March through July.

Elevation: 250' to above 4,000'.

Habitat: Moist, grassy or rocky sites in conifer forest.

Comments: This herbaceous perennial grows mainly near the coast, in the Coast Ranges from Monterey County to southwestern Oregon, and in the Cascades northeast of Redding. Northern two-eyed violet or wedge-leaf violet (*Viola cuneata*), which occurs in northwestern California, has shiny leaves with bases that taper to the petiole. Its sepals aren't fringed, and although the petals resemble western heart's ease from the front, the backs of all five are dark reddish violet.

REDWOOD VIOLET

Family: Violaceae (violet family)

Also called: Evergreen violet

Scientific name: *Viola sempervirens* Greene

Height: A few inches at most.

Leaves: Evergreen, alternate, the blades 0.4" to nearly 2" long, oval to round or slightly heart-shaped, hairless or sparsely bristly, sometimes with purplish spots on one or both sides; margins scalloped.

Flowers: Sepals 5, narrow; petals 5, yellow, the lower bases of 3 with delicate red or purple veins, the base of the bottom petal forming a short wide spur that protrudes slightly from among the sepals; stamens 5; ovary superior.

Blooms January through July.

Elevation: Sea level to 4,500'.

Habitat: Forest near the coast, often in deep shade.

Comments: This herbaceous perennial occurs in coastal areas from Monterey County to Alaska and in the Klamath Ranges. Its creeping aboveground stems, 1–3' long, can become woody with age. Where the plants aren't especially dense, the more or less round leaves spaced out at short intervals across the forest floor are a good clue to the presence of evergreen violet even when it's not in bloom.

337

AMERICAN MISTLETOE

Leaves and male flowers of American mistletoe (*Phoradendron leucarpum* subsp. *macrophyllum*).

American mistletoe on northern California black walnut (*Juglans hindsii*).

American mistletoe berries; each is about 0.2" in diameter.

338

Family: Viscaceae (mistletoe family)

Also called: Bigleaf mistletoe

Scientific name: *Phoradendron leucarpum* (Raf.) Reveal & M. C. Johnst. subsp. *macrophyllum* (Engelm.) J. R. Abbott & R. L. Thomps.

Height: Up to about 3'.

Leaves: Evergreen, opposite, the blade 0.6–2.5" long and up to 2" wide, yellowish green to almost yellow, often glossy, hairless or with minute hairs; margins smooth.

Flowers: Male and female flowers borne on separate plants, both types with 3 (occasionally 4) tiny, fleshy, yellowish sepals and no petals; male flowers with 3 very short stamens; female flowers with an inferior ovary. Blooms December through March.

Elevation: Sea level to 4,000'.

Habitat: On many different species of hardwood trees but *not* on oak (*Quercus* spp.).

Comments: In some texts this shrub-like perennial is called *Phoradendron macrophyllum*, *Phoradendron serotinum* subsp. *macrophyllum*, or *Phoradendron flavescens* var. *macrophyllum*. It's common in the North Coast Ranges, Sacramento Valley, and Sierra Nevada foothills and is very conspicuous in winter when its host trees are bare. Technically it's a "hemiparasite" because it doesn't draw *all* its nutrients from its host: Its leaves contain chlorophyll and hence are able to make carbohydrates, but it "steals" water and mineral nutrients through modified roots that invade the host tree's branches. Heavy infestations weaken the host, making it more susceptible to attack by insects or pathogens and sometimes killing it. Oak mistletoe (*Phoradendron leucarpum* subsp. *tomentosum*) blooms from July to September and attacks oak trees; only rarely does it grow on other species. Its densely hairy leaves are no more than 1.2" long by 0.8" wide, and their dull gray-green or olive-green color makes the plants harder to spot. Dense mistletoe (*Phoradendron bolleanum*) mainly attacks cedar (*Hesperocyparis* spp.), juniper (*Juniperus* spp.), and white fir (*Abies concolor*). European mistletoe (*Viscum album*) was introduced to the Sebastopol area around 1900 but so far has only spread a few miles. It has longer, narrower leaves and four sepals per flower. California's other native mistletoes have tiny, scale-like leaves. *Phoradendron* is dispersed by birds that feed on the berries, which have gelatinous, sticky flesh. If a bird gets some seeds stuck to its beak, it'll wipe the goo off on whatever branch it's perching on, inadvertently "planting" the seeds. And those seeds that it does consume pass through its digestive system unharmed, further spreading the infestation.

Oak mistletoe (*Phoradendron leucarpum* subsp. *tomentosum*) on valley oak (*Quercus lobata*).

Dense mistletoe (*Phoradendron bolleanum*) on western juniper (*Juniperus occidentalis*).

339

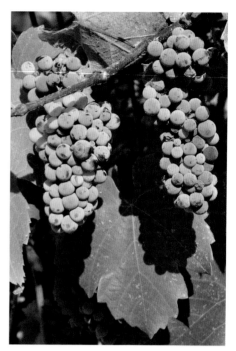

CALIFORNIA WILD GRAPE

Family: Vitaceae (grape family)

Scientific name: *Vitis californica* Benth.

Height: Climbs up to about 50'.

Leaves: Deciduous, alternate, the blade 3–6" long and wide, heart- or kidney-shaped, unlobed to shallowly palmately 3- or 5-lobed, somewhat hairy to densely woolly; margins toothed or scalloped.

Flowers: Male and female flowers borne on the same plant, both types with 5 greenish sepals and 5 yellowish petals, all tiny, the petals fused into a cap that falls off without expanding when the flowers open; male flowers with 5 spreading stamens that are the least inconspicuous part of the flower; female flowers with a superior ovary and nonfunctional stamens or no stamens at all.

Blooms April through June.

Elevation: Sea level to above 4,000'.

Habitat: Riparian areas and canyons.

Comments: This woody vine is widespread in northern California except on the Modoc Plateau. It often climbs high into nearby trees; if there's nothing to climb, it spreads across the ground, where it can provide good erosion control. The fruits are berries similar to table grapes except that they're only 0.2–0.3" wide with a fairly tough skin and containing one to four seeds. In fall, the leaves often turn golden yellow or deep red. When growing near vineyards the species can hybridize with wine grape (*Vitis vinifera*), which has bisexual flowers and is native to Europe.

PUNCTURE VINE

Family: Zygophyllaceae (caltrop family)

Also called: Caltrop, bullhead, goathead, or Texas sandbur

Scientific name: *Tribulus terrestris* L.

Height: Stems up to 3' long lying flat on the ground or mounded to a height of about 1'.

Leaves: Opposite, once pinnately compound with 6–12 leaflets per leaf, each leaflet 0.2–0.5" long, hairless to moderately hairy, the hairs white and silky or bristly; margins smooth except for a fringe of hairs.

Flowers: Less than 0.2" wide; sepals 5, green; petals 5, light yellow; stamens 10; ovary superior, topped by a 5-lobed, star-like green stigma.

Blooms April through October.

Elevation: Sea level to above 3,000'.

Habitat: Dry, disturbed sites.

Comments: Puncture vine is an annual that seems to have arrived from the Old World's Mediterranean region around 1900 and quickly became widespread throughout California. It's notorious for the stout spines on its fruit that easily punctured the tires on early cars and can injure people and animals— "caltrop" refers to the spiked iron balls that were thrown onto the ground to maim cavalry horses when wars were fought on horseback. Puncture vine is a pretty plant when you look at it closely but otherwise a thoroughly unpleasant one, highly poisonous to livestock. The roots sometimes contain bacteria that convert atmospheric nitrogen into forms usable by plants, helping this noxious weed thrive in poor soil. Two species of weevils from Italy that attack the stems and seeds are now being used to control it.

FLOWERING PLANTS: MONOCOTYLEDONS

CAMAS

Family: Agavaceae (century plant family)

Also called: Quamash

Scientific name: *Camassia leichtlinii* (Baker) S. Watson subsp. *suksdorfii* (Greenm.) Gould

Height: 8" to more than 3'.

Leaves: All basal, 8" to 2' long by 0.2–1" wide, grass-like in appearance from a distance, hairless; margins smooth.

Flowers: Sepals and petals very similar, 3 of each, 0.8" to more than 1.5" long, bright blue to violet or occasionally white; stamens 6, filaments blue, anthers bright yellow; ovary superior, apple-green.

Blooms May through August.

Elevation: 3,000–8,500'.

Habitat: Wet meadows.

Comments: This herbaceous perennial is common in the North Coast Ranges, Klamath Ranges, Cascades, Sierra Nevada, and as far north as British Columbia. The small bulbs were a mainstay in the diet of many Native American tribes, who carefully tended fields of camas. Probably some of the spectacular displays of flowers we now see are old Indian fields; unfortunately, they always seem to be at their showiest at the height of mosquito season. After the flowers have been pollinated, the petals and sepals twist together like a bit of rope, enclosing the developing seed capsule for a short time before dropping off. *Camassia quamash* subsp. *breviflora* grows in the same general area. It looks similar but has somewhat shorter, narrower leaves, and its petals and sepals are only 0.4–0.8" long; they don't twist as they dry out after pollination and fertilization have occurred and stay in place until the fruit is mature. The two species can hybridize.

Flowers in late afternoon.

Mature seed capsules that have split open, revealing the crinkled black seeds.

COMMON SOAP PLANT

Family: Agavaceae (century plant family)

Also called: Wavy-leaved soap root or amole

Scientific name: *Chlorogalum pomeridianum* (DC.) Kunth var. *pomeridianum*

Height: Up to more than 8'.

Leaves: Mainly basal, 8" to nearly 30" long by 0.2–1" wide; margins usually wavy; the few stem leaves much smaller, the uppermost reduced to papery bracts.

Flowers: Borne in branched inflorescences, opening late afternoon and closing the next morning; sepals and petals very similar, 3 of each, 0.6–1" long, very narrow, white with a green or purplish stripe down the middle; stamens 6, filaments white, anthers pale yellow; ovary superior, light green.

Blooms May through August.

Flowers from the same patch as those above left, around 10 a.m. the next day.

Elevation: Sea level to 5,000'.

Habitat: Open woodland, chaparral, and grassland.

Comments: This herbaceous perennial is common in the North Coast Ranges, Klamath Ranges, and Sierra Nevada. In a reasonably rainy winter, its leaves may start emerging as early as January. Later, when the plants are flowering, you'll probably be underwhelmed if you see them in the middle of the day. But go early in the evening, and you'll be rewarded by shimmering clouds of dainty white blossoms. The flower buds are said to open with an audible pop; I've watched them but I'm not sure that I've ever heard them. Maybe my dog did. Native Americans made soap and shampoo, brushes, glue, food, and a fish stupefactant from this versatile species. Narrow-leaved soap plant (*Chlorogalum angustifolium*), which grows in the same general region as common soap plant and also in the Cascade foothills, only gets 1–3' tall. Its leaves are 0.1–0.2" wide, usually with flat margins, and the sepals and petals are only 0.3–0.5" long.

LANCELEAF WATER-PLANTAIN

Family: Alismataceae (water-plantain family)

Scientific name: *Alisma lanceolatum* With.

Height: 4–40".

Leaves: Basal, the blade 2.5–5" long by 0.4–1.5" wide with a tapered base and long petiole; margins smooth.

Flowers: Borne in open, heavily branched inflorescences; sepals 3, small, green; petals 3, pink; stamens 6, anthers greenish yellow; pistils many, their ovaries superior, arranged in a circle on a flat disk (called the receptacle) that's essentially the end of the flower stalk.

Blooms June through August.

Elevation: Sea level to 1,600'.

Habitat: Marshy shores, ponds, and slowly moving water.

Comments: This herbaceous perennial, native to Eurasia and northern Africa, is a common weed in the Sacramento Valley's rice fields; it also occurs in the North Coast Ranges and Sierra Nevada foothills. Northern water-plantain (*Alisma triviale*), a widespread northern California native, has white petals and leaves with squared-off or even lobed bases. In both species the flowering stems are much taller than the leaves. The rare grass-leaved water-plantain or grass alisma (*Alisma gramineum*) mainly grows in ponds on the Modoc Plateau; its flowering stems are more or less equal in height to the leaves, which have blades 2.5–12" long by 0.3–0.8" wide.

SANFORD'S ARROWHEAD

Family: Alismataceae (water-plantain family)

Scientific name: *Sagittaria sanfordii* Greene

Height: 2–5'.

Leaves: Basal, the blade 5–10" long, narrow to very narrow with a tapered base, hairless, the petiole either flat like the blade or triangular in cross-section; margins smooth.

Flowers: 3 female flowers at the base of each inflorescence, each on a thick stalk that bends downwards as the fruit starts to develop, with 3 green sepals, 3 white petals, and many greenish pistils with superior ovaries spiraling around a rounded core (called the receptacle) that's essentially the end of the flower stalk; male flowers above, each with 3 green sepals, 3 white petals, and 7–30 yellow stamens.

Blooms May through October.

Elevation: Sea level to 1,000'.

Habitat: Ponds, sloughs, and slow-moving streams.

Comments: This rare herbaceous perennial grows in the Sacramento Valley, Klamath Ranges, Cascade foothills, and Del Norte County's coastal areas. It's one of six species of *Sagittaria* that occur in northern California. In sessile-fruited arrowhead (*Sagittaria rigida*), the female flowers are sessile; the leaves can be narrow, oval, or arrowhead-shaped. The other four species have arrowhead-shaped leaves; they include hooded arrowhead (*Sagittaria montevidenis* subsp. *calycina*), which has only two female flowers per inflorescence.

NARROW-LEAVED ONION

Family: Alliaceae (onion or garlic family)

Also called: Clasping onion

Scientific name: *Allium amplectens* Torr.

Height: 6–20".

Leaves: Basal, 2–4 leaves per plant, shorter than the stem, very narrow, more or less round in cross-section.

Flowers: Borne in umbels of 10–50 flowers, each flower on a stalk 0.2–0.6" long; sepals and petals very similar, 3 of each, spreading, white to pink; stamens 6; ovary superior, 3-lobed with 2 small, elongate bumps (called crests) on each lobe.

Blooms April through July.

Elevation: Sea level to 6,000'.

Habitat: Dry grassland and woodland.

Comments: This herbaceous perennial is widespread in northern California and farther north. Like all onions, it grows from a bulb, although wild onion bulbs are much smaller than the ones you cook with, typically only 0.4–1" in diameter. California has more than 50 species of *Allium*, and you often need bulbs as well as flowers and leaves to identify them; to make the task even harder, the leaves frequently wither before the plants bloom. The plants all smell like onions or garlic when picked. Common muilla (*Muilla maritima*), a member of the Themidaceae (brodiaea family), superficially resembles some species of *Allium* but is odorless.

SIERRA ONION

Family: Alliaceae (onion or garlic family)

Scientific name: *Allium campanulatum* S. Watson

Height: 4–12".

Leaves: Basal, usually 2 leaves per plant, roughly equal to the stem in length, very narrow, C-shaped in cross-section or flat; margins smooth.

Flowers: Borne in umbels of 10–50 flowers, each flower on a stalk 0.4–0.8" long; sepals and petals very similar, 3 of each, spreading widely, pink to purplish with a white base and a reddish "M" or inverted "V" in or just above the white area; stamens 6; ovary superior, 3-lobed with 2 small triangular bumps (called crests) on top of each lobe.

Blooms May through August.

Elevation: 2,000–9,000'.

Habitat: Dry mountain slopes.

Comments: Its common name notwithstanding, this herbaceous perennial also grows in the North Coast Ranges, Klamath Ranges, Cascades, and on the Modoc Plateau as well as in Oregon and Nevada. It tends to blend really well into the background, making it fairly hard to spot even though it often blooms in great profusion. Viewed close up, the pattern on the petals is distinctive. The flower stalks in each umbel tend to be a bit floppy.

345

VOLCANIC ONION

Family: Alliaceae (onion or garlic family)

Also called: Cascade onion

Scientific name: *Allium cratericola* Eastw.

Height: 1–4".

Leaves: Basal, 1 or 2 leaves per plant, usually 4–8" long, narrow, C-shaped in cross-section or flat; margins smooth.

Flowers: Borne in umbels of 20–30 flowers, each flower on a stalk 0.2–0.7" long; sepals and petals very similar, 3 of each, somewhat spreading, pink; stamens 6; ovary superior, 3-lobed with 1 tiny bump (called a crest) on top of each lobe.

Blooms March through June.

Elevation: 1,000–6,000'.

Habitat: Open, dry, gravelly or rocky sites, including fractured bedrock outcrops.

Comments: This herbaceous perennial occurs mainly around the perimeter of the Central Valley. Most onions reproduce not only by seed but also by small "baby bulbs" or offsets that form underground around the main bulb. In normal soil these offsets are pushed away from the parent plant by burrowing animals, from earthworms to gophers and badgers; but volcanic onion often grows in cracks in bedrock where few burrowing animals can live. As a result the bulbs stay clustered, collectively producing clumps of several to many leaves and flowering stems. Where the ground is softer, kangaroo rats dig up and eat the bulbs.

COASTAL ONION

Family: Alliaceae (onion or garlic family)

Scientific name: *Allium dichlamydeum* Greene

Height: 4–12".

Leaves: Basal, 3–6 leaves per plant, usually a bit longer than the stem, narrow, round or C-shaped in cross-section; margins smooth.

Flowers: Borne in umbels of 5–30 flowers, each flower on a stalk 0.2–0.8" long; sepals and petals very similar, 3 of each, not spreading very much, intense magenta; stamens 6; ovary superior, 3-lobed with 1 tiny bump (called a crest) on top of each lobe.

Blooms May through July.

Elevation: Sea level to 500'.

Habitat: Coastal bluffs and cliffs.

Comments: This herbaceous perennial occurs only in California along the state's north and central coast. Its rather stout stems help withstand the wind. When not growing among rocks, it seems to prefer heavy clay soils. Like volcanic onion (*Allium cratericola*), it often forms showy clumps.

SWAMP ONION

Family: Alliaceae (onion or garlic family)

Scientific name: *Allium validum* S. Watson

Height: 20" to more than 3'.

Leaves: Basal, 3–6 leaves per plant, usually about as long as the stem, narrow, V-shaped in cross-section or flat; margins smooth.

Flowers: Borne in umbels of 15–40 flowers, each flower on a stalk 0.3–0.5" long; sepals and petals very similar, 3 of each, narrow, upright, deep pink to almost white; stamens 6; ovary superior, 3-lobed without any additional bumps (or crests).

Blooms June through August.

Elevation: 4,000' to above 11,000'.

Habitat: Wet meadows.

Comments: This herbaceous perennial is one of a minority of *Allium* species with leaves that don't wither until after the plants have bloomed and set fruit, and the plants can be so abundant and dense that from a distance they look like a grassy meadow. The species grows in the North Coast Ranges, Klamath Ranges, Cascades, and Sierra Nevada, as well as the Modoc Plateau's Warner Mountains and as far north as British Columbia.

NAKED LADIES

Family: Amaryllidaceae (amaryllis family)

Scientific name: *Amaryllis belladonna* L.

Height: 1–2'.

Leaves: Basal, 12–18" long by 0.6–1.5" wide, glossy, withering before the leafless flowering stem emerges; margins smooth.

Flowers: Borne in clusters that splay out of a "cone" of large, greenish, partly fused bracts; sepals and petals very similar, 3 of each, 2–3.5" long, slightly fused at the base and forming a trumpet-like shape, pink, sometimes white or pale yellow at the base; stamens 6; ovary inferior.

Blooms July through September.

Elevation: Sea level to 2,500'.

Habitat: Dry disturbed sites, usually in partial shade.

Comments: This sweet-scented herbaceous perennial, native to southern Africa, grows from a bulb and is often found near abandoned home sites—it's an old-fashioned garden flower. In late winter and spring you'll only see clumps of its bright green, agapanthus-like leaves; unlike the wavy-edged leaves of soap root (*Chlorogalum pomeridianum*) that emerge about the same time, the leaf margins are smooth. Then, long after the leaves have become straw-colored debris, the unmistakable pink flowers appear. Some older references call the species *Brunsvigia rosea*. The many different kinds of daffodil and narcissus (all species of the genus *Narcissus*) belong to the same family.

347

LARGE CUCKOO PINT

Family: Araceae (arum family)

Also called: Italian lords and ladies or Italian arum

Scientific name: *Arum italicum* Mill.

Height: Up to about 3'.

Leaves: Basal, the blade up to 15" long on a sturdy petiole up to 17" long, arrowhead-shaped with outwards-flaring basal lobes, usually marbled white or pale green; margins smooth.

Flowers: Tiny, tightly packed near the bottom of a club-like flowering stem with an enlarged, yellow or cream-colored, flowerless tip (called a spadix); female flowers at the bottom of the spadix, each with 1 pistil with a superior ovary; male flowers above them, each with 2–3 stamens; all loosely enclosed in a large bract (called a spathe) that's green or purple-tinged at the base and white to pale yellowish green, thin, and sometimes papery above.

Blooms March through June.

Elevation: Sea level to 1,600'.

Habitat: Woodland and shady disturbed sites.

Comments: This herbaceous perennial, native to Eurasia and northern Africa, occurs mainly in the Sacramento Valley, North Coast Ranges, and coastal areas. It's one of those now-you-see-it-now-you-don't plants. The leaves are conspicuous when they first emerge, sometimes as early as December, but often they're soon overtopped by other vegetation and become hard to find. You really have to search for the inflorescences, which are shorter than the leaves; to see the actual flowers, you have to open the bottom of the spathe. By early summer, the leaves have collapsed and withered, and the brilliantly colored fruit are hard to miss. Come back a few days later, though, and you may only find bitten-off stalks—my guess is that deer relish the berries and quickly clear any patch they find.

DUCKWEED

Family: Araceae (arum family)

Scientific name: *Lemna turionifera* Landolt

Overall appearance: Small aquatic plants, free floating, usually clustered in 2s or 3s; each plant oval and 0.1–0.2" long with an unbranched root 0.1–0.2" long dangling in the water, upper side shiny green and convex with a row of small bumps along the midline that are visible with a good hand lens, lower side flat and often turning reddish in the winter.

Leaves: None.

Flowers: Borne in 2 minute pockets, one on each side of the plant, each pocket containing 2 male flowers and 1 female flower, the male flowers consisting of a single stamen, the female flowers of a single pistil.

Blooms in late summer.

Elevation: Sea level to 10,000'.

Habitat: Standing or slow-moving freshwater.

Comments: These diminutive plants are common in most of northern California. In fall, they produce "winter buds" that look like even tinier, brown or dark green versions of the parent plant and barely project from the pocket in which they were formed. Six other species of duckweed occur in California. *Lemna minor* is very similar to *Lemna turionifera* but lacks the row of bumps on the upper side, doesn't form winter buds, and is always green underneath, never reddish. *Lemna gibba* has a fairly flat upper surface but a "beer belly" below so that a cross-section of a plant is more or less semicircular or trapezoidal. Other species differ in the number of parent and offspring plants typically clustered together, the shape of each plant, the number of veins it has, and other details. Watermeal (*Wolfia* spp.) and mud-midget (*Wolfiella* spp.) are even smaller members of the family: The tiny apple-green specks in the right-hand photo are probably *Wolfia globosa*, which, at a maximum length of 0.03", makes duckweed look positively gigantic. Duckweed is sometimes confused with mosquito fern (*Azolla* spp.). Close up, they're easy to distinguish: Mosquito fern has short, branched stems with tiny, velvety, overlapping, scale-like leaves, and each plant is 0.5–1" wide.

YELLOW SKUNK CABBAGE

Family: Araceae (arum family)

Scientific name: *Lysichiton americanus* Hultén & H. St. John

Height: Up to 5'.

Leaves: Basal, the blade 1–5' long, fairly narrow with a thick midvein, tapered at the base to a short petiole, hairless; margins smooth.

Flowers: Tightly packed on the upper end of a long, club-like flowering stem (called a spadix) that's loosely wrapped by a light lemon-yellow, boat-shaped bract (called a spathe) up to 8" long; each flower sessile with 4 fleshy greenish sepals, no petals, 4 short stamens with off-white anthers, and 1 pistil with its ovary partly embedded in the core of the spadix.

Blooms March through June.

Elevation: Sea level to above 4,000'.

Habitat: Stream banks, marsh, and forested wetlands.

Comments: This uncommon herbaceous perennial grows near the coast from Santa Cruz County to Alaska. It's the only North American species in its genus and unlikely to be confused with anything else. The flowers smell bad, as do the leaves if bruised. According to many references, the leaves appear after the flowers, but the plants I've seen in the wild had flowers surrounded by well-developed leaves—my guess is that the flowers emerge early but last a long time. The "studded club" in the smaller photo consists of developing fruit, which stay green even when they're fully mature.

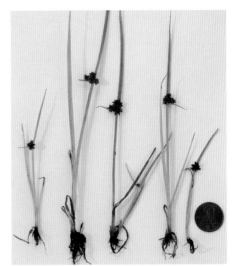

SANTA BARBARA SEDGE

Family: Cyperaceae (sedge family)

Also called: Whiteroot

Scientific name: *Carex barbarae* Dewey

Height: 1–3'.

Leaves: Grass-like, less than 0.2–0.4" wide, hairless, glossy, upper part flat, lower part with a keel-like ridge edged with tiny sharp teeth on the lower side.

Flowers: Male and female flowers borne on the same stem but in separate clusters, all with 6 small bristles instead of sepals and petals; male flowers with 3 stamens, filaments white, anthers long, slender, pale yellow; female flowers with 1 pistil, the superior ovary loosely enclosed in a minute flask-shaped structure from which protrude 2 fuzzy white stigmas.

Blooms May through August.

Elevation: Sea level to above 3,000'.

Habitat: Flat or gently sloping sites in oak woodland with moderately wet soil in winter and other seasonally moist areas.

Comments: This perennial, common in much of northern California except on the Modoc Plateau, spreads from creeping underground stems (called rhizomes). In summer and fall, when annual grasses have turned to straw, Santa Barbara sedge provides a lush green ground cover in many valley woodlands. Native Americans harvest the rhizomes and split the inner woody core into two strands, which are a choice material for weaving baskets.

VARIABLE FLATSEDGE

Family: Cyperaceae (sedge family)

Also called: Smallflower umbrella sedge

Scientific name: *Cyperus difformis* L.

Height: 1–16".

Leaves: Grass-like, 2–4 per stem, 0.1–0.2" wide; margins smooth except for minute hard hairs near the tip.

Flowers: Borne in flat oval clusters (called spikelets) that in turn are aggregated into a few small, compact groups with 2 or 3 leaf-like bracts just below them, 1 bract much longer than the others, each flower in the spikelets with a scale-like bract just below it, no sepals or petals, 1 or 2 stamens, and 1 pistil with a superior ovary and 3 thread-like stigmas.

Blooms July through November.

Elevation: Sea level to 1,600'.

Habitat: Shores of ponds and rivers and shallow, slow-moving water.

Comments: This annual, native to subtropical Asia and Africa, is common in the Sacramento Valley, where it's often a weed in rice fields. As in most sedges, the stems are triangular in cross-section. Although at first glance the flowers seem to grow roughly two-thirds of the way up the stem, they're actually at its tip, and what looks like the continuation of the stem is one of the two or three leaf-like bracts just below the flowers.

TALL FLATSEDGE

Family: Cyperaceae (sedge family)

Scientific name: *Cyperus eragrostis* Lam.

Height: 1–3'.

Leaves: Grass-like, 6–10 per stem, 0.2–0.4" wide, flat, glossy; margins look smooth but are edged with minute hard hairs that make them feel rough or sharp.

Flowers: Borne in flat oval clusters (called spikelets) that in turn are aggregated into a somewhat head-like shape with 4–8 leaf-like bracts just below it, each bract 1–20" long; each flower in the spikelets with a small scale-like bract just below it, no sepals or petals, 3 stamens, and 1 pistil with a superior ovary and 3 thread-like stigmas.

Blooms May through November.

Elevation: Sea level to above 2,000'.

Habitat: Stream banks, vernal pools, other sites with wet soil, and shallow water.

Comments: This weedy, very common perennial occurs in most of northern California except on the Modoc Plateau. It usually grows in small clumps created by short, thick, slightly spreading underground stems with many coarse, tough roots and can be hard to get rid of. The stems are triangular in cross-section. Although California has "only" 18 or so species of *Cyperus* (as compared to nearly 140 species of *Carex*), they can still be really hard to identify.

FALSE NUTSEDGE

Family: Cyperaceae (sedge family)

Also called: Straw-colored flatsedge

Scientific name: *Cyperus strigosus* L.

Height: 2–30".

Leaves: Grass-like, flat; margins edged with minute hard hairs.

Flowers: Borne in flat, very narrow clusters (called spikelets) aggregated into bottlebrush-like groups, which in turn are arranged in umbels with 3–6 leaf-like bracts just below the umbel, each of these bracts 2–12" long; each flower in the spikelets with a scale-like bract just below it, no sepals or petals, 3 stamens, and 1 pistil with a superior ovary and 3 thread-like stigmas.

Blooms July through October.

Elevation: Sea level to above 3,000'.

Habitat: Shores of rivers and ponds, flood plains, and other sites with moist soil.

Comments: This widespread perennial occurs throughout northern California, although it's probably most common in the Sacramento Valley. It overwinters in the form of short, upright underground stems (called corms). As in most sedges, the aboveground stems are triangular in cross-section. Sometimes the spikelets are straw-colored or tan, but just as often they seem to be greenish. Redroot flatsedge (*Cyperus erythrorhizos*) and white-margined flatsedge (*Cyperus flavicomus*) look very similar; the former has smaller fruit than false nutsedge, while the latter has only two stigmas per flower.

COMMON SPIKERUSH

Family: Cyperaceae (sedge family)

Scientific name: *Eleocharis macrostachya* Britton

Height: 8" to more than 3'.

Leaves: 2 per stem, reduced to thin, papery, sleeve-like sheaths at the base of the hairless stem.

Flowers: Borne in a single narrow cluster at the tip of the stem, a brown scale-like bract just below each flower; sepals and petals reduced to 4 or 5 bristles or completely absent; stamens 3; pistil 1 with a superior ovary and 2 narrow stigmas.

Blooms in spring and summer.

Elevation: Sea level to 7,500'.

Habitat: Freshwater and brackish wetlands, including vernal pools.

Comments: Despite its common name and stems that are round in cross-section, this species has flowers and tiny 1-seeded fruits typical of the sedge family and is *not* a member of the Juncaceae (rush family). (When it comes to *Eleocharis*, forget the saying, "Sedges have edges, rushes are round.") It's common in wetlands throughout northern California and has thin, tough, underground stems that form big patches. More than 20 other species of *Eleocharis* occur in the region, all essentially leafless. Squarestem spikerush (*Eleocharis quadrangulata*) stands out by its relatively stout stems, up to 0.2" thick, that are square in cross-section.

SMALL-FLOWERED HALFCHAFF SEDGE

Family: Cyperaceae (sedge family)

Scientific name: *Lipocarpha micrantha* (Vahl) G. C. Tucker

Height: 0.4–4".

Leaves: Basal, 1–3 per stem, 0.4–1" long, very narrow, hairless.

Flowers: Borne in tiny, narrow clusters (called spikelets) aggregated into 1–3 dense, egg-shaped, greenish brown inflorescences per stem, inflorescences 0.1–0.2" long with 2 or 3 leaf-like bracts just below them; each flower with 2 scale-like bracts just below it, no sepals or petals, 1–3 stamens, and 1 pistil with a superior ovary and 2-branched style.

Blooms August through October.

Elevation: Sea level to 5,000'.

Habitat: Wet soil.

Comments: This annual, one of three species of *Lipocarpha* found in northern California, grows in the Sacramento Valley, North Coast Ranges, and Sierra Nevada foothills. I might never have noticed it if I hadn't been photographing a butterfly resting on the ground; when I enlarged the photos, I noticed a curious little plant in the background. That, of course, woke up my inner "plant hound" and sent me back to the site ASAP to find a specimen or two for identification. Once I started looking, I found lots of these diminutive plants. Some older texts call them *Hemicarpha micrantha*.

DOUGLAS' IRIS

Family: Iridaceae (iris family)

Scientific name: *Iris douglasiana* Herb.

Height: Flowering stems usually 6–20".

Leaves: Basal leaves arranged in flat, fan-like configurations, each leaf up to more than 3' long, 0.4–1" wide; margins smooth; the 1–3 stem leaves similar in shape but alternate.

Flowers: Borne in clusters of 2–6 flowers, emerging from a pair of almost opposite bracts, only 1 flower per cluster open at a time; the bases of the sepals and petals fused into a slender tube 0.6" to more than 1" long; sepals (the free part above the sepal-petal tube) 3, 2–3.5" long by 0.6–1.2" wide, spreading, light to dark lavender, dark reddish purple, or cream-colored, with dark purple veins, the center of the lower half often paler or yellow; petals 3, 2–3" long by 0.4–0.7" wide, upright, the same color as the main color of the sepals; stamens 3; ovary inferior with 3 styles, each 1.2–2" long with a small triangular stigma.

Blooms May through July.

Elevation: Sea level to 700'.

Habitat: Grassland.

Comments: About 15 native species of *Iris* grow in northern California. They can be hard to identify: Many come in several colors, and it doesn't help that some of them hybridize. Douglas' iris is a highly variable, mainly coastal herbaceous perennial that's common from Santa Barbara County to southern Oregon; it also occurs in the western parts of the North Coast Ranges and Klamath Ranges. Like most species of *Iris*, it grows from fairly thick, creeping underground stems (called rhizomes). Occasionally you'll also find some of the many non-native horticultural species and varieties of *Iris* naturalized near abandoned home sites.

FERNALD'S IRIS

Family: Iridaceae (iris family)

Scientific name: *Iris fernaldii* R. C. Foster

Height: 8–16".

Leaves: Basal leaves arranged in flat, fan-like configurations, each leaf up to 16" long by 0.2–0.3" wide, gray-green with a waxy bloom; margins smooth; the 1–3 stem leaves similar in shape but alternate.

Flowers: Borne in clusters of 2 or 3, only 1 flower per cluster open at a time; the bases of the sepals and petals fused into a slender tube 1.5–2.5" long that flares gently near the top; sepals 3, 2–3" long by 0.3–0.8" wide, spreading, light yellow with darker yellow veins; petals 3, 1.5–2.5" long by 0.2–0.5" wide, upright, colored like the sepals; stamens 3; ovary inferior with 3 styles, each 1.2–2" long with a small triangular stigma.

Blooms April through May.

Elevation: 150–6,500'.

Habitat: Chaparral and forest.

Comments: In northern California, this common herbaceous perennial grows in the southern part of the North Coast Ranges. Yellow forms of *Iris macrosiphon*, which has light to golden yellow, lavender, or deep purple flowers, look similar except for their narrower leaves; also, the top of the floral tube widens abruptly, like the bell at the end of a length of PVC pipe.

YELLOW FLAG

Family: Iridaceae (iris family)

Scientific name: *Iris pseudoacorus* L.

Height: 20" to 5'.

Leaves: Basal leaves roughly equal to the stem in height, each leaf 0.4–1.5" wide with a conspicuous midvein, hairless, often with a waxy bloom; margins smooth; the 3–6 stem leaves similar in shape but alternate.

Flowers: Borne in clusters of 3–6, the bases of the sepals and petals fused into a barrel-shaped tube about 0.5" long; sepals 3, 2–3" long by 1.5–2" wide, spreading, bright yellow with brown veins; petals 3, 0.8–1.2" long by 0.2–0.3" wide, upright, yellow; stamens 3; ovary inferior with 3 styles, each up to 1" long with a small rounded stigma.

Blooms March through June.

Elevation: Sea level to 4,500'.

Habitat: Shores of rivers and ponds, shallow fresh water, and estuaries.

Comments: This invasive herbaceous perennial is native to Eurasia but has become established throughout much of the United States; in northern California it occurs in the Sacramento Valley, North Coast Ranges, and Sierra Nevada foothills. Western blue flag (*Iris missouriensis*) is the only other *Iris* in the region that likes very moist to wet sites; it grows at elevations of 3,000–11,000' and has pale to medium lavender flowers.

WESTERN BLUE-EYED GRASS

Family: Iridaceae (iris family)

Scientific name: *Sisyrinchium bellum* S. Watson

Height: Up to 2'.

Leaves: Grass-like, up to about 0.2" wide, mostly more or less basal and arranged in a single plane but usually with 1 leaf higher up on the stem; margins smooth.

Flowers: Sepals and petals very similar, 3 of each, their bases fused into a short funnel, light blue or violet to deep purple, often yellow at the base; stamens 6, filaments more or less fused to each other, purple, anthers bright yellow; ovary inferior.

Blooms March through July.

Elevation: Sea level to almost 8,000'.

Habitat: Fairly moist grassland and woodland.

Annual blue-eyed grass (*Sisyrinchium rosulatum*).

Comments: This herbaceous perennial, common throughout northern California, grows from short rhizomes, often forming small clumps. The stems are usually branched, and the fruit is a spherical brown capsule 0.1–0.3" wide. Idaho blue-eyed grass (*Sisyrinchium idahoense*) and the rare Hitchcock's blue-eyed grass (*Sisyrinchium hitchcockii*) also have blue to purple flowers but unbranched stems. Golden-eyed grass (*Sisyrinchium californicum*) and Elmer's blue-eyed grass (*Sisyrinchium elmeri*) have bright yellow flowers, usually with darker veins but no other markings. The flowers of annual blue-eyed grass (*Sisyrinchium rosulatum*) can be lavender, pink, maroon, or yellow, always with reddish or purple markings that resemble the outline of a 6-pointed star. Annual blue-eyed grass is native to the southeastern United States, where it can get weedy; how it got to California is a bit of a mystery. I've found the yellow form along the Lower American River, and the lavender form is a frequent lawn weed in my neighborhood in Sacramento; the species has also been reported from southern California.

GOLDEN FAIRY LANTERN

Family: Liliaceae (lily family)

Also called: Golden globe lily or Diogenes' lantern

Scientific name: *Calochortus amabilis* Purdy

Height: 4–20".

Leaves: Basal leaves 8–20" long, 0.2" to more than 1.5" wide, often with a waxy bloom; margins smooth; the 2–4 stem leaves alternate, 0.8–8" long.

Flowers: Nodding; sepals 3, 0.6–0.8" long, spreading, yellow; petals 3, equally long but curved towards the center to form a hollow ball, yellow, often with brown speckles, each petal with a large nectary that bulges to the outside of the flower, petal margins fringed with short, rather thick hairs; stamens 6; ovary superior.

Blooms April through June.

Elevation: 300' to above 3,000'.

Habitat: Woodland and chaparral.

Comments: This herbaceous perennial occurs in the North Coast Ranges and Klamath Ranges. The plants grow from bulbs, but it takes three to five years for a seedling to develop a bulb big enough to start producing flowers. This is one of five *Calochortus* species with nodding, closed flowers. They include white fairy lantern (*Calochortus albus*), which has white flowers tinged with pink. The rare *Calochortus raichei*, known only from Sonoma County, has oblong yellow flowers with petals that are a lot longer than the sepals.

LEICHTLIN'S MARIPOSA LILY

Family: Liliaceae (lily family)

Scientific name: *Calochortus leichtlinii* Hook. f.

Height: 8" to 2'.

Leaves: Basal leaves 4–6" long, very narrow, gray-green, often withered by the time the plants bloom; margins smooth; stem leaves smaller.

Flowers: Held upright; sepals 3, 0.4–0.8" long; petals 3, 0.4–1.6" long, white to smoky blue except for a yellow base and a red to dark maroon spot just above the yellow area, with an oval to almost round nectar-secreting depression in the yellow area that's nearly hidden by shaggy yellow hairs; stamens 6, anthers cream-colored or white; ovary superior.

Blooms June through August.

Elevation: 4,000' to above 13,000'.

Habitat: Open, gravelly or rocky sites.

Comments: This herbaceous perennial is common in the Cascades, Sierra Nevada, and on the Modoc Plateau. The rare Callahan's mariposa lily (*Calochortus syntrophus*), found only in Shasta and Tehama counties, looks similar but is taller, with larger leaves and flowers and a crescent-shaped nectary on each petal. In other species that sometimes have mainly white petals, the base of each petal is heavily speckled and streaked with maroon, rather than clear yellow, and often the big red spot is surrounded by a yellow halo.

357

GOLD NUGGETS

Family: Liliaceae (lily family)

Scientific name: *Calochortus luteus* Lindl.

Height: 8–20".

Leaves: Basal leaves 4–8" long by 0.1–0.2" wide, often withered by the time the plants bloom; margins smooth; stem leaves smaller.

Flowers: Held upright; sepals 3, 0.8–1.2" long, curled downwards; petals 3, 0.8–1.6" long, bright yellow, usually with a maroon spot near the center and additional maroon streaks and speckles, with an oval to crescent-shaped nectar-secreting area that's nearly hidden by shaggy yellow or orange hairs; stamens 6, anthers yellow; ovary superior.

Blooms April through June.

Elevation: Sea level to above 2,000'.

Habitat: Grassland and open areas with heavy soil in woodland and forest.

Comments: Like other mariposa lilies, this herbaceous perennial grows from a bulb. It's common in the Sacramento Valley, Coast Ranges, Cascades, and Sierra Nevada foothills. The pattern of spots, streaks, and speckles on the petals is notoriously variable, and occasionally you'll find a plant with predominantly cream-colored or light yellow petals. Gold nuggets can hybridize with yellow mariposa lily (*Calochortus superbus*), further complicating the picture. Incidentally, despite its common name, the main color of the petals of *Calochortus superbus* frequently is white or pinkish lavender, less often light yellow. Yellow star tulip (*Calochortus monophyllus*), a bright yellow–flowered species that occurs in the Cascade foothills and northern Sierra Nevada, seems less variable: Its 0.6–0.8"-long petals are completely covered with shaggy yellow hairs, and the equally long, outward-pointing yellow sepals give the flower as a whole an almost triangular outline.

PUSSY'S EARS

Family: Liliaceae (lily family)

Also called: Hairy star tulip

Scientific name: *Calochortus tolmiei* Hook. & Arn.

Height: 4–16".

Leaves: Basal leaves 4–16" long by 0.1–1.2" wide; margins smooth; usually with 1 stem leaf.

Flowers: Upright; sepals 3, 0.4–0.6" long; petals 3, 0.5–1" long, white to pale pink or lavender with purple streaks and speckles, upper side and margins hairy except at the tip, with an oval to crescent-shaped nectar-secreting area that's nearly hidden by the hairs; stamens 6, anthers white or pale lavender; ovary superior.

Blooms April through July.

Elevation: 160–6,500'.

Habitat: Dry grassy slopes, chaparral, woodland, and conifer forest.

Comments: In northern California, this herbaceous perennial grows in the North Coast Ranges, Klamath Ranges, Cascades, Sierra Nevada, and the northern end of the Sacramento Valley. Its stems are usually branched, and the patterns of purple speckles and density of the hairs on the petals are quite variable. Blue star tulip (*Calochortus coeruleus*) and northwestern mariposa lily or cat's ear (*Calochortus elegans*) are similar, but their stems are generally unbranched and the petals are hairy all the way to the tip. In all three, the fruit is a 3-winged, nodding seed capsule.

TROUT LILY

Family: Liliaceae (lily family)

Also called: Sierra fawn lily

Scientific name: *Erythronium multiscapideum* (Kellogg) A. Nelson and P. B. Kenn.

Height: 3–8".

Leaves: 2 per plant, basal, 1.5–6" long by 0.4–1" wide, heavily mottled with brown; margins smooth or slightly wavy.

Flowers: Usually 1 per stem; sepals and petals very similar, 3 of each, 0.6–1.5" long, white with a bright yellow base; stamens 6, filaments slender, anthers white or cream-colored; ovary superior with 3 curved stigmas.

Blooms March through May.

Elevation: 160–4,000'.

Habitat: Woodland and shady cliff faces.

Comments: In many references the specific epithet of this herbaceous perennial, which grows in the Cascades and Sierra Nevada, is spelled *multiscapoideum*. Each plant grows from a bulb that sends out slender, creeping underground stems (called rhizomes), the tips of which produce more bulbs, forming big patches of these handsome plants. California fawn lily (*Erythronium californicum*), found in the North Coast Ranges, Klamath Ranges, and Cascades, looks similar but doesn't produce rhizomes and bulblets. Glacier lily (*Erythronium grandiflorum*) has yellow petals. Northern California has seven other species of *Erythronium*; they differ in the shape of the filaments and stigma and whether the leaves are solid green or mottled.

CHECKER LILY

Family: Liliaceae (lily family)

Also called: Mission bells

Scientific name: *Fritillaria affinis* (Schult. & Schult. f.) Sealy

Height: 4" to 4'.

Leaves: Lower stem leaves opposite or in whorls of 3–8, upper stem leaves alternate, 1.5" to more than 6" long, narrow to oval, sessile; margins smooth.

Flowers: Nodding; sepals and petals very similar, 3 of each, 0.4–1.5" long by 0.2–0.5" wide, mottled in some combination of brown, purple, yellow, or yellowish green, often with wavy margins; stamens 6, anthers yellow; ovary superior with a green or greenish yellow, 3-branched style.

Blooms March through June.

Elevation: Sea level to 6,000'.

Habitat: Grassland, chaparral, and open woodland.

Comments: This highly variable herbaceous perennial, previously called *Fritillaria lanceolata*, grows near the coast and in the North Coast Ranges, Klamath Ranges, and Cascade and Sierra Nevada foothills. Its mottled flowers make it hard to spot in the dappled shade where it's often found. The sepals and petals of spotted fritillary (*Fritillaria atropurpurea*) are mottled in similar colors but are only 0.2–0.3" wide with smooth margins, and the leaves are very narrow. All in all, more than a dozen species of *Fritillaria* grow in northern California, several of them rare.

FRAGRANT FRITILLARY

Family: Liliaceae (lily family)

Scientific name: *Fritillaria liliacea* Lindl.

Height: 4–14".

Leaves: 2–10 per plant, alternate, 1.5–5" long, very narrow to oval; margins smooth.

Flowers: Nodding; sepals and petals very similar, 3 of each, 0.4–0.7" long by about 0.2" wide, creamy white except for the base, which can be yellow, greenish yellow or striped or mottled in various combinations of green and purple; stamens 6, anthers yellow; ovary superior with a cream-colored to green, 3-branched style.

Blooms February through April.

Elevation: Sea level to about 600'.

Habitat: Grassland.

Comments: This rare herbaceous perennial occurs only from Solano and Sonoma counties southwards to Monterey County. Despite its common name, many plants have completely unscented flowers. It's the only northern California species of *Fritillaria* with predominantly white petals. The seed capsules are 0.5–0.6" long and have an odd boxy shape, a bit like some legless leather hassocks; each contains six tidy stacks of flat, orange-brown seeds.

SMITH'S FAIRY BELLS

Family: Liliaceae (lily family)

Scientific name: *Prosartes smithii* (Hook.) Utech et al.

Height: 1' to more than 3'.

Leaves: Alternate, 2–5" long, narrowly to widely oval, sessile, the base sometimes clasping the stem, lower side hairless or sparsely hairy; margins smooth.

Flowers: Dangling below the leaves; sepals and petals very similar, 0.6" to more than 1" long, narrow, white; stamens 6, hidden by the sepals and petals; ovary superior.

Blooms March through June.

Elevation: Sea level to 5,200'.

Habitat: Moist, shady forest.

Comments: This herbaceous perennial grows along the coast and in coastal mountains from the San Francisco Bay region to British Columbia. It spreads by means of creeping underground stems and bears bright yellowish orange berries that are 0.4–0.6" long and usually contain more than three seeds. Hooker's fairy bells (*Prosartes hookeri*) is very similar except for small hard hairs on the underside of its leaves, stamens that clearly protrude from the flowers, and marginally smaller, orange-red or red berries. It occurs at elevations up to 5,200' in most of northern California except in the Sacramento Valley and on the Modoc Plateau. Northern California's third species in this genus, Siskiyou bells (*Prosartes parvifolia*), is rare, occurring only in the Siskiyou Mountains and southwestern Oregon; its leaves have glandular hairs on both sides, and its berries are usually 2-seeded. All three species used to be included in the genus *Disporum*.

MEADOW DEATH CAMAS

Family: Melanthiaceae (false-hellebore family)

Scientific name: *Toxicoscordion venenosum* (S. Watson) Rydb. var. *venenosum*

Height: 6–28".

Leaves: Mainly basal, 4–16" long by 0.2–0.4" wide, usually folded lengthwise into a shallow V, upper and lower sides hairless; margins smooth except for a fringe of small rough hairs; stem leaves alternate, smaller.

Flowers: Sepals and petals very similar, 3 of each, 0.2–0.3" long, white with a greenish yellow base, sometimes with ruffled margins; stamens 6, at least as long as the sepals and petals, anthers white; ovary superior, yellowish green with 3 styles and stigmas.

Blooms May through July.

Elevation: Sea level to 8,500'.

Habitat: Moist meadows to dry, rocky slopes.

Comments: This highly poisonous herbaceous perennial used to be called *Zigadenus venenosus* var. *venenosus* and included in the Liliaceae (lily family). It grows from a bulb, has hairless stems, and occurs in the North Coast Ranges, Klamath Ranges, Cascades, and Sierra Nevada. Small-flowered star lily (*Toxicoscordion micranthum*) typically produces fewer flowers, and at least the lower part of its stem has some short, rough hairs. In Fremont's death camas (*Toxicoscordion fremontii*) and the rare marsh zigadenus (*Toxicoscordion fontanum*), the stamens are shorter than the sepals and petals.

GIANT TRILLIUM

Family: Melanthiaceae (false-hellebore family)

Also called: Giant wakerobin

Scientific name: *Trillium chloropetalum* (Torr.) Howell

Height: 8–28".

Leaves: 3 per plant, borne in a whorl at the top of a stout stem; each leaf 3" to more than 8" long and often nearly as wide, sessile, usually with irregular brown mottling; margins wavy.

Flowers: 1 per stem, nestled right on top of the leaves, often with a rose-like scent; sepals 3, green; petals 3, 0.2–0.4" long, green, greenish yellow, white, pink, or purple; stamens 6, anthers 0.6–1.2" long; ovary superior, dull purple, with 3 convoluted, usually cream-colored styles.

Blooms April through May.

Elevation: 300–6,500'.

Habitat: Moist shady sites in chaparral and forest.

Comments: This herbaceous perennial grows mainly in the North Coast Ranges. Giant white wakerobin (*Trillium albidum*) is similar but has a green ovary, and its petals only come in white or pink. The flowers of *Trillium angustipetalum* smell musty, and the narrow, upright, maroon petals hide the stamens. In western wakerobin (*Trillium ovatum*, with two subspecies), there's a distinct stalk between each plant's three whorled leaves and the solitary, upright or nodding, white-petalled flower; also, the leaves are usually solid green, not mottled.

CORN LILY

Family: Melanthiaceae (false-hellebore family)

Also called: Western false-hellebore

Scientific name: *Veratrum californicum* Durand var. *californicum*

Height: 3' to more than 6'.

Leaves: Alternate, 8–16" long by 4–8" wide, sessile, the bases clasping the stem, upper side hairless or sparsely hairy, lower side hairier; margins smooth.

Flowers: Borne in large branched clusters, the branches spreading sideways or angled upwards; sepals and petals very similar, 3 of each, 0.4–0.6" long, white or greenish white with a bright green, Y-shaped nectar-secreting gland at the base; stamens 6, anthers yellow; ovary superior with 3 styles.

Blooms July through August.

Elevation: Sea level to above 11,000'.

Habitat: Stream banks, moist meadows, and moist open areas in forest.

Comments: This species is common in northern California's mountains, including the Modoc Plateau's Warner Mountains. It spreads by means of thick, creeping underground stems and is one of the first herbaceous perennials to appear in spring, often emerging before the snow has melted. In dry summers the leaves may wither before the plants have started blooming, but in good years they turn a beautiful golden yellow in fall. It's a plant I try to avoid when camping: It likes moist sites, which usually means lots of mosquitos. Green false-hellebore (*Veratrum viride*) bears leaf-green flowers on drooping branches. The sepals and petals of the rare Siskiyou false-hellebore (*Veratrum insolitum*) have shallowly fringed margins, and there are two small, oval, dark green nectar-secreting glands at the base of each; its ovary is woolly. Fringed false-hellebore (*Veratrum fimbriatum*) has deeply fringed sepals and petals, each with two green or yellow nectar-secreting glands near the center, and a hairless ovary; it too is rare, only occurring near the coast in Sonoma and Mendocino counties.

BEAR GRASS

Family: Melanthiaceae (false-hellebore family)

Scientific name: *Xerophyllum tenax* (Pursh) Nutt.

Height: Flowering stem 6" to 5'.

Leaves: Basal leaves in large clumps, each leaf 12–40" long by 0.1–0.2" wide, grass-like, rough to the touch; stem leaves smaller.

Flowers: Borne in dense, unbranched clusters; sepals and petals very similar, 0.2–0.4" long, narrow, white or cream-colored; stamens 6; ovary superior with 3 thread-like stigmas.

Blooms May through August.

Elevation: Sea level to 7,500'.

Habitat: Conifer forest and dry, open slopes and ridges.

Comments: This herbaceous perennial occurs mainly in the Klamath Ranges, Cascades, and Sierra Nevada, near the coast, and as far north as British Columbia. It's the only species in its genus in California. It grows from a woody underground stem and doesn't bloom until the plant is several years old. The leaves of undisturbed plants are only about a foot long, but Native American basket weavers burn the plants annually, which then produce much longer, soft, pliable leaves. *Nolina microcarpa*, a member of the Ruscaceae (butcher's-broom family), is also called bear grass; it too is important in Indian basketry but grows in Arizona and New Mexico.

SPOTTED CORALROOT

Family: Orchidaceae (orchid family)

Scientific name: *Corallorhiza maculata* (Raf.) Raf. var. *occidentalis* (Lindl.) Ames

Height: 6" to almost 2'.

Leaves: None.

Flowers: Sepals 3, red, purplish, yellow, greenish, or various shades of brown; petals 3, the lower one (called the lip) with 2 small lobes at its base and a slightly widened tip, white, usually with purple spots, its margins slightly wavy to ruffled, the upper 2 petals similar to the sepals except for some purple speckles; stamens, style, and stigma fused into a complex structure (called the column), light yellow with purple speckles; ovary inferior.

Blooms February through August.

Elevation: Sea level to above 9,000'.

Habitat: Shady forest and stream banks.

Comments: This fairly common but inconspicuous herbaceous perennial can be found in most of northern California except in the Sacramento Valley. It grows from short, heavily branched underground stems, lacks chlorophyll, and obtains all its nutrients from fungi in the soil and decomposing leaf litter. *Corallorhiza maculata* var. *maculata* has the same geographic range and looks similar except that its lip doesn't widen near the tip; in places where both kinds occur, variety *maculata* usually blooms two to four weeks later than variety *occidentalis*.

STRIPED CORALROOT

Family: Orchidaceae (orchid family)

Scientific name: *Corallorhiza striata* Lindl.

Height: 6–20".

Leaves: None.

Flowers: Sepals 3, pale yellow, pinkish, or light tan with 3–5 reddish stripes; petals 3, the lower one (called the lip) unlobed and pale yellow to deep red with 5 yellowish stripes, the upper 2 petals colored like the sepals; stamens, style, and stigma fused into a complex yellowish structure (called the column), often speckled purple; ovary inferior.

Blooms February through July.

Elevation: 300' to above 7,000'.

Habitat: Shady forest with a deep layer of decomposing leaves.

Comments: This herbaceous perennial occurs in most of northern California except in the Sacramento Valley. It's less common than spotted coralroot (*Corallorhiza maculata*), but where it does grow can form big colonies; where the two species occur together, striped coralroot starts blooming earlier than spotted coralroot. In western coralroot (*Corallorhiza mertensiana*), the sepals and two upper petals are very narrow, and the predominant color of the flowers is deep pink to red. Northern coralroot (*Corallorhiza trifida*) has green stems, although they too are leafless, and yellowish or chartreuse flowers with a white lip; in California it has only been found in a few places in Plumas County.

COAST PIPERIA

Family: Orchidaceae (orchid family)

Scientific name: *Piperia elegans* (Lindl.) Rydb. subsp. *elegans*

Height: 5" to more than 3'.

Leaves: Mainly basal, often withering by the time the plants bloom, 2.5–15" long by 0.4–4" wide; margins smooth.

Flowers: Sepals 3, white; petals 3, white except for their green base, the lower one with a forward-pointing lip and a hard-to-see downward-pointing spur 0.3–0.6" long, longer than the lip; stamens, style, and stigma fused into a complex pale yellow structure (called the column); ovary inferior; fragrance musky.

Blooms May through September.

Elevation: Sea level to 1,600'.

Habitat: Conifer forest and coastal scrub.

Comments: This herbaceous perennial, called *Habenaria elegans*, *Platanthera elegans*, or *Piperia maritima* in some older texts, grows along the coast and adjacent mountains from Monterey County to British Columbia; occasionally it's also found farther inland. Plants growing in sunny locations, like the one shown here, have more densely packed flowers than plants in shade. *Piperia elegans* subsp. *decurtata* occurs only at Point Reyes. It doesn't exceed 14" in height; the sepals have a conspicuous greenish midvein; the scent, strongest at night, is similar to cinnamon; and the spur is about the same length as the lip.

366

CHAPARRAL ORCHID

Family: Orchidaceae (orchid family)

Also called: Wood rein-orchid

Scientific name: *Piperia elongata* Rydb.

Height: 4" to more than 4'.

Leaves: Mainly basal, usually withered by the time the plants bloom, 3–12" long by 0.4–2.5" wide; margins smooth.

Flowers: Loosely to very densely clustered; sepals 3, light green, often with a darker green stripe; petals 3, similar in color to the sepals, the lower one with a gently curved, downward-pointing spur that's 0.3–0.7" long; stamens, style, and stigma fused into a complex, yellow and pale green structure (called the column); ovary inferior; fragrance faint.

Blooms May through July.

Elevation: Sea level to above 7,000'.

Habitat: Chaparral and dry sites in forest.

Comments: This herbaceous perennial occurs in most of northern California except in the Sacramento Valley and on the Modoc Plateau. Mountain piperia (*Piperia transversa*), another fairly common species, has clove-scented white flowers with long, straight spurs that cross the stem almost at right angles. Alaska piperia (*Piperia unalacensis*) has small green flowers with short straight spurs that can be held at right angles to the stem or point down. A total of eight species of *Piperia* grow in northern California; several are rare.

WHITE-FLOWERED BOG-ORCHID

Family: Orchidaceae (orchid family)

Scientific name: *Platanthera dilatata* (Pursh) L. C. Beck var. *leucostachys* (Lindl.) Luer

Height: 6" to 5'.

Leaves: Alternate, 2–14" long by 0.3–1.2" wide, sessile, V-shaped in cross-section; margins smooth.

Flowers: Sepals 3, white or cream-colored; petals 3, the same color as the sepals, the lower one with a long narrow lip and a gently curved, downward-pointing spur that's 0.2–0.6" long; stamens, style, and stigma fused into a complex, pale yellow structure (called the column); ovary inferior; fragrance strong, with a hint of cloves.

Blooms May through September.

Elevation: Sea level to above 11,000'.

Habitat: Stream banks, seeps, and wet meadows.

Comments: This herbaceous perennial, called *Habenaria leucostachys* in some older texts, grows in most of northern California except in the Sacramento Valley. It's one of four species of *Platanthera* in the region, all of which can hybridize with each other; the other three species have green or yellowish green flowers, as do most hybrids. Some species of *Piperia* have fairly similar flowers, but unlike *Piperia*, in which the leaves are mainly basal and withering by the time the plants bloom, *Platanthera* has leafy stems, and the leaves stay green while the plants are flowering.

HOODED LADIES' TRESSES

Family: Orchidaceae (orchid family)

Scientific name: *Spiranthes romanzoffiana* Cham.

Height: Usually 2.5–12", occasionally up to 18".

Leaves: Mainly basal, 1–6" long; margins smooth.

Flowers: Sepals 3, greenish at the base, pure white at the tip; petals 3, colored like the sepals, the lower one (called the lip) narrowed in the middle giving it a somewhat violin-like shape, the 2 upper petals and the uppermost sepal partly fused into a more or less hood-like shape; stamens, style, and stigma fused into a complex structure (called the column) hidden inside the petals; ovary inferior; fragrance sweet.

Blooms May through September.

Elevation: Sea level to almost 11,000'.

Habitat: Moist meadows, stream banks, seeps, and freshwater marshes, usually in full sun.

Comments: This herbaceous perennial grows in most of northern California except in the Sacramento Valley. The flowers are borne in three intertwined spirals and can be tightly or loosely packed. The leaves of inland plants are still green when the plants are in bloom, but those of coastal plants often wither before then. Typically the species blooms rather late in the growing season, when the moist habitats it favors are getting drier. In western ladies' tresses (*Spiranthes porrifolia*), the flowers range from creamy white to pale yellow with light yellow centers, the lip is tongue-like, not widening at the tip, and the sepals and two upper petals spread outwards in a star-like pattern. The plants can reach nearly 30" in height; in larger plants the leaves, up to 10" long, may attach to the lower part of the stem, although in smaller plants they're all basal. Intermediate forms between the two species do occur, and sometimes it's hard to figure out which one you're looking at.

FALSE LILY-OF-THE-VALLEY

Family: Ruscaceae (butcher's-broom family)

Also called: May lily or deerberry

Scientific name: *Maianthemum dilatatum* (Alph. Wood) A. Nelson & J. F. Macbr.

Height: 4–16".

Leaves: Alternate, the blade 2–8" long by 2–4" wide, heart-shaped to arrow-shaped, hairless to sparsely hairy, glossy; margins smooth.

Flowers: 10–50 per flowering stem; petal-like parts 4, about 0.1" long, white; stamens 4, anthers tiny, pale yellow; ovary superior, white.

Blooms May through June.

Elevation: Sea level to 1,600'.

Habitat: Moist, shady conifer forest.

Comments: This herbaceous perennial grows mainly near the coast from the San Francisco Bay region to Alaska. It spreads by means of creeping underground stems, and the leaves make a handsome ground cover all summer. Botanists don't seem to have decided whether the tiny, star-like flowers have four sepals and no petals, four petals and no sepals, or two of each. The mottled berries are 0.2–0.3" wide and contain one to three seeds.

Two other species of *Maianthemum* are more widespread in northern California, occurring in the Cascades and Sierra Nevada as well as the Klamath Ranges and North Coast Ranges. The flowers of false Solomon's seal (*Maianthemum racemosum*, formerly called *Smilacina racemosa*) are borne in branched clusters of more than 20; each flower has six petal-like parts that are shorter than the six stamens. Star-flowered false Solomon's seal (*Maianthemum stellatum*, formerly called *Smilacina stellata*) also has six petal-like parts, but they're longer than the six stamens, and each inflorescence consists of only 5–15 flowers. Both species are fairly widespread in northern California except in the Sacramento Valley and on the Modoc Plateau. Older texts include *Maianthemum* in the Liliaceae (lily family).

HARTWEG'S DOLL'S-LILY

Family: Tecophilaeaceae (tecophilaea family)

Scientific name: *Odontostomum hartwegii* Torr.

Height: 5–20".

Leaves: Mainly basal, 4–12" long, very narrow; margins smooth; the few stem leaves smaller, their bases sheathing the stem.

Flowers: Sepals and petals very similar, white or cream-colored with light green veins, fused into a tube about 0.2" long with 6 equally long, narrow, folded-back lobes; stamens 6, filaments very short, anthers brown or purplish, alternating with 6 small, tooth-like sterile stamens (called staminodes); ovary superior.

Blooms April through May.

Elevation: Sea level to 2,000'.

Habitat: Grassland.

Comments: This herbaceous perennial, found in the Klamath Ranges, the eastern part of the North Coast Ranges, and the Cascade and Sierra Nevada foothills, grows from deeply underground, short, thick stems called corms. The flowering stems typically are branched and gently zigzag. It's the only species in its genus, and the entire family consists of only eight or nine genera, all of which, except for *Odontostomum*, are native to Chile or Africa. This odd distribution is probably the result of the family's evolving late in the reign of the dinosaurs, before the ancient continent of Gondwana split into Africa and South America and before the rise of the Andes.

GARLAND BRODIAEA

Family: Themidaceae (brodiaea family)

Scientific name: *Brodiaea coronaria* (Salisb.) Engl.

Height: 2–10".

Leaves: Basal, as long as the stem or longer, very narrow, crescent-shaped in cross-section, usually withered by the time the plants bloom.

Flowers: Sepals and petals fused into a narrow greenish funnel with 6 gently curved-back lobes, each lobe lavender to violet with a darker central stripe; stamens 3, alternating with 3 taller, flat or curved sterile stamens (called staminodes) that lean towards the center of the flower; ovary superior.

Blooms April through June.

Elevation: Sea level to 2,500'.

Habitat: Vernal pools and grassland.

Comments: Like northern California's 11 other species of *Brodiaea*, this herbaceous perennial grows from short, thick, upright, underground stems called corms. It occurs mainly in and around the perimeter of the Sacramento Valley. Features to examine closely when identifying species of *Brodiaea* include the flowers' profile and the shape and orientation of the staminodes; for example, are they flat or curved? Do they meet in the center, partly hiding the stamens? Are their tips rounded or flat, curved into a hood-like form, or notched? Are their margins smooth or wavy? And so on …

HARVEST BRODIAEA

Family: Themidaceae (brodiaea family)

Scientific name: *Brodiaea elegans* Hoover subsp. *elegans*

Height: 4–20".

Leaves: Basal, about the same length as the stem, less than 0.1" wide, crescent-shaped in cross-section, usually withered by the time the plants bloom.

Flowers: Sepals and petals fused into a narrow greenish funnel with 6 gently curved-back lobes, each lobe violet to very dark purplish blue with a darker central stripe; stamens 3, alternating with 3 white, more or less flat sterile stamens (called staminodes) that are slightly shorter than the stamens and held well away from the center of the flower; ovary superior.

Blooms April through August.

Elevation: Sea level to 8,000'.

Habitat: Grassland, open woodland, and chaparral.

Comments: This herbaceous perennial is common in much of northern California except on the Modoc Plateau. Usually it prefers relatively dry habitats, but once in a while you may find it in damp meadows. It can hybridize with other species of *Brodiaea*. Confusingly, some field guides also apply the name harvest brodiaea to garland brodiaea (*Brodiaea coronaria*). In California brodiaea (*Brodiaea californica*), another fairly common species in the Cascade foothills and northern Sacramento Valley, the inward-curled margins of the staminodes are wavy or toothed, and the tips of the staminodes bend rather abruptly away from the center of the flower. The rare narrow-flowered California brodiaea (*Brodiaea leptandra*) also has abruptly bent-back staminodes, but their margins are smooth; it only grows in Napa, Lake, and Sonoma counties. Older references usually include the genus *Brodiaea* in the Liliaceae (lily family) or Amaryllidaceae (amaryllis family).

VERNAL POOL BRODIAEA

Family: Themidaceae (brodiaea family)

Also called: Small broadiaea or low brodiaea

Scientific name: *Brodiaea minor* (Benth.)
S. Watson

Height: 4–10".

Leaves: Basal, very narrow, usually withered by
the time the plants bloom.

Flowers: Sepals and petals fused into a tube
that narrows above the ovary, then widens into
6 spreading lobes, each lobe pinkish lavender
to violet with a darker central stripe; stamens
3, filaments T-shaped in cross-section, anthers
butter-yellow, alternating with 3 white, sterile stamens (called staminodes) that are longer than the
stamens, curled towards the center of the flower
("inrolled") about three-quarters of their width, and
have notched tips; ovary superior.

Blooms April through July.

Elevation: Sea level to 5,000'.

Habitat: Vernal pools, grassland, open woodland,
and chaparral.

Comments: This herbaceous perennial tolerates
a wide range of soil moisture conditions; it grows
in the eastern part of the Sacramento Valley and
the adjacent foothills. In vernal pools, it generally
blooms after the pools have dried out. Dwarf brodiaea (*Brodiaea nana*) occurs in the same region; it's
very similar to vernal pool brodiaea except that its
staminodes are inrolled only half their width or less
and its filaments are V- or Y-shaped in cross-section.

DWARF BRODIAEA

Family: Themidaceae (brodiaea family)

Also called: Earth brodiaea

Scientific name: *Brodiaea terrestris* Kellogg
subsp. *terrestris*

Height: 0.2–3".

Leaves: Basal, often longer than the stem, very
narrow, crescent-shaped in cross-section, sometimes withered by the time the plants bloom.

Flowers: Sepals and petals fused into a narrow
bell with 6 gently curved-back lobes, each lobe
lavender or violet with a darker central stripe;
stamens 3, anthers light yellow, alternating with
3 white, sterile stamens (called staminodes) that
are longer than the stamens, C-shaped in cross-
section, and have notched tips with a tiny tooth in
the center of the notch; ovary superior.

Blooms April through July.

Elevation: Sea level to 1,500'.

Habitat: Dry, open pine forest, coastal prairie, and
woodland.

Comments: In northern California, this herbaceous
perennial grows in the Sacramento Valley, North
Coast Ranges, and coastal areas. The stems and
leaves can be a greenish brown. *Brodiaea nana*,
which occurs on the eastern side of the Sacramento Valley and in the adjacent foothills, is also
called dwarf brodiaea, but if you look at its flowers
in profile, you'll see that the tube formed by the
fused bases of the sepals and petals is constricted
above the ovary.

BLUE DICKS

Family: Themidaceae (brodiaea family)

Scientific name: *Dichelostemma capitatum* (Benth.) Alph. Wood subsp. *capitatum*

Height: 2" to more than 2'.

Leaves: Basal, 2 or 3 per plant, each 4–28" long by 0.2–0.5" wide, hairless, lower side often with a longitudinal rib or "keel"; margins smooth.

Flowers: Borne in compact umbels of 6–15 flowers emerging from a cone of papery, dark purple or green-and-purple striped bracts; sepals and petals fused at the base into a 6-lobed bell, light blue to deep lavender or occasionally pink or white, with a "crown" of white or lavender projections at the base of the lobes that lean towards the center of the flower and almost hide the stamens; stamens 6, anthers yellow; ovary superior.

Blooms February through June.

Elevation: Sea level to 7,500'.

Habitat: Grassland, open woodland, and chaparral.

Comments: In older texts, blue dicks is called *Dichelostemma pulchellum* or *Brodiaea pulchella* and included in the Liliaceae (lily family) or Amaryllidaceae (amaryllis family). It's common in most of northern California and one of our earliest spring wildflowers, usually blooming about the same time that pipevine swallowtail butterflies (*Battus philenor hirsutus*, shown above) start emerging from their chrysalises. Like other species of *Dichelostemma*, it's a herbaceous perennial that grows from short, thick, upright, underground stems called corms. *Dichelostemma capitatum* subsp. *pauciflorum* is a desert plant with pale bracts and 2–5 flowers per umbel.

FORK-TOOTHED OOKOW

Family: Themidaceae (brodiaea family)

Scientific name: *Dichelostemma congestum* (Sm.) Kunth

Height: 1–3'.

Leaves: Basal, 3 or 4 per plant, each 1.5–15" long by 0.2–0.5" wide, hairless, often with a waxy bloom, lower side with a longitudinal "keel"; margins smooth.

Flowers: Borne in slightly elongated clusters of 6–15 flowers above a whorl of papery, green or purplish bracts; sepals and petals fused at the base into a 6-lobed tube that's constricted above the ovary, lavender or light blue, with a "crown" of 3 forked, slightly spreading projections at the base of the lobes; stamens 3, anthers light yellow; ovary superior.

Blooms April through June.

Elevation: Sea level to 6,500'.

Habitat: Grassland and open woodland.

Comments: This herbaceous perennial grows mainly in the North Coast Ranges, Cascades, northern Sierra Nevada, and the eastern margin of the Sacramento Valley. It's less common than blue dicks (*Dichelostemma capitatum*) and blooms later. The differences in their flowers are subtle: In fork-toothed ookow, you can often see the individual flower stalks in each cluster, the floral tube is shaped like a narrow-necked vase, and each flower only has three stamens. Also, the stems of fork-toothed ookow can be slightly twining.

ROUND-TOOTHED OOKOW

Family: Themidaceae (brodiaea family)

Also called: Wild hyacinth

Scientific name: *Dichelostemma multiflorum* (Benth.) A. Heller

Height: 8" to 3'.

Leaves: Basal, 3 or 4 per plant, each 1–3' long by 0.1–0.3" wide, hairless, with a waxy bloom, without a longitudinal rib or "keel" on the lower side; margins smooth.

Flowers: Borne in dense, almost spherical umbels of 6–35 flowers above a whorl of pale, papery bracts with purple stripes; sepals and petals fused at the base into a 6-lobed tube that's constricted above the ovary, lavender or medium blue, with a "crown" of 3 round- or square-tipped, upright projections at the base of the lobes, each appendage C-shaped in cross-section; stamens 3, anthers pale yellow; ovary superior.

Blooms May through June.

Elevation: Sea level to 6,500'.

Habitat: Grassland, chaparral, and open woodland.

Comments: This herbaceous perennial tends to bloom slightly later than fork-toothed ookow (*Dichelostemma congestum*). It's fairly common in the Klamath Ranges, Cascades, northern and central Sierra Nevada, Sacramento Valley, the northern part of the North Coast Ranges, and on the Modoc Plateau. Some older texts call it *Brodiaea multiflora*. Confusingly, *Triteleia hyacinthina*, which has white flowers, is often called wild hyacinth too.

SNAKE LILY

Family: Themidaceae (brodiaea family)

Also called: Twining brodiaea

Scientific name: *Dichelostemma volubile* (Kellogg) A. Heller

Height: 16" to 5'.

Leaves: Basal, 3 or 4 per plant, each 12–28" long by 0.3–0.6" wide, hairless, lower side with a longitudinal "keel"; margins smooth.

Flowers: Borne in umbels of 6–30 flowers above a whorl of papery, pinkish or beige bracts; sepals and petals pink, fused at the base into a 6-flanged tube that's constricted above the ovary and topped with 6 lobes and a "crown" of 6 pale pink or white projections that partly hide the anthers; stamens 3 plus 3 sterile stamens (called staminodes) similar to the functional stamens; ovary superior.

Blooms April through June.

Elevation: 50' to above 5,000'.

Habitat: Chaparral and woodland.

Comments: Although the stems of fork-toothed ookow (*Dichelostemma congestum*) can be a little wavy, those of snake lily are strongly twining, helping the plants climb into nearby vegetation (alas, all too often that's poison oak). They're also unexpectedly brittle. Usually only a few flowers in each umbel are open at a time. The species grows in the foothills of the Cascades and Sierra Nevada and the eastern part of the North Coast Ranges.

WILD HYACINTH

Family: Themidaceae (brodiaea family)

Also called: Fool's onion or white brodiaea

Scientific name: *Triteleia hyacinthina* (Lindl.) Greene

Height: 1–2'.

Leaves: Basal, 1–3 per plant, each leaf 4–16" long by 0.2–0.9" wide, hairless, lower side with a longitudinal "keel"; margins smooth.

Flowers: Borne in umbels above a whorl of narrow papery bracts, individual flower stalks 0.2–2" long; sepals and petals fused at the base into a 6-lobed bell, lobes white with a green stripe; stamens 6, anthers white; ovary superior.

Blooms March through July.

Elevation: Sea level to 6,500'.

Habitat: Grassland.

Comments: This herbaceous perennial, common throughout northern California, grows from a short, thick underground stem called a corm. In glassy hyacinth (*Triteleia lilacina*), which only grows in the foothills of the Cascades and the northern and central Sierra Nevada, each sepal and petal has a light grayish purple stripe and glistens as if sprinkled with tiny glass beads. The anthers are blue or lilac. The sepals and petals of the rare *Triteleia hendersonii* sport a bold purple stripe. Individual flowers in the umbels of long-rayed or marsh triteleia (*Triteleia peduncularis*) have exceptionally long stalks, up to 7" long. These four are northern California's only white-flowered species of *Triteleia*.

FOOTHILL PRETTY FACE

Family: Themidaceae (brodiaea family)

Scientific name: *Triteleia ixioides* (W. T. Aiton) Greene subsp. *scabra* (Greene) L. W. Lenz

Height: 8–20".

Leaves: Basal, 1–2 per plant, each leaf 4–20" long, very narrow, hairless, lower side with a longitudinal "keel"; margins smooth.

Flowers: Borne in umbels above a whorl of narrow papery bracts, individual flower stalks 0.4" to nearly 4" long; sepals and petals fused at the base into a short funnel topped by 6 spreading lobes, lobes straw-colored to light yellow with a darker yellow to greenish stripe; stamens 6, anthers cream-colored or yellow, rarely blue; ovary superior.

Blooms March through May.

Elevation: 50' to above 7,000'.

Habitat: Grassland, woodland, and conifer forest.

Comments: This herbaceous perennial grows mainly in the Klamath Ranges, Cascades, Sierra Nevada, and the northern end of the Sacramento Valley. It's one of five subspecies of *Triteleia ixioides* that differ in features such as the number of leaves per plant, the color of the stamens, and the exact size, color, and shape of the sepals and petals. Three additional northern California species of *Triteleia* also have yellow flowers.

WALLY BASKETS

Family: Themidaceae (brodiaea family)

Also called: Grass nut or Ithuriel's spear

Scientific name: *Triteleia laxa* Benth.

Height: 4–28".

Leaves: Basal, 1–3 per plant, each leaf 8–16" long by 0.2–1" wide, hairless, lower side with a longitudinal "keel"; margins smooth.

Flowers: Borne in umbels above a whorl of narrow papery bracts, individual flower stalks 0.4–4" long; sepals and petals fused at the base into a wide 6-lobed funnel, blue to almost white; stamens 6, filaments the same color as the sepals and petals and rather randomly curved, anthers whitish or blue; ovary superior, borne on a stalk 2–3 times as long as the ovary itself, sagging to the bottom side of the flower.

Blooms March through June.

Elevation: Sea level to 5,000'.

Habitat: Grassland, woodland, and open forest.

Comments: This common, highly variable herbaceous perennial grows in most of northern California except on the Modoc Plateau. From a distance, *Triteleia bridgesii* looks similar, but its sepals and petals often darken towards the tip, the blue anthers are held upright, not higgledy-piggledy as in wally baskets, and the ovary is stalkless. Ithuriel, by the way, is the name of an angel in some 16th- and 17th-century writings.

BROAD-LEAVED CATTAIL

Family: Typhaceae (cattail family)

Also called: Common cattail or soft flag

Scientific name: *Typha latifolia* L.

Height: 5–10'.

Leaves: Alternate, up to 4' long by 0.4–1.2" wide, the base wrapped around the stem, the rest flat, hairless; margins smooth.

Flowers: Male and female flowers borne on the same plant; male flowers densely packed at the top of the stem, each flower embedded in a mass of thread-like, color-less "bractlets" and consisting of nothing more than 2–7 stamens with slender filaments; female flowers densely packed just below the male flowers, each flower consist-ing of a cluster of hairs, a superior ovary on a slender stalk, and a style and stigma that initially are green, then turn reddish brown to very dark brown with age.

Blooms June through July.

Elevation: Sea level to 7,500'.

Habitat: Marshes and other shallow fresh or brackish water.

The weak stems of narrow-leaved bur-reed (*Spar-ganium angustifolium*), here shown with three seed heads, often fall over when shallow water dries up.

Comments: This common herbaceous perennial, found throughout northern California, has creeping under-ground stems. It provides good cover for waterfowl and other animals but can spread so quickly that managers of wildlife preserves need to clear out their cattail beds every few years to maintain a balance of vegetated areas and open water. In narrow-leaved cattail (*Typha angustifolia*) and southern cattail (*Typha domingensis*), there's usually a 0.4–5" section of bare stem between the male and female flowers. The three species can hybridize and all have minute flowers, and it helps to have a microscope for positive identification of species. Bur-reed (*Sparganium*) is the only other genus in the family; it's hard to believe that it's a relative of *Typha*, but recent molecular studies have confirmed their relatedness. Northern California is home to four species of *Sparganium*, all but one occurring mainly in marshes, ponds, and other aquatic habitats.

GLOSSARY

Examples mainly pertain to photos in this book that show the feature described.

Alpine With regard to vegetation: above timber line, which is the highest elevation in the mountains at which trees can grow.

Alternate With regard to leaves: attached to the stem one at a time, not in 2s, 3s, 4s, etc. Example: *Brassica rapa* (Brassicaceae).

Annual Plant that germinates from seed, grows, flowers, produces a new crop of seeds, and dies, all in a single growing season.

Anther The pollen-producing part of a stamen, usually consisting of two pollen sacs.

Appendage Term used for any kind of normal (that is, not pathological) outgrowth when botanists don't know what else to call it. Example: the "crown" on the petals of *Dichelostemma multiflorum* and *Dichelostemma congestum* (Themidaceae).

Appressed hairs Hairs that more or less lie flat on the surface to which they're attached.

Arrowhead-shaped In this book, used to describe leaves with two pointed basal lobes directed towards the stem as well as those with basal lobes that angle outwards; the latter shape is often called hastate. If the basal lobes are rounded, they're usually considered cordate (heart-shaped).

Basal With regard to leaves: at or very close to the base of the stem.

Biennial Plant that germinates from seed and produces leaves in its first year, then blooms, produces seeds, and dies in its second year.

Bisexual Flower with functional stamens and one or more functional pistils; most flowers are of this type.

Blade The widened, flattened part of a leaf, which in some species is secondarily folded, curved, or rolled into a three-dimensional shape. Called the lamina by some botanists.

Bloom 1) Flower or blossom; 2) a coating on the surface of some stems, leaves, and fruits consisting of minute flakes of wax that give the underlying color a whitish, grayish, or blue cast.

Bolt (verb) To produce a flowering stem from a basal rosette of leaves.

Brackish water Saltier than freshwater but not as salty as the ocean.

Bract Flattened or thread-like, usually relatively small structure below a flower or cluster of flowers. In a few species, the bracts are more conspicuous than the actual flowers, for example, in western dogwood and flowering dogwood (*Cornus nuttallii* and *Cornus florida*, respectively, neither of them shown in this book) and the genus *Castilleja* (Orobanchaceae).

Bristle Stiff, fairly straight hair.

Bulb Short, upright underground stem enclosed by relatively large, fleshy leaves. Example: onion.

Burred Ending in a small hard hook, like a miniature crochet needle.

Calyx (plural: calyces) Collective term for all the sepals in a flower.

Capsule (or seed capsule) A kind of fruit that consists of a dry, papery to hard wall and that, when fully ripe, opens in several places to release the seeds inside.

Catkin Slender, elongate inflorescence of many wind-pollinated species, often dangling. Examples: *Alnus rhombifolia* (Betulaceae)—dangling; *Notholithocarpus densiflorus* (Fagaceae)—upright.

Chaparral Vegetation that largely consists of evergreen, stiff-branched shrubs, often with thick, leathery leaves.

Chromosome One of the strands of DNA in each cell. Sometimes related species are characterized by different numbers of chromosomes per cell. Of course, chromosome numbers are useless for identification unless you have access to a research laboratory and lots of the requisite time, money, and expertise.

Coastal scrub Vegetation near the coast that largely consists of fairly low-growing shrubs with flexible branches.

Compound leaf Leaf that instead of having a single blade has two or more flattened parts called leaflets.

Compound umbel Umbel in which, at the end of each flower stalk, there's a smaller secondary umbel instead of a single flower. Example: Most species of Apiaceae; in fact, an older name for the family was Umbelliferae, or "umbel-bearing plants."

Corm Short, thick, upright, unbranched underground stem, often enclosed by thin, dry leaves or scales. If the leaves are fleshy, it's a bulb; if the short, thick stem grows horizontally, it's a tuber. Potatoes are tubers.

Corolla Collective term for all the petals in a flower.

Deciduous Shedding all leaves at the end of each growing season. Also used to mean falling off naturally, such as the sepals off the unfolding flowers of some species. For plant parts that fall off very early, botanists sometimes use the terms *ephemeral*, *caducous*, or *fugaceous*.

Disk flower One of the small flowers in the center of the flower head in many species of Asteraceae. Typically the disk flowers are bisexual, but some species are characterized by male or sterile disk flowers.

Dissected A leaf that's so deeply lobed that at the base of each lobe there's only a narrow flange of tissue left along the midrib; almost but not quite compound.

Divided In this book, a synonym for dissected.

Ephemeral stream Stream that only flows for a short time after a rainstorm.

Epiphyte Plant that grows on top of another, using it for physical support but not taking water or nutrients away from it. Examples: ferns that grow on tree branches; many tropical orchids.

Evergreen Retaining leaves for more than one growing season so that the plant is never leafless.

Female (or pistillate) flower Flower with one or more functional pistils but no functional stamens; if stamens are present at all, they may just consist of a filament or have exceptionally small, sterile anthers.

Fertilization Fusion of a sperm nucleus (produced by a pollen grain) with an egg nucleus (inside an ovule, which is the precursor of a seed); not to be confused with pollination.

Filament The usually slender, stalk-like part of a stamen.

Flora 1) Collective term for all the plant species that grow in a particular area; 2) a book or other scientific publication listing (and often describing) all those species.

Floral tube Tube formed by fusion of the sepals and petals.

Free Not attached to anything else except at its base.

Fruit Ovary in which the ovules inside have been fertilized and become seeds; often the ovary matures into some kind of device for seed dispersal, for example, by attracting animals that will eat it and expel the unharmed seeds in their feces, by developing burs that catch in the fur or feathers of animals that brush against it, by growing wings or small "parachutes" that allow it to be carried away by wind, or by popping open and flinging out the seeds.

Fused Parts that have grown into a single structure so that you can't separate them without tearing them; the parts can be alike or different. Occasionally parts are held together by interlocking hairs, but technically they're still separate structures and considered free.

Genus (plural: genera) A group of related species.

Gland Structure that exudes a substance such as nectar, resin, or oils. The small, translucent spots in citrus peel are oil glands.

Glandular hair Hair that secretes some substance, often from a flattened or round head supported by a thin stem, the whole structure resembling a miniature tack or sewing pin. Example: *Centromadia fitchii* (Asteraceae).

Hair Very slender outgrowth from the surface of a plant.

Half-inferior ovary Ovary in which the lower parts of the sepals, petals, and filaments have fused with the lower half of the ovary wall, making it look as if they've sprouted from the side of the ovary.

Head Very dense cluster of flowers, typical of the Asteraceae but also occurring in some other plants, such as *Gilia capitata* (Polemoniaceae) and many species of *Trifolium* (Fabaceae).

Heart-shaped Resembling a stylized heart. When the heart is upside-down, botanists use the term cordate; when it's right side up, obcordate. Examples: leaves of *Cardamine* *cordifolia* (Brassicaceae), leaflets of *Oxalis* spp. (Oxalidaceae), and fruit of *Capsella bursa-pastoris* (Brassicaceae).

Herbaceous perennial Plant in which the underground parts live three or more years while the aboveground parts die after each growing season; generally such plants don't have much woody tissue in their stems, but there are exceptions, such as *Pterospora andromedea* (Ericaceae).

Inferior ovary Ovary in which the lower parts of the sepals, petals, and filaments have fused with the ovary wall, making it look as if they've sprouted from the top of the ovary. Examples: *Mentzelia laevicaulis* (Loasaceae), *Vaccinium uliginosum* (Ericaceae), apples, and pears.

Inflorescence A cluster of flowers. Botanists have a plethora of technical terms for different configurations.

Inrolled Curled towards the center. Example: the sterile stamens or staminodes of *Brodiaea minor* (Themidaceae).

Intergrade (verb) To form a continuum of shapes, sizes, and/or colors.

Intermittent stream Stream that flows only part of the year but not as briefly as an ephemeral stream.

Internode The section of stem between two successive leaves.

Leaf A usually green structure (typically with a flat part called the blade and a thin stalk called the petiole) attached to a stem with a small bud in the angle just above the point of attachment; the bud may stay dormant or grow into a branch, inflorescence, or flower.

Lens-shaped More or less round with a well-defined edge and a slightly bulging center, like a lentil.

Liana Woody vine. Example: *Vitis californica* (Vitaceae).

Lobe A big bulge or projection. If the United States were a plant, you could say that Florida is a long, narrow lobe.

Lobed With one or more lobes. As used in this book, includes terms such as *cleft*, *parted*, and *laciniate*.

Male (or staminate) flower Flower with functional stamens but no functional pistil; if a pistil is present at all, it's usually small and without ovules.

Matte Not shiny.

Midrib The thick vein in the center of the flat portion or blade of many leaves, essentially a continuation of the leaf stalk or petiole.

Narrow In this book, used loosely for leaf shapes that are a good deal longer than wide with a length to width ratio of roughly 3:1 or narrower; as used here, the term encompasses several more specific botanical terms such as *acicular*, *linear*, *lanceolate*, *oblanceolate*, *subulate*, and *falcate*. The shape of the tip and base can vary; e.g., a narrow leaf may have a rounded or pointed tip, a tapered, rounded, heart-shaped, or asymmetrical base, etc.

Native In this book, used to mean native to northern California unless specified otherwise.

Nectary Any structure or place on the surface of a plant that exudes a sweet, sugary solution that attracts pollinators, usually but not always located somewhere in the flower.

Node The point on a stem where a leaf is attached.

Notched With a sharp little indentation at the tip. Example: petals of *Claytonia sibirica* (Montiaceae).

Nucleus The part of a cell in which, except while a cell is actively dividing, its DNA is located.

Ocrea (plural: ocreae) In Polygonaceae, a papery sheath wrapped around the stem wherever a leaf is attached.

Opposite With regard to leaves: attached to the stem in pairs. Example: *Marrubium vulgare* (Lamiaceae).

Oval In this book, used loosely for leaf shapes somewhere between "narrow" and "round" with a length to width ratio somewhere in the neighborhood of 1.5:1 to 2.5:1; as used here, the term encompasses several more specific botanical terms such as *elliptic*, *ovate*, *obovate*, and *oblong*. The shape of the tip and base can vary; e.g., an oval leaf may have a rounded or pointed tip, a tapered, rounded, heart-shaped, or asymmetrical base, etc.

Ovary The bottom part of a pistil, often but not always somewhat swollen, consisting of a wall that encloses one or more ovules.

Ovule Small structure containing an egg nucleus; after fertilization of the egg, the ovule matures into a seed.

Palmate Radiating in two dimensions from a central area or central point of attachment, a bit like fingers spreading away from the palm of your hand. Examples: The leaves of *Lupinus* (Fabaceae) and *Aesculus californicus* (Sapindaceae) are palmately compound, while those of *Geranium carolinianum* and *Geranium molle* (both in Geraniaceae) and *Platanus racemosa* (Platanaceae) are palmately lobed.

Pappus In Asteraceae, the highly modified sepals, usually consisting of a few to many flattened scales, barbs, hooks, bristles, or unbranched or feathery hairs.

Perennial Plant that lives for more than two growing seasons, often for much longer, and typically blooms repeatedly.

Perianth Collective term for all the sepals and petals in a flower, regardless of whether they look alike or not.

Petal A flattened, usually non-green part of the flower that helps advertise the presence of the flower to pollinators such as insects or birds; in wind-pollinated plants, the petals are often tiny or absent. In many species, the petals are fused into three-dimensional shapes such as bells and funnels.

Petiole The stalk, considered part of the leaf, that in many species connects the flat part of the leaf or blade to the plant's stem. Leaves that lack a petiole are called sessile.

Phyllary In Asteraceae, one of the bracts on the outside or underside of each flower head.

Pinnate With leaflets, veins, or lobes arranged on both sides of a main axis. Example: leaves of *Polypodium calirhiza* (Polypodiaceae), many other ferns, *Schinus molle* (Anacardiaceae), and *Potentilla anserina* (Rosaceae). As used in this book, the term includes what botanists call ternate: pinnately compound with only three leaflets, the two lateral ones sessile, the terminal one stalked.

Pistil Female part of a flower, consisting of an ovary containing the ovules or future seeds, a stigma on which pollen needs to land, and usually a neck-like portion called the style between the ovary and stigma.

Pod Fruit produced by most members of the Fabaceae, differing from a capsule in some important technical details. Examples: *Vicia villosa*, snow peas, and green beans.

Pollen Minute, frequently more or less spherical, often but not always yellow structures produced in the anthers that carry sperm to the stigma; each tiny structure is called a pollen grain.

Pollination The process of delivering pollen grains to the stigma, most often effected by insects, birds, or wind.

Rare In this book, used as a general term for very uncommon plants, not in its legal sense, and so encompassing terms such as *rare*, *threatened*, *endangered*, *CNPS List 1B*, and so on, as defined by various state and federal laws and regulations.

Ray flower One of the flowers around the perimeter of the flower head in many species of Asteraceae, each ray flower superficially resembling a single petal. In some species, the ray flowers are female (that is, they lack stamens) or completely sterile.

Receptacle Tip of a flower stalk, sometimes enlarged, to which the sepals, petals, stamens, and one or more pistils are attached.

Rhizome In flowering plants, a long stem that grows more or less horizontally through the ground, periodically producing leaves and/or branches that grow upright into "normal" aboveground stems. It can be thin or fleshy. Confusingly, in ferns the term is applied to *all* horizontally growing stems, regardless of whether they're aboveground or underground.

Riparian Growing along or close to a creek or river.

Root Underground structure that anchors a plant, absorbs water and mineral nutrients, and sometimes also stores food. Roots never produce leaves, and their internal structure differs from that of stems.

Rosette Dense cluster of leaves more or less at ground level. Example: *Mentzelia laevicaulis* (Loasaceae).

Scale Small, flattened structure pressed flat against the surface to which it's attached, a bit like one of the scales covering a snake's skin.

Scalloped With rounded, not pointy teeth along the margin. Botanists often use the term *crenate* or, for very small rounded teeth, *crenulate*.

Seed Structure derived from a fertilized ovule and containing a plant embryo that will, when the seed germinates, grow into a new plant. Seeds vary in size from dust-like specks (as in many orchids) to as big as a coconut.

Sepal Typically a flattened, green structure, several of which protect each flower bud. In some species, the sepals are fused; in others they're free. Occasionally the sepals resemble petals; regardless of their appearance, though, their internal structure is slightly different than that of petals.

Sessile Attached directly to the stem, without a petiole or flower stalk.

Shrub Relatively short, woody plant that's heavily branched near the base.

Simple leaf A leaf that's not compound.

Smooth A leaf margin that's not toothed, scalloped, or lobed; botanists often use the term *entire*. Examples: leaves of *Arctostaphylos patula* and *Rhododendron macrophyllum* (both in Ericaceae) and *Umbellularia californica* (Lauraceae).

Sorus (plural: sori) In ferns, a small, distinct cluster of sporangia.

sp. (plural: spp.) Species.

Specific epithet The second word in a scientific name, identifying a particular species in the genus; always written lowercase and italicized or underlined.

Spoon-shaped Leaf with a petiole that gradually widens into an oval to roundish blade; unlike a real spoon, the blade is generally flat, not a shallow bowl. As used here, the term includes more technical ones such as *obovate* and *spatulate*.

Sporangium (plural: sporangia) In ferns, horsetails, and a few other kinds of plants not covered in this book, a small structure that produces spores.

Spore In ferns, horsetails, and a few other kinds of plants not covered in this book, a single cell that will eventually give rise to male and/or female organs respectively producing sperm and egg cells.

Sprawling In this book, loosely used to mean more or less lying on the ground and encompassing more specific terms such as *prostrate*, *procumbent*, *decumbent*, *trailing*, and (to some extent) *ascending*.

Spur A sack-like or tubular extension of a sepal or petal. Example: *Kickxia elatine* (Plantaginaceae).

Square stem More accurately, a stem that is square in cross-section. Example: *Lycopus americanus* (Lamicaceae).

Stamen Male part of the flower, consisting of a generally stalk-like filament and a pollen-producing anther. In some species, the lower part of the filament is fused to the petals.

Staminode Sterile stamen, often consisting merely of a filament or differing in appearance from the functional stamens in some other way.

Stem Leaf- or flower-producing axis. Usually but not always aboveground. A leafless stem that only bears one or more flowers is sometimes called a scape.

Sterile Not reproductively functional.

Stigma The top part of a pistil, modified to receive and hold onto pollen. Complex chemical interactions between the surface of the stigma and each pollen grain ensure that only the right kind of pollen fertilizes that particular flower.

Stipe Petiole of a fern leaf.

Stipules A pair of small outgrowths from the stem at the base of a petiole. Not all species have stipules. When present, their shape can be helpful in identification. Example: *Salix lasiolepis* (Salicaceae).

Stolon In flowering plants, a long, usually thin stem that grows more or less horizontally across the ground, periodically producing roots and clusters of leaves that become new plants. Also called a runner. Example: *Fragaria* spp. (Rosaceae).

Style The typically neck-like part of a pistil that connects the stigma at the top with the ovary at the bottom. Some species lack a style.

Subalpine At or just below timberline, which is the highest elevation at which trees grow in the mountains.

Subshrub Perennial plant in which the lower aboveground parts of the stem and main branches are woody and survive from year to year, while the upper parts die back each winter. Examples: *Brickellia californica* (Asteraceae) and *Monardella villosa* (Lamiaceae).

subsp. Subspecies. Sometimes abbreviated ssp. (not to be confused with spp., the plural abbreviation for species).

Substrate The medium in which a plant is growing, such as soil, gravel, or tailing piles.

Superior ovary Ovary that "sits on top of" the sepals, petals, and stamens, none of which are fused to its wall. In some species (e.g., many members of the Rosaceae), the bases of the sepals, petals, and filaments are fused into an urn-like shape with the ovary in the center, hiding it from view, but as long as the ovary isn't fused to the urn it's still considered superior.

Tailings Rocky or gravelly debris left behind by mining operations.

Talus Natural, fairly stable accumulation of large boulders, often at the base of a cliff.

Taprooted Having one main root that grows more or less straight downwards from the stem, with clearly smaller roots branching off it.

Tendril Slender, coiling structure, usually derived from the tip of a stem or branch or replacing leaflets at the tip of a compound leaf, that helps many climbing plants hold onto whatever they're climbing. Examples: *Lathyrus* spp. and *Vicia* spp. (Fabaceae).

Toothed With a zigzagged margin, rather like a serrated knife. Examples: leaves of *Mentzelia laevicaulis* (Loasaceae) and *Rosa californica* (Rosaceae). In this book, used loosely to include the terms *serrate*, *serrulate*, *dentate*, *denticulate*, *runcinate*, and *incised*. If the teeth are rounded, the margins are called scalloped or crenate. Some plants have leaves in which each main tooth is edged with even smaller, sharply pointed teeth; they're called double-toothed.

Tree Relatively tall woody plant with only one or at most a few main stems that don't branch until they're well above the ground.

Umbel Cluster of flowers in which all the flower stalks come together at the same point, rather like the ribs of an umbrella coming together at the top of the shaft. Examples: *Hydrocotyle umbellata* (Araliaceae) and *Triteleia hyacinthina* (Themidaceae). Also see *compound umbel*.

Urn-like or urn-shaped With a hollow, round body and a narrow neck. Examples: the fused petals of *Gaultheria shallon*, *Pterospora andromedea*, and all species of *Arctostaphylos* (all in Ericaceae).

var. Variety.

Vine Plant that climbs on some kind of support, usually holding on by means of tendrils or very small roots or by coiling its entire stem or branches around it.

Wavy Undulating in three dimensions. Example: basal leaves of *Eriogonum nudum* (Polygonaceae).

Waxy bloom A coating of minute flakes of wax on a leaf, stem, or fruit; the flakes partly hide the color of the underlying surface and give it a paler or even whitish appearance; rubbing the surface compresses the wax and brings out the "true" color. Example: *Vaccinium uliginosum* (Ericaceae).

Whorled With regard to leaves: attached to the stem in groups of three or more. Examples: *Mollugo verticillata* (Molluginaceae) and *Galium aparine* (Rubiaceae).

Wing A thin, flat extension. *Acer negundo* (Sapindaceae) and *Fraxinus latifolia* (Oleaceae) have winged fruit. When used in reference to stems or petioles, "winged" means a thin, ribbon-like extension, like the fins on an eel, rather than anything remotely resembling the wing of a bird, insect, or airplane.

Yellow pine forest Forest in which *Pinus ponderosa* is the most common tree.

SPECIES IN THIS BOOK LISTED BY COLOR

Plants are listed here by the main color of their flowers—the color you first notice—which is usually but not always the color of their petals. A few species are listed twice, such as carnival poppy, which has equal numbers of pure yellow and pure white petals, as are some that come in different colors or that look purple to some observers, pink to others. Once in a blue moon you may come across a white-flowered individual of a species that normally produces colored flowers, but the white list includes only those species that are always white-flowered or at least produce white flowers fairly often.

Bold text indicates plants native to northern California.

① Rare species, as defined in the glossary.

② Drought-tolerant, non-invasive species that might be suitable in a garden or for revegetation projects. I've not included primarily riparian species. This list is admittedly rather subjective, and some species may be hard to grow or not commercially available.

③ Invasive species.

White to cream-colored

Dicotyledons

Adoxaceae	**Sambucus nigra subsp. caerulea**	**Blue elderberry** ②
Adoxaceae	**Sambucus racemosa var. racemosa**	**Red elderberry**
Anacardiaceae	*Schinus molle*	Pepper tree ③
Anacardiaceae	**Toxicodendron diversilobum**	**Poison oak**
Apiaceae	**Angelica breweri**	**Brewer's angelica**
Apiaceae	**Angelica hendersonii**	**Coast angelica**
Apiaceae	*Anthriscus caucalis*	Bur-chervil
Apiaceae	*Conium maculatum*	Poison hemlock ③
Apiaceae	*Daucus carota*	Queen Anne's lace
Apiaceae	**Daucus pusillus**	**Southwestern carrot**
Apiaceae	**Heracleum maximum**	**Cow parsnip**
Apiaceae	**Sphenosciadium capitellatum**	**Ranger's buttons**
Apiaceae	*Torilis arvensis*	Tall sock-destroyer ③

Apocynaceae	**Apocynum cannabinum**	**Indian hemp** ②
Apocynaceae	**Asclepias fascicularis**	**Narrow-leaved milkweed** ③
Apocynaceae	Nerium oleander	Oleander ②
Araliaceae	**Hydrocotyle umbellata**	**Marsh pennywort**
Asteraceae	**Achillea millefolium**	**Yarrow** ②
Asteraceae	Anthemis cotula	Mayweed
Asteraceae	**Baccharis pilularis** subsp. **consanguinea**	**Coyote brush (female flowers)** ②
Asteraceae	**Baccharis salicifolia** subsp. **salicifolia**	**Mulefat**
Asteraceae	**Calycadenia multiglandulosa**	**Rosin weed** ②
Asteraceae	**Eclipta prostrata**	**False daisy**
Asteraceae	**Erigeron canadensis**	**Horseweed**
Asteraceae	**Gnaphalium palustre**	**Cudweed**
Asteraceae	Logfia gallica	Daggerleaf cottonrose
Asteraceae	**Micropus californicus** var. **californicus**	**Cottontop**
Asteraceae	**Pseudognaphalium beneolens**	**Fragrant cudweed**
Asteraceae	**Pseudognaphalium californicum**	**California cudweed** ②
Asteraceae	Pseudognaphalium luteoalbum	Red-tip rabbit-tobacco
Asteraceae	**Psilocarphus brevissimus** var. **brevissimus**	**Dwarf woolly marbles**
Bignoniaeae	Catalpa speciosa	Northern catalpa
Boraginaeae	**Eriodictyon californicum**	**California yerba santa** ②
Boraginaeae	**Eucrypta chrysanthemifolia** var. **chrysanthemifolia**	**Spotted hideseed**
Boraginaeae	**Heliotropium curassavicum** var. **occulatum**	**Alkali heliotrope**
Boraginaeae	Heliotropium europaeum	European heliotrope
Boraginaeae	**Hesperochiron californicus**	**California hesperochiron**
Boraginaeae	**Nemophila heterophylla**	**Canyon nemophila**
Boraginaeae	**Nemophila maculata**	**Fivespot**

Boraginaeae	*Nemophila menziesii* var. *atomaria*	*Baby blue-eyes*
Boraginaeae	*Pectocarya penicillata*	*Sleeping combseed*
Boraginaeae	*Phacelia imbricata* subsp. *imbricata*	*Imbricate scorpionweed*
Boraginaeae	*Plagiobothrys canescens* var. *canescens*	*Valley popcornflower*
Boraginaeae	*Plagiobothrys nothofulvus*	*Rusty popcornflower* ②
Boraginaeae	*Plagiobothrys stipitatus* var. *micranthus*	*Vernal pool popcornflower*
Brassicaceae	*Arabidopsis thaliana*	Mouse-ear cress
Brassicaceae	*Athysanus pusillus*	*Common sandweed*
Brassicaceae	*Capsella bursa-pastoris*	Shepherd's purse
Brassicaceae	*Cardamine cordifolia*	*Heart-leaved bittercress*
Brassicaceae	*Cardamine oligosperma*	*Little western bittercress*
Brassicaceae	*Draba verna*	Whitlow grass
Brassicaceae	*Nasturtium officinale*	*Watercress*
Brassicaceae	*Raphanus sativus*	Wild radish ③
Brassicaceae	*Thysanocarpus curvipes*	*Lacepod*
Brassicaceae	*Thysanocarpus radians*	*Spokepod*
Campanulaceae	*Downingia cuspidata*	*Toothed downingia*
Caprifoliaceae	*Lonicera japonica*	Japanese honeysuckle ③
Caryophyllaceae	*Cerastium glomeratum*	Sticky mouse-ear chickweed
Caryophyllaceae	*Cerastium viride*	*Field chickweed*
Caryophyllaceae	*Minuartia californica*	*California sandwort*
Caryophyllaceae	*Saponaria officinalis*	Soapwort ③
Caryophyllaceae	*Silene gallica*	Small-flowered catchfly
Caryophyllaceae	*Silene noctiflora*	Night-flowering catchfly
Caryophyllaceae	*Stellaria media*	Common chickweed
Convolvulaceae	*Calystegia occidentalis* subsp. *occidentalis*	*Chaparral false bindweed*
Convolvulaceae	*Convolvulus arvensis*	Field bindweed ③
Cucurbitaceae	*Marah fabacea*	*California man-root*

Cucurbitaceae	*Marah watsonii*	*Taw man-root*
Ericaceae	*Arbutus menziesii*	*Madrone* ②
Ericaceae	*Orthilia secunda*	*One-sided wintergreen*
Ericaceae	*Vaccinium ovatum*	*Evergreen huckleberry*
Ericaceae	*Vaccinium parvifolium*	*Red huckleberry*
Euphorbiaceae	*Croton setiger*	*Turkey mullein*
Fabaceae	*Astragalus nuttallii* var. *virgatus*	*Nuttall's milkvetch*
Fabaceae	*Lupinus microcarpus* var. *densiflorus*	*Chick lupine* ②
Fabaceae	*Robinia pseudoacacia*	Black locust ③
Fabaceae	*Rupertia physodes*	*California tea*
Fagaceae	*Chrysolepis sempervirens*	*Bush chinquapin*
Fagaceae	*Notholithocarpus densiflorus* var. *densiflorus*	*Tan oak*
Gentianaceae	*Frasera albicaulis* var. *nitida*	*Whitestem frasera* ②
Gentianaceae	*Gentiana newberryi* var. *tiogana*	*Alpine gentian*
Geraniaceae	*Geranium carolinianum*	*Carolina crane's bill*
Grossulariaceae	*Ribes cereum* var. *cereum*	*Wax currant*
Grossulariaceae	*Ribes menziesii* var. *menziesii*	*Canyon gooseberry*
Hydrangeaceae	*Philadelphus lewisii*	*Wild mock orange* ②
Hydrangeaceae	*Whipplea modesta*	*Modesty*
Lamiaceae	*Clinopodium douglasii*	*Yerba buena*
Lamiaceae	*Lepechinia calycina*	*Pitcher sage* ②
Lamiaceae	*Lycopus americanus*	*Bugleweed*
Lamiaceae	*Marrubium vulgare*	Horehound
Lamiaceae	*Salvia sonomensis*	*Sonoma sage* ②
Limnanthaceae	*Limnanthes douglasii* subsp. *nivea*	*Meadowfoam*
Malvaceae	*Hibiscus lasiocarpos* var. *occidentalis*	*California hibiscus* ①
Malvaceae	*Sidalcea calycosa* subsp. *calycosa*	*Vernal pool checkerbloom*

Molluginaceae	*Mollugo verticillata*	Carpet-weed
Montiaceae	***Claytonia parviflora* subsp. *parviflora***	**Narrow-leaved miner's lettuce**
Montiaceae	***Claytonia perfoliata* subsp. *perfoliata***	**Miner's lettuce**
Montiaceae	***Claytonia sibirica***	**Candy flower**
Montiaceae	***Lewisia nevadensis***	**Nevada bitter-root**
Montiaceae	***Lewisia triphylla***	**Three-leaved lewisia**
Oleaceae	*Olea europea*	Olive ③
Onagraceae	***Clarkia arcuata***	**Glandular clarkia**
Onagraceae	***Epilobium brachycarpum***	**Tall annual willowherb**
Orobanchaceae	***Castilleja ambigua* subsp. *ambigua***	**Johnny-nip**
Orobanchaceae	***Castilleja attenuata***	**Valley tassels**
Oxalidaceae	***Oxalis oregana***	**Redwood sorrel**
Papaveraceae	***Hesperomecon linearis***	**Carnival poppy**
Papaveraceae	***Platystemon californicus***	**Cream cups**
Parnassiaceae	***Parnassia palustris***	**Grass-of-Parnassus**
Phrymaceae	***Mimulus bicolor***	**Yellow and white monkeyflower**
Phytolaccaceae	*Phytolacca americana* var. *americana*	Pokeweed ③
Plantaginaceae	***Gratiola ebracteata***	**Bractless hedge-hyssop**
Plantaginaceae	***Lindernia dubia***	**False pimpernel**
Plantaginaceae	***Plantago erecta***	**Dwarf plantain**
Plantaginaceae	*Plantago lanceolata*	English plantain ③
Plantaginaceae	***Veronica peregrina* subsp. *xalapensis***	**Purslane speedwell**
Polemoniaceae	***Leptosiphon bicolor***	**True baby stars**
Polemoniaceae	***Leptosiphon liniflorus***	**Narrow-leaved flaxflower**
Polemoniaceae	***Navarretia leucocephala* subsp. *leucocephala***	**White-headed navarretia**

Polemoniaceae	*Phlox diffusa*	*Spreading phlox*
Polygonaceae	*Bistorta bistortoides*	*Western bistort*
Polygonaceae	*Eriogonum latifolium*	*Coast buckwheat*
Polygonaceae	*Eriogonum nudum* var. *pubiflorum*	*Fremont's wild buckwheat* ②
Polygonaceae	*Persicaria punctata*	*Dotted smartweed*
Polygonaceae	*Polygonum shastense*	*Shasta knotweed*
Primulaceae	*Primula clevelandii* var. *patula*	*Padre's shooting star*
Ranunculaceae	*Caltha leptosepala*	*Marsh marigold*
Ranunculaceae	*Clematis lasiantha*	*Chaparral clematis* ②
Ranunculaceae	*Delphinium hansenii* subsp. *hansenii*	*Hansen's larkspur* ②
Ranunculaceae	*Ranunculus aquatilis*	*White water crowfoot*
Rhamnaceae	*Ceanothus cuneatus* var. *cuneatus*	*Buckbrush* ②
Rhamnaceae	*Ceanothus integerrimus* var. *macrothyrsus*	*Deerbrush*
Rosaceae	*Adenostoma fasciculatum* var. *fasciculatum*	*Chamise* ②
Rosaceae	*Chamaebatia foliolosa*	*Mountain misery*
Rosaceae	*Fragaria chiloensis*	*Beach strawberry*
Rosaceae	*Heteromeles arbutifolia*	*Toyon* ②
Rosaceae	*Horkelia tridentata* var. *tridentata*	*Three-toothed horkelia*
Rosaceae	*Prunus emarginata*	*Bitter cherry*
Rosaceae	*Pyracantha fortuneana*	Chinese firethorn ③
Rosaceae	*Rosa multiflora*	Rambler rose
Rosaceae	*Rubus parviflorus*	*Thimbleberry*
Rosaceae	*Rubus ursinus*	*California blackberry*
Rubiceae	*Cephalanthus occidentalis*	*Button willow*
Rubiceae	*Galium aparine*	*Goose grass*
Rutaceae	*Ptelea crenulata*	*California hop tree* ②

Sapindaceae	*Aesculus californica*	**California buckeye** ②
Saxifragaceae	*Lithophragma bolanderi*	**Bolander's woodland star** ②
Scrophularia-ceae	*Verbascum blattaria*	Moth mullein ②
Simaroubaceae	*Ailanthus altissima*	Tree-of-heaven ③
Solanaceae	*Datura stramonium*	Thorn-apple
Solanaceae	*Datura wrightii*	**Jimson weed** ②
Solanaceae	*Nicotiana acuminata* var. *multiflora*	Many-flowered tobacco
Solanaceae	*Solanum douglasii*	**Douglas' nightshade**
Styracaceae	*Styrax redivivus*	**Snowdrop bush** ②
Valerianaceae	*Valerianella locusta*	Lamb lettuce
Violaceae	*Viola ocellata*	**Western heart's ease**

Monocotyledons

Agavaceae	*Chlorogalum pomeridianum* var. *pomeridianum*	**Common soap plant** ②
Alismataceae	*Sagittaria sanfordii*	**Sanford's arrowhead** ①
Alliaceae	*Allium amplectens*	**Narrow-leaved onion**
Amaryllidaceae	*Leucojum aestivum*	Summer snow ②
Araceae	*Arum italicum*	Large cuckoo pint
Cyperaceae	*Carex barbarae*	**Santa Barbara sedge (female flowers)**
Cyperaceae	*Eleocharis macrostachya*	**Common spikerush**
Liliaceae	*Calochortus leichtlinii*	**Leichtlin's mariposa lily** ②
Liliaceae	*Calochortus tolmiei*	**Pussy's ears**
Liliaceae	*Erythronium multiscapideum*	**Trout lily**
Liliaceae	*Fritillaria liliacea*	**Fragrant fritillary** ①
Liliaceae	*Prosartes smithii*	**Smith's fairy bells**
Melanthiaceae	*Toxicoscordion venenosum* var. *venenosum*	**Meadow death camas**
Melanthiaceae	*Trillium chloropetalum*	**Giant trillium**
Melanthiaceae	*Veratrum californicum* var. *californicum*	**Corn lily**

Melanthiaceae	***Xerophyllum tenax***	***Bear grass***
Orchidaceae	***Piperia elegans*** subsp. ***elegans***	***Coast piperia***
Orchidaceae	***Platanthera dilatata*** var. ***leucostachys***	***White-flowered bog-orchid***
Orchidaceae	***Spiranthes romanzoffiana***	***Hooded ladies' tresses***
Ruscaceae	***Maianthemum dilatatum***	***False lily-of-the-valley***
Tecophi-laeaceae	***Odontostomum hartwegii***	***No common name*** ②
Themidaceae	***Triteleia hyacinthina***	***Wild hyacinth*** ②

Yellow to orange

Dicotyledons

Aizoaceae	*Carpobrotus edulis*	Freeway iceplant ③
Apiaceae	*Foeniculum vulgare*	Fennel ③
Apiaceae	***Lomatium caruifolium*** var. ***denticulatum***	***Foothill lomatium***
Apiaceae	***Lomatium marginatum*** var. ***marginatum***	***Butte desert-parsley***
Apiaceae	***Lomatium utriculatum***	***Biscuit root***
Apiaceae	***Sanicula arctopoides***	***Footsteps of spring***
Apiaceae	***Sanicula bipinnatifida***	***Purple sanicle***
Asteraceae	***Achryachaena mollis***	***Blow-wives***
Asteraceae	***Artemisia douglasiana***	***Mugwort***
Asteraceae	***Baccharis pilularis*** subsp. ***consanguinea***	***Coyote brush (male flowers)*** ②
Asteraceae	***Bidens frondosa***	***Devil's beggartick***
Asteraceae	***Blennosperma*** var. ***nanum***	***Yellow carpet***
Asteraceae	***Brickellia californica***	***California brickellbush***
Asteraceae	*Centaurea solstitialis*	Yellow star-thistle ③
Asteraceae	***Centromadia fitchii***	***Fitch's tarweed***
Asteraceae	***Centromadia pungens*** subsp. ***pungens***	***Common spikeweed***
Asteraceae	*Chondrilla juncea*	Skeleton weed ③

Asteraceae	*Cotula australis*	Southern brass buttons ③
Asteraceae	*Cotula coronopifolia*	Brass buttons ③
Asteraceae	*Dittrichia graveolens*	Stinkwort ③
Asteraceae	**Eriophyllum lanatum var. grandiflorum**	**Large-flowered woolly sunflower**
Asteraceae	**Eucephalus breweri**	**Golden aster**
Asteraceae	**Euthamia occidentalis**	**Western goldenrod**
Asteraceae	**Grindelia camporum**	**Great Valley gumweed**
Asteraceae	**Grindelia stricta var. platyphylla**	**Beach gumweed**
Asteraceae	**Helenium puberulum**	**Sneezeweed**
Asteraceae	**Helianthus annuus**	**Common sunflower** ②
Asteraceae	*Helminthotheca echioides*	Bristly ox-tongue ③
Asteraceae	**Heterotheca grandiflora**	**Telegraph plant**
Asteraceae	**Heterotheca oregona var. compacta**	**Rayless golden aster**
Asteraceae	**Holocarpha virgata subsp. virgata**	**Pitgland tarweed**
Asteraceae	*Hypochaeris glabra*	Smooth cat's ear③
Asteraceae	*Lactuca serriola*	Prickly lettuce ③
Asteraceae	**Lagophylla glandulosa**	**Hare-leaf**
Asteraceae	*Lapsana communis*	Nipplewort
Asteraceae	**Lasthenia californica subsp. californica**	**California goldfields** ②
Asteraceae	**Lasthenia fremontii**	**Fremont's goldfields**
Asteraceae	**Layia fremontii**	**Fremont's tidy-tips** ②
Asteraceae	*Leontodon saxatilis* subsp. *longirostris*	Hairy hawkbit
Asteraceae	**Lessingia pectinata var. tenuipes**	**Sticky lessingia**
Asteraceae	**Madia elegans**	**Common madia** ②
Asteraceae	**Madia gracilis**	**Gumweed**
Asteraceae	**Madia sativa**	**Coast tarweed**
Asteraceae	*Matricaria discoidea*	Pineapple weed

Asteraceae	*Senecio flaccidus* var. *douglasii*	*Douglas' threadleaf ragwort*
Asteraceae	*Senecio triangularis*	*Arrowleaf ragwort*
Asteraceae	*Senecio vulgaris*	Common groundsel
Asteraceae	*Solidago velutina* subsp. *californica*	*California goldenrod* ②
Asteraceae	*Sonchus asper* subsp. *asper*	Spiny sow thistle ③
Asteraceae	*Sonchus oleraceus*	Common sow thistle ③
Asteraceae	*Tragopogon dubius*	Yellow salsify
Asteraceae	*Wyethia mollis*	*Woolly mule's ears*
Asteraceae	*Wyethia helenioides*	*Gray mule's ears* ②
Berberidaceae	*Berberis aquifolium* var. *aquifolium*	*Oregon grape*
Boraginaeae	*Amsinckia lycopsoides*	*Bugloss-flowered fiddleneck*
Boraginaeae	*Emmenanthe penduliflora* var. *penduliflora*	*Whispering bells*
Brassicaceae	*Brassica rapa*	Field mustard ③
Brassicaceae	*Hirschfeldia incana*	Shortpod mustard ③
Brassicaceae	*Rorippa curvisiliqua*	*Western yellow cress*
Caprifoliaceae	*Lonicera japonica*	Japanese honeysuckle ③
Caprifoliaceae	*Lonicera interrupta*	*Chaparral honeysuckle* ②
Caprifoliaceae	*Lonicera involucrata* var. *ledebourii*	*Black twinberry*
Cistaceae	*Crocanthemum scoparium*	*Peak rush-rose* ②
Convolvulaceae	*Cuscuta howelliana*	*Vernal pool dodder*
Crassulaceae	*Dudleya cymosa* subsp. *cymosa*	*Canyon live-forever* ②
Crassulaceae	*Dudleya farinosa*	*Bluff lettuce*
Crassulaceae	*Sedella pumila*	*Dwarf stonecrop*
Ericaceae	*Pterospora andromedea*	*Pine drops*
Ericaceae	*Rhododendron occidentale*	*Western azalea*
Euphorbiaceae	*Euphorbia oblongata*	Eggleaf spurge ③
Fabaceae	*Acacia dealbata*	Silver wattle ③
Fabaceae	*Acmispon brachycarpus*	*Foothill deervetch*

Fabaceae	*Acmispon glaber* var. *glaber*	*Deerweed* ②
Fabaceae	*Acmispon nevadensis* var. *nevadensis*	*Sierra Nevada lotus*
Fabaceae	*Acmispon strigosus*	*Bishop's lotus*
Fabaceae	*Lupinus arboreus*	*Yellow bush lupine* ③
Fabaceae	*Lupinus microcarpus* var. *densiflorus*	*Chick lupine* ②
Fabaceae	*Spartium junceum*	Spanish broom ③
Fabaceae	*Trifolium campestre*	Hop clover
Fagaceae	*Chrysolepis sempervirens*	*Bush chinquapin*
Fagaceae	*Notholithocarpus densiflorus* var. *densiflorus*	*Tan oak*
Gentianaceae	*Cicendia quadrangularis*	*Timwort*
Grossulariaceae	*Ribes montigenum*	*Western prickly gooseberry*
Hypericaceae	*Hypericum anagalloides*	*Tinker's penny*
Hypericaceae	*Hypericum mutilum* subsp. *mutilum*	Dwarf St. John's wort
Hypericaceae	*Hypericum perforatum* subsp. *perforatum*	Klamath weed ③
Lauraceae	*Umbellularia californica*	*California bay*
Loasaceae	*Mentzelia laevicaulis*	*Smooth-stem blazing star*
Malvaceae	*Fremontodendron californicum*	*Flannelbush* ②
Malvaceae	*Modiola caroliniana*	Carolina bristle-mallow
Moraceae	*Maclura pomifera*	Osage orange
Myrsinaceae	*Lysimachia arvensis*	Scarlet pimpernel
Nyctaginaceae	*Abronia latifolia*	*Sand verbena*
Oleaceae	*Fraxinus latifolia*	*Oregon ash*
Onagraceae	*Camissonia contorta*	*Contorted sun cup*
Onagraceae	*Camissoniopsis cheiranthifolia* subsp. *cheiranthifolia*	*Beach evening-primrose*
Onagraceae	*Ludwigia hexapetala*	Uruguayan water-primrose ③
Onagraceae	*Oenothera biennis*	Common evening-primrose
Onagraceae	*Oenothera elata* subsp. *hirsutissima*	*Hooker's evening-primrose*

Orobanchaceae	***Castilleja ambigua*** subsp. ***ambigua***	***Johnny-nip***
Orobanchaceae	***Castilleja campestris*** subsp. ***campestris***	***Field owl's clover***
Orobanchaceae	***Castilleja foliolosa***	***Woolly paintbrush*** ②
Orobanchaceae	***Castilleja pruinosa***	***Frosted paintbrush***
Orobanchaceae	***Castilleja wightii***	***Wight's paintbrush***
Orobanchaceae	*Parentucellia viscosa*	Yellow glandweed ③
Orobanchaceae	***Triphysaria eriantha*** subsp. ***eriantha***	***Butter-and-eggs***
Oxalidaceae	*Oxalis corniculata*	Creeping wood-sorrel ③
Oxalidaceae	*Oxalis micrantha*	Dwarf wood-sorrel
Oxalidaceae	*Oxalis pes-caprae*	Bermuda buttercup ③
Papaveraceae	***Dendromecon rigida***	***Bush poppy*** ②
Papaveraceae	***Eschscholzia californica***	***California poppy*** ②
Papaveraceae	***Eschscholzia lobbii***	***Frying pans*** ②
Papaveraceae	***Hesperomecon linearis***	***Carnival poppy***
Papaveraceae	***Platystemon californicus***	***Cream cups***
Phrymaceae	***Mimulus aurantiacus*** var. ***aurantiacus***	***Bush monkeyflower*** ②
Phrymaceae	***Mimulus bicolor***	***Yellow and white monkeyflower***
Phrymaceae	***Mimulus floribundus***	***Many-flowered monkeyflower***
Phrymaceae	***Mimulus guttatus***	***Seep-spring monkeyflower***
Phrymaceae	***Mimulus moschatus***	***Musk monkeyflower***
Phrymaceae	***Mimulus primuloides*** var. ***primuloides***	***Primrose monkeyflower***
Plantaginaceae	*Kickxia elatine*	Sharp-leaved fluellin
Platanaceae	***Platanus racemosa***	***Western sycamore (male flowers)***
Polemoniaceae	***Collomia grandiflora***	***Large-flowered collomia***
Polygonaceae	***Eriogonum nudum*** var. ***pubiflorum***	***Fremont's wild buckwheat*** ②

Portulacaceae	*Portulaca oleracea*	Common purslane ③
Ranunculaceae	**Ranunculus alismifolius var. hartwegii**	**Plantain-leaved buttercup**
Ranunculaceae	*Ranunculus muricatus*	Prickle-fruited buttercup
Ranunculaceae	**Ranunculus occidentalis var. occidentalis**	**Western buttercup**
Rosaceae	**Cercocarpus betuloides var. betuloides**	**Birch-leaf mountain mahogany** ②
Rosaceae	**Drymocallis lactea var. austiniae**	**Austin's woodbeauty**
Rosaceae	**Potentilla anserina subsp. pacifica**	**Pacific silverweed**
Rosaceae	**Purshia tridentata var. tridentata**	**Bitterbrush** ②
Rubiceae	**Galium porrigens var. porrigens**	**Climbing bedstraw**
Rutaceae	**Ptelea crenulata**	**California hop tree** ②
Salicaceae	**Populus fremontii subsp. fremontii**	**Fremont's cottonwood (male flowers)**
Salicaceae	**Salix exigua var. hindsiana**	**Hind's willow (male flowers)**
Salicaceae	**Salix lasiolepis**	**Arroyo willow (male flowers)**
Sarraceniaceae	**Darlingtonia californica**	**California pitcher-plant** ①
Saxifragaceae	**Tellima grandiflora**	**Fringe cups**
Scrophulariaceae	**Scrophularia californica**	**California bee-plant**
Scrophulariaceae	*Verbascum blattaria*	Moth mullein ②
Scrophulariaceae	*Verbascum thapsus*	Woolly mullein ③
Simaroubaceae	*Ailanthus altissima*	Tree-of-heaven ③
Solanaceae	*Nicotiana glauca*	Tree tobacco ③
Violaceae	**Viola bakeri**	**Baker's violet**
Violaceae	**Viola douglasii**	**Douglas' violet**
Violaceae	**Viola lobata subsp. lobata**	**Pine violet**
Violaceae	**Viola sempervirens**	**Redwood violet**
Zygophyllaceae	*Tribulus terrestris*	Puncture vine ③

Monocotyledons

Araceae	***Lysichiton americanus***	***Yellow skunk cabbage***
Cyperaceae	***Carex barbarae***	***Santa Barbara sedge (male flowers)***
Iridaceae	***Iris douglasiana***	***Douglas' iris***
Iridaceae	***Iris fernaldii***	***Fernald's iris*** ②
Iridaceae	*Iris pseudoacorus*	Yellow flag ③
Iridaceae	*Sparaxis elegans*	Cape buttercup ②
Iridaceae	*Sisyrinchium rosulatum*	Annual blue-eyed grass
Liliaceae	***Calochortus amabilis***	***Golden fairy lantern***
Liliaceae	***Calochortus luteus***	***Gold nuggets*** ②
Orchidaceae	***Corallorhiza striata***	***Striped coralroot***
Themidaceae	***Triteleia ixioides*** subsp. ***scabra***	***Foothill pretty face*** ②

Pink to red or maroon

Dicotyledons

Aizoaceae	*Carpobrotus edulis*	Freeway iceplant ③
Apiaceae	***Angelica hendersonii***	***Coast angelica***
Apiaceae	***Sanicula bipinnatifida***	***Purple sanicle***
Apocynaceae	***Apocynum androsaemifolium***	***Bitter dogbane***
Apocynaceae	***Asclepias cordifolia***	***Purple milkweed*** ②
Apocynaceae	***Asclepias fascicularis***	***Narrow-leaved milkweed*** ③
Apocynaceae	***Asclepias speciosa***	***Showy milkweed*** ②
Apocynaceae	*Nerium oleander*	Oleander ②
Asteraceae	*Carduus pycnocephalus* subsp. *pycnocephalus*	Italian thistle ③
Asteraceae	*Cirsium vulgare*	Bull thistle ③
Asteraceae	***Pseudognaphalium ramosissimum***	***Pink cudweed***
Asteraceae	*Silybum marianum*	Milk thistle ③
Asteraceae	***Stephanomeria exigua*** subsp. ***coronaria***	***White-plume wire lettuce***
Betulaceae	***Alnus rhombifolia***	***White alder (female flowers)***

Brassicaceae	*Cakile maritima*	Sea rocket ③
Brassicaceae	*Cakile edentula*	American sea rocket
Brassicaceae	*Raphanus sativus*	Wild radish ③
Calycanthaceae	**Calycanthus occidentalis**	**Spice-bush**
Caprifoliaceae	**Lonicera conjugialis**	**Twinberry honeysuckle**
Caprifoliaceae	**Lonicera hispidula**	**Pink honeysuckle**
Caprifoliaceae	**Symphoricarpos albus** var. **laevigatus**	**Common snowberry** ②
Caryophyllaceae	*Petrorhagia dubia*	Grass pink ②
Caryophyllaceae	*Saponaria officinalis*	Soapwort ③
Caryophyllaceae	**Silene laciniata** subsp. **californica**	**California pink** ②
Caryophyllaceae	**Spergularia macrotheca** var. **macrotheca**	**Sticky sand-spurrey**
Caryophyllaceae	*Velezia rigida*	Velezia
Chenopodiaceae	*Salsola tragus*	Tumbleweed ③
Ericaceae	**Arctostaphylos viscida**	**Whiteleaf manzanita** ②
Ericaceae	**Gaultheria shallon**	**Salal**
Ericaceae	**Pterospora andromedea**	**Pine drops**
Ericaceae	**Rhododendron macrophyllum**	**California rhododendron**
Ericaceae	**Rhododendron occidentale**	**Western azalea**
Ericaceae	**Sarcodes sanguinea**	**Snow plant**
Ericaceae	**Vaccinium ovatum**	**Evergreen huckleberry**
Ericaceae	**Vaccinium parvifolium**	**Red huckleberry**
Ericaceae	**Vaccinium uliginosum** subsp. **occidentale**	**Western blueberry**
Fabaceae	**Acmispon americanus** var. **americanus**	**Spanish clover**
Fabaceae	*Albizia julibrissin*	Silk tree
Fabaceae	**Cercis occidentalis**	**Western redbud** ②
Fabaceae	*Lathyrus hirsutus*	Caley pea
Fabaceae	**Lathyrus jepsonii** var. **californicus**	**California tule pea**

Fabaceae	*Lathyrus latifolius*	Everlasting pea
Fabaceae	*Lathyrus tingitanus*	Tangier pea
Fabaceae	**Pickeringia montana var. montana**	**Chaparral pea** ②
Fabaceae	*Sesbania punicea*	Rattlebush ③
Fabaceae	**Trifolium depauperatum**	**Cowbag clover**
Fabaceae	**Trifolium variegatum var. major**	**Large white-tipped clover**
Fabaceae	**Trifolium willdenovii**	**Tomcat clover**
Fabaceae	**Vicia gigantea**	**Giant vetch**
Fabaceae	*Vicia sativa* subsp. *nigra*	Spring vetch
Fabaceae	*Vicia villosa* subsp. *varia*	Winter vetch
Gentianaceae	*Centaurium tenuiflorum*	Slender centaury
Geraniaceae	*Erodium botrys*	Broadleaf filaree
Geraniaceae	*Erodium cicutarium*	Redstem filaree ③
Geraniaceae	**Geranium carolinianum**	**Carolina crane's bill**
Geraniaceae	*Geranium molle*	Dovefoot geranium
Grossulariaceae	**Ribes cereum var. cereum**	**Wax currant**
Grossulariaceae	**Ribes malvaceum var. malvaceum**	**Chaparral currant** ②
Grossulariaceae	**Ribes menziesii var. menziesii**	**Canyon gooseberry**
Grossulariaceae	**Ribes montigenum**	**Western prickly gooseberry**
Lamiaceae	*Lamium amplexicaule*	Henbit
Lamiaceae	**Salvia spathacea**	**Pitcher sage** ②
Lamiaceae	**Stachys rigida var. quercetorum**	**Hedge-nettle**
Malvaceae	**Sidalcea calycosa subsp. calycosa**	**Vernal pool checkerbloom**
Montiaceae	**Calandrinia menziesii**	**Red maids** ②
Montiaceae	**Claytonia parviflora subsp. parviflora**	**Narrow-leaved miner's lettuce**
Montiaceae	**Claytonia perfoliata subsp. perfoliata**	**Miner's lettuce**
Montiaceae	**Claytonia sibirica**	**Candy flower**

Montiaceae	*Lewisia rediviva* var. *rediviva*	*Bitter-root* ②
Onagraceae	*Chamerion angustifolium* subsp. *circumvagum*	*Fireweed*
Onagraceae	*Clarkia arcuata*	*Glandular clarkia*
Onagraceae	*Clarkia purpurea* subsp. *quadrivulnera*	*Four spot*
Onagraceae	*Clarkia unguiculata*	*Elegant clarkia* ②
Onagraceae	*Epilobium brachycarpum*	*Tall annual willowherb*
Onagraceae	*Epilobium canum* subsp. *canum*	*California fuchsia* ②
Orobanchaceae	*Castilleja ambigua* subsp. *ambigua*	*Johnny-nip*
Orobanchaceae	*Castilleja exserta* subsp. *exserta*	*Purple owl's clover* ②
Orobanchaceae	*Castilleja foliolosa*	*Woolly paintbrush* ②
Orobanchaceae	*Castilleja lemmonii*	*Lemmon's paintbrush*
Orobanchaceae	*Castilleja pruinosa*	*Frosted paintbrush*
Orobanchaceae	*Castilleja wightii*	*Wight's paintbrush*
Orobanchaceae	*Cordylanthus tenuis* subsp. *tenuis*	*Slender bird's beak*
Orobanchaceae	*Orobanche californica* subsp. *californica*	*California broomrape*
Orobanchaceae	*Orthocarpus cuspidatus* subsp. *cryptanthus*	*Short-flowered owl's clover*
Orobanchaceae	*Pedicularis attollens*	*Little elephant's head*
Orobanchaceae	*Pedicularis densiflora*	*Warrior's plume*
Oxalidaceae	*Oxalis oregana*	*Redwood sorrel*
Paeoniaceae	*Paeonia brownii*	*Western peony*
Phrymaceae	*Mimulus angustatus*	*Pansy monkeyflower*
Phrymaceae	*Mimulus douglasii*	*Purple mouse-ears*
Phrymaceae	*Mimulus kelloggii*	*Kellogg's monkeyflower* ②
Phrymaceae	*Mimulus lewisii*	*Lewis's monkeyflower*
Phytolaccaceae	*Phytolacca americana* var. *americana*	Pokeweed ③

Plantaginaceae	*Antirrhinum orontium*	Syrian snapdragon
Plantaginaceae	**Keckiella breviflora** var. **breviflora**	**Gaping beardtongue** ②
Platanaceae	**Platanus racemosa**	**Western sycamore (female flowers)**
Plumbaginaceae	**Armeria maritima** subsp. **californica**	**Thrift**
Polemoniaceae	**Ipomopsis aggregata** subsp. **aggregata**	**Scarlet gilia** ②
Polemoniaceae	**Ipomopsis tenuituba**	**Slender-flowered skyrocket**
Polemoniaceae	**Leptosiphon bicolor**	**True baby stars**
Polemoniaceae	**Leptosiphon ciliatus**	**Whisker brush**
Polemoniaceae	**Navarretia leptalea** subsp. **leptalea**	**Bridge's gilia**
Polemoniaceae	**Phlox diffusa**	**Spreading phlox**
Polygalaceae	**Polygala californica**	**California milkwort**
Polygonaceae	**Chorizanthe membranacea**	**Pink spineflower**
Polygonaceae	**Eriogonum latifolium**	**Coast buckwheat**
Polygonaceae	**Eriogonum roseum**	**Wand wild buckwheat** ②
Polygonaceae	*Persicaria maculosa*	Lady's thumb
Polygonaceae	**Polygonum shastense**	**Shasta knotweed**
Polygonaceae	*Rumex acetosella*	Sheep sorrel ③
Primulaceae	**Primula clevelandii** var. *patula*	**Padre's shooting star**
Primulaceae	**Primula hendersonii**	**Mosquito bills** ②
Primulaceae	**Primula jeffreyi**	**Sierra shooting star**
Ranunculaceae	**Aquilegia formosa**	**Western columbine**
Rosaceae	*Prunus amygdalus*	Almond
Rosaceae	**Rosa californica**	**California rose**
Rosaceae	**Rosa gymnocarpa** var. **gymnocarpa**	**Wood rose**
Rosaceae	**Rosa nutkana** var. **nutkana**	**Nootka rose**
Rosaceae	**Rubus spectabilis**	**Salmonberry**
Rosaceae	**Spiraea douglasii**	**Douglas' spiraea**

Rosaceae	*Spiraea splendens*	*Rose-colored meadow-sweet*
Rubiceae	*Galium porrigens* var. *porrigens*	*Climbing bedstraw*
Salicaceae	*Populus fremontii* subsp. *fremontii*	*Fremont's cottonwood (male flowers)*
Sapindaceae	*Acer negundo*	*Box elder*
Sapindaceae	*Acer saccharinum*	Silver maple
Sarraceniaceae	*Darlingtonia californica*	*California pitcher-plant* ①
Saxifragaceae	*Tellima grandiflora*	*Fringe cups*
Scrophulariaceae	*Scrophularia californica*	*California bee-plant*
Valerianaceae	*Plectritis congesta* subsp. *congesta*	*Sea blush*
Verbenaceae	*Phyla nodiflora*	*Common lippia*

Monocotyledons

Alismataceae	*Alisma lanceolatum*	Lanceleaf water-plantain
Alliaceae	*Allium amplectens*	*Narrow-leaved onion*
Alliaceae	*Allium campanulatum*	*Sierra onion*
Alliaceae	*Allium cratericola*	*Volcanic onion* ②
Alliaceae	*Allium dichlamydeum*	*Coastal onion*
Alliaceae	*Allium validum*	*Swamp onion*
Amaryllidaceae	*Amaryllis belladonna*	Naked ladies ②
Iridaceae	*Ixia flexuosa*	Ixia ②
Iridaceae	*Sparaxis elegans*	Cape buttercup ②
Iridaceae	*Sisyrinchium rosulatum*	Annual blue-eyed grass
Liliaceae	*Fritillaria affinis*	*Checker lily*
Melanthiaceae	*Trillium chloropetalum*	*Giant trillium*
Orchidaceae	*Corallorhiza maculata* var. *occidentalis*	*Spotted coralroot*
Orchidaceae	*Corallorhiza striata*	*Striped coralroot*
Themidaceae	*Dichelostemma volubile*	*Snake lily* ②

Blue to purple

Dicotyledons

Apiaceae	*Sanicula bipinnatifida*	*Purple sanicle*
Apocynaceae	*Asclepias cordifolia*	*Purple milkweed* ②
Apocynaceae	*Vinca major*	Greater periwinkle ③
Asteraceae	*Carduus pycnocephalus* subsp. *pycnocephalus*	Italian thistle ③
Asteraceae	*Cichorium intybus*	Chicory
Asteraceae	*Cirsium vulgare*	Bull thistle ③
Asteraceae	*Erigeron glacialis* var. *glacialis*	*Wandering daisy*
Asteraceae	*Erigeron glaucus*	*Seaside daisy*
Asteraceae	*Silybum marianum*	Milk thistle ③
Asteraceae	*Symphyotrichum spathulatum* var. *spathulatum*	*Western mountain aster*
Boraginaeae	*Eriodictyon californicum*	*California yerba santa* ②
Boraginaeae	*Myosotis laxa*	*Bay forget-me-not*
Boraginaeae	*Nemophila menziesii* var. *menziesii*	*Baby blue-eyes*
Boraginaeae	*Phacelia imbricata* subsp. *imbricata*	*Imbricate scorpionweed*
Boraginaeae	*Phacelia tanacetifolia*	*Lacy phacelia* ②
Brassicaceae	*Raphanus sativus*	Wild radish ③
Campanulaceae	*Campanula californica*	*Swamp harebell* ①
Campanulaceae	*Campanula rotundifolia*	*Bluebell*
Campanulaceae	*Downingia bicornuta* var. *picta*	*Two-horned downingia*
Campanulaceae	*Downingia concolor* var. *concolor*	*Maroon-spotted downingia*
Campanulaceae	*Downingia cuspidata*	*Toothed downingia*
Campanulaceae	*Downingia insignis*	*Cupped downingia*
Campanulaceae	*Downingia pulchella*	*Valley downingia*
Caryophyllaceae	*Spergularia macrotheca* var. *macrotheca*	*Sticky sand-spurrey*

Fabaceae	*Lupinus albifrons* var. *albifrons*	Bush lupine ②
Fabaceae	*Lupinus benthamii*	Spider lupine ②
Fabaceae	*Lupinus bicolor*	Miniature lupine
Fabaceae	*Vicia gigantea*	Giant vetch
Fabaceae	*Vicia villosa* subsp. *varia*	Winter vetch
Fabaceae	*Vicia villosa* subsp. *villosa*	Winter vetch
Lamiaceae	*Clinopodium douglasii*	Yerba buena
Lamiaceae	*Lamium amplexicaule*	Henbit
Lamiaceae	*Mentha pulegium*	Pennyroyal ③
Lamiaceae	*Monardella breweri* subsp. *lanceolata*	Mustang mint ②
Lamiaceae	*Monardella villosa* subsp. *villosa*	Coyote mint ②
Lamiaceae	*Pogogyne zizyphoroides*	Sacramento beardstyle
Lamiaceae	*Salvia sonomensis*	Sonoma sage ②
Lamiaceae	*Stachys rigida* var. *quercetorum*	Hedge-nettle
Lamiaceae	*Trichostema lanceolatum*	Vinegar weed
Linaceae	*Linum bienne*	Pale flax
Malvaceae	*Sidalcea calycosa* subsp. *calycosa*	Vernal pool checkerbloom
Myrsinaceae	*Lysimachia arvensis*	Scarlet pimpernel
Onagraceae	*Clarkia purpurea* subsp. *quadrivulnera*	Four spot
Orobanchaceae	*Castilleja exserta* subsp. *exserta*	Purple owl's clover ②
Orobanchaceae	*Castilleja lemmonii*	Lemmon's paintbrush
Orobanchaceae	*Orobanche uniflora*	Naked broomrape
Orobanchaceae	*Orthocarpus cuspidatus* subsp. *cryptanthus*	Short-flowered owl's clover
Oxalidaceae	*Oxalis oregana*	Redwood sorrel
Phrymaceae	*Mimulus douglasii*	Purple mouse-ears
Plantaginaceae	*Collinsia grandiflora*	Giant blue-eyed Mary ②

Plantaginaceae	*Collinsia heterophylla* var. *heterophylla*	*Chinese houses* ②
Plantaginaceae	*Collinsia linearis*	*Narrow-leaved blue-eyed Mary*
Plantaginaceae	*Collinsia torreyi* var. *wrightii*	*Wright's blue-eyed Mary*
Plantaginaceae	Kickxia elatine	Sharp-leaved fluellin
Plantaginaceae	*Lindernia dubia*	*False pimpernel*
Plantaginaceae	*Penstemon heterophyllus* var. *purdyi*	*Purdy's foothill penstemon* ②
Plantaginaceae	*Penstemon rydbergii* var. *oreocharis*	*Meadow penstemon*
Plantaginaceae	Veronica anagallis-aquatica	Water speedwell
Plantaginaceae	Veronica persica	Persian speedwell
Polemoniaceae	*Gilia capitata* subsp. *pedemontana*	*Bluehead gilia* ②
Polemoniaceae	*Gilia tricolor* subsp. *tricolor*	*Bird's-eye gilia* ②
Polemoniaceae	*Ipomopsis tenuituba*	*Slender-flowered skyrocket*
Polemoniaceae	*Navarretia filicaulis*	*Thin-stemmed navarretia*
Polemoniaceae	*Navarretia pubescens*	*Downy pincushion*
Polemoniaceae	*Navarretia squarrosa*	*Skunkweed*
Polemoniaceae	*Navarretia tagetina*	*Marigold pincushion*
Polemoniaceae	*Phlox diffusa*	*Spreading phlox*
Polemoniaceae	*Polemonium californicum*	*Jacob's ladder*
Polygalaceae	*Polygala californica*	*California milkwort*
Ranunculaceae	*Aconitum columbianum* subsp. *viviparum*	*Monkshood*
Ranunculaceae	*Delphinium hansenii* subsp. *hansenii*	*Hansen's larkspur* ②
Ranunculaceae	*Delphinium patens* subsp. *patens*	*Spreading larkspur* ②
Ranunculaceae	*Delphinium variegatum* subsp. *variegatum*	*Royal larkspur* ②
Rhamnaceae	*Ceanothus lemmonii*	*Lemmon's ceanothus* ②

Rhamnaceae	*Ceanothus prostratus* var. *prostratus*	*Mahala mat*
Solanaceae	*Solanum douglasii*	*Douglas' nightshade*
Solanaceae	*Solanum xanti*	*Chaparral nightshade*
Verbenaceae	*Phyla nodiflora*	*Common lippia*
Verbenaceae	*Verbena bonariensis*	Tall vervain
Verbenaceae	*Verbena lasiostachys* var. *scabrida*	*Western vervain*
Violaceae	*Viola adunca* subsp. *adunca*	*Western dog violet*

Monocotyledons

Agavaceae	*Camassia leichtlinii* subsp. *suksdorfii*	*Camas*
Alliaceae	*Allium campanulatum*	*Sierra onion*
Iridaceae	*Iris douglasiana*	*Douglas' iris*
Iridaceae	*Sisyrinchium bellum*	*Western blue-eyed grass* ②
Iridaceae	*Sisyrinchium rosulatum*	Annual blue-eyed grass
Liliaceae	*Calochortus leichtlinii*	*Leichtlin's mariposa lily* ②
Liliaceae	*Calochortus tolmiei*	*Pussy's ears*
Melanthiaceae	*Trillium chloropetalum*	*Giant trillium*
Themidaceae	*Brodiaea coronaria*	*Garland brodiaea*
Themidaceae	*Brodiaea elegans* subsp. *elegans*	*Harvest brodiaea* ②
Themidaceae	*Brodiaea minor*	*Vernal pool brodiaea*
Themidaceae	*Brodiaea terrestris* subsp. *terrestris*	*Dwarf brodiaea*
Themidaceae	*Dichelostemma capitatum* subsp. *capitatum*	*Blue dicks* ②
Themidaceae	*Dichelostemma congestum*	*Fork-toothed ookow* ②
Themidaceae	*Dichelostemma multiflorum*	*Round-toothed ookow* ②
Themidaceae	*Triteleia laxa*	*Wally baskets* ②

Green or brown

Dicotyledons

Apiaceae	*Eryngium armatum*	**Coastal button-celery**
Apiaceae	*Eryngium castrense*	**Great Valley coyote thistle**
Aristolochiaceae	*Aristolochia californica*	**Pipevine** ②
Asteraceae	*Ambrosia psilostachya*	**Western ragweed**
Asteraceae	*Artemisia dracunculus*	**Tarragon**
Asteraceae	Logfia gallica	Daggerleaf cottonrose
Asteraceae	Matricaria discoidea	Pineapple weed
Asteraceae	*Psilocarphus tenellus*	**Slender woolly marbles**
Asteraceae	Soliva sessilis	Burweed
Asteraceae	*Xanthium strumarium*	**Common cocklebur**
Betulaceae	*Alnus rhombifolia*	**White alder (male flowers)**
Chenopodiaceae	Dysphania ambrosioides	Mexican tea
Ericaceae	*Orthilia secunda*	**One-sided wintergreen**
Euphorbiaceae	*Croton setiger*	**Turkey mullein**
Fagaceae	*Quercus agrifolia* var. *agrifolia*	**Coast live oak** ②
Fagaceae	*Quercus douglasii*	**Blue oak** ②
Fagaceae	*Quercus lobata*	**Valley oak** ②
Fagaceae	*Quercus vacciniifolia*	**Huckleberry oak**
Fagaceae	*Quercus wislizeni* var. *wislizeni*	**Interior live oak** ②
Gentianaceae	*Frasera speciosa*	**Monument plant**
Grossulariaceae	*Ribes montigenum*	**Western prickly gooseberry**
Juglandaceae	*Juglans hindsii*	**Northern California black walnut**
Oleaceae	*Fraxinus latifolia*	**Oregon ash**
Plantaginaceae	*Plantago erecta*	**Dwarf plantain**
Plantaginaceae	Plantago lanceolata	English plantain ③
Plantaginaceae	*Plantago maritima*	**Seaside plantain**
Polygonaceae	Rumex crispus	Curly dock ③
Rhamnaceae	*Frangula californica* subsp. *tomentella*	**California coffee berry** ②

Rhamnaceae	*Frangula purshiana* subsp. *purshiana*	*Cascara sagrada*
Rhamnaceae	*Rhamnus ilicifolia*	*Hollyleaf redberry* ②
Rutaceae	*Ptelea crenulata*	*California hop tree* ②
Salicaceae	*Populus fremontii* subsp. *fremontii*	*Fremont's cottonwood (female flowers)*
Salicaceae	*Salix exigua* var. *hindsiana*	*Hind's willow (female flowers)*
Salicaceae	*Salix lasiolepis*	*Arroyo willow (female flowers)*
Sapindaceae	*Acer negundo*	*Box elder*
Saxifragaceae	*Tellima grandiflora*	*Fringe cups*
Viscaceae	*Phoradendron leucarpum* subsp. *macrophyllum*	*American mistletoe*
Vitaceae	*Vitis californica*	*California wild grape*

Monocotyledons

Cyperaceae	*Cyperus difformis*	Variable flatsedge
Cyperaceae	*Cyperus eragrostis*	*Tall flatsedge*
Cyperaceae	*Cyperus strigosus*	*False nutsedge*
Cyperaceae	*Lipocarpha micrantha*	*Small-flowered halfchaff sedge*
Liliaceae	*Fritillaria affinis*	*Checker lily*
Orchidaceae	*Corallorhiza striata*	*Striped coralroot*
Orchidaceae	*Piperia elongata*	*Chaparral orchid* ②
Typhaceae	*Sparganium angustifolium*	*Narrow-leaved bur-reed*
Typhaceae	*Typha latifolia*	*Broad-leaved cattail*

SELECTED REFERENCES

General

Bailey, L. H. 1949. *Manual of Cultivated Plants* (revised edition). MacMillan Publishing Company, Inc., New York.

Baldwin, B. B., D. H. Goldman, D. J. Keil, R. Patterson, T. J. Rosatti, and D. H. Wilken, eds. 2012. *The Jepson Manual: Vascular Plants of California*, 2nd edition. University of California Press, Berkeley, Los Angeles, and London. Digital version available at http://ucjeps.berkeley.edu/eflora.

Barbour, M., T. Keeler-Wolff, and A. A. Schoenherr, eds. 2007. *Terrestrial Vegetation of California*, 3rd edition. University of California Press, Berkeley, Los Angeles, and London.

Coleman, R. A. 2002. *The Wild Orchids of California*. Comstock Publishing Associates and Cornell University Press, Ithaca, New York.

Heywood, V. H., R. K. Brummitt, A. Culham, and O. Seberg. 2007. *Flowering Plant Families of the World*. Firefly Books, Richmond Hill, Ontario, Canada.

Hickman, J. C., ed. 1993. *The Jepson Manual: Higher Plants of California*. University of California Press, Berkeley, Los Angeles, and London.

Jepson, W. L. 1925. *A Manual of the Flowering Plants of California*. University of California Press, Berkeley, Los Angeles, and London. (For what is now called *The Jepson Manual*, see Baldwin et al. 2012.)

Mason, Herbert L. 1957. *A Flora of the Marshes of California*. University of California Press, Berkeley and Los Angeles.

McMinn, H. E. 1939. *An Illustrated Manual of California Shrubs*. University of California Press, Berkeley and Los Angeles.

Munz, P. A., with D. D. Keck. 1968. *A California Flora with Supplement*. University of California Press, Berkeley, Los Angeles, and London.

Nakamura, G., and J. K. Nelson, eds. 2001. *Selected Rare Plants of Northern California*. University of California, Agriculture and Natural Resources Publication 3395.

Niehaus, T. F., and C. L. Ripper. 1976. *A Field Guide to Pacific States Wildflowers*. The Peterson Field Guide Series, Houghton Mifflin Company, Boston, Massachusetts.

Parkinson, P. G. 1975. "The International Code of Botanical Nomenclature: A historical review and bibliography." *TANE: Journal of the Auckland University Field Club* 21: 153–73. Available at http://www.thebookshelf.auckland.ac.nz/docs/Tane/Tane-21/23%20The%20International%20Code%20of%20Botanical.pdf.

Sampson, A. W., and B. S. Jespersen. 1981. *California Range Brushlands and Browse Plants*. University of California, Division of Agricultural Sciences, California Agricultural Experiment Station Publication No. 4010.

Smith, J. P., Jr. 2014. *Field Guide to Grasses of California*. University of California Press, Berkeley, Los Angeles, and London.

Stromberg, M. R., J. D. Corbin, and C. M. d'Antonio, eds. 2007. *California Grasslands: Ecology and Management*. University of California Press, Berkeley, Los Angeles, and London.

van Rijckevorsel, P. 2014. "A brief history of the *Code*." Available at http://www .iapt-taxon.org/historic/history.htm.

Local Floras

Bills, A., and S. Mackey. 2011. *Wildflowers of Table Mountain: A Naturalist's Guide*. Studies from the Herbarium No. 15, California State University, Chico.

Cole, R., and W. W. Weathers, eds. 1985. *Flora and Fauna of the Stebbins Cold Canyon Reserve*. Institute of Ecology Publication No. 29, University of California, Davis.

Horn, E. L. 1993. *Coastal Wildflowers of the Pacific Northwest*. Mountain Press, Missoula, Montana.

Howell, J. T., F. Almeda, W. Follette, and C. Best. 2007. *Marin Flora: An Illustrated Manual of the Flowering Plants, Ferns, and Conifers of Marin*. California Academy of Sciences and California Native Plant Society, Marin Chapter.

Oswald, V. H. 1986. *Vascular Plants of Upper Bidwell Park, Chico, California*. Studies from the Herbarium No. 3, California State University, Chico.

Oswald, V. H., and L. Ahart. 1994. *Manual of the Vascular Plants of Butte County, California*. California Native Plant Society, Sacramento.

Redbud Chapter, California Native Plant Society. 2014. *Trees and Shrubs of Nevada and Placer Counties, California*. California Native Plant Society Press, Sacramento.

Redbud Chapter, California Native Plant Society. 2017. *Wildflowers of Nevada and Placer Counties, California*, 2nd edition. California Native Plant Society Press, Sacramento.

Trees

Fowells, H. A. 1965. *Silvics of Forest Trees of the United States*. Forest Service, U.S. Department of Agriculture, Washington, D.C., Agriculture Handbook No. 271. 762 pp.

Johnston, V. R. 1994. *California Forests and Woodlands: A Natural History*. University of California Press, Berkeley, Los Angeles, and London.

Keator, G. 1998. *The Life of an Oak: An Intimate Portrait.* Heyday Books, Berkeley, California, and the California Oak Foundation.

Lanner, R. M. 1999. *Conifers of California.* Cachuma Press, Los Olivos, California.

Pavlik, B. M., P. C. Muick, S. Johnson, and M. Popper. 1991. *Oaks of California.* Cachuma Press, Los Olivos, California, and the California Oak Foundation.

Peattie, D. C. 1950. *A Natural History of Western Trees.* University of Nebraska Press, Lincoln and London.

Sudworth, G. B. 1967. *Forest Trees of the Pacific Slope.* Dover Publications, New York. (Unabridged republication of 1908 U.S. Department of Agriculture handbook.)

Weeds

DiTomaso, J. M., and E. A. Healy. 2003. *Aquatic and Riparian Weeds of the West.* University of California, Agriculture and Natural Resources Publication 3421.

DiTomaso, J. M., and E. A. Healy. 2007. *Weeds of California and Other Western States.* University of California, Agriculture and Natural Resources Publication 3488.

Whitson, T. D., ed., L. C. Burrill, S. A. Dewey, D. W. Cudney, B. E. Nelson, R. D. Lee, and R. Parker. 2012. *Weeds of the West*, 11th edition. Western Society of Weed Science and University of Wyoming.

Native American Uses of Plants

Anderson, M. K. 2005. *Tending the Wild: Native American Knowledge and the Management of California's Natural Resources.* University of California Press, Berkeley, Los Angeles, and London.

Balls, E. K. 1962. *Early Uses of California Plants.* University of California Press, Berkeley, Los Angeles, and London.

Farmer, J. P. 2010. *Basketry Plants Used by Western American Indians.* The Justin Farmer Foundation, Fullerton, California.

Moerman, D. E. 1998. *Native American Ethnobotany.* Timber Press, Portland, Oregon.

Rawls, J. R. 1984. *Indians of California: The Changing Image.* University of Oklahoma Press, Norman and London.

INDEX

ABOUT THE AUTHOR

Eva Begley holds a Ph.D. in botany from the University of California at Davis, has enjoyed plants ever since she was a toddler, and has been exploring northern California for more than 40 years. She has taught undergraduate courses in botany and general biology as well as plant identification classes for the general public, worked in botanical and agricultural research labs, and served as a senior environmental scientist and senior environmental planner for several state agencies. Her articles on various natural history topics have been published in *Outdoor California* and other magazines, along with photographs taken by her husband, Paul Begley, and herself; she is also the author or coauthor of a number of scientific papers. She and her husband live in Sacramento, California.